# THE POLITICS OF JUDICIAL INDEPENDENCE IN THE UK'S CHANGING CONSTITUTION

Judicial independence is generally understood as requiring that judges be insulated from political life. The central claim of this work is that far from standing apart from the political realm, judicial independence is a product of it. It is defined and protected through interactions between judges and politicians. In short, judicial independence is a political achievement. This is the main conclusion of a three-year research project on the major changes introduced by the Constitutional Reform Act 2005, and the consequences for judicial independence and accountability. The authors interviewed over 150 judges, politicians, civil servants and practitioners to understand the day-to-day processes of negotiation and interaction between politicians and judges. They conclude that the greatest threat to judicial independence in future may lie not with politicians' actively seeking to undermine the courts, but rather with their increasing disengagement from the justice system and the judiciary.

GRAHAM GEE is a Senior Lecturer at the University of Birmingham.

ROBERT HAZELL is Professor of Government and the Constitution and Director of the Constitution Unit at University College London.

KATE MALLESON is a Professor of Law at Queen Mary University of London.

PATRICK O'BRIEN is an LSE Fellow in Law.

# THE POLITICS OF JUDICIAL INDEPENDENCE IN THE UK'S CHANGING CONSTITUTION

GRAHAM GEE

ROBERT HAZELL

KATE MALLESON

PATRICK O'BRIEN

CAMBRIDGE
UNIVERSITY PRESS

**CAMBRIDGE**
**UNIVERSITY PRESS**

University Printing House, Cambridge CB2 8BS, United Kingdom

Cambridge University Press is part of the University of Cambridge.

It furthers the University's mission by disseminating knowledge in the pursuit of education, learning and research at the highest international levels of excellence.

www.cambridge.org
Information on this title: www.cambridge.org/9781107066953



First published 2015

*A catalogue record for this publication is available from the British Library*

*Library of Congress Cataloguing in Publication Data*
Gee, Graham, author.
The politics of judicial independence in the UK's changing constitution / Graham Gee, University of Birmingham; Robert Hazell, University College London; Kate Malleson, Queen Mary, University of London; Patrick O'Brien, London School of Economics and Political Science
pages cm
"This book is the product of a three-year research project carried out between 2011 and 2013, funded by the Arts and Humanities Research Council (AH/H039554/1)" – Introduction.
ISBN 978-1-107-06695-3 (hardback)
1. Judicial independence – Great Britain. 2. Great Britain – Politics and government – 2007- Gee I. Hazell, Robert, author. II. Malleson, Kate, author. III. O'Brien, Patrick, 1977- author. IV. Title.
KD4645.G44 2015
347.42'012–dc23
2014034655

ISBN 978-1-107-06695-3 Hardback

## CONTENTS

# FIGURES AND TABLES

## Figures



## Tables

# PREFACE

This book is the product of a three-year research project carried out between 2011 and 2013, funded by the Arts and Humanities Research Council (AH/H039554/1). The project set out to explore the implications for judicial independence and judicial accountability of the profound constitutional changes which have taken place in the UK in recent years.

To enable us to understand the full impact of those changes, which are still working their way through the system, we interviewed over 150 people. These included judges, government ministers, parliamentarians, senior civil servants in the Ministry of Justice and other parts of Whitehall, officials in Parliament, the Courts Service and the Judicial Appointments Commission, plus a similar range of people in Scotland and Northern Ireland. Most of the interviews were carried out on the basis of anonymity and so we cannot name the interviewees here; but we are immensely grateful to them for their time and trouble, and for subsequently commenting on our chapters in draft. One person we can name is Lord Judge, who as Lord Chief Justice generously gave us a great deal of his time and encouraged his colleagues to do likewise.

During the course of the project we held ten seminars conducted under the Chatham House Rule and attended by senior judges, politicians, officials and academics. Each seminar had a panel of speakers and addressed one particular aspect of the project. The topics covered were: separation of powers, judges and the media, judges and Parliament, judicial appointments, the Supreme Court, Northern Ireland, judges and the executive, tribunals, the Lord Chancellor and Scotland. We are grateful to the Northern Ireland Attorney General for hosting a seminar in Belfast, to the Faculty of Advocates for hosting an event in Edinburgh, to the Clerk of the House of Commons for hosting us in Parliament, and to the Supreme Court for hosting an event there. In January 2014 we held a closing conference at St George's House, Windsor Castle, which followed a similar format.

We are grateful to all our speakers and participants. The views expressed at these seminars by very senior figures from the judicial, legal and political worlds, who had personal and detailed knowledge of the topics covered, provided us with rich data which has informed this book. We owe special thanks to our Advisory Committee of twenty-eight people who formed a core group at the seminars and provided invaluable advice and input, individually and collectively, as the work progressed.

Brian Walker, the Constitution Unit's media adviser, patiently attended all our project meetings and reminded us of the wider picture whenever we risked becoming too narrowly academic. A succession of Constitution Unit interns did huge amounts of library and Web research for us, and we owe a special debt to John Adenitire, Will Allchorn, Srijanee Bhattacharyya, Stephen Clark, Jack Connah, John Crook, Eleanor Forbes, Matt Gayle, Shyam Kapila, Ed Lucas, Ruchi Parekh and Nick Perkins. Our thanks also go to Vicki Spence and Ben Webb, Constitution Unit administrators, for managing the project's finances and creating its Web pages. The Web pages are at ucl.ac.uk/constitution-unit, and contain blog posts and other project outputs.

Finally we should thank Jane Robertson, our copy-editor, and Finola O'Sullivan, our commissioning editor at Cambridge University Press. The book went to press in early 2014, and we have tried to update it to end 2013.

*Patrick O'Brien*
*Kate Malleson*
*Robert Hazell*
*Graham Gee*
*March 2014*

# ABBREVIATIONS

| | |
|---|---|
| CAFCASS | Child and Family Court Advisory Support Service |
| CRA | Constitutional Reform Act 2005 |
| DCA | Department for Constitutional Affairs |
| HMCS | Her Majesty's Courts Service |
| HMCTS | HM Courts and Tribunals Service |
| JABS | Judicial Appointments Board for Scotland |
| JAC | Judicial Appointments Commission |
| JACO | Judicial Appointments and Conduct Ombudsman |
| JCHR | Joint Committee on Human Rights |
| JCIO | Judicial Conduct Investigations Office |
| JCO | Judicial Communications Office |
| LCD | Lord Chancellor's Department |
| LCJ | Lord Chief Justice |
| LCJ-NI | Lord Chief Justice of Northern Ireland |
| LCO | Lord Chancellor's Office |
| MoJ | Ministry of Justice |
| NAO | National Audit Office |
| NICTS | Northern Ireland Courts and Tribunals Service |
| NIJAC | Northern Ireland Judicial Appointments Commission |
| NMGD | non-ministerial government department |
| OJC | Office for Judicial Complaints |
| SCS | Scottish Court Service |
| SNP | Scottish National Party |
| SPJ | Senior Presiding Judge |
| SPT | Senior President of Tribunals |
| SSRB | Senior Salaries Review Body |
| UKSC | United Kingdom Supreme Court |

# 1

# Introduction

This book is about the politics of judicial independence. These two concepts are not usually coupled in accounts of the UK's constitutional arrangements, at least not in any positive way. Rather, they are seen as being in tension. Judicial independence is understood as requiring that judges be insulated from the pressures and temptations of political life, not least so that they can resolve politically sensitive disputes impartially and hold those who exercise political power answerable to the law. Politics tends to be considered relevant to judicial independence only to the extent that judges must remain above the political fray in order to supply an effective check upon it. The premise of this work is that far from standing apart from the political realm, judicial independence is a product of it. It is defined and protected through interactions between judges and politicians. In short, judicial independence is a political achievement.

Our arguments are based on an analysis of empirical data gathered from confidential interviews with over 150 judges, politicians, civil servants, lay officials, practitioners and academics carried out between 2011 and 2013. In addition, we held a series of ten private seminars in London, Edinburgh and Belfast at which these groups discussed the challenges of nurturing judicial independence against the background of a changing constitution. The politicians who are the focus of this study are principally government ministers and their officials. They also include MPs, peers, parliamentary clerks and officials associated with a variety of public bodies (for example, the Courts Service, the Judicial Appointments Commission, the Judicial Conduct and Investigations Office and the Senior Salaries Review Body). More recently, these politicians and officials have been joined by senior laypeople who sit as members of these judiciary-related bodies. We have generally focused on leadership figures, particularly in the senior judiciary, but we have also interviewed judges who sit in courts up and down the judicial hierarchy in order to develop a picture of the system as a whole.[1]

[1] For an account of the daily experiences of judges at all levels of the judicial hierarchy, see P. Darbyshire, *Sitting in Judgment: The Working Lives of Judges* (Oxford: Hart Publishing, 2011).

We have also tried to capture the full range of interactions between judges and politicians and officials, from those occurring at the highest levels to the lowest and most ordinary; in high-profile constitutional arguments as well as in everyday negotiations about issues like budgets and judicial complaints. The primary objective of the empirical research was to explore how these negotiations are conducted during a period of rapid constitutional change.

Two main and related constitutional developments underpin this book. First, the expanding role of EU law, the Human Rights Act 1998, devolution and the increasing scope and intensity of judicial review have combined to draw judges into a range of politically sensitive disputes. Second, a raft of legislation has reshaped the institutional terrain throughout the UK by instigating greater formal separation between the judicial and political realms. In Scotland and Northern Ireland this process was triggered by the devolution legislation in the late 1990s. In England and Wales the Constitutional Reform Act 2005 (CRA) was the catalyst for change, leading to the reform of the office of Lord Chancellor, the creation of the Supreme Court and new judicial appointments processes. These changes have increased judicial power in two respects: first, the courts increasingly deliver judgments which encroach into areas of public policy once considered the preserve of elected politicians; second, and less widely acknowledged, the judiciary today enjoys greater power over the justice system in matters such as judicial selection, discipline, deployment and the funding and management of the courts.

Ascendant power in the first respect supplies essential background to this book, but not its focus. It is the increasing judicial power in the second respect that is our main interest. We are concerned with the way that constitutional reforms have changed the 'hidden wiring' governing relationships between judges and politicians, and our objective is to capture and describe these evolving relationships in order to investigate the implications for the independence and accountability of the judiciary.

## The nature of the politics of judicial independence

It is these relationships that we have in mind when we speak of the politics of judicial independence. They can be formal, such as when representatives of the judiciary negotiate with officials from the Ministry of Justice about changes to the structure of the Courts Service or the funding of the courts. But they can also be informal, and even indirect, such as when the President of the Supreme Court used a public lecture to argue that the budget for the Court was insufficient, and the Lord Chancellor responded in a radio interview. Much of the negotiation is routine, mundane, even, with its full significance drowned out by the high-profile tensions between judges and politicians that occur from time to time. But it is the day-to-day processes of negotiation and interaction that form the backbone of the politics of judicial independence in the UK. We seek to explain their significance and to understand the various tools and arguments that politicians, judges and officials use when delineating the constitutional position of the judiciary and the relationships between the political and judicial branches of government.

We elaborate more fully on what we mean by the politics of judicial independence in Chapter 2. We do not address the more familiar concept of 'the politics of the judiciary' which is concerned with possible connections between patterns of judicial decision-making and the ideological dispositions of judges.[2] Others have conducted research into the effects of judges' backgrounds and values, as well as other external influences, on their decision-making.[3] However, our book is not about judicial politics in this sense. Nor do we seek to address the effects on judicial decision-making of public opinion or the media.[4] Our emphasis is instead on the relations between the judiciary and the other branches of government, including new official bodies with judiciary-related functions. We also scrutinise relations within the judiciary itself, a topic largely neglected by public lawyers and political scientists, but which requires the tools of both. By analysing these relationships, we seek to understand how the meaning, content and limits of judicial independence are negotiated now that judges exercise more power in formally more separate, but in some respects less stable, institutional settings.

[2] See, for example, J. Griffith, *The Politics of the Judiciary*, 5th edn (London: Fontana, 1997); S. Lee, *Judging Judges* (London: Faber 1988); D. Robertson, *Judicial Discretion in the House of Lords* (Oxford: Clarendon Press, 1998); A. Paterson, *The Law Lords* (London: Macmillan, 1982).

[3] See the seminal work positing a link between ideological disposition and patterns of decision-making on the United States Supreme Court by Jeffrey Segal and Harold Spaeth: J. Segal and H. Spaeth, *The Supreme Court and the Attitudinal Model* (Cambridge: Cambridge University Press, 1993); J. Segal and H. Spaeth, *The Supreme Court and the Attitudinal Model Revisited* (Cambridge: Cambridge University Press, 2002); J. Knight and L. Epstein, 'The Norm of *Stare Decisis*' (1996) 40 *American Journal of Political Science* 1018.

[4] On this see, for example, M. Potter, *Do the Media Influence the Judiciary?* (Oxford: Foundation for Law, Justice and Society, 2011).

We start from the premise that judicial independence in the UK, as elsewhere, is not a fixed point of reference.[5] It is only at a relatively high level of generality that there is a clear consensus about what judicial independence means in practice. Most people agree that it requires that judges should be equipped, personally and professionally, to decide disputes impartially, according to the law and free from any inappropriate pressure.[6] However, the interactions explored in this book disclose competing claims about what is required by judicial independence in the day-to-day reality of running the justice system, such as the way judges are appointed, trained, disciplined and remunerated, as well as in relation to the structure, funding and management of the courts and tribunals. The protection of judicial pay and pensions from cuts which we explore in Chapter 3 is a good example of this disputed territory. From the perspective of many lawyers and judges, the practical bottom line of judicial independence is the protection of judges' remuneration. But tracing the interactions between politicians and judges over judicial pay and pensions shows how the relationship between the principle of judicial independence and its implementation in practice is highly contested. Appeals to the language of judicial independence in negotiations about issues of this sort can be a powerful card to play, but it is a card that cannot be played too often without losing its value.

It is the varied and sometimes rival interpretations of judicial independence in these interactions, including the alternative interpretations adopted by different judges, that are explored in this book. The question 'what is judicial independence in the UK?' can only be answered by offering an account of how the politics of judicial independence are transacted on a daily basis. Judicial independence depends on, amongst many other things, contested negotiations about the accounting lines of the Chief Executive of the Supreme Court, the rules governing the questions that Parliamentary select committees ask of judges, and the criticisms which ministers make of court judgments with which they disagree. This is not as straightforward or convenient as a list of abstract and universal rules but it provides a more accurate and complete account of judicial independence in the UK today.

[5] P. Russell, 'Towards a General Theory of Judicial Independence', in P. Russell and D. O'Brien (eds.), *Judicial Independence in the Age of Democracy* (Charlottesville: University Press of Virginia, 2001).

[6] For example, S. Burbank, 'What Do We Mean by "Judicial Independence"?' (2003) 64 *Ohio State Law Journal* 323; J. Ferejohn and L. Kramer, 'Independent Judges, Dependent Judiciary: Institutionalizing Judicial Restraint' (2002) 77 *NYU Law Review* 962.

Although the title of the work is *The Politics of Judicial Independence*, we have as much to say about judicial accountability. Throughout the book we highlight areas where judicial accountability has increased or where accountability gaps have opened up. Judicial independence presupposes judicial accountability, so that the politics of judicial independence is as intimately and inevitably concerned with defining the accountability of judges as it is with their independence (as we elucidate in Chapter 2).[7] Just as we argue for a more interconnected approach to the relationship between politics and judicial independence, so we also challenge the view that accountability is necessarily in tension with and distinct from independence. Until recently, work on judicial accountability generally placed weight on the individual independence of the judge in the courtroom, rather than on the collective independence of the judiciary as a branch of government. One effect of a greater formal separation of powers, however, has been to place heightened stress on collective independence and collective accountability and this is reflected throughout the book.[8] Chapters 3 and 4 explore the accountability of the judiciary to the executive, especially in relation to finance and discipline, while Chapter 5 describes their growing accountability to Parliament, with the big increase in judicial appearances before select committees.

## The old and the new politics of judicial independence

To provide a framework to help analyse the different interactions between judges and politicians, in Chapter 2 we distinguish between the 'old' and 'new' politics of judicial independence. The old politics were secretive and informal, with a great deal going on behind closed doors, but they were also flexible. The new politics tend to be more formal, institutionalised and open. They are less centred on the Lord Chancellor and offer more prominent roles for senior judges such as the Lord Chief Justice, as well as a wider array of other actors. The old and the new politics are crude distinctions which provide a framework for analysing the changing relationship between judges and politicians, but we do not claim any tidy movement from one to the other or a neat division between them.

[7] S. Burbank, 'The Architecture of Judicial Independence' (1999) 72 *Southern California Law Review* 315; A. Le Sueur, 'Developing Mechanisms for Judicial Accountability in the UK' (2004) 24 *Legal Studies* 73.

[8] R. Masterman, *The Separation of Powers in the Contemporary Constitution* (Cambridge: Cambridge University Press, 2011), Part IV.

One example of an important theme which transcends the old and the new politics of judicial independence, and which recurs throughout the book, is the role which personalities play in determining institutional relationships. Despite the greater formality, openness and institutionalisation of the new politics, powerful individuals – whether judges, politicians, officials or lay participants – continue to exert a strong influence in shaping the way in which the politics of judicial independence are played out. Many of the interactions, negotiations and indeed formal reform processes which we trace might have been very different with other individuals at the helm.

This is particularly true of the office of Lord Chancellor. In Chapter 4 we explore how the office of Lord Chancellor changed forever in 2003, but how its historical role still colours how judges, in particular, understand judicial independence and how it should be protected. Traditionally the Lord Chancellor was viewed as the indispensable guardian of judicial independence at the very heart of government. In combining executive, legislative and judicial roles, Lord Chancellors helped to nurture common interpretations of judicial independence in both political and legal spheres. Stripped of their judicial responsibilities, the new-style Lord Chancellors have become conventional ministers like any other. Many of the judges with whom we spoke still mourn the passing of the old-style Lord Chancellors and feel more exposed without this unique voice to represent the judicial view inside government. Our evidence suggests, however, that the individual approach of the person appointed as Lord Chancellor continues to be a significant factor in the day-to-day politics of judicial independence.

One effect of the changes to the office of Lord Chancellor is to prompt important questions about who now serves as the effective guardian of judicial independence, given that this task no longer falls to one pre-eminent minister. We scrutinise the role of a number of different potential guardians of judicial independence, some old and some new, who can be found in a range of institutions such as Parliament, the Judicial Office, the Judicial Appointments Commission, the Judicial Appointments and Conduct Ombudsman, the Courts Service, the Judicial Conduct Investigations Office and the administrative structure of the UK Supreme Court. Out of sight, and largely hidden behind the Whitehall and Westminster curtains, the full significance of these figures in nurturing judicial independence has not generally been recognised. Nor are they the only ones engaged in the politics of judicial independence. Non-state actors, most obviously those in the media and the legal professions, also perform critical roles. Though touching lightly on these actors in various parts of the book, we concentrate on those in public offices, explaining how and why the responsibility for safeguarding judicial independence has dispersed more widely in light of the recent retreat of successive Lord Chancellors from judiciary-related matters.

While our main focus is on the relationship between judges and external actors, we also chart the increasing burden on senior judges in defending their own independence and the impact this has had on the leadership structure of the judiciary. In Chapter 3 we consider how the formal system of partnership established in 2006 between the judiciary and the executive is working in practice before moving on in Chapter 4 to focus on the way judges have been drawn into the process of negotiating budgets for the courts, particularly in the context of severe public-sector cuts. A consequence of this economic pressure has been the growing interest of judges in England and Wales in pushing for more independent management of the courts, as judges have already done in Scotland.

One effect of moving to a more independent Courts Service could be to expand even further the responsibility borne by the judicial leadership. Chapter 6 explores the ever-expanding role of the Lord Chief Justice since replacing the Lord Chancellor as head of the judiciary and the professionalisation of the judicial senior management team. We review how the leadership of the judiciary has been strengthened and formalised while the commitment to the ideal of the 'judicial family' has been maintained – if at times it has been strained. Whereas the judges of the past defended their independence from each other almost as vigorously as their independence from government and Parliament, the judges of today, influenced in part by the integration of the tribunals judiciary into their ranks, must accept management and training and even performance appraisal by their colleagues as part and parcel of a well-run, modern and independent judiciary. Not all judges agree that these changes are compatible with judicial independence, although attitudes are shifting. In contrast, one area in which the judiciary has stood united was in the need to retain its central role in the new arrangements established for appointing the judges. In Chapters 7, 8 and 9 we analyse the extent to which judges in all three jurisdictions and the UK Supreme Court have retained a strong (and we argue excessive) influence in the independent judicial appointments bodies, based upon our analysis of how the judges interact with the lay members of those bodies and with politicians where they have a residual involvement in the appointments process.

The politics of judicial independence are played out differently in the UK now that the three legal jurisdictions of England and Wales, Scotland and Northern Ireland are located in more separated polities linked by an overarching UK Supreme Court. In Chapters 6 and 8 we chart how this multi-level system adds greater complexity and diversity to the politics of judicial independence. The Supreme Court is new, but the other jurisdictions are of long standing, and until recently the politics of judicial independence played out in similar ways in Scotland, England and Wales, and Northern Ireland. Devolution has changed this. Different approaches can be found in the systems for running the Courts Service, the judicial appointments processes, and judicial complaints and discipline.

## The future politics of judicial independence

In mapping out the different locations in which the politics of judicial independence are played out, we do not suggest that the relationship between judges and politicians is on a simple trajectory towards greater tension. Occasional tensions must be understood as just one part of the dynamic rhythm of the politics of judicial independence. Relations ebb and flow. However, whereas this once involved relatively moderate undulations, there are now more erratic patterns emerging. As we consider various challenges to the institutional independence of the judiciary, it is important to keep in mind that the baseline for our discussion is one of a long-standing and vibrant culture of judicial independence in the UK. The challenge is to ensure that this culture endures. A major point that we return to in the conclusion is that the greatest threat to judicial independence in the future may not be from the actions of politicians but rather from their disengagement and disinterest. Political will is required to sustain judicial independence. There are many challenges confronting judges in their day-to-day work, including heavy caseloads, ineffectual IT systems and reduced resources. All of our interviewees agreed, however, that the degree of independence of individual judges in the UK is rightly the subject of both international envy and respect. They remain free to resolve disputes impartially, according to the law and free from improper pressure. This is no small matter and could easily be taken for granted. In the light of the increased instability in the institutional arrangements and the growing formal separation between politicians and judges, it is even more important that there is a sizeable corps of politicians and officials who appreciate the value, over the long haul, of independent judicial decision-making.

## 2

# The politics of judicial independence and accountability

Throughout this book we use the term 'the politics of judicial independence' as shorthand for the ways in which politicians, judges and civil servants negotiate the meaning, content and limits of judicial independence and accountability in the UK. Our aim is to investigate how these negotiations operate in the real world to shed light on the practices and relationships generated by them. This chapter differs from later chapters in being conceptually rather than empirically oriented. It has two tasks: to anchor our account of independence and accountability, and to justify the political lens that we use throughout this book. The central claim developed in this chapter is that the content of independence and accountability is largely settled by politics. Politics, like independence and accountability, is a broad and flexible term, and we note various senses of it later in the chapter. However, we primarily mean politics in a transactional sense of negotiations about the day-to-day implementation of judicial independence and accountability undertaken by actors in the political and legal systems.

The chapter opens with a discussion of judicial independence, before turning to judicial accountability. That independence appears before accountability is not a signal that it is more important. On the contrary, across this book we seek to show how the two must be – and in the UK increasingly are – taken together. In practice, when judges, politicians and civil servants are negotiating the fine details of the judicial appointments process or the management of the court system, they are transacting the politics of independence and accountability simultaneously. In other words, the politics of independence defines the limits of accountability, and vice versa.

## Judicial independence

Judges should be independent. Some might disagree about whether judges are as independent as is commonly supposed. Others might dispute whether judges are sufficiently independent. But few would disagree that judges should be equipped, personally and professionally, to resolve disputes impartially, according to law and free from improper pressure – whether from the parties to the dispute, governmental actors, pressure groups or other judges. This core understanding of judicial independence is based on 'the social logic of courts'.[1] If judges are induced to decide disputes and hold the government to account other than through a good-faith adjudication of the facts and determination of the relevant law, then the logic of courts as a method of impartial dispute resolution breaks down. The losing party no longer has a reason to accept the legitimacy of the court's decision. Even the appearance or suspicion of interference or undue influence subverts that legitimacy.[2]

From this starting proposition it is possible to identify a number of generally accepted conditions for judicial independence.[3] But it is not possible to articulate a definitive checklist which guarantees judicial independence since the importance of any particular condition depends on the unique blend of political, social and historical circumstances in any one country at any one time. The following ten conditions are therefore inevitably set at a high level of generality:

(a) Judges should enjoy guaranteed tenure until the expiry of their terms of office or a mandatory retirement age. Judges must only be removed earlier for reasons of incapacity or misconduct that renders them unfit for judicial office.
(b) There should be a merit-based appointment process that ensures that persons selected as judges not only have an appropriate knowledge of and training in the law, but also exhibit a willingness to decide disputes with an open and fair mind and according to law. Promotions must be made only on merit.
(c) There should be arrangements in place to ensure that judges receive fair and secure remuneration. Any changes to, and in particular reductions in, salaries and pensions should not be used as a means of influencing judicial decision-making.

[1] M. Shapiro, *Courts: A Comparative and Political Analysis* (Chicago: The University of Chicago Press, 1981), p. 1.

[2] 'Justice must not only be done; it must manifestly and undoubtedly be seen to be done,' Lord Hewart, giving judgment in *R.* v. *Sussex Justices ex p. McCarthy* [1924] 1 KB 256, 259.

[3] We avoid speaking of 'principles' of judicial independence, preferring instead to speak of 'conditions' that typically contribute towards judicial independence. This terminology allows us to more readily grasp the contextual and contestable nature of the conditions listed below.

(d) The judicial system as a whole should receive adequate funds to enable judges to fulfil their functions.
(e) There should be rules to protect the jurisdiction of the courts. Judges must have authority to decide matters of a judicial nature according to their own view of the relevant law and facts. They should also have exclusive authority to determine whether any particular issue submitted for judicial decision falls within their competence as defined by law.
(f) Judges should have personal immunity against suit for improper acts or omissions in the exercise of their judicial functions.
(g) There should be rules providing for the recusal and disqualification of individual judges from particular cases, as well as rules banning judges from activities deemed to be incompatible with judicial office.
(h) The system for investigating judicial misconduct should ensure that complaints are not used improperly to influence how individual judges decide particular cases.
(i) There should be an independent legal profession that remains vigilant in ensuring that the law and the legal system are free from political manipulation. Well-qualified persons from the legal profession should be selected for appointment to the bench.
(j) There must be a general attitude of respect for the law and the legal system within politics.

In any particular political system, this list may be incomplete or need refining. But whether the list is drawn narrowly or widely, it is not inherently difficult to identify the core conditions derived from the concept of judicial independence.[4] Much more problematic is their implementation. Most of this book is concerned with implementation: how the practical requirements of judicial independence and accountability have been negotiated, defined and redefined in the UK in recent years. This is the point at which judicial independence moves from being an abstract ideal that almost everyone accepts to a set of rules, practices and institutions that are contextual and contestable.

[4] There are numerous international documents articulating basic principles – or, as we would put it, considerations – generated by the intuition that courts should decide impartially: see, for example, *Tokyo Principles on the Independence of the Judiciary in the LAWASIA Region* (1982); UN General Assembly, *UN Basic Principles on the Independence of the Judiciary* (1985); *Commonwealth (Latimer House) Principles on the Three Branches of Government* (2003); UN Office on Drugs and Crime: Judicial Integrity Group, *Bangalore Principles of Judicial Independence* (The Hague, 2002).

### *Contextual*

Judicial independence is 'a highly contextual concept that has changed over time and varies with circumstance and other developments'.[5] In particular, the conditions which promote or undermine judicial independence differ according to whether judicial independence is being used in an individual or a collective sense; the former relates to the decision-making of the individual judge and the latter to the judiciary as an institution.[6] Several conditions listed above seek to ensure that individual judges resolve disputes impartially, according to law and without fear or favour. Collective independence concerns the judiciary's financial and administrative relationships with the executive and the legislature, such as rules relating to the funding of the judicial system or the jurisdiction of the courts. The individual and collective dimensions are related. The insistence on the independence of the judiciary as an institution seeks to render more likely the independence of the individual judge. As the former Lord Chief Justice Lord Judge has noted, 'Without institutional independence the critical environment on which the independence of judicial decision-making depends would gradually wither'.[7]

Despite the close link between collective and individual judicial independence, the structural and procedural arrangements which are required to ensure the collective independence of the judiciary are neither necessary nor sufficient to guarantee judicial independence at the level of the individual judge. A consequence of this is that potential evidence of judicial independence is difficult to evaluate.[8] Experience in new democracies has shown that formal structures are

[5] A. Dodek and L. Sossin, 'Introduction', in A. Dodek and L. Sossin (eds.), *Judicial Independence in Context* (Toronto: Irwin Law, 2010), p. 1.

[6] For alternative accounts of the multiple dimensions, see P. Russell, 'Towards a General Theory of Judicial Independence', in P. Russell and D. O'Brien (eds.), *Judicial Independence in the Age of Democracy* (Charlottesville: University Press of Virginia, 2001); S. Shetreet, 'Judicial Independence: New Conceptual Dimensions and Contemporary Challenges', in S. Shetreet and J. Deschênes (eds.), *Judicial Independence: The Contemporary Debate* (Dordrecht: Martinus Nijhoff, 1985); S. Burbank and B. Friedman, 'Reconsidering Judicial Independence', in S. Burbank and B. Friedman (eds.), *Judicial Independence at the Crossroads: An Interdisciplinary Approach* (Thousand Oaks: Sage, 2002), p. 9.

[7] Lord Judge, 'Constitutional Change: Unfinished Business' (the Constitution Unit, 4 December 2013), para. 7.

[8] C. Larkins, 'Judicial Independence and Democratization: A Theoretical and Conceptual Analysis' (1996) 44 *American Journal of Comparative Law* 605, 610–12.

no guarantee of individual judicial behaviour or of political respect for judicial independence.[9] Conversely, experience in jurisdictions with long traditions of the rule of law – including the UK – has demonstrated that judges can behave impartially, and politicians can respect the decision-making of the courts, even in the absence of much of the structural and procedural formality often associated with institutional judicial independence. Formal protections are clearly useful in 'sustaining social conventions', for example, by providing bright-line demarcations of what is appropriate and what is not.[10] But there is no settled relationship between structures and behaviour – or what is sometimes called '*de jure*' and '*de facto*' independence.[11] What is clear is that there is increasing emphasis in the UK on ensuring that there are adequate structural arrangements in place to promote judicial independence, even though there has been no suggestion that at an individual level judicial independence has been under threat.

Threats to judicial independence can come from both internal and external sources. Judges can be subject to influence not just from outsiders, like politicians, but also from insiders – from fellow judges. Influence might arise out of decisions by senior judges about issues like judicial deployment, working conditions, remuneration or promotion. Some internal influences will not raise any concerns, such as the influence that higher courts exercise over lower courts through the appellate system. Others would be clearly inappropriate. It would be wrong for a senior judge to deploy a junior colleague to a remote court with the aim of influencing how a case is decided or as punishment for an earlier decision. In the UK, the traditional concern with the external dimension of judicial independence is being augmented by an awareness of the need to think through the internal controls in the light of increasingly hierarchical and tightly managed judicial governance systems.

[9] Y. Vyas, 'The Independence of the Judiciary: A Third World Perspective' (1992) 11 *Third World Legal Studies* 127; P. Spiller and M. Tomasi, 'Judicial Decision-Making in Unstable Environments: Argentina 1935–1998' (2002) 46 *American Journal of Political Science* 699.

[10] C. Cameron, 'Judicial Independence: How Can You Tell It When You See It? And Who Cares?', in S. Burbank and B. Friedman (eds.), *Judicial Independence at the Crossroads: An Interdisciplinary Approach* (Thousand Oaks: Sage, 2002), p. 140.

[11] B. Hayo and S. Voigt, 'Explaining De Facto Judicial Independence' (2007) 28 *International Review of Law and Economics* 269; G. Helmke and F. Rosenbluth, 'Regimes and the Rule of Law: Judicial Independence in Comparative Perspective' (2009) 12 *Annual Review of Political Science* 345.

Differing stress will be placed on these various dimensions in different countries at different times, because judicial independence is ultimately contingent on the particular political, legal and historical context in which courts operate. Judicial independence will take the form of a context-specific 'package' of rules,[12] practices and institutions that are moulded by larger cultures and traditions in politics and the law. Countries with a more 'legal' constitution might rely in large part on judicially enforceable guarantees of judicial independence found in a constitutional text, while those with a more 'political' constitution might rely more on non-legal rules and conventions. Countries will differ in their detailed approach to the implementation of particular considerations of judicial independence. Take appointments to top courts.[13] In some countries, ministers appoint the most senior judges. Other countries have legislative hearings for those nominated to top courts, while independent appointment commissions are used in an increasing number of countries. Even within any one country, and from time to time, there may be differences, largely because judicial independence is a reflection of the historical and political context in which judges operate.[14]

To be successfully realised, the independence of the judiciary depends ultimately on a general culture across the political and legal systems that values judges and the rule of law. Nurturing this culture presents a variety of challenges at different periods in different countries. The challenge in new democracies will usually stem from the relative weakness of courts. In these cases it is often difficult to foster confidence in and support for judges if courts have traditionally been closely controlled by the ruling regime. In established democracies, difficulties can arise out of the relative strength of courts, where it is a challenge to maintain support for independent judges – especially among politicians – while courts continue to wield substantial power over public policy.

### *Contestable*

Judicial independence is contestable as well as contextual and this is a key issue underpinning our book. Everyone agrees that judges should be

[12] V. Jackson, 'Judicial Independence: Structure, Context, Attitude', in A. Seibert-Fohr (ed.), *Judicial Independence in Transition* (New York and Heidelberg: Springer, 2012), p. 25.

[13] K. Malleson and P. Russell (eds.), *Appointing Judges in an Age of Judicial Power: Critical Perspectives from around the World* (Toronto: University of Toronto Press, 2006).

[14] J. Bell, 'Judicial Cultures and Judicial Independence' (2001) 4 *Cambridge Yearbook of European Legal Studies* 47, 50.

independent in a broad and abstract sense. Beyond this, however, the scope for disagreement is 'unusually wide'.[15] People have different views on the appropriate combination of the various individual and collective, structural and behavioural, internal and external dimensions described above. The scope for contesting issues such as these derives from the fact that independence is ultimately a question of degree, and people have different views about what is the appropriate degree.[16] It is plain, after all, that judges cannot be independent in the sense of being completely autonomous. They have to be appointed, promoted and, in cases of misconduct or incapacity, removed. Their salaries have to be negotiated and the courtrooms in which they sit have to be built, furnished and staffed. Their decisions have to be enforced. Since political actors typically have a say in the appointment, promotion, removal and remuneration of judges, and in the funding of the courts as a whole, as well as a role in enforcing judicial decisions, judges can never be independent in the sense of the complete absence of any dependence on others.

It is equally plain that most people would not want judges to be independent in this absolute sense. To permit those who wield power to be wholly free from any control contradicts the basic democratic impulse. This is true for judicial as well as political institutions, even if the exact blend of dependence and control inevitably varies between different institutional types. The challenge is not to release judges from each and every type of dependence and control. It is to strive for a balance within which judges are equipped to decide disputes impartially without exercising wholly unchecked power. How much institutional independence is necessary is notoriously difficult to determine.[17] Too little and our worry will be that the impartiality of judges is at risk. Too much and our concern will be for the accountability of judges, especially if they regularly overturn the policy preferences of elected politicians. The most that can be said in the abstract is that we strive for judges who

[15] J. Ferejohn and L. Kramer, 'Independent Judges, Dependent Judiciary: Institutionalizing Judicial Restraint' (2002) 77 *NYU Law Review* 962, 963.

[16] Although few dispute that judicial independence is a matter of degree, some political scientists come close to treating judicial independence as absolute: e.g. T. Jennings Peretti, 'Does Judicial Independence Exist? The Lessons of Social Science Research', in S. Burbank and B. Friedman (eds.), *Judicial Independence at the Crossroads: An Interdisciplinary Approach* (Charlottesville: University Press of Virginia, 2002).

[17] J. Finn, 'The Rule of Law and Judicial Independence in Newly Democratic Regimes' (2004) 13 *The Good Society* 12, 14.

are sufficiently independent to perform their judicial functions while also seeking appropriate mechanisms of judicial accountability.

## Judicial accountability

So far we have suggested that judicial independence is contextual and contestable. Something similar can be said of judicial accountability, which is also an essentially contested concept, with understandings that differ from country to country, time to time and person to person.[18] But more than this, the relationship between accountability and independence adds to the contextual and contestable nature of judicial independence. In the final analysis, debates about the practical implications of independence and accountability go hand in hand, culminating in difficult and disputed decisions about how to ensure that judges have sufficient independence to fulfil their judicial role and manage their collective affairs, while at the same time ensuring adequate accountability. Throughout this book, we encounter questions about the practical requirements of independence (for example, should judges be responsible for managing the court system?) that ought to be answered only after reflecting on the practical requirements of accountability (for example, what sort of accountability should accompany greater judicial involvement in the management of the courts, and what would happen if things go wrong?).

### *Accountability: six questions*

Accountability is a notion used throughout public life, and with increasing force in recent decades as politics and administration have moved away from systems based on trust to systems based on openness and public explanation.[19] It has been extended to institutions and walks of life previously sheltered from it.[20] No longer is accountability limited to narrow ideas of legality and probity, but instead extends to value for money, efficiency, fairness and equality. Sites of accountability have expanded beyond the traditional stress on ministerial responsibility to

[18] M. Bovens, 'Analysing and Assessing Accountability: A Conceptual Framework' (2007) 13 *European Law Journal* 447, 448.

[19] See, for example, R. Dalton, *Democratic Challenges, Democratic Choices* (Oxford: Oxford University Press 2004).

[20] C. Scott, 'Accountability in the Regulatory State' (2000) 27 *Journal of Law and Society* 38, 48.

Parliament or electoral accountability to the voters, to encompass notions such as corporate accountability, administrative accountability and social accountability, with a new emphasis on mechanisms such as complaints procedures, ombudsmen, audits and reporting obligations. With all of this, accountability has become a slippery notion, sometimes at risk of being all things to all people, since it seems to be 'one of those concepts that no one can be against'.[21] Within the academic literature, there is a proliferation of labels and variants, pulling the notion in many different directions.

At its heart, however, it remains a simple idea. Accountability involves the giving of reasons or explanations for decisions or conduct. This implies that accountability, in its most rudimentary sense, is a relationship where someone offers an account of their conduct to another. Here are six key questions that help to define any accountability relationship: (a) Who must provide the account? (b) To whom? (c) About what? (d) Through what processes? (e) Assessed by what standards? (f) And with what effect?[22] Answering these questions fleshes out every conceivable accountability regime, with different types – legal, political, financial, administrative – ultimately answering these questions in more or less distinct ways, each with their own complexities and variations.

In the courtroom, the judge is both an account-receiver and an account-giver. The court is a forum of legal accountability, where judges hold disputants, including public actors, to account for legal wrongs. As an account-giver, the judge provides detailed reasons to the litigants, the public at large and appellate courts (*to whom*) through a written and publicly promulgated judgment (*process*) for their decision to resolve a legal dispute one way rather than another (*about what*). Their reasoned decision is assessed according to the relevant legal rules (*standards*), with shortcomings liable to render the decision vulnerable to appeal (*to what effect*). Supplying reasoned decisions reduces the scope for judges themselves to abuse their decision-making power.

Until recently, this might have been the beginning and end of many discussions of the accountability of individual judges. It is now generally accepted, however, that individual judges are subject to multiple, overlapping (and, as illustrated across this book, increasingly formal

[21] Bovens, 'Analysing and Assessing Accountability', 448.

[22] J. Mashaw, 'Accountability and Institutional Design: Some Thoughts on the Grammar of Governance', in M. Dowdle (ed.), *Public Accountability: Designs, Dilemmas and Experiences* (Cambridge: Cambridge University Press 2006), pp. 117–18.

and transparent) accountability regimes. A judge is liable to account not just for their decisions in the courtroom, but also for their conduct in it (e.g. do they treat litigants, lawyers, the public and the court staff respectfully?). They are increasingly liable to account to senior colleagues for how long they take to reach a decision, as well as for its content. There continue to be limited experiments with judicial appraisal, whereby a judge accounts to a more senior colleague for his or her judgecraft. In short, individual judges today engage in a variety of concrete practices of account-giving to a wide range of people (higher courts, senior judicial colleagues, the legal profession and the public), through multiple processes (reasoned decisions, disciplinary processes, appraisal schemes) about all aspects of their judicial working lives.

Collectively, the judiciary is subject to increasing regimes of accountability as well. Senior judges in leadership roles, in particular, are both account-receivers and account-givers on behalf of the wider judiciary. Administrative staff account to them for their performance in supporting senior judges in the day-to-day work of managing the judiciary, as does the chief executive responsible for the running of the Courts Service. Junior colleagues will account to more senior colleagues for their performance. Drawing on all this information, judicial leaders must in turn offer accounts for their stewardship of the judiciary. Throughout this book, we will see examples of senior judges offering explanations of their management, administrative and policy decisions to ministers, Parliament, the legal professions and the public at large. These occur in annual reports, business plans, appearances before parliamentary committees, speeches and press conferences. The information is then assessed by reference to a range of standards (financial probity, value-for-money, transparency, fairness and equality). Consequences include criticism or praise for the use of resources, and the imposition of statutory duties, targets or limits to improve performance. Providing an account of their stewardship encourages senior judges more generally to reflect on their performance, to obtain feedback from stakeholders and to ensure that they are focused on achieving desirable societal outcomes.

### *Sacrificial accountability and explanatory accountability*

Our suggestion, then, is that judges – individually and collectively – are subject to numerous accountability regimes. Individual and collective regimes are themselves interrelated: for example, senior judges must offer an account for the efficiency of the judiciary as a whole, which will draw on accounts offered by each judge for their individual performance. This is as it should be: in a democracy all public officials who wield significant power – whether the substantive decision-making power in the courtroom or management decision-making that is part of judicial leadership – should make themselves accountable, and usually in several different ways. Yet the richness of these interconnected regimes of accountability might surprise some judges. One judge we interviewed said that he was 'not accountable at all, apart from to the head of the judiciary'. We suspect that this is because some judges remain wedded to a narrow understanding that assumes that accountability necessarily carries some sanction, or sacrificial element.

'Sacrificial accountability' implies that a failure to render a satisfactory explanation or justification for poor performance will result in a sanction or, in the event of seriously poor performance, the account-giver's dismissal.[23] In the UK, sacrificial accountability has a strong hold on the constitutional imagination because of the emphasis traditionally placed on the requirement that ministers account to Parliament for their actions and also those of their department, with the possibility of a minister resigning in the event of a serious failure. Within the political realm, elections also supply a form of sacrificial accountability, with MPs liable to lose their jobs at the hands of the electorate. While there is a strong association between sacrificial accountability and political life, there is a much weaker one with judicial life. Many of the core conditions of judicial independence that we listed earlier seek to preclude the sort of sacrificial accountability that can attach to political office. The first condition was that judges only be removed for incapacity or misconduct that renders them unfit to hold judicial office. Judges occasionally resign or are dismissed for serious personal misconduct, but the precariousness of ministerial tenure, including accountability for the failures of others, is clearly inapposite for judges. Judges are also protected against sanctions for certain mistakes made in their judicial capacity; for example, judges are personally immune from liability for judicial acts.

If judges assume that the only relevant type of accountability is sacrificial, then it is not surprising if they conclude that they are not really accountable 'at all'. After all, judicial independence requires taking

[23] V. Bogdanor, 'Parliament and the Judiciary: The Problem of Accountability' (Third Sunningdale Lecture on Accountability, 9 February 2006).

steps to insulate judges against the types of sacrificial accountability found in the political sphere. But accountability is much broader than this, with no necessity for formal sanction, penalty or risk of removal.[24] Even within the political sphere, the greater part of accountability has no connection with sanction but can be summarised simply as a duty to give an account, to explain, to inform or to justify. This 'explanatory accountability'[25] is how most ministers, MPs and public bodies offer accountability for their activity most of the time. The classic example mentioned above of the individual judge giving reasons in public for their decisions fits comfortably with this explanatory model, as does the more recent idea of an individual judge offering an account of their professional performance through an appraisal with a senior colleague. Similarly, senior judges providing accounts of their stewardship of the judicial system exemplifies explanatory accountability. Our book not only charts an explosion of explanatory accountability within the judicial system, but also to a significant degree could only be written because of it. Without the information and explanations that are now routinely made available to the public by senior judges, our ability to explain how the judicial system operates would have been seriously impoverished.

Even in this context, however, there is reason for judges to be cautious. Trust is especially important to the judicial function. Safeguarding trust in the impartiality of judges is part of the rationale for protecting judicial independence in the first place. However, as Onora O'Neill has explained, greater accountability does not necessarily enhance trust. Specialist information is liable to be misinterpreted in the public domain if it is not properly contextualised, while constantly challenging someone to justify their actions might encourage suspicion that they have committed some wrong.[26] Public trust in the UK judiciary is in fact very high,[27] but, as Le Sueur argues, accountability regimes must be properly tailored when

[24] We follow Harlow and Rawlings in concluding that sanction is not essential to the concept. C. Harlow and R. Rawlings, 'Promoting Accountability in Multi-level Governance: A Network Approach' (2007) 13 *European Law Journal* 542, 545–6.

[25] Bogdanor, 'Parliament and the Judiciary'.

[26] J. Gardner, 'The Mark of Responsibility', in M. Dowdle (ed.), *Public Accountability: Designs, Dilemmas and Experiences* (Cambridge: Cambridge University Press, 2006), p. 239.

[27] The Ipsos MORI Veracity Index consistently records levels of trust in 'judges' at above 75 per cent of the population. Figures for the 2013 survey were 82 per cent, by contrast with a meagre 18 per cent for 'politicians generally'. Source: ipsos-mori.com.

applied to judges if this trust is not to be jeopardised.[28] He notes that 'content accountability' (that is, for the substance of judicial decisions) is a particularly sensitive matter. Independence requires that judges must be free – and feel free – to render what they see as the correct decision on the basis of the applicable law and the facts of the case. For this reason, judges are accountable for their decisions almost exclusively to the appellate courts. However, 'probity accountability' for matters like personal misconduct, conflicts of interest and the administration of budgets is less troubling from this standpoint and more readily amenable to existing accountability mechanisms, such as Parliamentary oversight, audit requirements, reporting obligations and so on.[29] The failure of an expensive courtroom IT procurement exercise, for example, is a legitimate object of public concern that may require senior judges to account for the underlying decisions and strategies. Between these two poles of content and probity accountability lie a myriad of difficult issues, such as the listing of cases and case management.

### *Independence and accountability*

Judicial independence and judicial accountability are sometimes described as 'two sides of the same coin'.[30] This is a helpful metaphor insofar as it encourages us to grasp that independence and accountability are not in inevitable and irreconcilable tension. At the same time, this metaphor is misleading if it is taken to suggest that there are easy answers about how best to promote independence while also ensuring adequate accountability. As we will see, there have been tensions – felt particularly keenly by the judges – between traditional understandings of judicial independence and increasing pressure from ministers for accountability initiatives designed to secure value for money in the justice system. If implemented sensitively, accountability can, however, bolster trust in judges,[31] which in turn fosters conditions in which judicial independence is likely to thrive. Sensibly designed accountability

[28] A. Le Sueur, 'Developing Mechanisms for Judicial Accountability in the UK' (2004) 24 *Legal Studies* 73, 74–5.

[29] Le Sueur, 'Developing Mechanisms for Judicial Accountability in the UK', 81–7.

[30] S. Burbank, 'The Architecture of Judicial Independence' (1998) 72 *Southern California Law Review* 315, 339.

[31] D. Brody, 'The Use of Judicial Performance Evaluation to Enhance Judicial Accountability, Judicial Independence, and Public Trust' (2008) 86 *Denver University Law Review* 115.

regimes can help, for example, to weed out incapable judges or to provide greater clarity about the operations of the judicial system. Accountability can enhance independence more directly: a robust system for declaring judges' conflicts of interest will, for example, protect their independence as well as ensuring accountability.

If we adopt an explanatory or account-giving definition of judicial accountability, then many of the conditions for judicial independence listed above – for example, those relating to tenure, merit-based appointment and recusal – are also relevant for judicial accountability. A central claim made in this book is that, despite their apparent distinctiveness, independence and accountability are realised together in the politics of judicial independence. When judges and politicians negotiate issues like judicial appointments or the management of judicial misconduct, they are in fact transacting the politics of judicial independence and accountability simultaneously. Negotiations around real issues are rarely explicitly acknowledged as being about independence and accountability, but in discussions about how much involvement senior judges should have in the running of the courts, or politicians should have in the selection of judges, concerns about independence and accountability are woven together. The politics of judicial independence define the limits of judicial accountability and vice versa.

## The political lens

One consequence of the difficulty of agreeing what exactly is meant by judicial independence and accountability, let alone the proper relationship between them, is that it can be hard to pin down the ways in which these notions are expressed in everyday practices. For these purposes we need a 'lens' to help us decide what to study, why and how. In this book, politics supplies our lens. A political lens encourages us to locate politics, politicians and day-to-day political processes at the heart of the study of independence and accountability. It supplies an important corrective to the propensity (of lawyers and judges in particular) to adopt overly legalistic accounts that exaggerate the importance of judges and the law. Judicial independence and accountability are not just about judges, but also about the general attitudes and everyday decisions of ministers, legislators, civil servants and many others. Many important parts of political life are largely ignored or given short shrift in most accounts of judicial independence. Day-to-day practices inside the

Ministry of Justice and the Courts Service, for example, have a significant effect on the realisation of judicial independence and accountability. As well as statutes and case law,[32] the study of judicial independence involves soft law – concordats, framework documents and codes of conduct – as well as informal interactions. Reflecting this, the language of independence and accountability today includes the political and managerial lexicon of Westminster and Whitehall: of select committee hearings, business plans and annual reports. All of this would have seemed alien to the judges of thirty years ago – if not a threat to judicial independence in itself.[33]

Above all, a political lens helps us to grasp that independence and accountability are ultimately political achievements. Given their contestability, this should be no surprise, since politics arises whenever questions in the public sphere do not have clear or easily agreed solutions. Independence and accountability result, in large measure, from politics and as a product of the everyday practices of a wide variety of political and judicial actors. The political actors that we have in mind are primarily ministers and their officials, but also parliamentarians and their officials. The day-to-day practices include decisions by ministers to adjust the level of court fees or judicial pensions, decisions by MPs and peers to refrain from commenting in Parliament on legal proceedings, and the role of parliamentary clerks to disallow questions that might undermine the judicial function. These are just a flavour of the everyday political practices explored in this book. These practices are everyday in an almost literal sense: routine, mundane even, with their significance often drowned out by the clamour of partisan politics, and by occasional but high-profile clashes that occur between politicians and judges.

These everyday political practices point to a broad-based coalition behind judicial independence, which is built on the stake that political actors share in a system of independent courts.[34] In the UK's constitutional traditions, this political support has proven sufficiently

[32] See, for example, the Constitutional Reform Act 2005, sections 3–4; Judiciary and Courts (Scotland) Act 2008, section 1; *Duport Steel* v. *Sirs* [1980] 1 WLR 142, *Starrs* v. *Ruxton* (2000) JC 208.

[33] See, for example, N. Browne-Wilkinson, 'The Independence of the Judiciary in the 1980s' [1988] *Public Law* 44.

[34] S. Holmes, 'Judicial Independence as Ambiguous Reality and Insidious Illusion', in R. Dworkin (ed.), *From Liberal Values to Democratic Transition: Essays in Honor of Janos Kis* (Budapest and New York: Central European University Press), pp. 11–14.

strong to withstand the tensions between politicians and judges that inevitably arise from time to time. Yet most commentators are apt not only to overstate the extent to which legal rules help to secure independence and accountability, but also to overstate the significance of occasional but inevitable tensions – even as they understate the extent to which both are secured via political practices that shape and are shaped by an enduring political commitment. What, though, do we mean by politics? There are three key senses of politics that inform our understanding of independence and accountability.

### *Politics as government*

Insofar as judicial independence is sometimes confused with judicial isolation, this first sense of politics is a useful reminder that judges always remain part of the 'political' – as in governmental – apparatus of the state, even when they hold other political actors to account on legal grounds.[35] Judges exercise considerable coercive powers in the name of the state and can help to secure socially and economically desirable goals, and in this sense are not so different from other power-wielding governmental actors, albeit they fulfil their governmental functions by creating, applying and interpreting law. We do not mean to suggest that judges are simply politicians in judges' robes, nor to deny the distinctiveness of law and legal reasoning. Judicial independence entails recognising that judges perform a different and rather specialised government function. By envisaging judges as part of government and politics, we are, however, able to address the practical puzzle presented by judicial independence: how can we arrange the apparatus of the state in a manner that confers on one part of it a degree of independence from the rest?

No matter how we answer this question there is likely to be a convoluted package of institutional rules that define the constitutional position of the judiciary. Even where this package embraces a formal separation of powers there will be an intricate web of relationships and interactions between the judicial and political realms. While recent reforms in the UK have created a more formal separation between the judicial and political branches, relationships between judges, politicians and civil servants are closer in some significant ways, as a result of new

[35] This draws on insights of political jurisprudence in M. Shapiro, 'Political Jurisprudence' (1963) 52 *Kentucky Law Journal* 294.

approaches to issues like judicial discipline and judicial selection, responsibility for which is now shared between politicians and judges. In the chapters that follow, our political lens is not directed at the separation of powers as an abstract idea. Indeed, if this work suggests anything, it is that recent reforms have been more about 'power' than 'separateness'; about how powers are now divided and shared, and how the judicial systems in the UK work as a result.

### *Politics as power*

A commonly applied understanding of politics relates to the distribution, exercise and consequences of power. Judicial power has two elements. The first is jurisdictional, and concerns the substantive decision-making powers in legal disputes, especially in realms traditionally viewed as the exclusive preserve of elected politicians. The second is institutional, and concerns the influence that judges now wield in areas such as the selection, conduct, deployment, funding and management of the judiciary. This embraces the ability of the judiciary to alter its own internal arrangements, to set the agenda, to initiate and make policy on issues relating to the judiciary and courts, and the ability to shape the thinking of the other branches of government and to influence public debate.[36] This second element of judicial power not only depends on, but also finds expression in, resources: the funds and staff to support judges, the ability to influence the level and allocation of money in the court system, and the ability to select and direct staff.

Most discussions of the judiciary in the UK's changing constitution have focused on judicial power in the first sense; that is to say, on the growing scope of the substantive decision-making power of the courts, especially in light of the increasing scope and intensity of judicial review and the courts' powers under the Human Rights Act 1998. The considerable growth of the institutional power of the judiciary is rarely discussed.[37] In the last ten years or so, the judiciary has assumed increasing influence over judicial appointments, deployment and discipline, and the management of the courts service. This has led to

[36] This draws on the account of power in S. Lukes, *Power: A Radical View* (Basingstoke: Palgrave Macmillan, 1974) as developed in R. Rhodes, *Control and Power in Central–Local Government Relations* (Aldershot: Gower, 1981).

[37] One exception being R. Masterman's book, *The Separation of Powers in the Contemporary Constitution* (Cambridge: Cambridge University Press, 2011), especially Part IV.

increasingly prominent roles for senior judges, such as the Lord Chief Justice and the Senior President of Tribunals. The Judicial Office, which supports and enables the leadership and governance of the judiciary, now has over 200 staff. Across this book we chart the increasing institutional power of the judiciary, examining the implications of this in terms of the judiciary's external relations with other parts of government (including Parliament), but also in terms of the judiciary's internal relationships, given the considerable concentration of power in a handful of very senior judges. A particular concern is whether this growth in the institutional power of the judiciary has been accompanied by sufficiently robust mechanisms of judicial accountability.

### *Politics as negotiation*

This final sense is, for us, the most important, and concerns the contestation and compromise that is the basic ingredient of most political activity – or what we term the politics of judicial independence and accountability. The key actors in these negotiations span the political and legal worlds. Some fall squarely into one realm, some into the other, and some straddle both. Negotiations about the judiciary's relations with other parts of the political system are always carried out within this distinctively dual context. It is important to correct the tendency to foreground judges and sideline political actors when discussing independence and accountability. It is equally important not to make the opposite mistake by downplaying the increasing importance of judges in defining and defending their own independence. Senior judges play increasingly prominent roles in leading, and safeguarding the interests of, the judiciary as a whole.

These negotiations are an unusually subtle form of politics. There is a general reluctance in the politics of judicial independence to draw on the common tools of political negotiation. It is rare, for example, for judges or politicians to publicise their cause in the media. Negotiations usually take place quietly, often informally and behind closed doors. The gloves rarely come off, at least not in public. Politicians and judges generally recognise that they each have more to gain by adhering to the rules of a game in which judicial independence is a trump card to be played with restraint. Judges seldom resort to explicit claims that politicians are undermining judicial independence, while politicians are equally reluctant to accuse judges of invoking independence as a cloak for their self-interest. This represents a counter-intuitive and unique feature of the politics of judicial independence. The players rarely invoke judicial independence directly; and in fact they generally deny that the process is political at all.

Politicians hold potentially powerful tools that could be used to undermine the independence of the judiciary; for example, ministers could withhold the funds necessary for the efficient running of the courts or parliamentarians could misuse powers to remove judges. And there is no doubt that from time to time political actors in the UK encroach upon judicial independence, although encroachments have not generally been egregious. Clashes between judges and politicians – and with ministers and their officials in particular – are inevitable. But as Alan Hutchinson notes, 'the clash between government and judiciary occupies only a small corner of the overall terrain on judicial independence'.[38] This insight is evident through the rest of this book. There are *positive* and *negative* limbs to the politics of judicial independence. The mistake of many people, and of legal commentators in particular, is to focus too much on the negative – on those relatively rare occasions where political actors seem to undermine independence. Too little attention is paid to the positive – to the willingness of most political actors to act in ways that promote and protect that independence. A political lens enables us to keep in sight both the positive and the negative limbs of the politics of judicial independence.

## The 'old' and 'new' politics

Our central claim in this chapter is that judicial independence and accountability, in day-to-day terms, are secured through political negotiations. A secondary claim is that a political lens supplies a way of understanding how these negotiations are transacted via the everyday decisions and interactions of a wide range of politicians, judges and officials. It is these negotiations that we have in mind when referring to 'the politics of judicial independence'. We now want to suggest that, in the UK, it is possible to contrast the *old* and *new* politics of judicial independence. These terms capture something significant about how independence and accountability have been negotiated before and after recent reforms, and in particular they reflect a move away from informality and reliance on conventions towards more formal legal rules and institutional separation. The Constitutional Reform Act 2005

[38] A. Hutchinson, 'Judges and Politics: An Essay from Canada' (2004) 24 *Legal Studies* 275, 287.

(CRA), in particular, has substantially modified the office of Lord Chancellor, established the UK Supreme Court and introduced new methods of selecting judges involving an independent body. The labels 'old' and 'new' create a broad-brush distinction. There is no settled division between the two, and some characteristics of the new politics can be detected long before 2005. Nonetheless, the term 'new politics' expresses a discernible change in how judicial independence and accountability are both understood and negotiated.

The old politics were characterised by informality, secrecy and flexibility. They were focused on a very narrow range of institutional actors, with the Lord Chancellor at the centre as an essential buckle between the judiciary and the government. Incumbent Lord Chancellors were often perceived to be on the judges' side when negotiating with ministerial colleagues, and with the Treasury in particular. Regular meetings between the Lord Chancellor and senior judges were essentially the only contacts between the judiciary and the government. Each side preserved the confidences of the other and institutional boundaries were blurred. The Lord Chancellor was a Cabinet minister, a parliamentarian and the head of the judiciary. The UK's most senior judges sat in, and delivered judgments as a committee of, the House of Lords. There was relatively little concern about these institutional anomalies. Indeed, they were often seen as strengths. Far from being viewed as a threat to judicial independence, the Lord Chancellor's overlapping ministerial and judicial roles were generally deemed an indispensable safeguard for the judges. The Lord Chancellor represented judicial interests inside government, cautioning ministerial colleagues not to do anything to endanger the constitutional position of the judiciary. Generally speaking, the old politics were relatively stable, with far-reaching changes few and far between. Underpinning the old politics was a narrow understanding of independence, with a weight traditionally only attached to the 'hallmarks'[39] of individual independence, such as security of tenure and the rules safeguarding judicial remuneration. Little, if any, attention was paid to judicial accountability.

The new politics of judicial independence is spurred by the removal of many of the overlaps between the political and judicial realms. Informality is replaced with formality, and institutional linkages are

[39] R. Stevens, 'Judicial Independence in England: A Loss of Innocence', in P. Russell and D. O'Brien (eds.), *Judicial Independence in the Age of Democracy: Critical Perspectives from around the World* (Charlottesville: University Press of Virginia, 2001), p. 159.

replaced by more formal separation. With the creation of the Supreme Court, judges have been removed from Parliament. Many of the judiciary-related responsibilities of the Lord Chancellor have been either transferred to senior judges or hived off to new independent bodies. There has been a move to rationalise relationships more in keeping with a formal account of the separation of powers. Formal processes have been introduced to regulate such matters as the selection of judges and the administration of the court system. There is less reliance on the single channel of the Lord Chancellor as the buckle between the judiciary and the government, with a much wider range of people involved in negotiating the parameters of independence and accountability. In addition to the increasingly crucial leadership role played by the Lord Chief Justice, there are important leadership functions for a range of senior judges, in particular the Senior Presiding Judge and the Senior President of Tribunals. Individual judges are often charged with negotiating specific issues with politicians and administrators. In the new politics, there are multiple channels for communication between politicians and judges. The new politics are more open and transparent, with senior judges occupying more visible roles: they appear frequently before Parliamentary committees, hold press conferences and give interviews.

Driving the new politics is the importance attached by legal and political elites to a more expansive notion of judicial independence that emphasises its collective, structural and internal dimensions. This goes hand in hand with rising recognition in the legal and political worlds of the importance of promoting judicial accountability. Amidst all of this change, some aspects remain the same. The new more formal structures that have been created still rely heavily on informal relationships and are often shaped by individual personalities. The new politics rely on informal channels, personal relationships and individual diplomacy to avoid conflicts and to achieve compromise. For all the emphasis on openness and transparency, considerable secrecy shrouds negotiations between senior judges and ministers. Perhaps, above all, the new politics still depend on politicians who understand the importance of an independent judiciary.

## Conclusion

Judicial independence is ultimately a political achievement, and we have argued that this arises out of its contextual and contestable nature. The rest of this book describes and analyses the political processes of negotiating and defining judicial independence and accountability, and the detailed arrangements that result. We trace the move from the old to new politics, even as we see that the features that made the old politics distinctive have often reappeared, in modified form, in the new. Many of the institutional debates of the last decade are to some extent perennial. The appropriate role of the House of Lords and of the Lord Chancellor, the need for a Ministry of Justice, and the degree to which judges should control the administration of the courts have been debated back and forth since at least the 1860s. The constitutional reforms of the early twenty-first century will not be the last word.[40]

[40] Indeed, important parts of the Constitutional Reform Act 2005 were changed after just a few years. See, in particular, the Crime and Courts Act 2013.

3

# The new Lord Chancellors and the executive

The relationship between the judiciary and the executive is pivotal to the politics of judicial independence. At the heart of that relationship is the office of Lord Chancellor, an ancient office that can be traced back to the eleventh century, and possibly earlier.[1] Often described as the buckle or linchpin of the two branches of government, it has traditionally been the locus at which the relationship between the two is played out. Since 2005, the office has undergone a transformation that has impacted on the politics of judicial independence in ways that are only now beginning fully to emerge. The formal changes to the office of Lord Chancellor are only one part of the story. The changing political culture is equally important, as is the burgeoning of the Lord Chancellor's Department, which has grown from a small Whitehall backwater in the early 1970s into a major government department today.

In this chapter we trace the changes in order to compare the old- and new-style Lord Chancellors and to identify how, in turn, these changes are reconfiguring relations between the judiciary and the executive and affecting the independence and accountability of the judiciary. As with the distinction between 'old' and 'new' politics in the last chapter, there is no sharp divide between old and new Lord Chancellors. Nonetheless there is an identifiable trend towards the new Lord Chancellor becoming an ordinary Minister of Justice. In the light of this change, we ask how power is now divided between the two branches of government and how much consultation and co-operation is required to make the system work. We consider how effectively the new form of partnership operates, where the problems lie and whether there are now sufficient shared understandings between the ministers and senior judges to enable new Lord Chancellors to serve as effective guardians of judicial independence inside government. We also trace the ways in which the

[1] See N. Underhill, *The Lord Chancellor* (Lavenham: Terence Dalton, 1978).

judiciary is accountable to the Lord Chancellor. Later chapters then look in more detail at the relationship between the judiciary and the executive in the funding and management of the courts, the UK Supreme Court and judicial appointments.

## Comparing old and new Lord Chancellors

### *Roles and responsibilities*

Every law student knows that the old-style office of Lord Chancellor was a bizarre blend of executive, legislative and judicial roles. As a Cabinet minister, the Lord Chancellor was bound by collective responsibility and accountable to the Westminster Parliament for the fair, efficient and effective administration of justice. He was also Speaker of the House of Lords, entitled to preside over proceedings in Parliament's upper chamber and to speak on behalf of the government in debates. This trinity of institutional roles was completed by the Lord Chancellor's position as the head of the judiciary.[2] The Lord Chancellor's unusual hybrid role persisted, at least in part, because the office was ancient, but in fact even the old-style Lord Chancellor changed significantly between 1970 and 2005. At the beginning of the 1970s, the Lord Chancellor's Office (LCO) was a very small department that primarily dealt with the appointment of judges; its 'major concern was patronage'.[3] As we explain in the next chapter, this changed with Courts Act 1971, which turned the LCO into the Lord Chancellor's Department (LCD), responsible for most aspects of court administration. The Lord Chancellor now had responsibility for judicial appointments, case listing, court organisation and the summoning of juries, and with all of this a much bigger administration which continued to grow as it acquired more power and more responsibilities.[4] Some judges became concerned that in this acquisition of power by the Lord Chancellor and his department there lay a threat to independence.[5] As Sir Nicholas Browne-Wilkinson

[2] Our focus in this chapter is on England and Wales, but the Lord Chancellor was also head of the judiciary in Northern Ireland and had some functions in relation to Scotland. See O. Gay/House of Commons Parliament and Constitution Centre, *Role of the Lord Chancellor* (SN/PC/2105 2003).

[3] D. Woodhouse, *The Office of Lord Chancellor* (Oxford: Hart Publishing, 2001), p. 44.

[4] The LCD acquired responsibility for criminal legal aid in 1989 and for magistrates' courts in 1993.

[5] Woodhouse, *The Office of Lord Chancellor*, pp. 44–5.

commented, 'Judges are sitting in an environment wholly determined by executive decision in the Lord Chancellor's Department, which is in turn operating under the financial constraints and pressures imposed by the Treasury'.[6] While its culture in the 1970s was that of a small office and owed more to legal culture than to civil service norms – Sir Derek Oulton, its Permanent Secretary, liked to conceive of it 'as a set of chambers around the Lord Chancellor'[7] – its increased size and budgetary responsibility created pressure for the LCD to operate as a normal Whitehall department.

Although chary of the increasing administrative power of the department, judges generally felt that the Lord Chancellor was a valuable advocate in Cabinet, their 'friend at court',[8] as a former Lord Chancellor put it, whose 'essential function' was 'defending and preserving the independence of the judiciary'.[9] This did not mean that Lord Chancellors were mouthpieces of the judges. The protection of judicial independence and the protection of the judges' interests were closely aligned in the minds of the judiciary. Challenges to their interests – for example by Lord Mackay when he pushed through reforms to judges' pensions and the legal profession – were often fiercely opposed as threats to their independence.[10] Nonetheless Lord Mackay is remembered as an exemplary Lord Chancellor because of his total commitment to the core values of judicial independence; his battles with the judges are largely forgiven, if not forgotten. However, Lord Elwyn-Jones is viewed less well because of his refusal, for political reasons, to promote Mr Justice Donaldson to the Court of Appeal in the mid-1970s.[11]

The success with which old-style Lord Chancellors were able to defend judicial independence at the heart of government depended to a

[6] N. Browne-Wilkinson, 'The Independence of the Judiciary in the 1980s' [1988] *Public Law* 44, 50.

[7] In conversation with one of the authors (Robert Hazell, then a young civil servant).

[8] Lord Hailsham, 'The Office of Lord Chancellor and the Separation of Powers' [1989] *Civil Justice Quarterly* 308, 314.

[9] Hailsham, 'The Office of Lord Chancellor and the Separation of Powers', 311.

[10] F. Purchas, 'The Constitution in the Market Place' (1993) 143 *New Law Journal* 1604; F. Purchas, 'Lord Mackay and the Judiciary' (1994) 144 *New Law Journal* 527; F. Purchas, 'What Is Happening to Judicial Independence?' (1994) 144 *New Law Journal* 1306.

[11] Sir John Donaldson had been President of the National Industrial Relations Court (1971–4), seen as hostile to the trade unions. One hundred and eighty-one Labour MPs signed a Commons motion for his dismissal. He was promoted to the Court of Appeal in 1979, two months after the election of the Thatcher government, and became Master of the Rolls (1982–92).

considerable degree on the status of the office and its occupants. By the end of the twentieth century, the Prime Minister would by convention appoint as Lord Chancellor a person at the pinnacle of a successful legal and political career, who did not share the political ambition of their Cabinet colleagues. It was this relative absence of political ambition that empowered Lord Chancellors to stand up to ministerial colleagues, especially over measures that might undermine the independence of the judiciary. In addition, as a member of the House of Lords, the Lord Chancellor was removed from the hurly-burly of frontline politics and thus in a better position to appreciate constitutional niceties than their colleagues in the Commons.

The new-style Lord Chancellor occupies a much pared-down post: no longer Speaker of the House of Lords and no longer a judge. Crucially, the Lord Chief Justice (LCJ) has replaced the Lord Chancellor as head of the judiciary.[12] While the Lord Chancellor retains ultimate responsibility for the court system and the terms and conditions of the judiciary, significant areas like court administration and judicial appointments have been delegated or transferred to other agencies. The Courts Service, for example, is now jointly responsible to the Lord Chancellor and the LCJ. Lines of accountability to Parliament still run through the Lord Chancellor, but significant parts of the system are now run independently of, or at arm's length from, the Lord Chancellor and the Ministry of Justice (MoJ).

The office of the new-style Lord Chancellor is now a conventional ministerial office with a heavyweight portfolio: 'We've gone from a Lord Chancellor's Department that was about six men and a dog to a Ministry of Justice now that's a major government department,' according to a District Judge. Since 2007, the position of Lord Chancellor has been twinned with that of the Secretary of State for Justice. Strictly speaking, these are two separate offices to which the Prime Minister appoints the same person, with legislation relating to judges and the courts usually designating the Lord Chancellor as the responsible minister.[13] A practical consequence of the twinned offices is that the judiciary-related functions of the Lord Chancellor sit alongside the Secretary of State's responsibilities for the criminal justice system, prisons and probation. Hence, the individual appointed as Lord Chancellor has an expansive

[12] Constitutional Reform Act 2005, section 7(1).

[13] A. Le Sueur, 'Parliamentary Accountability and the Judicial System', in N. Bamforth and P. Leyland (eds.), *Accountability in the Contemporary Constitution* (Oxford: Oxford University Press, 2013).

ministerial portfolio and heads a sizeable department, and the judiciary and the courts must compete for attention and resources alongside several more politically salient priorities.[14] The judiciary-related functions of the Lord Chancellors also remain fairly extensive. Underpinning these various responsibilities is the statutory duty on the Lord Chancellor, and indeed all ministers, to uphold the independence of the judiciary.[15] The Lord Chancellor is under an additional duty to 'have regard to the need to defend that independence'.[16]

Many judges view the transfer of judicial leadership from the Lord Chancellor to the LCJ as potentially undermining the protection of judicial independence within government. As Lord Judge told us:

> The really important consideration is that the Lord Chancellor is no longer the head of the judiciary and the Lord Chief Justice has become head of the judiciary. That means there is nobody representing the judiciary around the Cabinet table, at all. The Lord Chancellor has an obligation to represent the interests of the judiciary but he is, in reality, a deflated figure for this purpose . . . the Lord Chancellor may express a view, but he's simply now expressing a departmental view.

We will discuss the new Lord Chancellor's reduced role in judicial appointments in Chapter 7. For now, though, it is important to sketch the very different levels of discretion enjoyed by the old and new Lord Chancellors. Old Lord Chancellors enjoyed wide discretion over appointments, restricted only by the convention that they would consult the senior judiciary before making any appointment. For very senior appointments, the senior judges would consider a list of possible candidates for the High Court and above, which would be discussed at a meeting of the Lord Chancellor, the department's Permanent Secretary and the Heads of Division. But, as one former senior official put it, Lord Chancellors 'would take advice from the judiciary but wouldn't necessarily follow it'. Ultimately, the Lord Chancellor would decide. Lord Bingham was, notably, appointed Lord Chief Justice over the objections of the senior judiciary. Though nominally the decision-maker for appointments to the High Court and above, and while responsible to Parliament for the operation of the selection process as a whole, the new Lord Chancellor has little discretion in practice over appointments when presented with just

[14] See, for example, Jack Straw's wide-ranging policy objectives following his appointment as Lord Chancellor in 2007: J. Straw, *Last Man Standing: Memoirs of a Political Survivor* (London: Macmillan, 2012), pp. 498–9.

[15] Constitutional Reform Act 2005 Act, section 3(1).

[16] Contained in section 3(6) and in the Lord Chancellor's oath in section 17.

a single candidate for each vacancy by the Judicial Appointments Commission or the *ad hoc* selection commission for the Supreme Court. In the 3,500 or so judicial appointments made between 2006 and 2013, the Lord Chancellors rejected a nomination, or requested reconsideration, on just five occasions. The Lord Chancellor's role in appointments was further reduced under the Crime and Courts Act 2013, with the decision-making power in respect of appointments to courts below the High Court and tribunals transferred to the LCJ and the Senior President of Tribunals respectively.[17]

### *The 2005 changes: from old to new Lord Chancellor*

Reflecting the peculiar mix of political and legal responsibilities that distinguished the old-style office, Lord Chancellors were usually either party politicians with significant experience in legal practice or leading barristers (occasionally judges) with similar political sympathies to the government of the day.[18] Though there were no formal qualifications for the post, it was generally accepted that as well as being a political supporter of the party in power, the Lord Chancellor had to be 'a lawyer of first-class ability, capable of evoking the respect, and even fear, of lawyers, politicians, and civil servants'.[19] Thus the position differed from other Cabinet ministers who tended to be amateurs and might be able to bring political and perhaps administrative skills to their department, but not necessarily relevant expertise.[20] If not already a peer, the appointee would be elevated to the Lords.

Like other Cabinet ministers, the Lord Chancellor held office at the pleasure of the Prime Minister. Though at least three were abruptly dismissed,[21] they enjoyed longer-than-average tenure. Eleven Lord Chancellors served between 1945 and 2003, each holding the office for an average of just over five years, or roughly twice the average tenure of other Cabinet ministers.[22] Being a senior and respected

[17] Crime and Courts Act 2013, Schedule 13, Part 4.

[18] Lord Schuster, 'The Office of the Lord Chancellor' (1948) 10 *Cambridge Law Journal* 175, 177.

[19] R. Heuston, *Lives of the Lord Chancellors: 1940–1970* (Oxford: Clarendon Press, 1997), p. 3.

[20] R. Brazier, *Ministers of the Crown* (Oxford: Clarendon, 1997), p. 61.

[21] Lord Simonds (1954), Lord Kilmuir (1962) and Lord Irvine (2003).

[22] Cabinet ministers remain in post, on average, for 28.7 months: S. Berlinksi, T. Dewan and K. Dowding, *Accounting for Ministers: Scandal and Survival in British Government 1945–2007* (Cambridge: Cambridge University Press, 2012), p. 36.

figure at the end of a successful career, the Lord Chancellor had little to fear from standing up to ministerial colleagues or even the Prime Minister.

The foundations of the changes to the office of Lord Chancellor set out in the Constitutional Reform Act 2005 (CRA) were laid much earlier. Starting with Michael Howard in the early 1990s, successive Home Secretaries had seen the Lord Chancellor as an obstacle to a more efficient criminal justice system and tried to find ways around this. It was under Howard that plans were drawn up for a Ministry of Justice.[23] In 2001 the Prime Minister's office made a bold attempt for the Home Office to take over the whole courts system. Alerted by the Lord Chancellor, Lord Irvine, senior judges met the Prime Minister to protest, and Prime Minister Tony Blair backed down. Irvine was also opposed to the creation of a UK Supreme Court and a Judicial Appointments Commission. The Labour government became so frustrated with the Lord Chancellor's opposition to reform that it determined to sweep away his office as well as reforming the whole justice system. To prevent the judges from stifling reform, the changes were prepared in strict secrecy. In June 2003, abruptly and with no consultation, 10 Downing Street announced the resignation of Lord Irvine alongside plans to abolish the office of Lord Chancellor and to create a new Supreme Court and Judicial Appointments Commission.[24] The Lord Chancellor was to be replaced by a Secretary of State for Constitutional Affairs, who no longer had to be a lawyer and could sit (as most government ministers do) in the House of Commons. The senior judges were taken completely by surprise, as were almost all the Lord Chancellor's senior officials, who were away at a conference at the time: 'The reform of the Lord Chancellor was an earthquake, the tremors of which lasted throughout Charlie Falconer's time. The judiciary were outraged at the idea that you could just come in [and abolish the Lord Chancellor] and they never quite got over that' (senior official in the Lord Chancellor's Department). The judges were equally outraged at the lack of any consultation. The Lord Chief Justice,

[23] But the idea of a Ministry of Justice responsible for the whole administration of justice, criminal and civil, goes back a long way – to the Haldane report of 1918, and earlier.

[24] Lord Irvine was effectively sacked. For a detailed account of the episode, see HL Constitution Committee, 'Memorandum by Lord Irvine of Lairg', *The Cabinet Office and the Centre of Government* (HL 30 2009); Judicial Independence Project, 'The Abolition of the Office of Lord Chancellor: 10 Years On: Note of Seminar Held at Queen Mary, University of London' (12 June 2013).

Lord Woolf, postponed his retirement in order to moderate the proposals and negotiate a new settlement. Working intensively with the Lord Chancellor's Permanent Secretary, Sir Hayden Phillips, the two hammered out a new division of responsibilities:

> I think I must have had twenty meetings . . . with the Lord Chief Justice . . . We had actually to write down what it was that the judges were going to do and what it was the Lord Chancellor and his civil servants were going to do under this new arrangement. Harry [Woolf] and I agreed from the start that we needed a written document, the Concordat . . . on how to make the new system work.
>
> *(Sir Hayden Phillips)*

After six months of intensive negotiations between Lord Woolf and Lord Falconer, the Concordat was published in January 2004.[25] The Concordat provided the basis for a new division of roles and responsibilities which heavily influenced the content of the CRA 2005 and has since developed into a new form of partnership. The Concordat covered a range of issues: leadership of the judiciary, provision of resources, deployment, leadership posts, complaints and appointments. Reflecting the judges' main concerns, over half of the twenty-seven-page document was taken up with just two topics: judicial discipline and judicial appointments. The judges sought protection from political influence through very detailed legal drafting of the new processes.

The judges were also concerned at losing the influence of a powerful protector at the Cabinet table. There may have been relatively few occasions when the Lord Chancellor actually intervened in Cabinet, but there was little doubt that when he did so he had a special standing and authority. Even Margaret Thatcher, who had a famously uncompromising manner at Cabinet, would defer to her Lord Chancellors and pay careful attention to any concerns or reservations they expressed. As a former Cabinet secretary, Sir Robin Butler, put it, 'there was a certain grandeur about the office which everyone respected. It was one of [Thatcher's] points of principle that Government should not interfere with judicial matters'. Another government adviser noted that the change came with the removal of Lord Irvine:

> [Derry Irvine] had a special status, there is no doubt about it. Derry was definitely in a different category. But I think that basically changed when Derry went. Charlie Falconer was very much a creature of the Prime

[25] 'The Lord Chancellor's Judiciary-Related Functions: Proposals', commonly referred to as 'the Concordat'.

> Minister; owed his political career entirely to the Prime Minister's patronage. And was doing a job which we were trying to normalise and turn into a normal Secretary of State. We were even trying to avoid calling him the Lord Chancellor.
>
> *(senior government adviser)*

It is the loss of this special status that caused most anxiety to the judges. Many of the judges whom we interviewed were still in mourning for the passing of the old-style Lord Chancellor. A particular concern has been the fact that under the CRA there is no requirement for the Lord Chancellor to be a lawyer. Rather, the appointee must seem to be 'qualified by experience'.[26] The Prime Minister effectively has a free hand in the appointment.[27] The fear is that a Lord Chancellor without any legal background will not have been brought up 'understanding the way the system works . . . and where those lines are and what you do and don't do' (District Judge).

A number of interviewees told us, however, that while they had originally objected to the proposal to allow non-lawyers to be appointed Lord Chancellor, they had come to realise that this was less significant than the status of the office-holder. A respected senior figure at the end of their career had nothing to lose by defending judicial independence if that was threatened by their political colleagues. Since 2005, the first three Lord Chancellors have been legally qualified, although Jack Straw's experience of legal practice amounted to only a couple of years at the bar, while Kenneth Clarke's days in practice were rather distant. Despite their limited legal experiences, both were considered by the judges to be appropriately senior and respected politicians. The fear that this would not always be the case was summarised by Lord Judge in an interview with him when he was LCJ:

> I can envisage the day coming when a Minister of Justice will be appointed as Lord Chancellor, who will have no real idea of how the system is supposed to work. Have no real idea, for example, of what judicial independence means . . . So we could end up with a politician who has serious further political ambitions, who will, as a human being, be anxious to demonstrate to the Prime Minister of the day and the party and the public that he is, she is, just the right person to move up the political

[26] Constitutional Reform Act 2005, section 2(1).

[27] The Prime Minister may take into account experience as a minister, parliamentarian, lawyer, law tutor or any 'other experience that the Prime Minister considers relevant': CRA, section 2(2).

> ladder, and may therefore lose sight of the responsibilities of the Lord Chancellor or may allow them to be obfuscated by a sense of his or her political ambitions. Now if that happens I can't see a Lord Chief Justice, any Lord Chief Justices I've known, being too pleased.

For some judges, that day arrived with the appointment of Chris Grayling as Lord Chancellor in 2012. As the first non-lawyer to hold the office in the modern era, his appointment marked a turning point, but, more importantly, he was also the first mid-career politician to become Lord Chancellor. Though some senior judges commented in private that they were 'quite impressed' with Grayling and his willingness to articulate his support for judicial independence,[28] others were less sanguine. Writing in 2013, Sir Stephen Sedley, a retired Court of Appeal judge, expressed a view that many sitting judges shared in private: 'The decision in 2012 to put a political enforcer, Chris Grayling, in charge of the legal system carried a calculated message: the rule of law was from now on, like everything else, going to be negotiable.'[29] The post-2005 Lord Chancellor is still a young office and there may yet be a reversion to something that more closely resembles the old-style Lord Chancellor. It is likely, though, that the focus of future Lord Chancellors will be more firmly on the task of implementing government policy and that they will be less concerned about upsetting the judiciary as they do so.[30]

Thus judges may find new-style Lord Chancellors uncongenial. There may, however, be political gains from the appointment of career politicians as Lord Chancellors. Powerful Commons figures may wield more influence within government and may be more adept at securing funding from the Treasury. Judges, with their longer terms in office, may also sometimes be at an advantage in negotiating with ministers who have been in post for only a short time.

[28] Participating in the BBC programme *Question Time* on 15 November 2012, Grayling criticised a judicial decision but refused to criticise the judge who reached the decision, stressing that '[j]udges have a right in an independent society, in an independent judiciary, to reach the verdicts they believe are right according to law. And that's a principle we have to hold sacrosanct'.

[29] S. Sedley, 'Beware Kite-Flyers' (2013) 35 *London Review of Books* 13.

[30] Some of Chris Grayling's initiatives have been modified in response to judicial concerns, for example over the government's 2013 proposals to restrict judicial review. J. Rozenberg, 'Despite the Tough Talk, Grayling Has Listened to the Judges on Judicial Review', *Guardian*, 5 February 2014.

## The evolving partnership between the judiciary and the executive

Whether or not the new Lord Chancellor and the judiciary can work together in an effective partnership depends on the structural arrangements and the political culture within which the office operates. In the days of the old-style Lord Chancellor, close co-operation with the judiciary was bred in the bone. Sir George Coldstream was Permanent Secretary in the department in the 1960s and saw the Lord Chief Justice every morning before court. Although such frequent engagement did not continue under his successors Sir Derek Oulton or Sir Tom Legg, a significant proportion of their time was also spent in regular face-to-face meetings with the judges. The Lord Chancellor and departmental officials were formally in charge, but they ran the justice system and the Courts Service through close consultation with the senior judges.

The partnership was managed on the basis of tradition and slow evolution. The particular personalities and preferences of the Lord Chancellor and the senior officials in the department were highly influential. The tendency was for them to stay in office for a long stretch and to stamp their mark on the relationship between the judges and politicians. Very little was written down.

This system was swept away in January 2004 when a detailed description of shared responsibilities was set out in the Concordat. The judges regarded detailed drafting as the best way to protect their position in this febrile new world, but the result (expressed in the Concordat and later in the CRA 2005) was often felt to be *too* detailed. A frequent complaint from our interviewees was that the CRA was overly constraining:

> I don't think I've ever worked with such a well-thumbed piece of legislation ... because it's such a constant reference to what we can or cannot resolve. It just had a feeling of being too prescriptive.
>
> *(Ministry of Justice official)*

> [T]he Act was far, far too prescriptive. I mean absurd. I mean when you look at it now it's unbelievable how prescriptive it was.
>
> *(senior judge)*

Once its provisions had been enacted in the CRA 2005, the Concordat became largely redundant. Officials refer to the Act a lot, but almost never go back to the Concordat. But that is also because the Concordat engendered a new way of working in partnership with the judiciary:

> I also think part of the Concordat is around a way of working with the judiciary as well. And I think once that gets into your blood you probably have to be referred back to the original document less.
>
> *(another Ministry of Justice official)*

The new partnership was to be severely tested within a couple of years. In 2007 there was a further upheaval in Whitehall; again the judges had no warning. It started with a Home Office leak that the government was planning to create a Ministry of Justice, adding prisons, probation and criminal law reform to the responsibilities of the Lord Chancellor. The then Home Secretary, John Reid, wanted to get rid of these functions so that the Home Office could become a classic Ministry of the Interior, focusing solely on policing, terrorism, security and immigration. He wanted to offload the remainder onto the Lord Chancellor.[31]

Overseeing prisons would be a huge additional responsibility for the Lord Chancellor and would dominate the budget of the new Ministry, and the judges were concerned that the courts would be the losers. They felt this was a constitutional shift, not just a change to the machinery of government.[32] Under the 2004 Concordat, the Courts Service had been left accountable to the Lord Chancellor alone. The judges now wanted to see the Courts Service budget protected, and to have greater involvement in its administration. The Lord Chancellor reluctantly set up a working group with the Lord Chief Justice – but with tight parameters – and insisted that the Ministry of Justice would come into being anyway.[33] There followed another round of intense negotiations, partly in public and before Parliament,[34] which after nine months resulted in a Framework Document for the Courts Service, published in January 2008. It was a document written, as one senior official put it, in the 'white heat of judicial anxiety about what they described as ill-considered

[31] HL Constitution Committee, *Relations between the Executive, the Judiciary and Parliament* (HL 151 2007), para. 61.

[32] HL Constitution Committee, *Relations between the Executive, the Judiciary and Parliament*, para. 58.

[33] The working group was set up on 19 March, seven weeks before the creation of the Ministry of Justice on 9 May 2007. The tight parameters were that there must be no change to legislation, to the Concordat or to the executive-agency status of the courts service, and no ring-fencing of its budget.

[34] The House of Lords Constitution Committee held an immediate inquiry into the creation of the new Ministry of Justice and its consequences for the judiciary, to which the Lord Chancellor and Sir Igor Judge (President of the Queen's Bench Division) both gave evidence twice. See report of HL Constitution Committee, *Relations between the Executive, the Judiciary and Parliament*, para. 61.

constitutional reform' and in an atmosphere of intense suspicion. The judges wanted a framework document which was extremely detailed about who was responsible for what and who was accountable for what; the resulting document was an agreement that made life difficult for both sides.

The Framework Document proclaimed that in future the Courts Service would operate as a partnership between the Lord Chancellor and Lord Chief Justice. But the House of Lords Constitution Committee criticised the government for not treating the judiciary as partners in the creation of the Ministry of Justice:

> We are disappointed that the Government seem to have learnt little or nothing from the debacle surrounding the constitutional reforms initiated in 2003. The creation of the Ministry of Justice clearly has important implications for the judiciary. The new dispensation created by the Constitutional Reform Act and the Concordat requires the Government to treat the judiciary as partners, not merely as subjects of change. By omitting to consult the judiciary at a sufficiently early stage, by drawing the parameters of the negotiations too tightly and by proceeding with the creation of the new Ministry before important aspects had been resolved, the Government failed to do this.[35]

The 2008 Framework Document was revised and updated in 2011 to incorporate the Tribunals Service, and this time the judiciary was fully involved in the process. The drafting was also streamlined and clarified: 'the original [2008] document was far too complicated and convoluted, and it left open a number of areas of ambiguity' (senior judge). The result was that by 2012 a partnership which had operated for centuries on a largely informal basis, rooted in convention, was, within less than ten years, described in four different governing documents: the 2004 Concordat, the CRA 2005, and the 2008 and 2011 Framework Documents.

### *The department: from Lord Chancellor's Department to Ministry of Justice*

The creation of these governing documents changed the formal basis of the partnership between politicians and judges, but equally influential was the longer-term transformation of the department itself. Over a

[35] HL Constitution Committee, *Relations between the Executive, the Judiciary and Parliament*, para. 67.

period of forty years it evolved from a quiet government backwater to a large, resource-intensive department subject to the same public management regime of accountability, efficiency and value for money as any other government department. Before the early 1970s, Lord Chancellors were supported by a handful of lawyers whose work focused on the judiciary and the courts, with the result that they sometimes seemed to be no more than lobbyists for judges.[36] Until 2003 the LCD was exempted from routine select committee scrutiny, and only in 1998 was a non-lawyer appointed Permanent Secretary.[37] These idiosyncrasies, together with the department's very narrow policy remit, reinforced a legalistic departmental culture oriented towards judicial interests. The judiciary felt that the department had to be 'wholly different from any other department of State'[38] in order to protect judicial independence.

The significant growth of the LCD and its gradual acquisition of more power and functions between 1972 and the turn of the century widened the department's policy remit and increased its budget, resulting in the gradual reorientation of its officials 'away from the judges and towards the executive'.[39] This shifting focus was consolidated by the creation in 1995 of an independent courts service responsible for managing the courts, which liberated 'the centre of the department ... to consider wider policy issues regarding the provision and administration of justice'.[40] By 2003, however, there was a feeling inside Downing Street that the Lord Chancellor still led an antiquated department that remained an obstacle to new policy development.[41] The tendency of

[36] According to Harlow, the department saw itself 'as a cart rather than a horse and [was] ... insufficiently active in developing policy and promoting reform': C. Harlow, 'Refurbishing the Judicial Service', in C. Harlow (ed.), *Public Law and Politics* (London: Sweet and Maxwell, 1986), p. 206.

[37] This in itself required an amending statute, the single-purpose Supreme Court (Offices) Act 1997, which abolished all prior restrictions on the appointment of the Permanent Secretary. Eligibility had previously been extended to civil servants with five years' service in the Lord Chancellor's Department.

[38] Browne-Wilkinson, 'The Independence of the Judiciary in the 1980s', 48.

[39] Woodhouse, *The Office of Lord Chancellor*, pp. 47–8. See also D. Woodhouse, 'The Office of Lord Chancellor: Time to Abandon the Judicial Role – The Rest Will Follow' (2002) 22 *Legal Studies* 128. As Gavin Drewry notes, this shifting focus was in large measure 'successfully camouflaged by successive Lord Chancellors': G. Drewry, 'Ministers, Parliament and the Courts' (1992) 142 *New Law Journal* 50, 52.

[40] Lord Mackay, 'The Lord Chancellor's Role within Government' (1995) 145 *New Law Journal* 1650, 1651.

[41] J. Powell, *The New Machiavelli: How to Wield Power in the Modern World* (London: Vintage, 2010), p. 153.

the Lord Chancellor to resist his criminal justice reforms had led, as Tony Blair put it, 'to priorities that didn't coincide with those of the government'.[42]

There is an interesting symmetry in this: if by the start of the twenty-first century political elites at the centre of government worried that Lord Chancellors focused *insufficiently* on policy – Tony Blair was almost obsessively focused on the efficiency of the criminal justice system – some legal elites were increasingly concerned that Lord Chancellors were *excessively* focused on it. For them, the relentless drive to improve the efficiency of the criminal justice system led Lord Chancellors to prioritise their executive role over their judicial role. Some concluded that Lord Chancellors had become unwilling and ineffective guardians of judicial independence, and doubted that the office should continue to mix the twin roles of judge and minister.[43] The political imperative of reorienting the Lord Chancellor and his officials to deliver the government's criminal justice reforms motivated the first attempt to abolish and eventually to remodel the office.[44] Further developments led two years later to the creation of a Ministry of Justice, which became the leading department for criminal justice policy. Thus by 2007 the Lord Chancellor was in charge of a department responsible not only for constitutional issues, civil and administrative justice, the courts and legal aid, but for criminal justice policy as well.

### *Communications between judges and the executive*

In the light of the new division of powers between the two branches and the radical structural changes to the department and its increasing policy-orientated focus, there was an acute need for good communications between the judges and politicians in order to maintain a smoothly running partnership. When Jack Straw was Lord Chancellor, he told his Permanent Secretary that one of his key priorities was rebuilding relations with the judges. Since then, both sides have recognised that the

42 T. Blair, *The Journey* (London: Hutchinson, 2010), p. 632.

43 See, for example, Lord Steyn, 'The Case for a Supreme Court' (2002) 118 *Law Quarterly Review* 382.

44 See the summary of our seminar from June 2013 where participants familiar with the planning of the 2005 reforms emphasised that Blair was concerned about the 'department's structure and policy delivery': Judicial Independence Project, 'The Abolition of the Office of Lord Chancellor'.

need for consultation and regular meetings is as great as ever, and in some respects even greater. As Lord Judge told us, 'There has had to be a much closer relationship. For a start I have to talk about money to the Lord Chancellor; well that was inconceivable before the changes'.

The Permanent Secretary may no longer drop in to see the LCJ daily on his way to work, but there is a regular meeting once a month between the Lord Chancellor, his Permanent Secretary and Director-General, and the Lord Chief Justice and his Chief Executive. The LCJ and the Lord Chancellor also speak on the phone when the need arises. There are also frequent meetings between other senior officials and senior judges, in particular the Senior Presiding Judge, who is the LCJ's main deputy in running the Courts Service and dealing with the executive. Judges also sit on the Sentencing Council, the Criminal Justice Operational Board, the Civil Justice Council, the Family Justice Council, and numerous other boards and committees which engage with other agencies in the justice system.

These are just the formal channels of communication through which judges and politicians speak to each other. There are also the usual informal channels – dinners and legal and academic events in the Inns of Court, universities and law firms. There have also been more systematic attempts to develop stronger informal channels, with mixed results. Famously, Charles Clarke as Home Secretary issued an invitation in 2005 to the Law Lords to discuss detention powers under the anti-terrorism legislation after their decision in the *Belmarsh* case. The senior law lord, Lord Bingham, refused, saying that 'they should not discuss with anyone – least of all a minister – a question that may compromise them if the same question should come before them judicially'.[45] Charles Clarke publicly expressed his frustration at this stance, which he felt placed a misguided understanding of the principle of judicial independence above the need for judges and politicians to work together to create fair and enforceable anti-terrorism legislation.

He might have felt even more frustrated if he had known that, a few years earlier, when Michael Howard was Home Secretary, Lord Bingham and his colleagues had agreed to attend a briefing in the Home Office from senior officials about their difficulties in areas like prisons and immigration. The Permanent Secretary, Sir Richard Wilson, was invited back to a sandwich lunch in the Court of Appeal. As Wilson acknowledged, nothing came of this except slightly better relations; it had no impact on the judicial review cases that so exercised Michael Howard.

[45] J. Rozenberg, 'Not the Usual Channels', *Daily Telegraph*, 10 November 2005.

A few years before that, as judicial review was taking off in Britain and starting to have an impact on government, Sir Robin Butler suggested a similar initiative to Margaret Thatcher (then Prime Minister). He proposed joint training sessions for judges and senior civil servants about how government works, so that judges would be better informed when handling judicial review applications. A former barrister herself, Thatcher firmly slapped him down. She regarded the proposal as a form of interference by the government with the independence of the judges and as such was completely out of the question. These three episodes show that within government there can be differing interpretations of the requirements of judicial independence, and also different interpretations amongst senior judges.

### *Judges criticising ministers; ministers criticising judges*

The communications outlined above, whether formal or informal, involve judges and politicians speaking directly to each other (or trying to). Equally important to the working of their relationship is the way that the two sides speak *about* each other through the media and other channels; how judges express their views on government policy and how politicians respond to judicial decisions.

In terms of formal channels, judges feed in their views on government policy related to the justice system through responses to government consultations. A committee of the most senior judges meets every Friday to canvass views on proposed changes to criminal law and criminal justice. Judges' representative bodies, as well as individual judges, also offer responses on occasion. When the Home Office published proposals to change the law for victims of rape, the Council of Circuit Judges issued a largely critical response.[46]

When the Law Lords sat in Parliament, some of them felt free to criticise the government's legislative proposals and to move amendments against them. Now that the judges are no longer involved in the legislative process, they are expected to be more circumspect once the consultation is closed and the government has made up its mind. As Sir Igor Judge explained in evidence to the House of Lords Constitution Committee:

[46] Council of HM Circuit Judges, 'Convicting Rapists and Protecting Victims: A Consultation', 2006.

> [Negative responses] may create tension [but] we do not expect our response to carry the day . . . in the end Parliament legislates, and then it does not really matter what the judges think . . . the judges apply the law that Parliament has produced.[47]

What is less clear is whether this convention limiting judicial comment on government policy will survive. If senior judges come to feel that the new-style Lord Chancellor no longer defends them in Cabinet, or conclude that the executive largely ignores their views, they may feel free to lobby Parliament during the passage of a Bill. Public channels – speeches, lectures and media interviews – have become increasingly important to senior judges as a means of expressing views on government policy. In a 2004 lecture, for example, Lord Woolf as LCJ was extremely critical of the ouster clause in the Asylum and Immigration Bill, which would have restricted the jurisdiction of the High Court in certain judicial review cases.[48] Similarly, his successor Lord Judge used his 2010 Mansion House dinner speech to attack the increasing use by governments of Henry VIII clauses in primary legislation (these empower the government to amend or repeal statutes using delegated legislation).[49] Retired judges who take up seats in the Lords may also speak to the viewpoint of senior judges on occasion, a point to which we return in Chapter 5.

On occasion, ministers respond publicly to judicial criticisms. In 2011, for example, Lady Hale commented in a speech to the Law Society that proposed cuts in legal aid would have a 'disproportionate impact upon the poorest and most vulnerable in society'.[50] The then Lord Chancellor, Kenneth Clarke, responded by insisting that Lady Hale had 'misunderstood the effect of our proposals'. On the floor of the Commons, he said he would be willing to meet her to reassure her that he would be giving £20 million that year in legal aid to 'not-for-profit' neighbourhood advice and law centres. Such public criticism by judges can be irritating for ministers and civil servants: a senior civil servant commented that judges are right to be uncomfortable with ministers

[47] HL Constitution Committee, *Relations between the Executive, the Judiciary and Parliament*, para. 55 and Q. 297.

[48] Lord Woolf, 'The Rule of Law and a Change in the Constitution' (the Squire Centenary Lecture, Cambridge, 3 March 2004).

[49] Lord Judge, 'Lord Mayor's Dinner for the Judiciary: The Mansion House Speech' (Mansion House, 13 July 2010).

[50] Lady Hale, 'Equal Access to Justice in the Big Society: Sir Henry Hodge Memorial Lecture' (the Law Society, 27 June 2011).

commenting on individual cases, but that the judges themselves 'also have to learn to shut up'.

Ministerial criticism of judicial decisions is generally unproblematic unless it is personalised, intemperate or inaccurate. Media comments by Michael Howard and David Blunkett, as Home Secretaries, were widely felt to have overstepped the line. In 1995, Michael Howard remarked in a response to a judicial review case which went against him, 'the last time this particular judge found against me, which was in a case which would have led to the release of a large number of immigrants, the Court of Appeal decided unanimously that he was wrong'. In 2003 David Blunkett wrote a critical piece in the *News of the World* newspaper under the headline 'It's Time for Judges to Learn Their Place'. Theresa May stated in 2011 that the government was 'disappointed and appalled' by a Supreme Court decision concerning the rights of those placed on a sex offenders' register to have their registration reviewed.[51] These episodes are keenly felt by the judges, but there is no evidence that their incidence is increasing, and they occurred just as much under the old Lord Chancellors as under the new.[52] Provided such outbursts are occasional aberrations and not routine responses to judgments, it is unlikely that they will undermine the partnership between the judges and politicians any more than equivalent judicial criticism of the government. However, judges do worry that sustained criticism of judges by politicians may undermine public trust in the judiciary more generally. The Lords Constitution Committee recommended in 2007 that the Ministerial Code should be amended to include 'strongly worded guidelines setting out the principles governing public comment by ministers on individual judges', but this recommendation has not been acted upon.[53]

A notable development in relation to political criticisms of judges is the idea that senior judges have a role to play in educating politicians about the requirements of judicial independence. As Lord Judge commented in interview:

51 *Hansard*, HC, vol. 523, col. 959, 16 February 2011.

52 For a contrary view, see D. Feldman, '"Which in Your Case You Have Not Got": Constitutionalism at Home and Abroad' (2011) 64 *Current Legal Problems* 117, 132–3.

53 HL Constitution Committee, *Relations between the Executive, the Judiciary and Parliament*, 51. The Committee reiterated this recommendation in a follow-up report the next year. Although it does not contain a direct reference to this convention, the Cabinet Manual (2011) notes that ministers are obliged to uphold the administration of justice (para. 3.46).

> There is a new government. Like the previous government, ministers got carried away every time they didn't like decisions reached by judges ... It took some time to persuade Mr Blair that he had to curb his ministers. It's taking some time to persuade the new government that when you don't like a judicial decision, you don't boo, and when you like it you don't cheer.

Prime Minister David Cameron (though himself guilty of intemperate booing on occasion) summed up a view which most of our interviewees, both judicial and political, would probably subscribe to:

> [T]here are occasions we all know when judges make critical remarks about politicians and there are occasionally [times] when politicians make critical remarks about judges. To me, this is part of life in a modern democracy and I think we should try to keep these things as far as possible out of the courts.[54]

Maintaining a tolerant and respectful partnership between judges and politicians requires political skill and commitment on both sides. The success or failure of the relationship ultimately rests with the Lord Chancellor and this brings us to the question whether new Lord Chancellors have the same capacity to defend judicial independence as their predecessors.

## Defending judicial independence

Judges and lawyers doubt whether new Lord Chancellors can be effective guardians of judicial independence. These doubts are the product of two overlapping assumptions. The first is that old Lord Chancellors were uniquely well equipped to defend judicial independence inside government because of their judicial role, and in particular the relationships that developed with senior judges as a result of being head of the judiciary. The second assumption is that there is a problematic divide between the legal and political cultures that no new office-holder can bridge in the way required of an effective guardian of judicial independence.

For many, old-style Lord Chancellors personified the shared understanding between the legal and political spheres about the proper boundaries between the government and the judges. By virtue of their hat-trick of institutional roles, the Lord Chancellors spent time with and nurtured the confidence of both their ministerial and judicial colleagues,

[54] Speaking at Prime Minister's Questions, *Hansard*, HC, vol. 543, col. 317, 18 April 2012.

expressing the values and concerns of the one to the other. The various roles of the Lord Chancellors, and the relationships that sprang from them, fostered shared values between the political and legal realms. With the reform of the office, 'the relationships that have promoted a sharing of values are changing'.[55] The Lord Chancellor no longer has any judicial role and important functions relating to appointments, deployment and discipline are now effectively or primarily exercised by the LCJ or judicial agencies. A senior civil servant put it to us this way:

> [Chris Grayling's] predecessors would have done a lot of the things that Lord Chancellors and indeed Attorneys General do, which is to go to Inns of Court dinners and just interact at that kind of organisational – cultural – level. He doesn't do that. He'll go along to a dinner and deliver a set speech, like a minister would at a stakeholder event.

New Lord Chancellors (and perhaps non-lawyers in particular) are more likely to treat the judiciary simply as an ordinary minister would treat any major stakeholder group. As a result, there is concern that the office is no longer an effective channel for inculcating within the government the respect for the rule of law and the independence of the judiciary. Or, in the words of one senior judge: 'the sort of culture in which we are working and have worked since 2005 ... perhaps pose[s] more threat to judicial independence than before'. The growth of the Ministry of Justice (MoJ) and its portfolio of responsibilities is a source of concern. Speaking in a lecture in 2013, Lord Judge commented that the expansion of the MoJ had been 'detrimental to institutional independence. It is not a tidal wave, but rather the consistent steady drip'.[56]

It is increasingly clear that when Lord Chancellors now engage in negotiations with judges, and when they represent judges in negotiations with their Cabinet colleagues, they are primarily acting as the Secretary of State for a large government department and not as the rarefied Lord Chancellors of old. Gone is the traditional deference that even Margaret Thatcher exhibited towards her Lord Chancellors. Special pleading on behalf of judges is likely to be received in the same sceptical spirit as arguments made on behalf of other stakeholder groups. The new-model Lord Chancellor is a guardian of the courts and of the judiciary in much the same way that the Health Secretary is the

[55] D. Woodhouse, 'The Constitutional Reform Act 2005: Defending Judicial Independence the English Way' (2007) 5 *International Journal of Constitutional Law* 153, 158.

[56] Lord Judge, 'Constitutional Change: Unfinished Business' (the Constitution Unit, 4 December 2013).

guardian of the National Health Service. Just as in respect of health policy there will be iconoclastic ministers who take a radical approach, braving the ire of doctors, new Lord Chancellors may be more willing to upset the judiciary and the legal community, and indeed to introduce headline-grabbing initiatives for party political reasons.[57] Equally, however, there will be sober and more consensual figures who will operate in much the same way as did the pre-2005 Lord Chancellors. Indeed, a senior civil servant told us that from the perspective of the judiciary, Lord Falconer and Jack Straw could, because they were political heavyweights, be regarded as *better* than their predecessors:

> The two new Labour Lord Chancellors were, from the judicial perspective, something of a golden age because you had all of the benefits of the old Lord Chancellor with the added heft of the Secretary of State for Justice. Because in the old days the Lord Chancellor was not such a powerful player.

Negotiations with judges and justice policy are now transacted to a greater extent as part of the knockabout culture of politics, and less as part of the deferential and innately conservative culture of the legal profession. The politics of judicial independence, shorn of their judicial mantle, are now part of ordinary politics.

It is not difficult to see why judges might find this new environment uncongenial. The new culture is less deferential and more uncertain. Newer, more political Lord Chancellors will be less receptive to judicial arguments and may define judicial independence more narrowly than do judges, drawing a sharper distinction between threats to the interests of judges and threats to their independence. Section 3(6) of the CRA 2005 imposes a duty on the Lord Chancellor to have regard to:

(a) the need to defend [judicial] independence;
(b) the need for the judiciary to have the support necessary to enable them to exercise their functions; and
(c) the need for the public interest in regard to matters relating to the judiciary to be properly represented in decisions affecting those matters.

The old Lord Chancellors had no such statutory duty but were immersed in legal culture. New Lord Chancellors may read the statutory duty much

[57] Compare, for example, J. Legge, 'Health Secretary Jeremy Hunt Says NHS Must Adapt to Survive' *Independent*, 11 August 2013; and S. Moss, 'Hammer Falls on Free Sky TV for Judges', *Guardian*, 14 October 2013.

more strictly and narrowly than their predecessors would have, placing significance on the reference to 'public interest' in subsection (c) and drawing a sharper distinction between judicial independence and the interests of the judges.[58] Potential threats to judicial independence may not always be dealt with as carefully as they might have been under the old system: for example, between 2009 and 2011 there was a shortfall in funding for the Supreme Court, because the Courts Service in England and Wales failed to provide monies it owed. At one point the shortfall became so serious that the court was only a matter of days away from being unable to pay its staff. Despite negotiations with both the Courts Service and the Ministry of Justice, it was only after the Supreme Court chief executive wrote to the Permanent Secretary to convey the gravity of the financial position that then Lord Chancellor Kenneth Clarke agreed to make up the shortfall.[59] In the small judge-focused department of the old-style Lord Chancellor, matters would not have got so far. In the much larger MoJ, an issue like this is liable to pass below the Lord Chancellor's radar until it becomes a serious problem. Officials in the Ministry of Justice may also be less adept than their predecessors at advising Lord Chancellors, because MoJ officials are less engaged with the judiciary. As one senior judge observed, 'senior civil servants do not really have an in-built understanding of the constitutional lines and why they are important, why they matter'. Whereas their predecessors might have spent their whole career in the Lord Chancellor's Department and developed long and productive personal relationships with senior judges, senior civil servants today rotate throughout the government and MoJ officials may only work in the department for a few years at a time.

There have always been more guardians of legal values inside government than the Lord Chancellor alone. Others include the Attorney General, as the UK government's senior law officer; parliamentary counsel, in the principles they apply to drafting legislation; and the Government Legal Service, which reminds ministers where they risk transgressing constitutional proprieties. Hidden behind the Whitehall curtain, the daily work of these 'guardians' in upholding the rule of law and judicial independence is largely invisible to outsiders and may often concern only small aspects of the overall picture of judicial independence – but it remains vital. As one senior official observed, 'ministers, civil servants and the

[58] For example, in the negotiations over judicial pensions discussed in Chapter 4.

[59] G. Gee, 'Guarding the Guardians: The Chief Executive of the UK Supreme Court' [2013] *Public Law* 538.

executive accept judicial independence as a basic part of the context within which they have to operate' and recognise that 'interference with judicial independence carries a very high risk of being counter-productive'.

Whereas old-style Lord Chancellors might have defended judicial independence because, as judges themselves, they were personally committed to it as a core value, new-style Lord Chancellors will defend it for political and practical reasons. They do so in two key contexts: first, in respect of the system as a whole. Though relieved of much of the day-to-day decision-making concerning the judiciary and the courts, the Lord Chancellor's continuing responsibilities for designing, funding and supervising the appointment system, the court system and the complaints system ensure that she or he must negotiate and engage regularly with the senior judges.

The second context in which they safeguard judicial independence is in internal Cabinet relations, particularly by encouraging ministers to refrain from publicly criticising judicial decisions or the judges who deliver them. The Lord Chancellor's officials are alert to forthcoming court decisions that might embarrass the government and seek in advance to dissuade ministers in other departments from venting their frustration in public. Although these efforts do not always succeed, the majority of potentially inappropriate comments by ministers are headed off before they are made.

There have been occasions in recent years when the Lord Chancellor has privately rebuked colleagues for criticising judges. In 2011, Kenneth Clarke wrote to the Home Secretary to remind her of the duty on ministers to uphold judicial independence, copying the letter to the Prime Minister, after both Theresa May and David Cameron were widely felt to have been excessively critical of the Supreme Court's decision in *R (F)* v. *Secretary of State for the Home Department* to allow people on the sex offenders' register to apply for their inclusion to be reviewed.[60] Admittedly, the LCJ and President of the Supreme Court had both written to the Lord Chancellor to remind him of the statutory duty imposed on all ministers; however, at least one senior judge suggested that the Lord Chancellor did not require encouragement.

[60] *R (F) v. Secretary of State for the Home Department* [2010] UKSC 17. May and Cameron described the government as 'appalled' at a decision that the Prime Minister said seemed 'to fly completely in the face of common sense': *Hansard*, HC, vol. 523, cols. 955 and 959, 16 February 2011.

## Judicial accountability to the executive

The demotion of the office of Lord Chancellor from that of a senior statesperson who straddled the judicial and political spheres to that of an ordinary Justice Minister may have come at the cost of destabilising traditional arrangements for protecting judicial independence, but it has had the benefit of increasing democratic accountability. As we discussed in Chapter 2, despite judicial concern about the term, the greater part of accountability in public life does not refer to the imposition of sanctions (sacrificial accountability) or the control of judges' decision-making, but is explanatory – giving reasons for one's actions. The classic understanding of the judges' role can be framed as this form of accountability.[61] Individual judges give detailed reasons for their decision-making in public, while being subject to appeal to a higher court for any errors made. Equally important, however, is the collective accountability of the judiciary for matters outside the courtroom: for the greater administrative and managerial powers that they now hold. The judiciary now enjoys greater institutional autonomy than it did before 2005, but it is not wholly self-regulating. Judges are held to account by the executive and by Parliament in a number of ways. They give account to Parliament primarily through reporting requirements, but also through dialogue with Parliament in arenas such as select committees (see Chapter 5). There is executive and/or external agency involvement in judicial discipline, deployment and appointments, and of course the MoJ plays a key role in negotiating budgets for the courts system and must be convinced that budgets are justified. Primarily, this accountability is explanatory and dialogic – the judiciary publish statistics about the performance of court centres, for example – but in some respects, particularly in the context of discipline, it involves the imposition of sanctions. Judges are now disciplined more formally and more publicly.

### *Political accountability*

Since 2005, three of the four Lord Chancellors have sat in the House of Commons. That the last three office-holders have been MPs reflects the fact that justice policy is politically important, and the Ministry of Justice a very big department, which requires public accountability through an elected politician. This was indeed part of the impetus for the reforms to

[61] V. Bogdanor, 'Parliament and the Judiciary: The Problem of Accountability' (Third Sunningdale Lecture on Accountability, 9 February 2006).

the role announced in 2003. As an elected politician, the Lord Chancellor is now able to offer some democratic accountability (albeit of an indirect kind) for those aspects of the courts system and the judiciary for which the office bears responsibility. But this formal democratic link between the judiciary and the electorate is only one element of the role of the Lord Chancellor's accountability function.

The role of the executive in checking the judiciary is recognised in statute. As noted above, the duty imposed by section 3 of the CRA 2005 on Lord Chancellors to defend judicial independence and provide the judiciary with adequate support also requires that they have regard to the public interest. Politicians increasingly define judicial independence separately from the interests of the judiciary. The statute does not spell it out, but the public interest is different from the interests of the judiciary: in terms of pay and pensions, the Lord Chancellor must consider what the country can afford, not just what the judges might believe they should be paid. Similarly with the programme of court closures: the courts exist for the convenience of the public, not the judges. In terms of judicial recruitment, the public interest includes the need for greater diversity as part of a merit-based appointment process. The Lord Chancellor is the ultimate judge of the public interest in this context and is accountable to Parliament for his or her decisions on where the public interest lies.

### *Judicial reports*

The judiciary gives an account of its work through the publication of annual reports, some of which the Lord Chancellor lays before Parliament, and others of which the judiciary itself lays before Parliament. The Supreme Court produces an annual report for the Lord Chancellor, which also goes to the First Ministers in Scotland, Wales and Northern Ireland (whose governments help to fund the court).[62] No equivalent duty has been imposed upon the LCJ or the courts of England and Wales. Annual reporting has become more haphazard since the Lord Chief Justice became head of the judiciary. The intention had been that the LCJ would produce an annual review:

> Our principal focus has been on accountability through reporting on what the judiciary does. As one of the most important steps in that direction is the Annual Review the Lord Chief Justice agreed to publish . . . A body

[62] Constitutional Reform Act 2005, section 54.

which makes decisions which affected the public ought to set out annually an account of what it did.[63]

In practice, however, incumbent LCJs have produced reports only irregularly (about once every two years). The reports offer a selective, high-level account, and their irregular frequency makes it impossible to compare performance with earlier periods.[64] There used to be annual reports by the Civil and Criminal Divisions of the Court of Appeal, by the Commercial and Admiralty Courts, and the Technology and Construction Court, together with regional reports by the Crown, County, Family and Magistrates Courts. Now only two of those courts produce an annual report.[65] The annual report of HM Courts and Tribunals Service (HMCTS) does not bridge the gap either, being mainly financial.[66] Detailed information on the workload of the courts is now located in the Judicial and Court Statistics produced by the Ministry of Justice.

The Judicial Statistics and HMCTS reports are important tools for external scrutiny, with data on cracked trials, waiting times, costs per sitting day, etc. They provide essential information for the executive to work with the judges in seeking to improve the efficiency of the courts and judicial performance. A gap in the reporting system has occurred in that recent LCJs have not used the annual review to explain how they plan to improve judicial performance, and how that improvement will be monitored and measured in subsequent years. Court performance and judicial performance are closely linked; but to preserve judicial independence, improving judicial performance is seen as the business of the judiciary. The executive acts as constructive critic, and coach, and there are many different forums in which it can make suggestions and put its point of view across, from the formal board meetings of the Courts Service to the informal meetings which take place every month between the Lord Chancellor and LCJ. The executive can also offer help and

[63] Lord Justice Thomas, 'The Position of the Judiciaries of the United Kingdom in the Constitutional Changes: Address to the Scottish Sheriffs' Association' (Peebles, 8 March 2008) 6.

[64] There have been four such reports, covering the periods April 2006 to March 2008, April 2008 to February 2010, January 2010 to June 2012, and July 2012 to August 2013. The intention is to produce these reports on an annual basis, perhaps matching the annual Business Plan produced by the Judicial Office.

[65] The Court of Appeal (Criminal Division) and Technology and Construction Court.

[66] The annual report contains five pages on workload and performance summary, and six on performance review; with over a hundred on the annual accounts, and notes to the accounts.

advice, as it has done in providing information about appraisal systems, to help the judiciary in evaluating individual judicial performance; and to help develop more systematic succession planning for recruitment to the senior levels of the judiciary. These are matters where the judiciary has limited experience, but the executive has valuable expertise.

### *Judicial discipline*

In terms of regulating misconduct in the judiciary, the executive still plays a central role, sharing the responsibility for judicial complaints and discipline jointly with the Lord Chief Justice, under detailed procedures set out in the Concordat[67] and implemented in the Judicial Discipline (Prescribed Procedure) Regulations 2006. The old Lord Chancellors enjoyed considerable discretion over judicial discipline, though the department was generally thought to handle dismissals and discipline 'with considerable natural justice',[68] with a 'quiet word'[69] often used to encourage judges to step aside. Today, responsibility for complaints is shared between the LCJ and the Lord Chancellor, supported by a Judicial Conduct Investigations Office (JCIO) staffed by civil servants. The Lord Chancellor is accountable to Parliament for the operation of the discipline system.[70] The JCIO filters out unfounded or trivial complaints, referring serious ones to a nominated judge, who acts as a further filter, then to an investigating judge. This triage system ensures that non-trivial complaints receive proper consideration and that judges are investigated by their peers. If at the end of the process the LCJ and Lord Chancellor wish to take disciplinary action, they must refer the case to a review body composed of two judges and two lay members.

The LCJ and Lord Chancellor must decide jointly on disciplinary sanctions but cannot take any action more severe than that recommended by the review panel.[71] At the end of the process only the Lord Chancellor can formally remove a judge from office, and only at Circuit Judge level and below.[72] For judges of High Court level or above,

[67] Concordat, paras. 73–113; and CRA, section 115.

[68] R. Stevens, 'Judicial Independence in England: A Loss of Innocence', in P. Russell and D. O'Brien (eds.), *Judicial Independence in the Age of Democracy: Critical Perspectives from around the World* (Charlottesville: University Press of Virginia, 2001), p. 160.

[69] Woodhouse, *The Office of Lord Chancellor*, p. 27.

[70] The Office for Judicial Complaints (OJC) was replaced by the JCIO in October 2013: CRA, sections 108–19.

[71] Concordat, para. 80; and CRA, section 108(2).

[72] Concordat, para. 81; and CRA, section 108(1).

the decision to dismiss must be approved by both Houses of Parliament (this has not occurred since 1830).[73] There is also a process for reviewing the JCIO process itself. Complainants or judges can raise concerns about the handling of a complaint (but not the merits of the decision made) with the Judicial Appointments and Conduct Ombudsman (JACO).[74] Allegations of serious misconduct remain very rare amongst the senior judiciary. That said, the JCIO and the JACO receive significant numbers of complaints – an average of around 1,700 a year. This, in turn, requires significant resources: the JCIO has fifteen staff and the JACO ten. A significant proportion of complaints received (normally 50 per cent or more) relate to judicial decisions rather than alleged misconduct and are dismissed for this reason. Between 2008 and 2013 an average of fifteen court judges were disciplined each year for misconduct. A similar number (eighteen) resigned. The average figure for judges removed from office is very low – less than two per year – but if the total for judicial officers (including court-based judges, tribunal judges, coroners and magistrates) is considered an average of twenty-six are removed each year.[75]

As the head of the judiciary, the Lord Chief Justice can impose lesser penalties: suspension, or a formal warning, reprimand or advice. The LCJ may do this only with the agreement of the Lord Chancellor.[76] Agreement is not merely formal: the Lord Chancellor has adjusted penalties both upwards and downwards. So in terms of complaints and discipline, the judiciary is more self-regulating than it used to be, but the system operates under the close eye of the Lord Chancellor, who must agree to any disciplinary sanction, and has sole responsibility for imposing the ultimate sanction of removal from office. In this, the complaints system in England and Wales may be regarded as more accountable than those in Scotland and in Northern Ireland, where the systems are run by the judiciary with little external oversight (see Chapter 9).

There is, however, a gap in the process when it comes to disciplining the LCJ. Unlike in the case of the Supreme Court or the LCJ of Northern

73 The subject of that case, Sir Jonah Barrington, was a judge of the Irish Court of Admiralty. The Act of Settlement procedure has never been invoked in respect of a judge in England and Wales. See P. O'Brien, 'When Judges Misbehave: The Strange Case of Jonah Barrington', ukconstitutionallaw.org (7 March 2013).

74 CRA, section 110.

75 Based on the figures from OJC and JCIO annual reports from 2008–9 through to 2012–13. Figures for the averages are rounded.

76 CRA, section 108.

Ireland, there are no specific rules governing complaints against the LCJ in England and Wales.[77] While the prospect of a future LCJ being removed from office is, hopefully, a remote one, it is not impossible to imagine a scenario in which a future LCJ is the subject of a complaint. Given the joint role of the LCJ and Lord Chancellor in disciplinary matters, the conventional process might, theoretically, lead to the LCJ effectively disciplining herself or himself. In practice, the LCJ will recuse himself or herself from such a decision, passing the matter on to the Master of the Rolls (as is currently done where the LCJ knows the subject of a complaint or has some other conflict of interest), but the absence of a formal and agreed procedure to cover this scenario is problematic.

The Lord Chancellor also has the power to remove a senior judge on grounds of incapacity. In the case of the LCJ, however, this can only be done on the basis of a medical certificate confirming physical or mental incapacity and with the concurrence of two other Heads of Division.[78] It is therefore likely to be difficult in practice to remove an LCJ from office in this way. Nor is this a far-fetched concern. Lord Widgery (LCJ 1971–80) suffered from what was later diagnosed as dementia in the later years of his period of office. He was unable to discharge his duties for at least eighteen months prior to his resignation. He had long resisted private pressure to resign and the Lord Chancellor, Lord Hailsham, was very reluctant to intervene. Lord Widgery was finally persuaded to go in 1980. It is not obvious that if a similar case arose today it would be dealt with any more effectively.[79] Now that Lord Chancellors no longer head the judiciary, they may be even more wary of exercising this power unless it is absolutely unavoidable.

### *Judicial deployment, and leadership posts*

A final respect in which the judiciary is accountable to the executive relates to the deployment of judges, and their appointment to leadership posts. Chapter 7 records how the Lord Chancellor has been largely removed from the process of judicial appointments. But once a judge is

[77] See para. 2 of the Supreme Court's Judicial Complaints Procedure (complaints against the President or Deputy President) and the Code of Practice for Complaints against the Lord Chief Justice, published by the Office of the Lord Chief Justice of Northern Ireland.

[78] Senior Courts Act 1981, section 11(8).

[79] Section 11 of the 1981 Act was enacted in order to ensure that a situation like that of Lord Widgery would not be repeated, but identical provisions had already been in place in section 12 of the Administration of Justice Act 1973 – they simply had not been used.

appointed, the 2004 Concordat provides that the Lord Chief Justice must consult the Lord Chancellor before 'determining which individual judge should be assigned to which Division, Circuit, District, Court'.[80] This is within a framework in which the Lord Chancellor determines the overall number of judges required, including the number required for each Division, jurisdiction and region, and at each level of the judiciary.[81] The nomination of judges to the most senior leadership posts requires not just consultation but the concurrence of the Lord Chancellor. Appointment of the Senior Presiding Judge, the Presiding Judges and the Resident Judges all require the concurrence of the Lord Chancellor.[82] There is a longer list of other leadership posts which require the LCJ to consult the Lord Chancellor: Vice-President, Court of Appeal (Civil, and Criminal); Vice-President, Queen's Bench Division; Chancery Supervising Judges; Family Division Liaison Judges; President of the Employment Appeal Tribunal; and Temporary Chairmen of various tribunals.

## Conclusion

A healthy politics of judicial independence has always depended on a functioning partnership between judges and politicians. This partnership has occasionally been strained, but has generally been stable for long periods of time. Traditionally it was mediated by the blurred and overlapping roles of the Lord Chancellor. That office remains pivotal, but today there is a more formal division of power and explicit joint responsibilities between the judiciary and the executive. The working arrangements of the new relationship are still in flux but some conclusions can be drawn about the potential effect of the new partnership on judicial independence and accountability.

The first is that the changing role of the Lord Chancellor has led to a shift in the power relations between the branches. The Lord Chancellor no longer commands the authority that came with the occupation of an ancient office by a senior and respected legal figure. Instead, she or he now exercises the more familiar ministerial power that is legitimised by greater democratic accountability as an elected politician in the House of Commons responsible for the workings of the justice system in both a

[80] Concordat, para. 31.

[81] After consultation with the Lord Chief Justice: Concordat, para. 29.

[82] Concordat, para. 45. The Lord Chancellor can object to the appointment within a specified time period, after which his consent will be assumed.

sacrificial and an explanatory sense. On the face of it, this change from judge–politician to fully fledged minister suggests an increase in judicial accountability at the cost of judicial independence. This is certainly a view that many judges subscribe to. But the picture is more complex than that. While the Lord Chancellor no longer commands automatic authority by virtue of the office, there is scope to carve out an effective role as a political guardian of judicial independence. A political heavyweight drawn from the Commons may be as effective a guardian as the old-style Lord Chancellors.

Moreover, there are sufficient channels of communication in place, both formal and informal, to allow a new relationship to evolve between the judges and politicians through which the judges can articulate the needs of judicial independence. Given the increasingly frequent turnover of Lord Chancellors and senior civil servants in the Ministry of Justice, the onus will fall more on senior judges, and particularly the Lord Chief Justice, to work harder at nurturing an understanding of the requirements of judicial independence and to encourage political engagement with the judiciary.

Under the new system, the danger lies as much in the judiciary being sidelined as in their being the subject of political sabotage. As both Lord Woolf and Lord Judge understood as they worked their way into the new system, the judiciary must put its weight behind the Lord Chancellor of the day and persuade each new government that judicial independence is not a cloak for judicial interest, but is an essential public interest. The judges must be conscious that every move which takes the Lord Chancellor further out of the process, for example by reducing responsibility for judicial appointments, or the courts system, runs the risk of increasing the disinterest and disengagement of the executive in the partnership. The judges must also continue to develop and extend their engagement with politicians and the public through the media, speeches, lectures and press releases in order to strengthen the political culture that respects and protects judicial independence.

Lastly, it is important to remember the importance of personalities. Whatever the formal processes and cultures in which the different office-holders operate, there is still surprising scope for different approaches by individuals to shape the politics of judicial independence as it is played out between the judges and the executive. The evidence of the last decade shows that different personalities take a different view of the conventions, and play the game in different ways. As the office of Lord Chancellor no longer carries with it a status above that of ordinary ministers, more will depend on the personality and reputation of the individual office-holder and the esteem in which they are held by politicians and judges. The different relationship between the judges and the executive under Lord Irvine, Lord Falconer, Jack Straw, Kenneth Clarke and Chris Grayling are not solely the consequence of the changing office. The same is true of the judicial side of the partnership. Lords Woolf, Phillips and Judge have now retired and each will have left their individual mark. The future development of the partnership will inevitably be influenced by the individuals who succeed them.

# 4

# The Courts Service, salaries and pensions

The previous chapter examined the transformation of the historic office of Lord Chancellor. This change was accelerated by the Constitutional Reform Act 2005, but its evolution is traceable back over at least forty years. By centralising most of the running of the courts in the Lord Chancellor's Department, the Courts Act 1971 triggered the process by which the office of Lord Chancellor evolved from a judicial to an executive orientation, with less stress on championing the judiciary's interests and more on efficiency, budget savings and the interests of court users.[1] The first half of this chapter concerns the changing arrangements for the funding and administration of the courts, which began in the early 1970s but have accelerated since 2008, and we focus particularly on these more recent developments. In examining the evolution of the courts service, we can identify some of the reasons for, and consequences of, the changing roles and responsibilities of the Lord Chancellor.

Towards the end of the chapter, we discuss how ministers, judges and officials negotiate judicial remuneration not only in the context of continuing constitutional change, but also in a cold economic climate that has required the Ministry of Justice to reduce its budget by 23 per cent between 2010 and 2014. And the age of austerity does not end there, with the Ministry required to make a further 10 per cent cut in 2015–16 and indications that there might be more cuts to come.[2] The administration of the judicial system in such challenging economic circumstances has tested the durability not only of prevailing institutional arrangements but also of relationships of trust between senior judges, ministers and their officials.

[1] D. Woodhouse, *The Office of Lord Chancellor* (Oxford: Hart Publishing, 2001), p. 52.

[2] See, for example, National Audit Office, 'The Performance of the Ministry of Justice 2012–13' (2013), paras. 1.12, 1.9.

## Three models of court administration

Running a court system in a large and complex society is inevitably time-consuming and expensive. It involves assessing differing needs up and down the court hierarchy; organising internal structures so that courts can effectively manage their caseload; setting pre-trial and trial procedures; measuring and monitoring performance; and devising and implementing reforms, large and small, to the practices and structures of courts.[3] A central question is how much responsibility ministers and judges should each have for these issues. On the one hand, the more control that ministers exercise over the resources, policies and structures of courts, the greater the opportunity for the government of the day to interfere, directly or indirectly, in the judicial work of the courts.[4] On the other hand, it is neither desirable nor possible to exclude government entirely, not least insofar as ministers should remain answerable to the legislature for the use of public money.[5] Around the common law world, there is a range of different models for running the courts, spanning those effectively controlled by the executive to those run by judges.[6] For these purposes, there are three main, if simplified, models.

The first is an *executive* model, where the administration of the courts falls within the remit of a government department, with the minister answerable to the legislature. The judiciary has no formal responsibility for court administration. Whether the advice of senior judges is sought is a matter for ministerial discretion, although typically the judiciary has minimal (if any) input into decisions about levels and allocation of resources. In practice, departmental officials usually take most of the key decisions, with judges often regarded in this model as little more than 'professional mercenaries' who come to court day-in-day-out 'to do the judging'.[7] As a consequence of weak consultative practices, judges not

[3] I. Scott, 'The Council of Judges in the Supreme Court of England and Wales' [1989] *Public Law* 379, 381.

[4] See, generally, P. Sallmann and T. Smith, 'Constitutionalism and Managerial Effectiveness: Revisiting Australian Courts' Governance', in Australasian Institute of Judicial Administration (ed.), *Australian Courts: Serving Democracy and Its Publics* (Melbourne, 2013), p. 266.

[5] See, for example, N. Browne-Wilkinson, 'The Independence of the Judiciary in the 1980s' [1988] *Public Law* 44, 54.

[6] For an excellent account of various possible models that informs the discussion presented on these pages, see Canadian Judicial Council, *Alternative Models of Court Administration* (Ottawa, ON, 2006), pp. 87–111; and P. S. Millar and C. Baar, *Judicial Administration in Canada* (Montreal: McGill-Queen's University Press, 1981), pp. 53–66.

[7] Scott, 'The Council of Judges in the Supreme Court of England and Wales', 384.

only lack scope to pursue the reforms that they deem necessary, but can also be reluctant to shape and implement reforms driven by the department, lest it make them appear 'political'.[8] Administrative staff in the courts are members of the executive, who are responsible to the minister and act under his or her control, though most of their day-to-day work involves interacting with judges. This can leave court staff feeling that they are pulled in two directions, although their primary loyalty may be to the head judge in his or her court. The success of the executive model is largely dependent on relationships of trust and respect between ministers and senior judges and, in the more everyday context of particular local courts, between the chief administrator and the presiding judge. It follows that the model's effectiveness is compromised when these relationships break down.[9] The system in England and Wales over the last forty years has followed the same trend as the rest of the common law world in loosening its embrace of the traditional executive model, although, as we explain in Chapter 9, this model still exists in Northern Ireland.

The second is a *judicial* model. In its strongest version, the judges effectively have complete control over almost all aspects of court administration. In theory, under such a model, the judiciary could set court fees at such a high level that the courts would be self-funding. In practice, the courts will require at least some funding from government but it is for the judges to determine the total amount and allocation of the court budget, to hire and sack personnel and create administrative policies. The senior judiciary will generally appoint an administrator as a chief executive who has responsibility for day-to-day operations in the courts and who is answerable to the senior judge. The chief executive typically reports to the legislature on the administration of the courts and liaises with government ministers and officials with responsibility for the justice system. In a weaker version of this model, judges are responsible for most of the court administration, but the overall budget is determined by the government and approved by the legislature. The courts operate within budgetary limits set by the government, but the judges can decide for themselves how best to allocate the resources. In either its stronger or weaker forms, this model is said to encourage judges to engage more fully in long-term strategic planning. The flip side of greater judicial

[8] See, generally, P. Sallmann, 'Courts Governance: A Thorn in the Crown of Judicial Independence?' (2007) 16 *Journal of Judicial Administration* 139.

[9] Canadian Judicial Council, *Alternative Models of Court Administration*, p. 15.

responsibility for running the courts is heavy administrative workloads for senior judges – and accountability to a minister, which not all judges welcome. While addressing several of the concerns with the executive model, a judicial model raises serious questions about whether there remains sufficient democratic accountability for the running of the courts. As we explain in Chapter 9, the Scottish Court Service is now run on the judicial model.

These models sit at either end of a continuum of executive and judicial control. A third, falling somewhere between these two, is a *partnership* model, distinguished by a blend of executive and judicial involvement.[10] It compensates for the weaknesses of the executive model by heightening judicial involvement in decision-making on a range of management matters, including the levels and allocation of resources, staffing and information systems. By retaining a significant role for the executive, the model addresses concerns about accountability for the use of public money. A board with judicial and executive representatives is responsible for court administration. Responsibility for the everyday running of the courts lies with a chief executive, appointed jointly by the executive and judiciary. This model requires close working relationships between the minister, judges and officials; constant consultation; and exchanges of information and a shared set of clearly defined policy objectives.[11] In practice, the partnership can sometimes seem more symbolic than real, for example if there are more executive than judicial members on the board or if departmental officials take the important decisions in private, with the board effectively a rubber stamp. In such circumstances, the partnership involves little more than the formalisation of the weak consultative approaches often seen under the executive model. From 2011, the partnership model operated in England and Wales.

## The Courts Service: from an executive to a partnership model

### *The executive model (1972–2008)*

Court administration in England and Wales has gradually evolved over forty years from the traditional executive model to a partnership model. The Courts Service's history began with the Courts Act 1971, which established a unified administrative courts service under the Lord

[10] Canadian Judicial Council, *Alternative Models of Court Administration*, pp. 99–100.

[11] I. Scott, 'Judicial Involvement in Court Administration' [1988] *Civil Justice Quarterly* 153, 156.

Chancellor.[12] In 1972, the Courts Service commenced its work managing all the courts in England and Wales (except for magistrates courts and administrative tribunals). Previously, court administration had been fragmented across 'a motley collection of almost independent fiefs'.[13] There was no central or uniform system of administration for the staffing, servicing, timing and location of the courts and their work. Among those involved in managing the various courts were the Lord Chancellor, the Lord Chief Justice (LCJ), local authorities and individual judges and court clerks.[14] In practice, judges had often held sway in local courts. Thus the creation of a courts service not only centralised control in the executive, but also shifted power away from judges to officials in Whitehall. This, in turn, helped to refashion the Lord Chancellor's Department from a small private office staffed mainly by lawyers into a modern and resource-intensive department of state with around 10,000 civil servants.[15]

Judicial concerns about the running of the courts grew as the culture of the Lord Chancellor's Department lost its distinctive legal flavour and came closer to a mainstream government department. Changes in government attitudes to public spending in the 1980s left the Lord Chancellor's Department subject to the same financial disciplines driven by the Treasury as any other Whitehall department. As officials placed increasing stress on efficiency, effectiveness and value for money, concerns intensified in legal circles that 'managerialism, by stealth and unnoticed, [was] taking over from constitutionalism in the Lord Chancellor's Department'.[16] This translated into complaints that judges had been sidelined in decision-making and that officials were 'flexing their newly acquired administrative muscles'.[17] In a 1987 lecture, Sir

[12] See, generally, J. Donaldson and I. Scott, 'Court Administration in England and Wales', in G. Moloney (ed.), *Seminar on Constitutional and Administrative Responsibilities for the Administration of Justice: The Partnership of Judiciary and Executive* (Canberra: Australian Institute of Judicial Administration, 1985), p. 43.

[13] P. Polden, *Guide to the Records of the Lord Chancellor's Department* (London: HMSO, 1988), p. 38.

[14] R. Baker, 'The New Courts Administration: A Case for a Systems Theory Approach' (1974) 52 *Public Administration* 285, 285–6.

[15] See S. Shetreet and S. Turenne, *Judges on Trial: The Independence and Accountability of the English Judiciary* (Cambridge: Cambridge University Press, 2013), p. 72; R. Stevens, *The Independence of the Judiciary: The View from the Lord Chancellor's Office* (Oxford: Clarendon Press, 1993), p. 118.

[16] D. Oliver, 'The Lord Chancellor's Department and the Judges' [1994] *Public Law* 157, 163.

[17] F. Purchas, 'The Constitution in the Market Place' (1993) 143 *New Law Journal* 1604, 1606.

Nicolas Browne-Wilkinson famously criticised the department's failure to consult judges, complaining that judges were 'sitting in an environment wholly determined by executive decision', where the yardstick for decision-making was 'financial value for money, not the interests of justice'.[18] While conceding that 'nobody [was] trying to erode the independence of the legal system', he concluded that this was 'happening unperceived and unappreciated'.[19]

While formally part of the Lord Chancellor's Department, the Courts Service had in practice operated as a separate unit within it.[20] In 1995, the Courts Service was reconfigured as an executive agency led by a chief executive, who was answerable to the Lord Chancellor. This was in line with the trend in the 1990s of carving out executive functions to be carried out by well-defined business units that were focused on delivering specified policy goals within a framework of accountability to ministers.[21] For the judges, this reconfiguration heightened concerns that court administration would be driven by the Treasury's cost-cutting agenda. In 1998, Ian Magee was appointed chief executive, the first non-lawyer to hold the post. He had previously served as chief executive of the Information Technology Services Agency, which provided IT services to the Department of Social Security. This signalled a shift in approach at the top of the Courts Service. As one official put it, the requirement was for management skills, 'not necessarily a set of legal skills'.

The Framework Document regulating the objectives and workings of the Courts Service required the chief executive and their officials to work closely with the LCJ and other senior judges 'to ensure that all parties are able to carry out their responsibilities in the management and administration of justice'.[22] Much of the chief executive's contact was with the Senior Presiding Judge, with informal discussions when the Courts Service was preparing its budget. Frequent meetings were also held with representative bodies such as the Council of Circuit Judges and a sub-committee of the Judges' Council to discuss such matters as resources and court closures. While this represented a formalisation of judicial participation in funding and management decisions, judicial input remained limited. There was no formal 'partnership' between ministers and judges, although its rhetoric often featured in speeches

[18] Browne-Wilkinson, 'The Independence of the Judiciary in the 1980s', 51.
[19] Browne-Wilkinson, 'The Independence of the Judiciary in the 1980s', 51.
[20] Our discussion draws on Woodhouse, *The Office of Lord Chancellor*, pp. 52–8.
[21] Cabinet Office, *Executive Agencies: A Guide for Departments* (London, 2006), p. 2.
[22] Court Service Agency, *Framework Document* (1995), Annex 4.

by Lord Chancellors.[23] Yet it was clear to officials involved in the day-to-day running of the courts that 'if you did not have the judges with you, or at least not against you, there was not going to be very much progress'.

### *The partnership model (2008–)*

The trigger for the formal shift from an executive to a partnership model was the creation of the Ministry of Justice in 2007, but the progression was more gradual. The Lord Chancellor's responsibility to ensure 'an efficient and effective' system of court administration had been formalised in a statutory duty under the Courts Act 2003.[24] The Concordat in 2004 envisaged 'arrangements to ensure that the judiciary can be effectively involved' in resource-planning by a unified service that now incorporated the magistrates' courts, including a senior judge serving as a non-executive board member of the Courts Service, which from 2005 was known as Her Majesty's Courts Service (HMCS).[25] A senior judge was also a non-executive member on the department's corporate board.[26] Expectations of real participation in decision-making about budgets and resource allocation were soon dashed, as judges again found themselves sidelined. As the LCJ, Lord Phillips, subsequently complained, departmental officials had not recognised the need for judges 'to be involved in a meaningful way in forward planning'.[27] Officials informed the judges of budget details only after the process had been effectively completed, withheld information on court closures and estate planning and interfered with HMCS's day-to-day operations.[28]

In early 2007, the judges were presented with a second chance to negotiate a more meaningful involvement, occasioned by the unexpected creation of a new Ministry of Justice, which had been precipitated by the then Home Secretary's wish to remove prisons and the probation service

23 'Real and effective partnership between the government and the judiciary is seen as being paramount, particularly in this area. Therefore, all significant issues should be decided after consultation or, for those where responsibility must be equally shared, by concurrence.' Department of Constitutional Affairs, Constitutional Reform: The Lord Chancellor's Judiciary Related Functions: Proposals ('the Concordat') (2004), para. 28.

24 Courts Act 2003, section 1(1). See also Constitutional Reform Act 2005, section 17.

25 Department of Constitutional Affairs, *Constitutional Reform*, para. 20.

26 Department of Constitutional Affairs, *Constitutional Reform*, para. 25.

27 Lord Phillips, 'Courts Governance' (Australian Institute of Judicial Administration Oration, 15 May 2008).

28 Phillips, 'Courts Governance'.

from the Home Office's policy remit in order to concentrate on security and counter-terrorism.[29] As in 2003, the judges were again taken by surprise, with the LCJ first learning of the proposed new department in a leaked newspaper report.[30] Over and above concerns about lack of consultation, the judges were anxious that the more politically pressing areas of prisons and probation would eclipse the Lord Chancellor's statutory duty to defend judicial independence; that the prisons budget would crowd out the courts; and that an expanded ministerial remit rendered litigation against the Lord Chancellor more likely, making meetings between the senior judges and the Lord Chancellor more difficult.[31] The judiciary argued that the Ministry should not be brought into existence until their concerns had been addressed, but received short shrift. Instead, in March 2007, ten days before the Prime Minister formally announced the creation of the Ministry, the Lord Chancellor and the LCJ agreed to establish a working group to consider judicial concerns.[32] For the second time, Lord Falconer had to soothe ruffled judicial feathers. And for the second time in four years, the Lord Chancellor – initially Lord Falconer and, from mid-2007, his successor, Jack Straw – negotiated the fine details of court administration with the judiciary.

These negotiations ushered in a *partnership* model in the guise of HMCS's 2008 Framework Document. HMCS was to be managed as a partnership between the Lord Chancellor and the LCJ, with judges to enjoy a stronger voice in decision-making. The Lord Chancellor and the LCJ would set objectives for HMCS.[33] The leadership and direction of HMCS were placed in the hands of the board, headed by a chief executive and a non-executive chair.[34] The Senior Presiding Judge and two other judges would sit on the board,[35] with a remit to keep HMCS updated on the LCJ's views and to update the judiciary on HMCS's work.[36] The Lord

29 HC Constitutional Affairs Committee, *The Creation of the Ministry of Justice* (HC 466 2007).

30 See QQ. 62 and 64 of the evidence of Lord Phillips and Lord Justice Thomas, HC Constitutional Affairs Committee, *The Creation of the Ministry of Justice*.

31 Lord Phillips, 'Courts Governance'.

32 HL Constitution Committee, *Relations between the Executive, the Judiciary and Parliament* (HL 151 2007), para. 63.

33 Ministry of Justice, *HM Courts and Tribunals Service Framework Document* (Cm 8043 2011), para. 2.1. All references are to this revised 2011 Framework Document. Similar provisions appeared in its 2008 predecessor document.

34 Ministry of Justice, *HM Courts and Tribunals Service Framework Document*, paras. 3.1 and 4.6.

35 Ministry of Justice, *HM Courts and Tribunals Service Framework Document*, para. 4.5.

36 Ministry of Justice, *HM Courts and Tribunals Service Framework Document*, para. 4.5.

Chancellor would seek to agree HMCS's budget with the LCJ, but ultimately had the final say. If he was concerned about the proposed or actual allocation to HMCS, the LCJ could record his concerns in writing to the Lord Chancellor, and also, if he or she wished, to Parliament.[37] All HMCS staff would owe a joint duty both to the Lord Chancellor and to the LCJ.[38] But in issues such as listing, case allocation and case management, staff would work subject to judicial direction.[39]

Lord Phillips was initially optimistic that these arrangements gave the judiciary all that it could reasonably expect. He had no enthusiasm for a judge-run model where the judges have control over and responsibility for the court system, largely because he did not want judges burdened with further administrative responsibilities.[40] But only months after his initial optimistic assessment, the economic crisis struck and court funding has been severely reduced ever since, with further cuts to come. In the Comprehensive Spending Review announced in October 2010, the Ministry of Justice's target was to reduce expenditure by 23 per cent in real terms over the next four years.[41] Prisons and probation is the largest item in the Ministry's budget at 45 per cent, with legal aid the next-largest (24 per cent), and the Courts Service the third-largest item at 12 per cent. Although confronting less severe cuts than the rest of the Ministry, HMCS was still expected to reduce its expenditure significantly in the 2010–11 and 2013–14 financial years. Because judicial salaries comprise a third of the budget for the court system, and are protected, this meant larger reductions in administrative costs, with significant reductions in staffing.

Budget cuts tested the partnership model, but there have been other challenges as well. Between 2008 and 2011, the judges complained that the Ministry was interfering in the running of HMCS, with the board exercising little discretion in practice. Or, as one senior judge put it, the board 'was really just a manifestation of the Lord Chancellor'. Concerns about Ministry interference, and continuing complaints that they were being sidelined, left the three judicial members feeling ambivalent about their role on the board. According to an official, the judicial members were 'allowed to wear two hats'. Although formally part of its decision-making process, they seemed reluctant to share any responsibility for the difficult decisions that the board was required to take in strained

[37] Ministry of Justice, *HM Courts and Tribunals Service Framework Document*, para. 7.2.
[38] Ministry of Justice, *HM Courts and Tribunals Service Framework Document*, para. 2.4.
[39] Ministry of Justice, *HM Courts and Tribunals Service Framework Document*, para. 2.5.
[40] Lord Phillips, 'Courts Governance'.
[41] HM Treasury, *Spending Review 2010* (London: TSO, 2010), pp. 55–6.

economic circumstances. The best example was in late 2010 when Lord Justice Goldring, then Senior Presiding Judge, criticised the proposal to close 157 courts that emanated from the board of which he was a member.[42] From HMCS's perspective, this was 'completely unsatisfactory', as one interviewee put it. Matters were further tested in December 2010 when the LCJ, Lord Judge, refused to agree HMCS's budget. Lord Judge felt that insufficient funds were being made available to the courts and informed the Lord Chancellor that he was not prepared to agree to the budget, although he decided not to communicate his concerns in writing to Parliament. As it turned out, the LCJ was overly pessimistic – eventually there proved to be sufficient funds available.

A second phase in the partnership model began in 2011. HMCS was merged with the Tribunals Service and relaunched as Her Majesty's Courts and Tribunals Service (HMCTS). This merger was intended to realise annual savings of £35 million by 2013–14.[43] Underlying the new Framework Document was an agreement by the Lord Chancellor, the LCJ and the Senior President of Tribunals (SPT) not to interfere with the executive management, leadership and direction of HMCTS, which are recognised as the responsibility of the chief executive, the chairman and the board.[44] The same judge who criticised the 2008–10 HMCS board as being a manifestation of the Lord Chancellor acknowledges that the HMCTS board is 'in control of its own business'. As important were personnel changes, following the appointment of Peter Handcock as chief executive and Robert Ayling as chair. With a long and impressive background in business, including as chief executive of British Airways in the late 1990s, Ayling lent 'credibility and clout' to HMCTS, as one senior judge put it. The leadership roles of chief executive and chair also became 'more clearly defined'.[45] In practice, the chief executive is responsible for day-to-day operations and is the chief adviser to the board – and, through it, to the Lord Chancellor, the LCJ and the SPT.

At the first meeting of the new HMCTS board, Ayling underscored the need for its members 'to act collegiately and not in representative

[42] Senior Presiding Judge, Response: Proposals on the Provision of Court Services in England and Wales (2010).

[43] HM Courts and Tribunals Service, *Annual Report and Accounts 2012–13* (HC 239 2013), p. 14.

[44] HM Courts and Tribunals Service, *Annual Report and Accounts 2011–12* (HC 323 2012), p. 3.

[45] HM Courts and Tribunals Service, *Annual Report and Accounts 2011–12* (HC 323 2012), p. 5.

capacities'.[46] No longer would the judicial members be allowed to stand aside from tough decisions about budgets and court closures. According to one official, the judges at times still 'find this very difficult, but by and large they meet their obligations'. Our interviews suggest that senior judges are indeed more engaged in increasing the efficiency of the courts, and of the judges who work in them. As one official observed, judges who work closely with HMCTS 'very much subscribe to the idea that they are providing a public service'. HMCTS produces monthly performance data on the workload and efficiency of each court centre. The judicial members of the board take this data back to the LCJ, and the Senior Presiding Judge then speaks with resident and presiding judges about how to improve the performance of their courts, which may involve tackling individual judges about their performance (in terms of case management, delays and so forth). Most judges do not feel that this threatens their independence, so long as it is senior judges that are managing performance, not court administrators (see Chapter 6). This is reflected in the Framework Document, which provides that performance measures that have an impact on the judiciary only bind judges when the LCJ 'has expressly agreed that they do so'. It continues that no performance measure 'fetters the exercise of judicial discretion or the interests of justice in any individual case'.[47]

As well as improving the dysfunctional board, Ayling has been pivotal in pushing forward the rationalisation of the court estate. From a total estate of about 650 courthouses, the first round of spending cuts in 2010 led to the closure of 142 magistrates courts and county courts.[48] Further spending cuts under the 2013 spending review will inevitably lead to more.[49] Two-thirds of courthouses had five courts or less; many were historic buildings, poorly suited to modern requirements; and few were capable of acting as centres for both courts and tribunals. The long-term vision is for a reduction to around 200 court centres, with centralised bulk processing centres for issuing writs, collecting fees and so on, supported by fully integrated and modernised IT systems. The difficulty is that this requires significant investment, at a time when public monies are in short supply.

[46] HM Courts and Tribunals Service, *Annual Report and Accounts 2011–12* (HC 323 2012), p. 3.

[47] Ministry of Justice, *HM Courts and Tribunals Service Framework Document* (Cm 8043 2011), para. 7.17.

[48] HM Courts and Tribunals Service, *Annual Report and Accounts 2012–13* (HC 239 2013), p. 10.

[49] F. Gibb, 'Magistrates Attack Plans for More Court Closures', *The Times*, 29 May 2013.

The first phase of the partnership model – that of 2008–11 – illustrates the risk that a partnership can be more symbolic than real if the government continues to hold sway. In its second phase, however, HMCTS's early years can be taken to suggest that the model is not necessarily flawed. HMCTS has secured genuine judicial involvement, including on difficult short-term decisions such as budget cuts as well as long-term strategic thinking about the future of the court estate. Above all, under its new leadership, and with the buy-in of senior judges, HMCTS's performance since 2011 demonstrates how 'the people are just as important as the model', as an interviewee put it.

Yet there are unresolved problems. Some have day-to-day implications. For example, HMCTS is hamstrung by its reliance on the Ministry's centrally negotiated contracts for estate management, human resources and IT services. The Ministry has imposed its own contracts on these matters in order to save money. However, HMCTS found these contracts inefficient: 'courts aren't cleaned and security guards do not turn up', as one official put it. Some of the problems are structural; for instance, the fees charged to court users are subject to elaborate controls set by the Treasury.[50] The courts in England and Wales require investment to modernise their estate and IT systems, but there is no way under the current partnership model to guarantee a sustained investment programme over several years. Even within its allocation of resources, HMCTS has found that it is allowed only limited discretion. As one interviewee noted, HMCTS 'has some control over the expenditure of the money allocated to it, but not very much'. Problems such as these lead some of those we interviewed to suggest that 'the current model is not sustainable' and that it may ultimately be 'a halfway house to a judge-run court service'.

### *Towards a judicial model?*

Ever since Sir Nicolas Browne-Wilkinson first floated the idea in the 1980s,[51] the judges have flirted with taking over the management of the courts – half-heartedly in the negotiations for the 2004 Concordat, and rather more determinedly in 2007 during the negotiations over the move to a partnership model. For example, Sir John Thomas told the House of Lords' Constitution Committee that 'an autonomous court

[50] HM Treasury, *Managing Public Money* (London: TSO, 2013), Annex 6.1.
[51] Browne-Wilkinson, 'The Independence of the Judiciary in the 1980s', 44, 54.

administration with a greater degree of judicial participation' had been 'very successful' in Ireland, Denmark and the Netherlands. He concluded that 'a new structure akin to these models is, in the view of the judiciary, a constitutional safeguard made necessary by the Ministry of Justice'.[52] In 2013, Sir John Thomas was appointed LCJ, and had the opportunity to put his views into practice when a radical proposal was floated for exploring private funding. Three factors explain the emergence of this proposal: first, Ayling's commercial background and his vision for running the courts on a modern business model; second, senior judges' dismay at continuing spending cuts, which cemented a wish to escape the constraints imposed by the Ministry and the Treasury; and third, the desire of Chris Grayling, who had been appointed Lord Chancellor in late 2012, to find a way of investing more of his shrinking budget into prisons and probation than in modernising the courts.

In May 2013, *The Times* reported that the courts were 'facing wholesale privatisation under revolutionary plans'.[53] It was said that HMCTS would be reconfigured as a commercial entity, freed from Treasury control, with the court estate and thousands of staff transferred into the hands of private companies, all of which was estimated to bring savings of £1 billion a year for the Ministry. The plans seemed so revolutionary as to be barely credible, until confirmed by a leaked letter with the senior judges' cautious responses. It seemed that the senior judiciary was giving serious consideration to the government's proposals, since 'continuing with the present model for HMCTS, both in governance and financial terms, was not an attractive option for the long term'.[54] The judges saw this as a chance to create a new courts and tribunals service ('new CTS') independent of ministerial control. But the caveats in their letter revealed contradictions in their own thinking as well as that of the government. They wanted continuing state funding, especially for the criminal courts, but expected the Ministry to remain only residually involved. They wanted closer judicial involvement, with the chief executive of a new CTS accountable to the LCJ, yet they did not envisage any significant increase in the management responsibilities of the senior judiciary.

[52] HL Constitution Committee, *Relations between the Executive, the Judiciary and Parliament* (HL 151 2007), para. 85.

[53] F. Gibb, 'Courts to Be Privatised in Radical Justice Shake-up', *The Times*, 28 May 2013.

[54] Senior Presiding Judge, *HMCTS Reform: Judicial Overview* (2013), paras. 3.1 and 4.6; 'Lord Judge's Correspondence with Chris Grayling on Court Privatisation: The Full Text', *Guardian*, 25 June 2013.

Weakest of all was their thinking about accountability. While desiring an increased role in shaping and directing a new CTS, they did not want further accountability requirements imposed on the LCJ. No mention was made of accountability to the executive, while accountability to Parliament was mooted through a 'non-partisan Joint Committee of both Houses'.

At the time of writing the outcome was still unknown. But it seems a measure of the frustration of the senior judges with the current model that they were willing to consider such radical proposals. It was also arguably a measure of their political naivety. It is a fantasy to suppose that greater independence would solve funding problems. The courts budget has to come from somewhere. Browne-Wilkinson recognised in 1987 that, 'in the last resort, the amount of the total legal budget must be determined politically and controlled by Parliament'.[55] The judges often refer to the Irish and Scottish models (and we consider the latter in Chapter 9), but the Department of Justice still sets the budget in both these cases. The only material difference is that the courts service boards have a judicial majority, and are chaired by the head of the judiciary. Comparisons with Scotland and Ireland risk ignoring the significant difference in scale. Scotland and Ireland are small jurisdictions, one-tenth the size of that of England and Wales, with fewer courts and smaller budgets, and even then the administrative burden for the chief justice is significant. This would become an even greater burden of management and responsibility for the LCJ and other senior judges given the size and complexity of the courts and tribunal systems in England and Wales. Some might argue that it is possible to support a judicial model in purely governance terms, irrespective of whether it results in more stable and higher levels of funding.[56] However, if judges were responsible for management and budgetary decisions in the English and Welsh courts, they would be responsible for running a very substantial organisation. They might not be directly involved in any of the nitty-gritty of running registries, managing IT systems and handling industrial relations, but they would ultimately be responsible for all these things, even if they delegated most of them to professional managers.[57] This would require devoting far greater time to court administration. And the judges could not do so without

[55] Browne-Wilkinson, 'The Independence of the Judiciary in the 1980s', 54.

[56] Sallmann, 'Courts Governance: A Thorn in the Crown of Judicial Independence?', 148.

[57] Sallmann, 'Courts Governance: A Thorn in the Crown of Judicial Independence?', 149.

accepting more direct accountability for running a major public service that spends large amounts of public money. If there were mismanagement or financial crises, as occur in large organisations from time to time, the judiciary would have to be willing to shoulder the blame.

## Judicial remuneration

### *Judicial salaries*

The provision of secure and adequate judicial salaries is generally recognised as a central requirement of judicial independence.[58] It scarcely needs stating that some measure of protection is thought necessary to prevent governments or legislatures from using judicial remuneration as an indirect tool to influence the judiciary,[59] although similar concerns can also apply where there is scope for senior judges to award or withhold pay increases to junior colleagues.[60] Adequate levels of pay are also said to diminish the prospect of judicial corruption. While it may, exceptionally, be necessary to reduce judicial pay as part of a wider cut in public-sector salaries, especially during a period of economic austerity,[61] for judicial independence to be maintained it is essential that any such changes should not be used as a means of influencing judicial decision-making.

Judicial salaries in England and Wales – and throughout the UK – are regulated by statute. Statutory regulation stretches back to the Act of Settlement 1701, which provided that salaries should be ‘ascertained and established’, which was taken to mean fixed by Parliament, rather than being left to the executive's whim.[62] Today, the executive is authorised by statute to determine the level of judicial salaries – but the Lord Chancellor's discretion is severely circumscribed by the fact that he or

[58] See, for example, UN General Assembly, UN Basic Principles on the Independence of the Judiciary (1985), section 11; Commonwealth (Latimer House) Principles on the Three Branches of Government (2003), section IV(b).

[59] V. Jackson, ‘Judicial Independence: Structure, Context, Attitude’, in A. Seibert-Fohr (ed.), *Judicial Independence in Transition* (New York and Heidelberg: Springer, 2012), p. 37.

[60] See, for example, L. Muller, ‘Judicial Administration in Transitional Eastern Countries’, in A. Seibert-Fohr (ed.), *Judicial Independence in Transition* (New York and Heidelberg: Springer, 2012), p. 961.

[61] See International Bar Association, *Minimum Standards of Judicial Independence* (1982), para. 15(b).

[62] M. J. Beloff, ‘Paying Judges: Why, Who, Whom, How Much? Neill Lecture 2006’ [2006] *Denning Law Journal* 1, 10.

she can only raise, not reduce, salaries.[63] It was not always so, although the last time that salaries were reduced was in 1932 following the Great Crash when judicial salaries were cut, alongside the pay of all other senior public servants, by 20 per cent, and before that the last reduction was in 1832. A key protection today, therefore, is that salaries cannot be reduced, except by statute.[64] In addition, judicial salaries are paid out of the Consolidated Fund. This means that they do not form part of the annual supply and appropriations voted by the House of Commons through the Estimates process and so, as 'non-voted expenditure', they are immune from reduction by Parliament.

Pay increases are decided by the Lord Chancellor, whose discretion is guided by the important, albeit advisory, role of the Senior Salaries Review Body (SSRB), which has become an important guardian of judicial remuneration. Established in 1971, the SSRB advises the government on the salaries of certain senior public appointments. It makes annual recommendations on the pay of all full-time and part-time salaried judges in courts and tribunals across the UK.[65] The Lord Chancellor is under no obligation to accept these recommendations, but often does, although sometimes by staggering or delaying a recommended increase.[66] Lord Chancellors have occasionally rejected recommendations outright.[67] But the practical effect of the SSRB's advisory role has been to distance ministers from involvement in judicial pay, with few fierce battles being fought over judicial salaries in modern times. Not only does this present a sharp contrast with periodic quarrels over judicial salaries in the nineteenth century and the first part of the twentieth,[68] it is also markedly different from the heated clashes over judicial pensions, which we discuss below. A further effect has been to professionalise decision-making about judicial pay. The SSRB adopts a rigorous and systematic approach to evaluating the appropriate pay for different judicial roles and consults widely. In 2013, it received written evidence from, among others,

63 See, for example, Courts Act 1971, section 18(2); Administration of Justice Act 1973, section 9(3); and Senior Courts Act 1981, section 12(3).

64 Stevens, *The Independence of the Judiciary*, pp. 52–63.

65 Review Body on Senior Salaries, *35th Annual Report on Senior Salaries: Report No. 81* (Cm 8569 2013), para. 5.1.

66 Beloff, 'Paying Judges: Why, Who, Whom, How Much? Neill Lecture 2006', 23.

67 In 1992, for example, the Major government rejected a recommended 20 per cent increase, settling instead on a 4 per cent award: Woodhouse, *The Office of Lord Chancellor*, p. 31.

68 Beloff, 'Paying Judges: Why, Who, Whom, How Much? Neill Lecture 2006', 12–15; Stevens, *The Independence of the Judiciary*, pp. 44–56.

the LCJ, the Ministry of Justice, the Judicial Appointments Commission (JAC), the Association of District Judges and the Council of Circuit Judges. It also received oral evidence from the Lord Chancellor, the LCJ and the JAC.[69] The SSRB also undertakes major reviews every four or five years, which include examining the soundness of the current salary structure, and the differential pay between various judicial offices and the employment markets from which judges are recruited.[70]

Its terms of reference require the SSRB to have regard to the need 'to recruit, retain and motivate suitably able and qualified people',[71] so it attempts to prevent salaries falling far behind the earnings of people of the sort who are generally recruited as judges. The primary labour market from which judges in England and Wales have traditionally been drawn is private practice, particularly the bar. As a result, judges in this country are highly paid by international standards, with a 2008 study identifying the UK as paying the highest judicial salaries.[72] The top salaries are for those in senior leadership positions, with the LCJ top of them all, earning over 15 per cent more than Justices of the Supreme Court and Heads of Division in the Court of Appeal. Pay in March 2013 ranged from approximately £104,000 for District Judges and First Tier Tribunal Judges to £130,000 for Circuit Judges, £174,000 for High Court judges, £199,000 for the Court of Appeal, and just over £242,000 for the LCJ.[73] As well as having regard to the need to recruit suitably qualified judges, the SSRB must also have regard to 'the funds available to the department set out in the departmental expenditure limits',[74] which a former member of the SSRB's Judicial Sub-Committee described as a helpful reminder that the SSRB 'is not simply to accept judges' estimation of their own value'.[75]

Judicial pay was frozen from 2009–10 to 2012–13, in line with the government's broader freeze on senior public salaries. As a result, judicial salaries diminished significantly in real terms and are set to fall further, with

69 Review Body on Senior Salaries, *35th Annual Report on Senior Salaries: Report No. 81*, paras. 5.4–5.5.

70 See, for example, Review Body on Senior Salaries, *33rd Annual Report on Senior Salaries: Report No. 77* (Cm 8026 2011), paras. 4.14–4.81.

71 Review Body on Senior Salaries, *35th Annual Report on Senior Salaries: Report No. 81*, Foreword, p. iii.

72 R. Watson and M. Wolfe, 'Comparing Judicial Compensation: Apples, Oranges and Cherry Picking' [2008] SSRN Duke Law Working Paper Series.

73 Ministry of Justice, *Judicial Salaries 2013–14* (2013).

74 Review Body on Senior Salaries, *35th Annual Report on Senior Salaries: Report No. 81*, Foreword, p. iii.

75 Beloff, 'Paying Judges: Why, Who, Whom, How Much? Neill Lecture 2006', 23.

a below-inflation 1 per cent rise agreed in 2013. Although concerned about the remuneration of all the public-sector posts for which it is responsible, the SSRB's 'greatest concern is for the judiciary'.[76] Taking account of inflation and changes to tax and national insurance, it is estimated that the take-home pay of Circuit Judges fell by 18.3 per cent between 2009–10 and 2012–13.[77] Despite this, there is little evidence of recruitment difficulties. Because of cuts to legal aid, barristers and solicitors with criminal practices have been more willing to seek appointment to the bench. This has been called the 'stampede for the purple lifeboat' as hard-pressed criminal practitioners seek 'sanctuary on the bench'.[78] Competition for appointment varies depending on the level of appointment, with roughly twice as many applicants per vacancy for the district bench as for higher levels.[79]

It is at the High Court where there is concern about the number and quality of applicants, because of a widening gap between judicial salaries and the earnings of successful QCs who traditionally form the recruitment pool. In 2011, the SSRB's survey evidence showed that High Court judges, almost all of whom were QCs, experienced on average a 60 per cent drop in earnings on appointment, while District Judges, who were mainly solicitors, enjoyed a 30 per cent increase (in both cases after allowing for the judicial pension).[80] In a 2008 report, Professor Hazel Genn identified salary reduction as amongst the most common reasons why experienced barristers did not seek judicial office, with one-third of those interviewed citing this as the main reason why they would not seek a judicial position.[81] Genn found a widespread perception that pay in the High Court 'has fallen significantly behind earnings in private practice as well as other areas of the public sector and in comparison with the position of the judiciary in the past'.[82] This perception was problematic in light of demographic changes

[76] Review Body on Senior Salaries, *35th Annual Report on Senior Salaries: Report No. 81*, para. 5.43.

[77] Review Body on Senior Salaries, *35th Annual Report on Senior Salaries: Report No. 81*, para. 5.11.

[78] O. Bowcott, 'Legal Aid Cuts Prompt Top Lawyers to Leave the Bar for Careers on the Bench', *Guardian*, 16 May 2013.

[79] There were 8.63 applicants for every vacancy for District Judge in 2012 compared with 5.8 for the High Court and 4.62 for the Court of Appeal, from our calculations based on JAC official statistics.

[80] Review Body on Senior Salaries, *33rd Annual Report on Senior Salaries: Report No. 77*, Table 4.3.

[81] H. Genn, *The Attractiveness of Senior Judicial Appointment to Highly Qualified Practitioners: A Report to the Judicial Executive Board* (2008), paras. 50 and 56.

[82] Genn, *The Attractiveness of Senior Judicial Appointment to Highly Qualified Practitioners*, para. 99.

(e.g. higher rates of divorce and remarriage), which meant that financial commitments continue longer and to an older age than was perhaps the case in the past, and this might preclude many practitioners from seeking an appointment to the bench.[83] As those appointed to the bench traditionally cannot return to practice, '[b]ecoming a judge is a serious, life-changing decision'.[84]

For this reason, the SSRB proposed concentrating any available salary increase on the High Court and above, where they felt that there was the strongest evidence of recruitment difficulties. However, the judges felt that would be divisive, damaging morale and collegiality: whatever increase was proposed should be made available to all judges, and as a result the SSRB reflected this in their ultimate recommendation of an across-the-board rise of 1 per cent.[85] The concerns informing the SSRB's proposal are premised on the belief that the pool of eligible candidates from which High Court judges are drawn is, as the LCJ put it in 2013, 'extremely limited'.[86] While senior judges are quick to point to the rising quality of and increasing competition for appointments to the High Court, even from the narrow pool from which it is currently drawn, at the same time they hasten to warn that this may change unless judicial remuneration is increased.

Another factor which might change is the willingness of judges to observe the convention that they do not return to private practice. Their letters of appointment state that this is the expectation, but it is probably unenforceable. A tightening in the practice rules of the profession would be required to prevent judges from doing so: there is no system to control the behaviour of retired judges – neither the Lord Chancellor nor the Lord Chief Justice has any authority over them. The supposed rationale for the convention – that an ex-judge appearing before former judicial colleagues might enjoy undue influence – does not say much for the impartiality of the bench. Nor is the restriction applied in all other

[83] Genn, *The Attractiveness of Senior Judicial Appointment to Highly Qualified Practitioners*, para. 59.

[84] Review Body on Senior Salaries, *35th Annual Report on Senior Salaries: Report No. 81*, para. 5.44.

[85] Judges have not always shown such solidarity: in 1945–51 the County Court judges, and in periodic submissions to the salary board, their successors the Circuit Judges, argued strongly for a reduction in the differential between themselves and the High Court. In this they have largely succeeded. In 1950 a County Court judge was paid only 40 per cent of the salary of a High Court judge; in 2013 the proportion had risen to 75 per cent. See, generally, Stevens, *The Independence of the Judiciary*, pp. 119–26 and 137.

[86] Judicial Office, *Lord Chief Justice's Report 2013* (2013), 12.

judiciaries where judicial independence is highly valued. In Canada, for example, it has become increasingly common for Supreme Court Justices to retire early and return to practice.[87] If judicial salaries lag too far behind professional earnings, the convention could well break down in the UK. If that happens, it would put additional pressure on the government to pay closer to the market rate to retain as well as attract high-quality judges. It would also increase the pressure on the government to offer attractive pensions for judges, an issue which we deal with in the next section.

### *Judicial pensions*

One of the reasons why the High Court has traditionally been a popular career choice for successful barristers, despite the significant cut in pay, is the generous pension. As the SSRB has observed, the judicial pension scheme 'could not bridge the gap between private practice and public service but it had a psychological impact well beyond its financial value, signalling acknowledgement of what had been given up forever and marking public respect for the judiciary as an institution'.[88] In more prosaic terms, barristers, being self-employed, must make their own pension provision, and many reach middle age only to find they have not saved sufficiently for their retirement.[89] Before 1995, judges enjoyed a gold-plated non-contributory pension, to which they were entitled after only fifteen years' service. Like so many pension schemes, the benefits have been whittled away over the last twenty years. As a result, the judiciary has been involved in more frequent and more ferocious battles with the Lord Chancellor and the Treasury over pensions than over pay. And, unlike in the context of judicial salaries, there is no intermediary equivalent to the SSRB to whom the judges can make their case:[90] negotiations are direct

[87] In Canada, retiring Justices do not appear before the court, but offer advisory opinions. See, for example, J. McNish, 'The Supreme Court's Retired, but Hardly Retiring, Ian Binnie', *Globe and Mail*, 10 April 2012. Some British judges return to practice as arbitrators and mediators: examples include Lord Hoffmann, Sir Gavin Lightman, Sir Mark Potter, Sir Gordon Langley and Sir Simon Tuckey.

[88] Review Body on Senior Salaries, *35th Annual Report on Senior Salaries: Report No. 81* (Cm 8569 2013), para. 5.45.

[89] See Genn, *The Attractiveness of Senior Judicial Appointment to Highly Qualified Practitioners*, para. 26.

[90] The SSRB has said that it will seek to quantify the effect of pension changes on judicial remuneration: Review Body on Senior Salaries, *35th Annual Report on Senior Salaries: Report No. 81*, para. 5.38.

between the senior judges and the Lord Chancellor and can be bruising. There have been three main occasions when pensions have surfaced as a source of dispute over the last twenty years: in 1992–3, 2004–5 and 2011–13. On each occasion, senior judges strongly resisted the changes proposed by the government, arguing that they represented a worsening in the terms and conditions of judicial service, and hence a reduction in their total remuneration.

In the 1990s, the Lord Chancellor, Lord Mackay, soon became unpopular with the judges when he ended the bar's monopoly of audience rights in the Crown Court and the 'two counsel rule', which required junior counsel to be instructed to appear with QCs.[91] In 1992, he proposed reforms to lower the retiring age for judges from seventy-five to seventy and to introduce a unified pensions scheme that increased the service required to earn a maximum pension from fifteen to twenty years. While the bar and bench broadly welcomed the lower retirement age, the proposal for a longer period of judicial service to earn a full pension encountered fierce opposition. One retired Court of Appeal judge encapsulated the mood of the senior judiciary in characterising the proposals as securing 'economic advantage to the Treasury . . . to the prejudice of the judicial system'.[92] Several senior judges spoke publicly against the change in the House of Lords and came close to defeating the proposal.

In June 1992, at the second reading of the Judicial Pensions and Retirement Bill, Lord Mackay explained that the purpose was to rationalise the haphazard arrangements for judicial pensions at different levels of the judiciary and bring them more into line with other pension schemes in the public sector.[93] The LCJ, Lord Taylor, used his maiden speech in the Lords to criticise the government's plans.[94] Other senior judges also used their position as peers to criticise the proposal.[95] Much of their opposition focused on the perceived danger that the proposals would dilute the quality of the High Court bench by rendering judicial office less attractive for the bar's strongest performers,

[91] For the trenchant opinion of a recently retired Court of Appeal judge, see F. Purchas, 'Lord Mackay and the Judiciary' (1994) 144 *New Law Journal* 527.

[92] F. Purchas, 'What Is Happening to Judicial Independence?' (1994) 144 *New Law Journal* 1306, 1310.

[93] *Hansard*, HL, vol. 538, col. 117, 16 June 1992.

[94] *Hansard*, HL, vol. 538, col. 141, 16 June 1992.

[95] See, for example, contributions from Lord Donaldson and Lord Ackner: *Hansard*, HL, vol. 538, cols. 147–50 and 154–8, 16 June 1992.

fearing that 'no doubt serious harm will result'.[96] At report stage, Lord Donaldson, the Master of the Rolls, moved an amendment to preserve existing pension rights, but was narrowly defeated by the government by ninety-four votes to eighty-nine.[97] Lawyers and judges in the Lords mustered loyally in support of Lord Donaldson's amendment. However, in the lower levels of the judiciary there was less solidarity, because not all judges were equally affected, and this led to a public split in the views of the judges. Though the Council of HM Circuit Judges objected to the change,[98] the Association of District Judges broke ranks to express support for the government in a forthright letter to *The Times*, endorsing the new arrangements as providing a single unified scheme that would apply equally to the whole of the judiciary.[99] The Bill passed through its remaining stages with little further opposition. The Judicial Pensions and Retirement Act 1993 created a new scheme for all judges appointed after 31 March 1995. The pension entitlements of serving judges remained unaffected, which perhaps explains why opposition faded away.

The next clash over judicial pensions was in 2004–5, as a result of new rules in the 2004 Budget to cap the tax relief which individuals could claim on pension contributions at £1.5m. In November 2004, the *Daily Telegraph* reported a Cabinet row over a plan to introduce a Judicial Pensions Bill to exempt the judiciary from the new rules. The then Lord Chancellor, Lord Falconer, had 'apparently promised the pensions before clearing the move with Cabinet colleagues'.[100] Tony Blair's chief of staff Jonathan Powell related how, most unusually, the matter came to full Cabinet, with Lord Falconer concerned that 'there might be mass judicial resignations if we did not'.[101] But Chancellor of the Exchequer Gordon Brown, along with other Cabinet ministers, 'raised strong objections', and the decision was postponed.[102] A Judicial Pensions Bill was mentioned in the Queen's Speech in November 2004, and was included again in the Queen's Speech which opened the new Parliament in May 2005. However, the Bill was never introduced because of strong

96 Purchas, 'The Constitution in the Market Place' (1993) 143 *New Law Journal* 1608.

97 *Hansard*, HL, vol. 538, col. 1069, 27 October 1992.

98 *The Times*, 12 November 1992.

99 *The Times*, 2 November 1992.

100 B. Carlin, 'Blair Backs Judges after Cabinet Revolt over Pension Tax Controls', *Daily Telegraph*, 23 November 2004.

101 J. Powell, *The New Machiavelli: How to Wield Power in the Modern World* (London: Vintage 2010), p. 63.

102 Powell, *The New Machiavelli*, p. 63.

opposition in the Labour Party, which was not naturally sympathetic to the privileged financial position of judges.[103] The judges kept up the pressure, with rumours of resignation threats and of legal action.[104] The Concordat, which had been negotiated only the year before, must have felt particularly fragile. However, in December 2005 a complex alternative solution was found. In a written statement, Lord Falconer announced that the Judicial Pensions Bill would be dropped.[105] Instead, judicial pensions were to be de-registered from the Finance Act 2004 so they would not be subject to the £1.5m cap on tax-exempt pension pots. The judges had won a special exemption, and the Treasury had lost – but the Treasury did not forget, and managed to claw back the exemption with a new judicial pension scheme in 2013.

The renegotiation of judicial pensions in 2011–13 was the most contentious, because the government proposed to change the conditions of service for serving judges. The judges viewed this as a constitutional outrage, arguing that their remuneration could not be reduced. The government countered that their pensions were not the same as judicial salaries. However, at the conclusion of the negotiations, the new Lord Chancellor, Chris Grayling, acknowledged a breach of long-standing practice, but not of broader constitutional principle. He recognised that there was a tradition that total remuneration, including pension provision, should not be reduced for serving judges, but he contended that 'in the particular context of difficult economic circumstances and changes to pension provision across the public sector', the proposed reforms did not undermine 'the broader constitutional principle of judicial independence'.[106]

The background was the report of the Independent Public Services Pensions Commission (chaired by Lord (John) Hutton) in 2011, which had suggested that public servants should contribute more towards their pension costs. The initial tussle with the judiciary in 2011 was over contributions. The former LCJ Lord Woolf had argued publicly that it would be wrong to impose contributions when no such requirement had existed at the time at which serving judges had been

[103] Beloff, 'Paying Judges: Why, Who, Whom, How Much? Neill Lecture 2006', 17.

[104] See F. Gibb, 'Judges Threaten to Resign over Pensions Losses', *The Times*, 6 October 2005; S. Hoare and J. Harris, 'Senior Judges Threaten Legal Action against Government', *The Lawyer*, 7 November 2005.

[105] *Hansard*, HL, vol. 676, col. WS151, 15 December 2005.

[106] Ministerial Statement on Judicial Pensions Reform, *Hansard*, HC, vol. 558, col. 10WS, 5 February 2013.

appointed.[107] In reply, the Secretary of State for Work and Pensions, Iain Duncan Smith, explained to the House of Commons that judges paid nothing towards the cost of their own pensions, while taxpayers made a contribution equivalent to about 32 per cent of judges' gross salaries, which was 'unaffordable and unfair to the taxpayer'.[108] Section 34 of the Pensions Act 2011 required contributions to judicial pensions. This Act set the legislative framework for public-service pension reform, with the detail to be laid out in regulations. In March 2012, the Lord Chancellor, Kenneth Clarke, introduced the Judicial Pensions (Contributions) Regulations, announcing that judges would start to contribute 1.28 per cent of their salaries in 2012–13, with a further 1.28 per cent in 2013–14.

Later that year, the Lord Chancellor wrote to the LCJ outlining the government's plans for more radical changes. Intense negotiations followed, conducted in strict secrecy on both sides, albeit with the occasional press comment that the judges might threaten court action, but otherwise making no real disclosures.[109] When Grayling, Clarke's successor as Lord Chancellor, announced the details of the new Judicial Pension Scheme in early 2013, it became clear just how much had been at stake. The main features of the new scheme included a new stand-alone Judicial Pension Scheme, solely for judges. Judges who were aged fifty-five and over – which accounted for around 74 per cent of serving judges – would be excluded from the new scheme and would instead continue in their current scheme until retirement. The new pension scheme would be registered with HM Revenue and Customs for tax purposes, with the result that judicial pension accrual would in future be subject to annual and lifetime allowances. Benefits would be based on average earnings, not final salary. The accrual rate would be approximately 1/43 for each year of service, not 1/40, and there would be no automatic lump sum.

The real battle was for younger and newer judges; that is, the quarter of serving judges under fifty-five, whose pensions would be drastically changed by the new arrangements. The most radical change was that the new scheme would be registered for tax purposes, reflecting the determination of the Treasury to unpick the exemption negotiated by

107 Quoted in F. Gibb, 'Judges Set for Trial over Pension Plan', *The Times*, 14 March 2011.

108 *Hansard*, HC, vol. 530, col. 45, 20 June 2011.

109 F. Gibb, 'Chris Grayling Is Set to Trigger a Constitutional Clash with Judges', *The Times*, 14 March 2011; F. Gibb, 'Judges Threaten Court Action over Changes to Their Pensions', *The Times*, 10 October 2012; J. Rozenberg, 'Judicial Pensions: Will Judges Take Chris Grayling to Court?', *Guardian*, 28 September 2012.

Lord Falconer in 2005. And this time they prevailed. But the effect was to penalise younger judges who had already accumulated a pension pot close to the lifetime allowance of £1.5m, although this was subsequently addressed via transitional protection to judges under fifty-five with substantial pension savings. However, this protection would not be extended to new judges. Lawyers who had built up significant pension provision while in private practice would find the new pension arrangements much less attractive.

Such was their concern that 1,200 judges submitted representations to the Lord Chancellor, almost all protesting about the impact on the younger judges. First, they expressed grave concern that the government could change the terms of employment of serving judges. Second, they protested the magnitude of the change. In his evidence to the SSRB, the LCJ submitted advice from actuaries suggesting that existing judges would see a reduction in pension benefits of 34–46 per cent after April 2015.[110] The SSRB commented that the reforms 'may well have a detrimental effect on the motivation and morale of judges and especially of the younger judges whose pension benefits will be substantially reduced'. The SSRB were also concerned that the reforms could 'prejudice judicial recruitment since the reduction is clearly substantial and it would be surprising if it did not deter some people from applying to join the judiciary, especially at more senior levels'.[111]

The impact on recruitment is a recurrent theme in all the negotiations about judicial salaries and pensions. The underlying issue is not so much judicial independence, but concern about the future quality of the judiciary if judicial remuneration lags too far behind. This is a difficult argument for the judiciary to deploy, because its effects lie some way in the future and can never convincingly be proved or disproved. Generally, the judges have a weak hand in negotiations over salaries and pensions. With their strong sense of public duty, they are not going to strike. They are not unionised. Their repeated threats of resignations have proved empty. And to date their threats of litigation have proved equally empty;

[110] Review Body on Senior Salaries, *35th Annual Report on Senior Salaries: Report No. 81*, para. 5.21. The new Judicial Pension Scheme may not be the only pension scheme affected: one report suggests that the four largest public-sector schemes would be worth over one-third less to members as a result of the government reforms. See the Pensions Policy Institute, *The Implications of the Coalition Government's Reforms for Members of the Public Service Pension Schemes* (2012).

[111] Review Body on Senior Salaries, *35th Annual Report on Senior Salaries: Report No. 81*, paras. 5.36–5.37.

in any event, such litigation would raise the difficulty of finding a suitable person to hear such a dispute, given judges' obvious interest in the outcome. As other jurisdictions such as Canada illustrate, it is possible for judicial review to include questions about the adequacy of judicial remuneration, but such cases often lead to concerns about the legitimacy of such decisions.[112] Finally, their preference to negotiate in secret makes it harder to appeal to allies in Parliament, or to generate sympathy amongst the media and the public, even if such sympathy were likely.

In the 2012 negotiations, the judiciary felt particularly indignant that judges under fifty-five could not also be exempted from the new scheme, because there were relatively few of them (only one-quarter of the total), and so the sum of money required to leave their pensions unaffected was also relatively small: it was estimated at £70m. Ironically, within a month of the Lord Chancellor announcing the conclusion of the negotiations in February 2013, the judges inflicted a defeat on the government over judicial pensions that was to be far more costly – but this time the defeat was in court. A series of cases had been brought by part-time, fee-paid judges who claimed they were entitled to pensions under the judicial pension scheme. After referring the issue to the European Court of Justice, the UK Supreme Court held in *O'Brien* that the judge in the lead case was a worker, and thus entitled to a pension under the EU Part-Time Workers (Prevention of Less Favourable Treatment) Regulations 2000.[113] As Paterson notes, the Supreme Court reached this decision to backdate pension benefits even though none of the part-time judges could have any expectation of such benefits given the terms of their service when appointed.[114] The Ministry's emergency response was to seek a Supplementary Estimate of £2 billion to cover the cost of this large group of additional pension-holders, estimated at around 10,000 retired and serving fee-paid judges. To put this in perspective, the annual estimate for the judicial pension scheme in 2012–13 was just under £150m.[115]

The full significance of the *O'Brien* decision will only become clear over time, but it may have substantial implications for judicial appointments if it renders it uneconomical to employ practitioners in part-time, fee-paid

[112] See P. Hogg, 'The Bad Idea of Unwritten Constitutional Principles: Protecting Judicial Salaries', in A. Dodek and L. Sossin (eds.), *Judicial Independence in Context* (Toronto: Irwin Law, 2010).

[113] *O'Brien* v. *Ministry of Justice* [2013] UKSC 6.

[114] A. Paterson, *Final Judgment* (Oxford: Hart Publishing 2013), p. 321.

[115] Ministry of Justice, Judicial Pension Scheme Memorandum on Single Supplementary Estimate 2012–13 (2013).

judicial work. If so, there would be no opportunity for practitioners to experience judicial work before deciding whether to commit to a judicial career. Similarly, it would remove the opportunity which senior judges now have to assess the suitability of possible candidates for appointment, with those views being fed into the selection process.

## Conclusion

The age of austerity has been difficult for the judges, as for all those in the public sector. It has brought them into conflict with the executive over salaries, pensions and the budget for the courts. In these disputes, the government has tended to prevail. In many ways, each of these conflicts has tested the reach of the notion of judicial independence, and shown its limits: when it came to the crunch, the judiciary was not able to demonstrate that its independence was seriously under threat. Over salaries, the judges have acquiesced in a pay freeze which has eroded their take-home pay by almost 20 per cent; and over pensions, they have reluctantly accepted a new scheme which reduces the pensions of some serving judges and all new judges. However, they could not credibly characterise this as an attack on their independence because they were not being singled out for harsher treatment than any other public-sector professionals.

In disputes over money, the executive will almost always win, because it controls the purse strings. Judicial threats of litigation often seem fanciful, not least because of the problem of finding a judge to hear their case. They can also threaten resignation, but so far this has proved an empty threat. They can appeal to Parliament: over pensions they did so unsuccessfully in 1992, but chose not to in 2004–5 and 2012–13. The LCJ has yet to appeal to Parliament over the funding of the courts. The ultimate court to which the judges could appeal is the court of public opinion. That is why, in 2013, the LCJ reluctantly decided they should accept their pensions defeat in dignified silence. The LCJ held seventeen meetings up and down the country to explain the settlement, but also to persuade the judges not to engage in any public protest. They would not have garnered much sympathy. Judges are in the top 1 per cent of earners. Their pensions – even after the changes – are very generous, and any public complaints would risk incurring envy and derision rather than support from the public. If they are in any doubt about this, judges need only look at the referendum in the Republic of Ireland in 2011, when a constitutional amendment to remove the prohibition on reducing judicial salaries was carried by a majority of 80 per cent.

The changes to salaries and pensions may not threaten judicial independence in any immediate sense but the longer-term effects may be significant. This chapter has shown how the economic crisis and financial cutbacks can challenge long-held practices and beliefs about the nature of judicial independence and the working of the judicial system. It is unlikely that the judiciary would be willing to contemplate a radical new model for funding the Courts Service without the sense of desperation engendered by a further round of funding cuts. If they go down that road it seems inevitable that the senior judiciary will be drawn more deeply into the management of the Courts Service, and will have to accept the responsibility and more direct accountability that goes with it. As for salaries and pensions, here too the age of austerity may have longer-term consequences. If the decision in *O'Brien* undermines the system of employing part-time, fee-paid judges, that may accelerate the development of a career judiciary, perhaps one where judges who find they are ill-suited to judicial work or cannot live as comfortably on a reduced pension will more often seek to return to practice.

Many judges believe strongly that they would have weathered the economic storm better under an old-style Lord Chancellor and that the Courts Service has suffered through being part of the Ministry of Justice. Both these beliefs are misplaced, and those with longer memories will recall that Lord Mackay, an old-style Lord Chancellor, was the first to reform the generous judicial pensions. The financial difficulties of HMCTS would almost inevitably be the same in a small or a large department: 20 per cent cuts are, after all, 20 per cent cuts. As we explained above, HMCTS has actually suffered proportionately less than other parts of the Ministry. Yet the judiciary was perhaps right in one of their concerns about the consequences of the creation of the Ministry of Justice: prisons might not have squeezed HMCTS's budget, but successive new-style Lord Chancellors – Kenneth Clarke and Chris Grayling in particular – have arguably shown more interest in the prisons estate and the probation service than in the judiciary and the courts. The real risk to the judiciary and the courts is that they suffer from ignorance and neglect. The main threat to judicial independence today does not come from an overweening executive bent on undermining the constitutional position of the judges. It comes from the indifference of politicians to their partnership with the judiciary, and from political retreat from engagement with the judicial system.

# 5

# Relations between judges and Parliament

In the years following the passing of the Constitutional Reform Act 2005, the relationship between Parliament and the judiciary has undergone a structural change. The removal of the UK's highest court of appeal from the House of Lords formally separated the judges from the legislature and this has inevitably changed the institutional architecture within which judges and parliamentarians interact. But the provisions of the Act do not tell the whole story of those changes, which did not begin and end in 2005. The removal of the Law lords was a critical moment, but practices shaping relations between Parliament and judges were changing before then, and have evolved since. In this chapter, we explore how both sides understand this changing relationship. Our focus is on the ways that Parliament both acts as a guardian of judicial independence and also offers new and constructive avenues of judicial accountability. The findings set out in this chapter counterbalance the tendency of lawyers and judges to focus on the high-profile but relatively rare occasions when politicians fail to respect judges and their decisions. There will always be tensions between Parliament and the courts. Recent years have provided a number of high-profile examples: sustained wrangling over the proper scope of judicial review in human rights and national security cases, the role of the European Court of Human Rights, and the boundaries of parliamentary privilege. Decisions by courts in relation to human rights and judicial review are often points of friction between judges and politicians, but this is not our focus here. We are interested instead in the ways in which judges and politicians interact beyond judicial decision-making. Occasional tensions over high-profile cases must be distinguished from the quiet diplomacy and everyday practices that ensure that an effective dialogue is maintained.

## Judges as parliamentarians

Before the Supreme Court opened its doors in 2009, the relationship between the judiciary and Parliament in the UK was most notable for the role of certain judges – not just the Law Lords, but also other senior judges – as parliamentarians. Observers from other countries were often understandably baffled by the fact that the UK's highest court operated formally as a committee of the upper house of the legislature. But what looked like an arrangement that might undermine the independence of the UK's top court had in fact insulated it from political pressure since its creation in 1876.[1] As highly respected members of the Lords, with their budget and facilities provided by Parliament, the Law Lords carried out their judicial work with little interference from politicians. The arcane workings of the upper house served to promote the independence of the Law Lords, a point to which we return in Chapter 8. Debate tends to focus on the Law Lords and on the role of the Appellate Committee, but in fact the Law Lords were not the only 'judicial peers' in the House of Lords. The Lord Chief Justice of England and Wales (LCJ) was by convention given a peerage on appointment. Other senior judges, such as the Master of the Rolls and the Lord President in Scotland, tended also to receive peerages, and some judges held peerages for reasons unrelated to their judicial roles.[2] The significance of retired judges in the Lords should also not be overlooked. These judicial peers were full members of the upper house, enjoying the right to speak and vote in the legislative process and contribute to its scrutiny work. Some had prominent roles on Lords committees, such as the legal sub-committee of the EU Committee and the Joint Committee on Delegated Powers and Regulatory Reform. Here we generally refer to the Law Lords (meaning the members of the Appellate Committee), but use the term 'judicial peers' to refer to the wider group of judges with peerages.

Writing in the 1970s, Louis Blom-Cooper and Gavin Drewry argued that 'the fundamental advantage of having active judges in the House of Lords is that they provide a two-way channel of communication between the courts and the legislature'.[3] Judges tended to speak as legal experts

[1] See generally D. Steele, 'The Judicial House of Lords: Abolition and Restoration 1873–6', in L. Blom-Cooper, B. Dickson and G. Drewry (eds.), *The Judicial House of Lords, 1876–2009* (Oxford: Oxford University Press, 2009).

[2] In January 2014 eight judges were listed as being excluded from participation in the Lords by virtue of section 137 of the 2005 Act: five Supreme Court judges, two judges of the Court of Session, and the Lord Chief Justice of England and Wales. House of Lords, *The Grey Book: Who Does What in the House of Lords* (2014), p. 34. The two Scottish judges (Baroness Clark of Calton and Lord Boyd of Duncansby) both held peerages as a result of prior political careers.

[3] L. Blom-Cooper and G. Drewry, *Final Appeal* (Oxford: Oxford University Press, 1972), p. 209.

on constitutional matters and 'lawyers' law' (technical matters of construction).[4] Some argued strongly for the retention of the Appellate Committee precisely because of the contribution judicial peers could make to the work of the upper house as experts.[5] But with almost a hundred other lawyers and judges, the Lords was not short of legal expertise.[6] Judges also spoke on judicial 'trade union' interests, but the ability of the Law Lords to communicate judicial concerns was limited by the fact that they could not speak for the judiciary as a whole. They were unlikely to have much experience of the courts at the lower levels. True, the LCJ and Master of the Rolls were better placed to speak on behalf of the English and Welsh judges, but the occupants of these posts tended to contribute to parliamentary debates rarely, and only when there were matters of serious concern to the judiciary. A notable example of this kind of activity occurred in the early 1990s when the then Lord Chancellor, Lord Mackay, initiated reforms to judicial pensions and the regulation of the legal profession that enraged the judiciary, leading to a notable spike in contributions by judicial peers (see Figure 5.1).[7]

Participation by judicial peers in parliamentary debates had in fact largely fallen away before the Constitutional Reform Act 2005, with many judges in the Lords following a self-imposed vow of silence and debates in the chamber increasingly clashing with the business of the Appellate Committee.[8] In 1967, judicial peers contributed to debates twenty-six times and in 1980 the figure was thirty-three.[9] In 2000, by contrast, there were only eight contributions and from 2000 to 2004 the contributions averaged four per year.[10] The sharp decline that occurred around the year

[4] Such as the law on unfair contractual terms: for example, *Hansard*, HL, vol. 384, cols. 435–530, 20 June 1977.

[5] For example R. Cooke, 'The Law Lords: An Endangered Heritage' (2003) 119 *Law Quarterly Review* 49.

[6] This is the figure for 2009, taken from M. Russell and M. Benton, *Analysis of Existing Data on the Breadth of Expertise and Experience in the House of Lords* (London: The Constitution Unit, 2010), Table 10 and p. 6.

[7] Lord Lane, as Lord Chief Justice, was at one point prompted to such flights of hyperbole that he drew an analogy between the impending reforms to the legal profession and the rise of fascism: *Hansard*, HL, vol. 505, col. 1331, 7 April 1989.

[8] Lord Hope, 'Voices from the Past: The Law Lords' Contribution to the Legislative Process' (2007) 123 *Law Quarterly Review* 547, 566.

[9] The first figure is from Blom-Cooper and Drewry, while the second is our own. See Blom-Cooper and Drewry, *Final Appeal*, on p. 202. Both figures refer to serving members of the Appellate Committee plus serving LCJs and Masters of the Rolls.

[10] HL Committee on the Constitutional Reform Bill, *Constitutional Reform Bill [HL]* (HL 125-I 2004), Appendix 8.

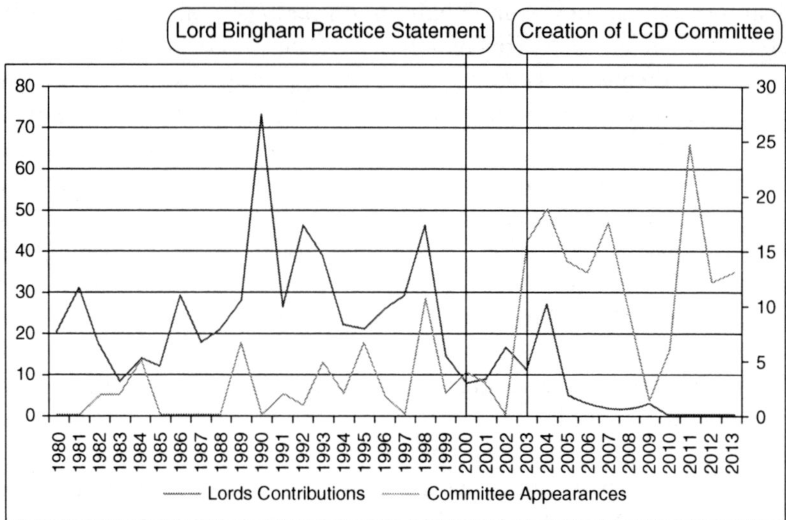


**Figure 5.1.** Debate contributions by Law Lords against committee appearances by judges 1980–2013[11]

2000 is largely explained by the hostility of Lord Bingham, then Senior Law Lord, to the practice.[12] The Wakeham Commission on reform of the legislative House of Lords did not accept in its report of the year 2000 that there was any immediate need for reform of the role played by the Appellate Committee.[13] It did, however, suggest that the Law Lords publish a statement clarifying how and when they would participate in debates in the Lords. Lord Bingham duly did so, explaining in a practice statement that the Law Lords 'do not think it appropriate to engage in matters where there is a strong element of party political controversy', and that they 'bear in mind' that they might render themselves ineligible

[11] The left vertical axis refers to 'Lords contributions' and the right axis to 'committee appearances'. Figures for 'Lords contributions' refer to contributions by serving members of the Appellate Committee, serving LCJs and serving Masters of the Rolls. Figures for 'committee appearances' (as elsewhere) refer to appearances by serving salaried UK judges.

[12] Lord Bingham, 'The Evolving Constitution' (the JUSTICE Annual Lecture, 4 October 2001), published in his *Lives of the Law: Selected Essays and Speeches, 2000–2010* (Oxford: Oxford University Press, 2011), p. 56. See also A. Le Sueur and R. Cornes, *The Future of the UK's Highest Courts* (London: The Constitution Unit, 2001).

[13] Royal Commission on the Reform of the House of Lords, *A House for the Future* (Cm 4534 2000), para. 9.5.

to sit judicially if they express opinion on matters which might later be relevant to an appeal.[14] This tentative phrasing was deliberate. The Law Lords were divided and could not agree on a stronger collective position. Some, notably Lord Hope, felt that participation in debates was of mutual benefit to the judiciary and to Parliament. Participation kept the top judges in touch with politics, while also providing Parliament with the benefit of their legal expertise. The Wakeham Report had reached the same conclusion.[15] However, shortly after his statement, Lord Bingham indicated that he regarded participation in debate as incompatible with the judicial role.[16] Most of his colleagues followed his example, accelerating an existing tendency for judicial peers to disengage themselves from parliamentary business that had been building for at least a decade, if not longer.

Yet as late as 2004 Lords Hoffmann and Scott participated in the controversial debates on proposed legislation to outlaw hunting with dogs. Lord Scott argued that '[t]o impose the ban would be a misuse of law' and 'profoundly undemocratic', and that 'a vast section of the community would think it unfair'.[17] Having expressed such vehement opinions and voted against portions of the Bill, both judges were precluded from hearing cases that arose out of the Hunting Act.[18] This highlighted the potential pitfalls of the Law Lords' association with Parliament. Interventions of this kind did not do them or the wider judiciary great credit, creating an impression of bias that, in later years, advocates cited in order to have individual Law Lords recused from appeals. At worst, comments of this kind risked the impression that certain Law Lords were reactionary and self-interested.[19]

## *The 2005 reforms*

By 2005, notwithstanding the high-profile contributions of Lords Hoffmann and Scott, judicial peers had largely withdrawn from participation in Lords debates and the apparent breach of the

[14] *Hansard*, HL, vol. 614, col. 419, 22 June 2000.

[15] Royal Commission on the Reform of the House of Lords, *A House for the Future*, paras. 9.6–9.7.

[16] Lord Bingham, 'A New Supreme Court for the United Kingdom' (the Constitution Unit Spring Lecture, 1 May 2002).

[17] *Hansard*, HL, vol. 623, col. 626, 12 March 2001.

[18] *R (Jackson)* v. *Attorney General* [2006] 1 AC 262; *R (Countryside Alliance)* v. *Attorney General* [2008] 1 AC 719.

[19] Lord Hoffman was also recused in *Reynolds* v. *Times Newspapers Ltd* [2001] 2 AC 127.

separation of powers arising from their presence in Parliament was more technical than real. Given the practical benefits of being in Parliament, it is not surprising that removal to a new Supreme Court was controversial and was strongly resisted by some of the senior judges. As Lord Hope expressed it when the Law Lords finally departed, 'the House of Lords has become a byword for judicial work of the highest quality ... Why give up something that seemed so valuable?'[20] But for the Labour government the reform had become an important element in its constitutional modernisation programme. It was not sufficient for the courts to be independent of politicians; they had to be seen to be independent. Two years after the proposal was first made, and after detailed scrutiny, including by a special *ad hoc* committee of the upper house, the Constitutional Reform Act was passed in 2005.[21] Because of the time taken to find and then to adapt a new building (Middlesex Guildhall), it took a further four years for the Law Lords to move to their new home across Parliament Square, breaking the formal link with Parliament.

As well as removing the top court from Parliament, the Constitutional Reform Act barred all judges with peerages from sitting and voting in the Lords while holding judicial office.[22] Lord Hope was not the only senior judge who lamented the loss of 'something that seemed so valuable'. Lord Judge regretted that as Lord Chief Justice he lacked the power enjoyed by his predecessors to speak in Parliament.[23] Our findings, however, suggest that judges have in fact lost little (if any) influence as a result of the changes. While judicial peers can no longer participate in debates, the judicial voice has not been extinguished from Parliament. In 2009, after the departure of the judicial peers, lawyers and judges were the largest single professional group in the Lords, comprising ninety-four peers, of whom twenty-six were retired judges.[24] The next-largest professional groups were from banking and finance (ninety-two) and academia

[20] See, for example, *Hansard*, HL, vol. 712, col. 1514, 21 July 2009 (Lord Hope).

[21] See, generally, A. Le Sueur, 'From Appellate Committee to Supreme Court: A Narrative', in Blom-Cooper, Dickson and Drewry, *The Judicial House of Lords, 1876–2009*.

[22] Constitutional Reform Act 2005, section 137.

[23] Lord Judge, 'Constitutional Change: Unfinished Business' (the Constitution Unit, 4 December 2013).

[24] Russell and Benton, *Analysis of Existing Data on the Breadth of Expertise and Experience in the House of Lords*, Table 10 and p. 6. On historical patterns of lawyer representation in Parliament, see M. Rush and N. Baldwin, 'Lawyers in Parliament', in D. Oliver and G. Drewry (eds.), *The Law and Parliament* (London: Butterworths, 1998), p. 155.

(eighty-one). The House of Commons elected in 2010 contained a similar number of lawyers, with ninety MPs who had been barristers or solicitors; fewer than there were fifty years ago, but still a large professional group.[25] On retirement from the bench, judicial peers resume the right to participate in the Lords. In 2013, the most active former judges were Lords Brown, Hope, Judge, Lloyd, Phillips and Scott, with Lords Hope and Judge becoming active as soon as they retired.[26] In the Lords, retired judges are the guardians of the interests of judges and the courts and can sometimes act as proxies for serving judges. Shortly after his retirement as President of the Supreme Court in 2012, Lord Phillips introduced an amendment designed to protect the independence of the Chief Executive of the Supreme Court.[27] He acted at the request of his successor, Lord Neuberger. One of our interviewees felt that, following the departure of the Law Lords, the Supreme Court ceased to have a relationship with Parliament, but this kind of interaction suggests that informal links do in fact persist.

It is not yet clear whether Supreme Court Justices appointed since 2009 who have been given only courtesy titles of 'Lord' will be automatically granted peerages on retirement. The granting of a peerage to Lord Thomas on being appointed the new LCJ in 2013 suggests that this tradition at least will continue. If so, the judiciary, through its retired members, will not be short of voices in the Lords to represent their interests and could form a very effective lobby group. Moreover, newly retired judges who go to the Lords may throw themselves into their new parliamentary role with less circumspection than did their predecessors, who were schooled in caution by their membership of the Appellate Committee. If, on the other hand, Supreme Court Justices are not routinely given peerages on retirement, a greater burden will fall on prominent lawyers – like Lords Lester and Pannick – to promote legal and judicial concerns in the upper chamber.

[25] D. Howarth, 'Lawyers in the House of Commons', in D. Feldman (ed.), *Law in Politics, Politics in Law* (Oxford: Hart Publishing, 2013), p. 41n2.

[26] Lord Hope and Lord Scott had been the most active contributors as serving Law Lords. In 2001–4, only four out of the twelve Law Lords contributed to debates: see HL Committee on the Constitutional Reform Bill, *Constitutional Reform Bill [HL]* (HL 125-I 2004), Appendix 8.

[27] *Hansard*, HL, vol. 741, col. 1488, 18 December 2012. The amendment was contained in section 29 of the Crime and Courts Act 2013 (amending sections 48 and 49 of the 2005 Act).

## Judges as account-givers

Prior to 2009, the judicial peers participated in debates as parliamentarians, not as account-givers. The question whether or how Parliament should hold them to account for their judicial roles did not usually arise. Yet Parliament has a role to play in promoting judicial accountability, both in a sacrificial sense – of holding judges to account for failings in the judicial system – and in an explanatory sense of judges giving an account of the system over which they exercise stewardship.[28] The ultimate form of sacrificial accountability held by Parliament is the power to dismiss a judge at High Court level or above by presenting an address by both Houses to the monarch.[29] This power has been used only once: in 1830, in relation to a judge of the Irish High Court who had misappropriated court funds. Parliament is very unlikely to use this dismissal power. There is instead a tradition of judges being encouraged by the Lord Chancellor and the LCJ to resign long before that stage is reached; of being 'eased out', as Robert Stevens delicately put it.[30] It is possible for Parliament to criticise an individual judge without calling for his or her dismissal, but this can only be done through a substantive motion, not in the course of ordinary parliamentary debate.[31] In practice, this significantly reduces the scope for parliamentarians to criticise individual judges.

In contrast, explanatory accountability takes place during the ordinary course of parliamentary work through a variety of channels including parliamentary questions, the laying of reports by the judiciary and HM Courts and Tribunals Service, and judicial appearances before select committees. Of the two senses of accountability, explanatory accountability is by far the more important. In practice, relatively few parliamentary questions concern the judiciary. Between January and July 2013, the Ministry of Justice was asked 1,617 questions in the Commons, of which 116 (7 per cent) concerned the court system. Questions about prisons, by contrast, made up 20 per cent of the total. Questions about the court system tend to focus on lower and mid-ranking courts

[28] V. Bogdanor, 'Parliament and the Judiciary: The Problem of Accountability' (Third Sunningdale Lecture on Accountability, 9 February 2006).

[29] The procedure was created by the Act of Settlement and re-enacted in the Senior Courts Act 1981, section 11(3).

[30] R. Stevens, *The English Judges: Their Role in the Changing Constitution* (Oxford: Hart Publishing, 2005), p. 80.

[31] M. Jack and others (eds.), *Erskine May: Parliamentary Practice*, 24th edn (London: LexisNexis Butterworths, 2011), pp. 443–4.

(e.g. coroners, magistrates courts and the Crown Court) and typically concerned current or local issues such as court closures or changes to sentencing policy, or restorative justice. Only six questions concerned the High Court level or above. Questions about individual judgments or the conduct of individual judges would be ruled inadmissible by the clerks.[32] These questions can offer only limited and indirect accountability for the judiciary, in large part because parliamentary questions are addressed to ministers and must raise an issue to which ministerial responsibility attaches (and as we have seen in Chapter 4, senior judges have increasing responsibility for the management, administration and efficiency of the judiciary as a whole).

Senior judges such as the LCJ issue reports, which are usually submitted to Parliament. Successive LCJs have demurred from a commitment to publish annual reports, instead issuing periodic reports. Under section 5 of the Constitutional Reform Act, the LCJ can lay written representations before Parliament. The use of this provision provides an illustration of some of the teething troubles that have arisen in relations between Parliament and the judiciary. In 2008 the Lords Constitution Committee encouraged the then LCJ, Lord Phillips, to submit annual reports to Parliament as a 'key mechanism of accountability'.[33] When Lord Phillips sought that same year to use section 5 to lay his report before Parliament, the parliamentary clerks resisted. Lord Phillips had previously described the section 5 power as a 'nuclear option',[34] and the clerks felt that its use to submit something as routine as a periodic report went against Parliament's intention in passing the section. After initially agreeing with the clerks to deposit the report as a paper with the parliamentary libraries, instead of via section 5, Phillips subsequently changed his mind and used section 5 anyway. His successor, Lord Judge, also sought to use section 5 to submit reports to Parliament – unsuccessfully in 2010 and 2012, following further resistance from clerks in the Commons, but successfully in 2013. In a private letter to the Lord Speaker, Lord Judge had argued that section 5 was an appropriate vehicle to submit the report since LCJs were no longer able to use their position as peers to voice concerns in Parliament. Of course such wrangling would be resolved if the LCJ were

32 Jack and others (eds.), *Erskine May: Parliamentary Practice*, p. 365.

33 HL Constitution Committee, *Relations between the Executive, the Judiciary and Parliament: Follow-up Report* (HL 177 2008), paras. 21–3.

34 HL Constitution Committee, *Relations between the Executive, the Judiciary and Parliament* (HL 151 2007), paras. 114–15.

under a statutory duty to submit an annual report, akin to that imposed on the Senior President of Tribunals.[35]

## Judges as witnesses

Parliamentary questions and judicial reports are useful means of producing factual information about the courts and the judiciary, but they are increasingly overshadowed by the role of select committee hearings, which have 'acquired a central role in accountability practices relating to the judicial system'.[36] These committees have become the primary forum for communication between judges and Parliament. This reflects changes not just to the judicial role, but also to the culture of Parliament itself. The centre of influence in Parliament has moved away from the debating chamber towards committees. The committees are 'hungrier and more self-confident', as one senior clerk put it, partly as a result of changes such as the election of committee chairs and increased resources, including the availability of specialist advisers.[37] A consequence of the growth in judicial appearances before select committees is that judges are now called to account in a more collective sense. When they spoke in Parliament, the judicial peers did not offer accountability for the courts system. The greatest number of them – i.e. the Law Lords – could not speak for the judiciary as a whole, nor did they claim to. More focused select committee inquiries allow greater scope for institutional accountability, with the agenda set principally by Parliamentarians rather than the judiciary.

### *Judicial appearances before select committees*

The level of judicial appearances before select committees is high. For the period of ten years from January 2003 to December 2013, we compiled 148 records of oral evidence by seventy-two salaried UK judges before select committees at Westminster.[38] If international judges, retired judges, deputy

[35] Tribunals, Courts and Enforcement Act 2007, section 43.

[36] A. Le Sueur, 'Parliamentary Accountability and the Judicial System', in N. Bamforth and P. Leyland (eds.), *Accountability in the Contemporary Constitution* (Oxford: Oxford University Press, 2013), p. 207.

[37] See R. Kelly, 'Select Committees: Powers and Functions', in A. Horne, G. Drewry and D. Oliver (eds.), *Parliament and the Law* (Oxford: Hart Publishing, 2013).

[38] The figure of 148 counts each judicial witness at each evidence session separately, including judges who have given evidence on multiple occasions and as part of a group.

High Court judges and magistrates are included, the number of judges who gave evidence rises to 185 individuals.[39] When the Lords Constitution Committee argued in 2007 that removal of the Lord Chancellor as head of the judiciary meant that select committees should play a 'central part' in facilitating understanding of the judicial role and in holding the judiciary to account, it was describing a constitutional trend that was already well developed.[40] As judicial contributions to debates in the Lords declined from the late 1990s, there was a significant and sustained (if erratic) increase in the number of judges who gave evidence before committees, with 2003 being a particular turning point.[41] In large part, this timing is due to the creation of a new select committee on the Lord Chancellor's Department in early 2003 and, just a few months later, the intense debate precipitated by the sacking of Lord Irvine and subsequently the introduction of the Constitutional Reform Bill. Prior to 2003, there was no designated committee to shadow the work of the Lord Chancellor's Department.[42] The new committee regularly invited judges to assist it in its work, and other committees also grew more confident in calling judicial witnesses. In 2004, the *ad hoc* Lords Committee on the Constitutional Reform Bill took extensive evidence from twenty-one judges anxious to express concerns about the proposed constitutional changes, as well as receiving collective submissions from the Judges' Council and the Law Lords.[43]

### *How are judicial appearances arranged?*

Judicial appearances before select committees are essentially a form of voluntary accountability. Committees have no power to compel or direct judges. Although a select committee could in theory order a judge to appear before it, it is extremely unlikely (amounting almost to a practical impossibility), and our interviewees agreed that to do so would be

[39] Except where otherwise stated, figures given here for the numbers of judges appearing before Select Committees refer to evidence given by serving salaried UK judges.

[40] HL Constitution Committee, *Relations between the Executive, the Judiciary and Parliament*, para. 126.

[41] The erratic nature of the increase reflects the fact that committee interest in judicial matters is episodic, often arising out of a particular inquiry (for example into judicial appointments or constitutional reform).

[42] See, generally, G. Drewry and D. Oliver, 'Parliamentary Accountability for the Administration of Justice', in D. Oliver and G. Drewry (eds.), *The Law and Parliament* (London: Butterworths, 1998), pp. 40–2.

[43] See HL Committee on the Constitutional Reform Bill, *Constitutional Reform Bill*, Appendix 4.

constitutionally inappropriate.[44] Attendance by judges as committee witnesses at Westminster is thus consensual in practice. Judges in Scotland and Northern Ireland have even greater protection as the Scottish Parliament and the Northern Ireland Assembly are precluded by statute from compelling judges to give evidence before them.[45] This protection is real, and the Lord President recently cited it when declining to appear before a Scottish committee.[46]

Until recently, evidence sessions were arranged informally between committee clerk and judges. Judges usually informed the Judicial Office, which provided advice and support.[47] Occasionally judges might submit written evidence on their own initiative or even volunteer to give evidence; an example an interviewee offered of the latter was in 2004 when the then LCJ, Lord Woolf, volunteered to give evidence as part of the Public Administration Committee's work on public inquiries.[48] Individual judges can take quite different attitudes to the process of giving evidence. One of our interviewees described the contrast between two judges attending the same session: judge *A* 'fell over themselves to come and give evidence', while judge *B* was 'far less happy' and the committee clerk had to 'talk to judge *B* on the phone to go through in painstaking detail' what the committee was going to ask. Judges seldom decline to appear outright, although the Judicial Office might seek to persuade a committee clerk that judicial evidence would be inappropriate, or that a different judge might be better placed to give evidence. Committees can be dogged at times in the face of an initial reluctance to appear: for example when the Public Accounts Committee's Chair, Margaret Hodge, wrote repeatedly to the President of the Family Division, Sir Nicholas Wall, asking him to give evidence in its inquiry into the Child and Family Court Advisory Support Service (CAFCASS). The committee has a fierce reputation and Wall was unwilling to be questioned about CAFCASS's value for money. In correspondence with Wall, Hodge acknowledged his concerns, but also

44 See Kelly, 'Select Committees: Powers and Functions', in Horne, Drewry and Oliver (eds.), *Parliament and the Law*, pp. 186–7.

45 Scotland Act 1998, section 23(7), and Northern Ireland Act 1998, section 44(5).

46 The Lord President declined to appear before the Petitions Committee to discuss a campaigner's call for a register of judicial interests, although subsequently he met with the Committee's convenor in private. Letter from Lord Gill to the Convenor of the Public Petitions Committee (28 May 2013).

47 See Judicial Executive Board, *Guidance for Judges Appearing before or Providing Written Evidence to Parliamentary Committees* (2008).

48 See HC Public Administration Committee, *Government by Inquiry: Minutes of Evidence* (HC 51-II 2005).

stressed that the committee felt that judges in the family court had a unique perspective as 'customers' of CAFCASS. Wall gave evidence in late 2010, in what one parliamentary clerk described as a productive session.

The joint appearance in November 2011 of the President of the Supreme Court, Lord Phillips, and the LCJ, Lord Judge, before the Joint Committee on Human Rights (JCHR) illustrates the intense behind-the-scenes negotiations that can occur. The session involved discussion of 'the legal issues with which . . . politicians have to wrestle' in the context of human rights.[49] Six weeks before the evidence session, the judges' officials contacted the JCHR's clerk to request more detailed information about the questions the President and the Lord Chief Justice were likely to be asked and expressed concerns about the areas into which questioning might lead. The clerks were unable to provide any cast-iron guarantees about the sort of question that the MPs and peers on the JCHR might ask, and in reply the judges indicated that they would think carefully before confirming their attendance. Their appearance was in doubt up until a matter of days before the session. Ultimately, the JCHR's chair, Dr Hywel Francis MP, spoke to the LCJ, who agreed to attend. At the session, the judges engaged with most of the topics about which they had previously expressed concern, even making tacit criticism of the Strasbourg Court. One parliamentary official was 'astonished' that the LCJ answered a question pertaining to a pending case before the Strasbourg Court. Only once, in response to a question about prisoner voting, did they refuse to answer. Lord Phillips declined to answer it 'because, although [it] may have been phrased as a matter of nice, pure constitutional law, this is one of the most hot political issues of the moment'.[50]

The process for arranging judicial appearances changed in 2012. According to revised guidance agreed between the LCJ and the Clerk of the House of Commons, a request to give evidence should now be made directly from the select committee in question to the private office of the LCJ.[51] The LCJ's office discusses with the committee's clerk whether a judicial appearance is appropriate, or whether written evidence might be more suitable. This is a tightening of control by the LCJ and is the product of increased dialogue between the senior judiciary and Parliament. A more centralised process, controlling who gives evidence and when,

[49] Joint Committee on Human Rights, *Human Rights Judgments: Minutes of Evidence* (uncorrected transcript of oral evidence) (HC 873-II 2011), Hywel Francis MP, Q. 1.

[50] Joint Committee on Human Rights, *Human Rights Judgments: Minutes of Evidence*, Lord Phillips responding to Q. 96.

[51] Judicial Executive Board, *Guidance to Judges on Appearances before Select Committees* (2012).

runs against the direction of travel since the abolition of the Kilmuir Rules in 1987 permitted greater public comment by judges. It remains for individual judges to decide when it is appropriate to venture public comments,[52] but appearances before select committees now fall into a more carefully controlled category. The more centralised process has resulted from judicial anxiety that there are now too many judicial appearances. Successive LCJs have voiced this worry,[53] as have other senior judges.[54] In private, one senior judge told us that judicial appearances presented 'a very serious danger'. Judicial concerns are threefold: first, that judges will become drawn unwittingly into politically contentious debates; second, that judges may express personal views that do not accord with the collective views of the judiciary; and third, that preparing for an appearance is time-consuming, with each appearance likely to cost a day or two of court time. It is certainly true that members of the judiciary are not always of one mind, as the Constitution Committee found during their inquiry into judicial appointments.[55] Equally valid are the human-resource implications. But as we explain below, the tone of questioning tends to be highly respectful, with MPs and peers conscious of the constraints on what judges are able to discuss publicly. Judicial concern seems overstated and, above all, understates the value of appearances before committees as an important and mutually beneficial mechanism of explanatory accountability.

### *What do judges talk about?*

To build up a picture of judicial evidence sessions, we looked at a selection of the transcripts, focusing primarily on fifty-two transcripts of the ten most frequent judicial witnesses between 2003 and 2012.[56] Evidence sessions with judges tend to cover a range of topics

[52] See, for example, Lord Neuberger, 'Where Angels Fear to Tread' (the Holdsworth Club, 2 March 2012).

[53] Lord Judge expressed this view in the course of the above appearance before the JCHR. See also Lord Phillips, 'Judicial Independence' (Commonwealth Law Conference, Nairobi, 12 September 2007).

[54] Letter from Lord Justice Toulson to Lord McNally (Minister of State at the Ministry of Justice), dated 9 December 2011 and published by the HL Constitution Committee as part of its inquiry into Judicial Appointments.

[55] HL Constitution Committee, *Judicial Appointments* (HL 272 2012).

[56] The judges were Igor Judge, Nicholas Phillips, John Thomas, Nicholas Wall, Michael Walker, Henry Hodge, David Neuberger, Nicholas Crichton, Thomas Bingham and Timothy Workman. We examined transcripts of some other judicial witnesses (outside this core group) where issues in specific sessions were raised by our interviewees, or where we were aware of features of a particular session that were of interest.

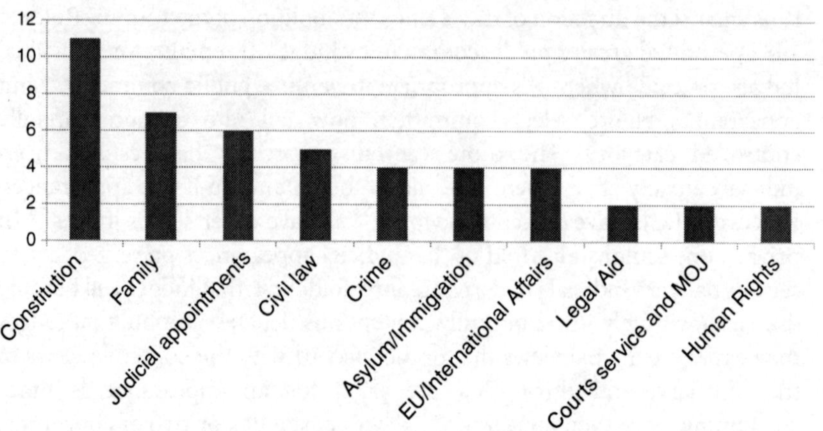


**Figure 5.2.** Top ten topics discussed by judicial witnesses 2003–2012[57]

rather than a single issue (See Figure 5.2). The prominence of constitutional matters and judicial appointments reflects their importance in the passage and implementation of the Constitutional Reform Act, and in its aftermath. By and large, the topics also reflect the priorities of parliamentarians, not the judges, since it is the select committees who choose the topics of their inquiries. Family law was prominent because of concerns about court delays. Judges are, unsurprisingly, more comfortable talking about the administration of the courts than about more substantive legal issues, and seek where possible to avoid politically sensitive issues altogether.

Judges appear most commonly before the Commons Justice Committee: sixty-five appearances between 2003 and 2013. Next are the Lords Constitution Committee (twenty-two) and the Commons Home Affairs Committee (eleven). The LCJ appears annually before the Constitution Committee and regularly, though less frequently, before the Justice Committee. The Lord Chancellor also appears annually before the Constitution Committee, which enables some 'triangulation' to take place, whereby each witness can comment on the evidence of the other.[58] In addition to these two, judges appear before a

[57] Top ten topics discussed by judicial witnesses between 2003 and 2012, based on the title of the inquiry or evidence session.

[58] Le Sueur, 'Parliamentary Accountability and the Judicial System', in Bamforth and Leyland (eds.), *Accountability in the Contemporary Constitution*, p. 208.

wide range of committees, including the Lords EU Committee and the Culture, Media and Sport Committee (particularly on press regulation) as well as Bill committees.[59] At times, judges have been reluctant to appear before select committees with which they were less familiar or those with combative reputations. The reluctance of the President of the Family Division to appear before the Public Accounts Committee is an example. But judges must recognise not only that select committees are increasingly important sites of parliamentary business, but also that the approach of individual committees can change. For example, with Hodge as its Chair, the Public Accounts Committee now invites a much wider range of witnesses. Although judicial leaders such as the LCJ and Heads of Division are the most frequent witnesses before select committees, there have been appearances from judges from across the judicial hierarchy.

By contrast, judicial appearances before the Scottish Parliament and Northern Ireland Assembly are rare, confined to senior judiciary and almost exclusively conducted by the respective Justice Committees. At Westminster, a broad range of committees call a much wider selection of judges to give evidence. Figure 5.3 compares the number of appearances before the Justice Committees at Westminster, Edinburgh and Belfast with the figure for all Westminster committees.[60] Unsurprisingly, given the big differences in size of both the legislature and the judicial systems, there were many more appearances each year before Westminster committees. What is more, the Northern Ireland Assembly's Justice Committee was only created in 2010, when justice powers were devolved to Stormont. It was not until 2008 that the Scottish Parliament's Justice Committee had more appearances than its Westminster counterpart, as a result of its scrutiny of the Bill that became the Judiciary and Courts (Scotland) Act 2008. The spike in the 'all Westminster' figure for 2011 is similarly accounted for in part by the Lords Constitution Committee's inquiry into judicial appointments, which coincided with the preparation of the Bill that became the Crime and Courts Act 2013.

While the primary function of appearances is for judges to explain the workings of the judicial system, the sessions also provide an opportunity for the committees to articulate Parliament's concerns to

[59] The Joint Committee on the Draft Defamation Bill, for example, heard from two judges in 2011.

[60] The Welsh Assembly does not have any powers over justice-related matters and so is omitted from the comparison.

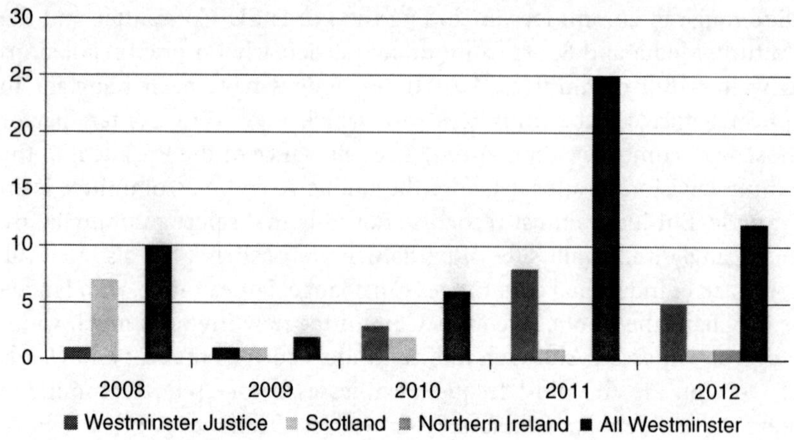


**Figure 5.3.** Judicial appearances before Justice Committees in Westminster, Edinburgh and Belfast[61]

the judiciary, including urging judicial witnesses to address problems that have been identified. In this way, there is a degree of dialogue in the select committee process. For example, the Lords Constitution Committee suggested in 2007 that the LCJ needed to change his strategy for media and public communication. Since then, the LCJ has developed a practice of giving an annual press conference, with the Judicial Communications Office also becoming more proactive.[62] During an inquiry into immigration asylum appeals before the Constitutional Affairs Committee, the predecessor of the Justice Committee, Mr Justice Hodge, responded to a question about delays in processing documentation by undertaking to investigate the matter and 'report to you as we go along how we are getting on, but we are looking at it in a major way now'.[63] Committee reports can also hold judges to account even without calling them before the committee. After criticism in a report by the House of Commons Home Affairs Committee about

[61] Total number of judicial appearances before Justice Committees in each legislature in each year, together with figures for all Westminster committees. Where the same judge gives evidence twice or more, each appearance is counted separately.

[62] Le Sueur, 'Parliamentary Accountability and the Judicial System', in Bamforth and Leyland (eds.), *Accountability in the Contemporary Constitution*, p. 210.

[63] HC Constitutional Affairs Committee, *Asylum and Immigration Tribunal: The Appeals Process* (HC 1006-I 2006).

the treatment of significantly vulnerable witnesses in cases of serious sexual crime, the LCJ announced a change in policy.[64]

In short, evidence sessions with judges are useful for Parliament because they can engage in a dialogue with the judiciary and influence judicial thinking. This dialogue can enrich Parliament's work of scrutiny. Several clerks told us that judicial witnesses typically have a 'unique perspective' and supply 'some of the best evidence'. But other clerks also noted that judicial appearances did not always attract much interest among committee members; one early appearance by the LCJ before the Justice Committee involved a struggle to find enough committee members to achieve quorum. This reflects the unavoidable truth that some aspects of the administration of justice will tend to be of only peripheral concern to many politicians, at least for as long as the judicial system is perceived to work satisfactorily. Evidence sessions are also of value to judges in offering a platform from which to educate Parliament and influence policy-making and can at the same time demonstrate their accountability to the democratic process.[65] Committee sessions also add to judicial influence in more subtle ways: the Ministry of Justice may be more willing to heed judges in the consultation phase of policy-making knowing that subsequently judges may be given a platform by select committees to publicise their concerns.

### *What are judges asked?*

In committee rooms, the committee's members, its clerks and the judges collaborate to create a 'constitutional safe space' in which judges can express concerns to Parliament and Parliament in return can seek a measure of accountability from the judiciary. Evidence sessions on specific areas of law, such as family law or small claims proceedings, tend to be almost entirely factual in tone. The judge acts as an expert witness, for example by outlining how custody hearings work in practice, identifying problems and offering solutions.[66] Opinions are

[64] Letter from Lord Judge to Keith Vaz MP (6 July 2013).

[65] Andrew Le Sueur argues that committee appearances have three functions: accountability, education and judicial criticism of government policy: A. Le Sueur, 'Parliamentary Accountability and the Judicial System', in Bamforth and Leyland (eds.), *Accountability in the Contemporary Constitution*, pp. 210–11.

[66] For example, Sir Nicholas Wall, Mrs Justice Pauffley and Mr Justice Ryder appearing before the HC Justice Committee, *Operation of the Family Courts* (HC 518-I 2011) Ev. 34–42.

offered, but are generally quite uncontroversial. Judges are most willing to talk about contentious issues when discussing constitutional change, judicial appointments and the running of the courts. They are willing to answer questions, provided that committees refrain from asking questions that could compromise their independence. The committees are schooled by the clerks to avoid doing so. In general, judges are given wide latitude by comparison with other committee witnesses. There is broad recognition that there are some issues on which judges cannot offer an opinion and committee chairs often take pains to explain to their members that judicial witnesses are subject to special constraints.

But not every evidence session is restrained and personality is important on both sides of the table. Individual committee members sometimes press judicial witnesses hard. One example cited by two judges in interview was the Home Affairs Committee's treatment in 2011 of retired judge Sir Scott Baker, who had chaired a committee on the US–UK Extradition Treaty.[67] One senior judge characterised some of the questioning as 'entirely inappropriate for a judge'. The committee's questioning was certainly sharp, as it often was under its chair, Keith Vaz, MP. But it is not immediately clear that retired judges need the same careful treatment as currently serving judges, nor is robust questioning (by itself) necessarily disrespectful or inappropriate. In any event, judges are generally very able witnesses; and Sir Scott Baker certainly gave a robust defence of his report. Those with good political skills can handle questioning very effectively, as in this case, where Lord Judge, who had clearly been well briefed, deflected a question on local court closures:

> There are courts that are in places where they are no longer needed . . . To take one from your area, I think Flint Crown Court is hard to justify . . . On the other hand, I do know very well there is a court not so far away from you at Pwllheli which is going to be closed, and I know that getting from Nefyn to Caernarfon is a very different journey on public transport than it is in getting to Pwllheli.[68]

The context in which judges appear may also be important. Judges who appear as chairs of an inquiry, like Sir Scott Baker or Sir Brian Leveson in

[67] HC Home Affairs Committee, *The US–UK Extradition Treaty* (HC 644 2012) Ev. 25–32; Judges' Council, *Guide to Judicial Conduct* (2008), para. 9.2.

[68] Lord Judge, appearing before the House of Commons Justice Committee on the topic of 'The Work of the Lord Chief Justice' on 26 October 2010.

relation to press regulation, tend to be treated more robustly than judges appearing in more clearly judicial roles.[69]

Guidance issued by the Judicial Executive Board in 2012 identifies four broad topics on which judges should not comment: (a) the merits of individual cases; (b) the personalities or merits of serving judges, politicians or other public figures; (c) the merits, meaning or likely effects of prospective legislation or government policy; and (d) issues which are subject to government consultation on which the judiciary intend to make a formal institutional response.[70] The last category is listed merely as 'desirable practice', discouraging individual judges from responding to consultations until after the judiciary has submitted a formal, collective response, whether via the LCJ, the Heads of Division, the Judicial Executive Board or the Judges' Council. However, this reflects and reinforces the increasingly hierarchical, closely managed nature of the judiciary, as discussed in Chapter 6 below. The third category covers political comment and attempts to prevent a judge's impartiality being impugned in the event of sitting in a case where those provisions are at issue. There is no absolute bar on discussing a Bill or government policy. Judges are permitted to comment on the merits of a Bill if it affects the independence of the judiciary; they can also comment on practical and technical aspects of a Bill or policy where it relates to the operation of the courts or the administration of justice. This reflects the judiciary's interest in the administration of the courts. But the distinction is difficult to draw even in the abstract and comments by judges often strain against this restriction. Lord Phillips, for example, expressed the following view in a discussion on penal policy, an issue of high political salience:

> If you are going to put somebody in prison for 30 years by way of punishment you are investing £1 million or more in that operation. I think Parliament ought to reflect whether that is the most desirable way of using resources having regard to, obviously, the viewpoint of the electorate.[71]

[69] Sir Brian Leveson appeared before the Culture, Media and Sport Committee on the topic of 'Press Regulation' on 10 October 2013. A senior civil servant we interviewed felt that in this session 'several lines were crossed'.

[70] Judicial Executive Board, *Guidance to Judges on Appearances before Select Committees.*

[71] At Q. 28 of his evidence before the House of Lords Constitution Committee inquiry into *Relations between the Executive, the Judiciary and Parliament* (HL Paper 177, 2008).

Yet, as we noted above, he refused to answer a question before the JCHR about the voting rights of prisoners because it was politically controversial.[72] Given that penal policy and voting rights for prisoners are both political issues, an important consideration will be whether or not a topic is currently attracting high levels of political and media attention. The likelihood of litigation will also be prominent in the mind of a judicial witness. Unlike the issue of prisoner voting, the question of how best to allocate resources within the realm of criminal justice is non-justiciable.

The other guidelines are also disregarded on occasion. Persistent questioning can push judges into saying more than they ought. Asked to interpret the words 'in good faith and without malice' in a statute, Lord Neuberger initially demurred out of fear that he might later be asked to interpret the words in court, but after persistent questioning offered a tentative definition.[73] At another session, several judges were willing to criticise the decision-making of an unnamed family judge in listing a case for hearing at a date six months after the initial hearing.[74] Only relatively rarely do committees ask questions about a specific judicial decision in a clear breach of convention.[75]

## Select committees as guardians of judicial independence

For non-UK readers, it may seem extraordinary that judges should appear before Parliamentary committees because this practice is not usual in many other jurisdictions. However, select committees perform a valuable dual role. Not only are they holding the judiciary to account, and in the process learning about the inner workings of the justice system – they also have developed into key guardians of judicial independence and the rule of law. Indeed, they are emerging as more systematic guardians than judicial peers could be in the past.

[72] He may also have been mindful that prisoners' voting was likely to come before the Supreme Court. Lord Phillips with Lord Judge before JCHR, October 2012.

[73] Lord Neuberger appearing before the Joint Committee on Privacy and Injunctions, 21 November 2011, at Q. 524.

[74] Sir Nicholas Wall, Mrs Justice Pauffley and Mr Justice Ryder appearing before the HC Justice Committee, *Operation of the Family Courts* Ev. 34–42.

[75] In an evidence session before the Justice Committee in 2007, for example, Judge Julian Hall appeared to have difficulty steering the Chairman away from questions about a recent sentence he had delivered which had attracted media controversy and was the subject of an appeal. HC Justice Committee, *Towards Effective Sentencing: Oral and Written Evidence* (HC 184-II 2008) Ev. 20–7.

Interventions by judicial peers in parliamentary debates can be eccentric and idiosyncratic, depending on the interests and time commitments of the individual. Select committees, by contrast, are far more systematic. Three new committees scrutinise all Bills in detail for adherence to legal and constitutional values: the JCHR, the Lords Constitution Committee and the Lords Committee on Delegated Powers.[76] They were all established at around the same time as contributions in the Lords by judicial peers were declining.[77] It is no coincidence that these are primarily Lords committees, since peers typically take the business of detailed legislative scrutiny more seriously than do MPs. Much – and even most – of the work of these committees does not directly relate to judicial independence. But their work helps shape a political culture that respects the authority of law and the legal system – and, in doing so, helps to nurture the political appreciation of judicial independence in ways that we outlined in Chapter 2.

The establishment of the Lords Constitution Committee resulted from a recommendation in the Wakeham Report that the upper chamber should serve as a constitutional guardian. With prominent retired judges and senior lawyers amongst its members, the Constitution Committee has largely fulfilled this expectation. As Le Sueur and Simson-Caird explain, it has evolved into an indispensable venue for institutional dialogue with the judiciary.[78] This dialogue fulfils four main goals. First, it facilitates the ventilation of judicial concerns. Second, it holds ministers, particularly the Lord Chancellor, to account for their judiciary-related responsibilities. Third, it calls the senior judiciary to account for operational and leadership matters. Fourth, it monitors the workings of the new institutional architecture across the judicial system. We refer to the Constitution Committee's reports throughout this book, especially its 2007 inquiry on relations between the judiciary, executive and Parliament and its 2011 inquiry on judicial appointments. Making use of detailed evidence from a wide range of stakeholders, and with clear findings and recommendations, these inquiries have more potential to educate parliamentarians and the

[76] R. Hazell, 'Who Is the Guardian of Legal Values in the Legislative Process: Parliament or the Executive?' [2004] *Public Law* 495.

[77] The Lords Constitution Committee and the Joint Committee on Human Rights were both established in 2001; the Delegated Powers Committee in 1997.

[78] A. Le Sueur and J. Simson-Caird, 'The House of Lords Select Committee on the Constitution', in Horne, Drewry and Oliver (eds.), *Parliament and the Law*, pp. 281, 304–6.

wider public than the occasional intervention from one of the Law Lords.[79]

Less well known is the Committee's legislative scrutiny role. Its legal advisers examine every Bill for constitutional issues. In its first eleven years, it produced eighty-six legislative scrutiny reports. In 2013, three academics used these reports to articulate the set of scrutiny standards that informs the Constitution Committee's work.[80] A number relate directly to issues covered in this book: the independence of the judiciary should not be undermined;[81] judges' security of tenure should be preserved;[82] the politicisation of the judicial appointments process should be avoided;[83] and where a government minister is to be made responsible for judiciary-related matters, then that minister should be the Lord Chancellor.[84] Several of the standards relate less directly to the constitutional position of judges and more to their constitutional role: the exercise of powers to combat terrorism should be subject to adequate judicial control;[85] the roles of Parliament and the judiciary should not be conflated;[86] coercive powers that restrict a constitutional right should be exercised by the judiciary rather than the executive;[87] ouster clauses should be avoided;[88] the nature of the judicial oversight of a ministerial power should be clear on the face of the Bill;[89] and laws should avoid creating the possibility of conflict between Parliament and the courts.[90] These standards were extracted from a number of Bills, illustrating the

[79] G. Drewry, 'Parliamentary Accountability for the Administration of Justice', in Horne, Drewry and Oliver (eds.), *Parliament and the Law*, p. 361.

[80] J. Simson-Caird, R. Hazell and D. Oliver, *The Constitutional Standards of the House of Lords Select Committee on the Constitution* (London: The Constitution Unit, 2014).

[81] HL Constitution Committee, *Counter-terrorism Bill: The Role of Ministers, Parliament and the Judiciary* (HL 167 2008), para. 38.

[82] HL Constitution Committee, *Justice (Northern Ireland) Bill* (HL 40 2004), Appendix 1.

[83] HL Constitution Committee, *Judicial Appointments*.

[84] HL Constitution Committee, *Northern Ireland Bill* (HL 50 2009), para. 14.

[85] HL Constitution Committee, *Counter-terrorism Bill: The Role of Ministers, Parliament and the Judiciary*, para. 5.

[86] HL Constitution Committee, *Counter-terrorism Bill: The Role of Ministers, Parliament and the Judiciary*, para. 39. 'Far from being a system of checks and balances, this is a recipe for confusion that places on Parliament tasks that it cannot effectively fulfil and arguably risks undermining the rights of fair trial for the individuals concerned.'

[87] HL Constitution Committee, *Welfare Reform Bill* (HL 79 2009), para. 10.

[88] HL Constitution Committee, *Justice and Security (Northern Ireland) Bill* (HL 54 2007), para. 2.

[89] HL Constitution Committee, *Coroners and Justice Bill* (HL 96 2009), para. 9.

[90] HL Constitution Committee, *Parliamentary Standards Bill: Implications for Parliament and the Courts* (HL 134 2009), para. 22.

wide range of legislative contexts in which judicial issues can arise – terrorism, coroners and welfare reform included.

One report notable for its impact was that on the Public Bodies Bill in 2011, in which the Constitution Committee strongly criticised the proposed use of Henry VIII powers, which enable ministers to amend primary legislation through the use of secondary legislation. Schedule 7 of the Public Bodies Bill proposed conferring on ministers powers to abolish a number of bodies, including the Judicial Appointments Commission and other bodies related to the judiciary. Alongside the private negotiations with senior judges, a speech in the House of Lords by the retired LCJ Lord Woolf,[91] and strong words from the serving LCJ during an evidence session before the Constitution Committee,[92] the committee's trenchant criticism helped persuade the government to remove the JAC and other judiciary-related bodies from the Schedule. The committee's work has been described as 'parliamentary constitutional review',[93] and with its help the House of Lords has developed into the constitutional guardian that the Wakeham Report envisaged.

Much of the Lords Constitution Committee's success is due to its composition: it includes experienced parliamentarians, distinguished lawyers and sometimes a former Lord Chancellor or Attorney General, and their work is supported by two specialist legal advisers.[94] At the same time, this can sometimes lend their evidence sessions a 'slightly surreal' air, insofar as the committee members and its witnesses are often 'all old mates', with the genteel tone of its evidence sessions risking the impression that it is a 'non-scrutinising body', in the words of one official at the Ministry of Justice. In reality, the detailed work of legislative scrutiny, drafting reports and deciding on recommendations is conducted out of sight. It is one thing for the Constitution Committee to make recommendations and propose changes to Bills; it is quite another for the government to accept them. There is no specific data on its success rate, although one experienced Ministry of Justice official told us that the prospect of the committee's scrutiny role 'scared the hell

[91] *Hansard*, HL, vol. 722, cols. 75–7, 9 November 2010.

[92] HL Constitution Committee, *Meetings with the Lord Chief Justice and the Lord Chancellor* (HL 89 2011).

[93] J. Simson-Caird, 'Parliamentary Constitutional Review: Ten Years of the House of Lords Select Committee on the Constitution' [2012] *Public Law* 4.

[94] See A. Le Sueur and J. Simson-Caird, 'The House of Lords Select Committee on the Constitution', in Horne, Drewry and Oliver (eds.), *Parliament and the Law*, pp. 281, 284–5.

out of [him]'. It is notable, however, that one-third of government defeats in the House of Lords arise from issues relating to justice and the courts.[95]

Other committees, such as the JCHR, foster a political culture respectful of the courts and the judges who work in them. The JCHR does so in part by engaging with ministers to ensure compatibility with the UK's human rights obligations. For example, in 2010 it engaged with the government over its response to the Supreme Court decision in *R (F)* v. *Home Secretary*,[96] which held that the absence of any review of whole-life reporting requirements for sex offenders in section 82 of the Sexual Offences Act 2003 was incompatible with Article 8 of the ECHR. The Court issued a declaration of incompatibility under section 4 of the Human Rights Act. The Prime Minister and Home Secretary criticised the decision in trenchant terms, prompting the Lord Chancellor to write and remind them of the ministerial duty to uphold judicial independence. The government initially proposed that the order remedying the incompatibility should only do so as minimally as possible. Despite its earlier criticisms, however, the government subsequently accepted the JCHR's recommendation that the order should address the incompatibility more fully by creating access for registered sex offenders to independent courts for the purposes of review.[97] Behind the scenes, the JCHR has also encouraged ministers to use temperate language when criticising judicial decisions, writing to explain that while ministers can criticise decisions they ought to do so in measured terms. In this way the JCHR has helped to sustain a political culture that respects the authority of judicial decisions. It is not just committees with a legal focus that contribute to the independence of the judiciary. In 2010, the Culture, Media and Sport Select Committee examined the privacy judgments of Mr Justice Eady and rejected the

[95] In the thirteen years from November 1999 until May 2012 the government lost 488 votes in the Lords. Of these a significant proportion (170, or 35 per cent) related to justice and the courts. In the case of sixty-two of these, the government either completely or substantially accepted the effect of the defeat. This data was provided by the Constitution Unit Parliament Project, which maintains a database of government defeats in the House of Lords since 1999. They relate to the period 17 November 1999 to 1 May 2012. Additional coding for 'justice and the courts' has been done by the authors and includes non-binding motions (for example, motions to express regret at a government decision) and votes to insist on an earlier defeat.

[96] *R (F)* v. *Secretary of State for the Home Department* [2010] UKSC 17.

[97] M. Hunt, 'The Joint Committee on Human Rights', in Horne, Drewry and Oliver (eds.), *Parliament and the Law*, p. 238.

complaints of newspaper editors that he was single-handedly developing a law of privacy. The committee concluded that the media's focus on the decisions of a single judge was misplaced, and mounted a strong defence of Mr Justice Eady.[98]

An account of the influence of select committees would not be complete without mention of the special select committee established by the Lords to examine the Constitutional Reform Bill in 2004. Four hundred and sixty-two amendments were made to the Bill as a result of the committee's work, including several to underpin judicial independence. These included amendments emphasising the special role of the Lord Chancellor in protecting the rule of law[99] and others tightening aspects of the judicial appointments process.[100] The independence of the new Supreme Court was also strengthened, by providing that selection committees would submit just one name to the minister, not between two and five,[101] and by giving the court more autonomy over the creation of its own rules.[102] The Lords were also responsible for retaining the office of Lord Chancellor. This was not in the select committee's report, but resulted from amendments tabled by the Shadow Lord Chancellor, Lord Kingsland. In the Commons, the Constitutional Affairs Committee took evidence on six occasions and closely questioned the Lord Chancellor, Lord Falconer. The result of efforts in both the Lords and Commons was a 'painstakingly slow process' of parliamentary scrutiny that 'contrasted with the casual abruptness of the initial announcement' of the reforms by Downing Street in 2003, all of which 'stood as a salutary reminder to ministers and their advisers that, unless and until approved by both Houses ... intended reforms calling for changes in the law were not at the disposal of government alone'.[103]

It is important not to overstate the significance of judicial accountability to select committees. This scrutiny is a relatively new phenomenon, accompanied by understandable hesitancy and occasional tensions between the committees and the judges. So far committees have shown

[98] HC Culture, Media and Sport Committee, *Press Standards, Privacy and Libel* (HC 362-I 2010), para. 76.

[99] Now section 1 of the Constitutional Reform Act 2005.

[100] For example what are now sections 74 and 95 of the CRA.

[101] Now sections 27(5) and 27(10) of the CRA.

[102] Now section 45 of the CRA. Section 36(2) of the Bill had given power to the minister to allow or disallow Rules submitted to him.

[103] Lord Windlesham, 'The Constitutional Reform Act: The Politics of Constitutional Reform – Part 2' [2006] *Public Law* 35, 50.

considerable deference towards judicial witnesses, who give an account of different parts of the justice system but are rarely held to account for any failings. Our research also understates the role of committee scrutiny in that this scrutiny goes far beyond the work of the judiciary to include all the other actors in the judicial system: most obviously the Lord Chancellor, but also specialist bodies such as the Judicial Appointments Commission, which has been scrutinised repeatedly by committees of both Houses.[104] But here too their role should not be overstated. Our interviews suggest that the JAC would welcome more interest in its work, but select committees do not have the time or the resources constantly to patrol all corners of the justice system. At best they shine the occasional searchlight on one part of the system before moving on. The JAC is unusual in having been reviewed so intensively in its early years. In the same period, the Courts Service, which has experienced a series of major changes, as we explained in Chapter 4, has been the subject of much less scrutiny.[105]

## Parliamentary proceedings

The work of select committees is at the heart of the day-to-day relationship between Parliament and the judiciary, but it rarely attracts extensive media coverage and is largely under the public radar. In contrast, speeches and comments in the debating chamber, particularly in the House of Commons, command wider interest, and constitute the more public face of the relationship between Parliament and the judges. It is in the chamber that MPs sometimes breach the rules regulating what parliamentarians can and cannot say about judges. These high-profile

[104] Much of this scrutiny took the form of evidence-only sessions. The JAC commissioners appeared before the Commons Constitutional Affairs Committee on 18 July 2006, 20 March 2007 and 20 June 2007, and before its successor the Justice Committee on 7 September 2010 and 31 January 2011 (the latter session being the pre-appointment scrutiny hearing for the new Chair Chris Stephens). They appeared on 4 June 2008 before the Joint Committee on the draft Constitutional Renewal Bill: for its report see Chapter 4 of HL 166, HC 551, August 2008. And they appeared several times before the Lords Constitution Committee for their 2011–12 inquiry into Judicial Appointments: for the report, see HL Constitution Committee, *Judicial Appointments.*

[105] The Lords Constitution Committee looked at the process for setting the budget of the courts: HL Constitution Committee, *Relations between the Executive, the Judiciary and Parliament*, paras. 75–87; HL Constitution Committee, *Relations between the Executive, the Judiciary and Parliament: Follow-up Report*, para. 12. There has been no inquiry into the structure or management of the Courts Service. The Commons Justice Committee held no evidence sessions with the Courts Service.

clashes are relatively uncommon, but they tend to be remembered. If judges or lawyers were asked about the interaction between Parliament and the judges, their immediate response might be to recollect occasions when parliamentarians had criticised court decisions, or used parliamentary privilege to breach injunctions or the *sub judice* rule. But these are rare events and behind the scenes parliamentary officials work hard to prevent them. When they do occur, they challenge the relationship of 'comity' – of mutual respect and understanding for each other's respective constitutional roles – that ought to exist between Parliament and judges.[106] However, as the Joint Committee on Parliamentary Privilege has noted, comity is not a static ideal: 'The principle of comity, which nobody would challenge, does not prevent constant evolution and occasional tension',[107] and in this section we reflect on some recent evolutions and tensions. First we describe the rules and breaches, and then explain how parliamentary officials and select committees have sought to police the boundary between Parliament and the courts, and minimise friction between the two.

### *The* sub judice *rule, and injunctions*

One of the clearest expressions of Parliament's respect for the courts and their independence is the *sub judice* rule. The rule is expressed in a pair of resolutions passed by the Commons and the Lords in 2001, though it can be traced back to the nineteenth century.[108] It prohibits discussion of matters that are before the courts, in order to avoid prejudicing judicial proceedings. The rule is not absolute. It affects neither the right of either House to legislate nor the right to discuss ministerial decisions.

The day-to-day work of applying the rule in the Commons is done by the Table Office, which screens questions tabled by MPs for admissibility.[109] The Office functions as a quiet guardian of judicial independence and will help MPs to rephrase their question or motion

[106] D. Oliver, *Constitutional Reform in the United Kingdom* (Oxford: Oxford University Press, 2003), pp. 19–20.

[107] Joint Committee on Parliamentary Privilege, *Parliamentary Privilege* (HL 30/HC 100 2013), para. 116.

[108] The *sub judice* rule was first formulated as a settled set of precedents in *Erskine May*, 10th edn, in 1893. It was first constructed as a formal rule of the House of Commons in 1962, and revised in 1972 and again in 2001, on each occasion following a report from the Procedure Committee. See also the HC Procedure Committee, *The Sub Judice Rule of the House of Commons* (HC 125 2005).

[109] We refer only to 'MPs', but everything discussed applies equally to the House of Lords.

in a more general way. If MPs are dissatisfied, they can seek a waiver: the Speaker has discretion to waive the rule, as do select committee chairs.[110] In the case of anonymous injunctions and super-injunctions (in which the very existence of the injunction is made confidential), the task of the Table Office is more difficult: because of the secrecy involved, it can be harder to identify whether litigation is still active.

The rules depend on the willingness of MPs to obey them. Obeying the rules at times carries a cost for MPs, who might find it difficult to explain to constituents why they are unable to raise in Parliament a matter of local concern, and might feel that the *sub judice* rule can result in an issue being discussed everywhere but Parliament.[111] In the vast majority of cases, MPs do adhere to the rule, though there have been a number of breaches. In 2011, John Hemming MP named footballer Ryan Giggs as the holder of a super-injunction. Hemming was cut off by the Speaker, and strongly criticised by his parliamentary colleagues.[112] In 2012, several MPs spoke in defence of Danny Nightingale, an SAS soldier tried by court martial whose case had become the subject of a well-organised media campaign.[113] Breaches of an injunction do not necessarily fall within the *sub judice* rule. If an injunction is permanent, and court proceedings are no longer active, the rule will also not apply. In 1996, Brian Sedgemore MP tabled a motion naming the daughter of Cecil Parkinson MP, in breach of an injunction.[114] If the matter had been raised outside Parliament, Sedgemore would have been in contempt of court; but because proceedings were no longer pending, the motion did not breach the *sub judice* rule.

Parliament has taken these breaches seriously, instigating several reviews to decide whether the rules needed tightening. After the Sedgemore affair, the Commons Procedure Committee held an inquiry, but concluded that such incidents arose so rarely that a new rule was unnecessary.[115] After more

[110] For a recent example of the former, see the debate on Ford's pensioners, *Hansard*, HC, vol. 572, col. 419, 12 December 2013, 'Ford and Visteon UK Ltd'. For the latter, see Justice Committee (30 November 2010), when Sir Alan Beith waived the rule in the context of discussion of the work of the Legal Services Commission.

[111] Appearance of John Denham MP before HC Procedure Committee, *The Sub Judice Rule of the House of Commons* Ev. 1–8.

[112] *Hansard*, HC, vol. 528, col. 638, 23 May 2011.

[113] *Hansard*, HC, vol. 553, cols. 553–8, 20 November 2012.The debate was timed so that technically it did not breach the *sub judice* rule, because it was after conviction but before an appeal had been lodged.

[114] The injunction arose out of *Re Z (a minor) (Freedom of Publication)* [1997] Fam 1.

[115] Lord Bingham MR expressed concern about the breach of the injunction in *Re Z*, and suggested in evidence to the Committee that if such incidents became more frequent a new resolution should be adopted (21 February 1996).

recent breaches, there were inquiries by Parliament and the judiciary. These went wider than breaches only in Parliament, because the main culprits were the media, who were hostile to privacy injunctions. The Master of the Rolls chaired an inquiry into super-injunctions, which recommended that they be granted only in very limited circumstances, and for very short periods of time.[116] Parliament established a Joint Committee of both Houses on Privacy and Injunctions. The Clerk of the House suggested that a new resolution on injunctions should be adopted, mirroring the *sub judice* rule. But after hearing evidence from legal experts, the judges and the media, the Joint Committee concluded that tightening the rules was not necessary.[117] In the event, the Joint Committee was proved right: the courts' use of super-injunctions declined, and so did the temptation to bust them amongst MPs. Injunction-busting had been a passing phase.[118] In 2012, the Joint Committee on Parliamentary Privilege looked at other aspects of the boundary between Parliament and the judges, including whether references to parliamentary proceedings in court cases amounted to the 'questioning' of proceedings in Parliament, thereby contravening Article 9 of the Bill of Rights 1689. In his evidence, the LCJ acknowledged that some judges had gone too far by praying in aid reports of select committees, but suggested that these aberrations did not justify legislation. The committee agreed, and concluded that codification was not required.

These various inquiries show how much effort Parliament and the judiciary devote to policing the boundaries, understanding each other's respective roles, and dealing with the difficulties that arise. It is not just through formal inquiries and committee reports that such difficulties get addressed. The Joint Committee on Parliamentary Privilege's report hinted at other channels of communication: 'We trust that less formal means than those above, building on the current good relations between the judiciary and the parliamentary authorities, will address recent problems'.[119] Informal contacts with the judiciary greatly increased following the appointment of Sir Robert Rogers as Clerk of the House of Commons in 2011. His view that 'good fences make good neighbours'

[116] Committee on Super-injunctions, *Super-injunctions, Anonymised Injunctions and Open Justice* (2011).

[117] Joint Committee on Privacy and Injunctions, *Privacy and Injunctions* (HL 273/HC 1443 2012).

[118] Joint Committee on Parliamentary Privilege, para. 5.

[119] Joint Committee on Parliamentary Privilege, para. 136.

is indicative of the priority he placed on working closely with the senior judiciary, while also remaining alert to protecting Parliament's privileges.[120] To develop better mutual understanding, Rogers began holding regular informal meetings with the LCJ and the President of the Supreme Court. He was invited to an away-day of the Judicial Executive Board, and in 2012 addressed an after-court seminar for seventy senior judges. The topics discussed at these informal meetings all concerned the boundaries between the courts and Parliament: the *sub judice* rule, the use of parliamentary materials in court cases, judicial appearances before select committees, how the judges collectively speak to Parliament, and parliamentary privilege. Dialogue between the senior judiciary and Parliament is conducted not just in the committee room, but also through regular informal contacts. These help to ensure a better understanding of the respective roles and responsibilities of the senior judges and Parliament, and to deal with difficulties that arise.

## Conclusion

The reforms of 2005 brought about a step change in the institutional setting within which the politics of judicial independence are played out between the judiciary and Parliament. Although there was concern amongst the judiciary about the removal of the Law Lords from Parliament, and the effects this might have on judicial independence, this has proved largely unfounded. Under the new system, judges have gained more than they have lost. Indeed, it is arguable that they have lost very little. Although serving judges no longer have any legislative role, they retain proxies – retired judges in particular – in the House of Lords, who articulate judicial concerns. It is unclear, however, whether senior judges – such as outgoing Justices of the Supreme Court – will continue to receive peerages. What is already clear is that it only takes one or two very active and engaged retired judges (such as Lords Phillips and Hope) to promote the interests of the judiciary in the Lords quite effectively, especially when they co-ordinate with prominent lawyer-peers (such as Baroness Kennedy and Lord Macdonald or, in their day, Lord Alexander and Lord Kingsland).

Engagement with a wide range of select committees allows judges to speak to a wider audience – to the politically powerful Commons as well as to the Lords. Judicial interventions in policy debates are now more

[120] Speaking at a seminar for this project on the Judges and Parliament, December 2011.

professional and systematic, and less dependent upon the idiosyncratic interests of the small group of judges who hold peerages. Co-ordinated and collective responses by the judiciary as a whole were almost impossible to deliver through the Law Lords, but are more easily facilitated by the committee process. Collective responses are also a product of the judiciary's evolution into a larger and more centralised corporate body headed by a more active leadership, as described in Chapter 6. With the increasing corporatisation of the judiciary, it is possible to speak of the emergence of an institutional dialogue between the senior judiciary and Parliament in a way that was not possible with the Law Lords. But corporatisation also enables a wide range of judicial voices to be heard. Whereas Parliament previously heard from the most senior appellate judges who could have had only limited knowledge of the lower courts and tribunals, judicial engagement with select committees encourages contributions from judges at all levels. The result is that select committees have the capacity to operate as more constant and effective guardians of judicial interests than the Law Lords.

Careful co-ordination takes place on both sides to foster mutual understanding and respect for each other's positions, although, as we have seen, not always successfully, with occasional flare-ups over fairly trivial matters, such as the appropriate use of the LCJ's powers under section 5 of the Constitutional Reform Act. As in all of the areas covered in this book, the interests and personalities of central players have an important role in shaping relationships. The appointment of Sir Robert Rogers as Clerk of the House of Commons in 2011 is widely acknowledged to have strengthened understanding on both sides through active engagement with the senior judiciary. Sir Robert sought to ensure that Parliament and the judiciary do not work at cross-purposes, while at the same time remaining conscious of his primary responsibility to ensure that courts do not trespass on the prerogatives of Parliament. The senior judges, for the most part, have been equally keen to develop a dialogue, although some are quick to note that relations with Parliament are 'still very green and new'. The new guidance issued in 2012 on judicial appearances before select committees is one product of the new relationship: parliamentary clerks must now ensure that select committees channel their requests through the private office of the LCJ, thus facilitating better co-ordination on both sides. It remains to be seen whether this constructive engagement between senior judges and senior officials will address the difficulties that parliamentary clerks at the coalface have sometimes encountered, such as the occasional wrangling over whether a particular judge should appear before a committee and what he or she can be asked.

Perhaps because of the Law Lords' traditional involvement in the House of Lords, the senior judiciary has been receptive to overtures and willing to engage with Parliament. By and large the engagement has been constructive and, for the judges, positive in terms of outcomes. More than once Parliament has provided a forum in which the judiciary can express serious concerns about government policy, and in effect negotiate with ministers in and via Parliament. That happened in 2004, when the House of Lords established a special Select Committee on the Constitutional Reform Bill, and again three years later when the Lords Constitution Committee launched a speedy inquiry into executive–judicial–parliamentary relations following creation of the new Ministry of Justice. At a time when relations between senior judges and ministers were strained, Parliament opened up a new channel of communication. And on the issues involved Parliament was a staunch supporter of the judiciary, strongly upholding judicial independence.

There have also been clear benefits for Parliament. Modern politics has become more separate from lawyers and legal practice, with fewer MPs having a background in the law.[121] Whereas in the twentieth century there were dozens of judges with parliamentary backgrounds, there are now almost none. As David Howarth (a lawyer-politician himself) has suggested, a perception has developed amongst lawyers and judges that politics is a 'kind of pollution' that must be kept apart from the law. Amongst politicians, there is a converse trend towards what many judges and lawyers view as a more 'lawless politics', especially in the field of human rights and relations with European institutions, with politicians more inclined to criticise the courts and to treat legislation as more akin to a press release.[122] Yet beneath the occasional din caused by high-profile political criticism of judicial decisions, the quieter and lower-profile work of Parliamentary committees is often enriched by the expertise and insights of judicial witnesses.

With greater engagement has come a more responsive and accountable judiciary. Judges at all levels are willing to explain themselves and, on occasion, to respond to criticism. This does not

[121] R. Cranston, 'Lawyers, MPs and Judges', in D. Feldman (ed.), *Law in Politics, Politics in Law* (Oxford: Hart Publishing, 2013); Howarth, 'Lawyers in the House of Commons', in Feldman (ed.), *Law in Politics, Politics in Law*, p. 41.

[122] Howarth, 'Lawyers in the House of Commons', in Feldman (ed.), *Law in Politics, Politics in Law*, pp. 61–3.

mean that relations between Parliament and the judiciary are never troubled. The boundaries and rules which govern the day-to-day communications between the two are still evolving. The running sores of Europe and human rights cases can stretch conventions of mutual respect to breaking point. But so far these episodes are the exception and angry outbursts at Prime Minister's Questions are not replicated in Parliament's everyday business. In general, Parliament takes great pains to ensure that rule of law values are upheld. The work of the committees is unpublicised and unglamorous, but judicial independence and the rule of law are upheld through small particulars, not grand pronouncements.

The occasional points of tension serve to emphasise our central claim that judicial independence is a political achievement. The aim is not to avoid tensions, since tensions are an inevitable part of the interplay of law and politics. It is to ensure that there are effective channels of communication through which the politics of judicial independence can be played out and better understandings can be forged. The transformation of judges from parliamentarians to expert witnesses before select committees has facilitated this process. And the willingness of Parliament and its senior officials to reach out and engage with the judges has also helped to smooth the way.

# 6

# Judicial leadership and the internal governance of the judiciary

Much of this book is concerned with the changing relations between the judiciary and the political branches of government. Equally important for the politics of judicial independence is the way in which relationships between judges at all levels of the judiciary are developing. Changes to external and internal relationships are interlinked. The new politics of judicial independence requires active judicial leadership and more formalised systems of internal governance. Occupying a more separate constitutional space, and with Lord Chancellors no longer as involved in judicial administration, the judiciary has had to develop new systems of self-governance. This has been partially driven by a wider political push over the last two decades to remodel the judicial system as a public service,[1] but is also the consequence of increasing political pressure for judges 'to do more with less' in an age of austerity.[2] But the requirements of judicial independence mean that governance structures cannot be determined solely by the concerns of efficiency, effectiveness and competence that are at the heart of a public-service model. And just as there is little agreement between judges and politicians about what exactly judicial independence requires in their interactions, so judges often sharply disagree amongst themselves over what it implies about their internal organisation.

Against this background our aim in this chapter is threefold. First, we trace a shift away from a culture of judicial individualism towards one of corporatism, and ask whether this strikes an appropriate balance between judicial efficiency and effectiveness on the one hand and the independence of individual judges on the other. Second, we outline the increasing importance of leadership at the very top of the judiciary, in

[1] A. Zuckerman, 'Civil Litigation: A Public Service for the Enforcement of Civil Rights' (2007) 26 *Civil Justice Quarterly* 1.

[2] S. Shetreet and S. Turenne, *Judges on Trial: The Independence and Accountability of the English Judiciary* (Cambridge: Cambridge University Press, 2013), p. 10.

particular through the ever-expanding management roles of the Lord Chief Justice. Lastly, we review the changing institutional architecture through which the judiciary is governed, outlining the ways in which it is moving towards a more centralised, formalised and hierarchical organisation. Our focus is primarily on the judiciary in England and Wales, where these changes are most evident, although parallels can be identified with Scotland and Northern Ireland and these are drawn out further in Chapter 9.

## From individualism to corporatism

Judicial self-governance is notably free of external scrutiny compared to many other public institutions. However, senior judges do not enjoy a free hand to impose change from above. They are limited by the links traditionally made between judicial independence and a 'culture of individualism'.[3] At its most literal, this requires that each individual judge is treated as an adjudicative island, with senior judges prohibited from interfering in a judge's work in any way (except through the ordinary working of the appellate process). The historical resistance to any form of performance appraisal is the best illustration of this approach. For much of the twentieth century, this culture of judicial individualism was sustained by the relatively solitary working lives of judges. It was underpinned by the fact that the judiciary was a small and extremely homogeneous group.[4] As a 'club' of people similar in terms of sex, age, race, education and social and professional background, the judiciary could accommodate highly individualistic approaches while retaining a strong core coherence.[5]

Today, individualism and independence remain linked in the minds of some judges. This can make it difficult for senior judges to introduce changes to the internal organisation and management of the judiciary: 'the need to bring people with you can be harder than herding cats', as one official put it. In truth, this image of individual judges completely insulated from each other was always an exaggeration. It was, as the same official described it, 'a creation myth'. In practice, no judge was allowed

[3] K. Malleson, 'Judicial Training and Performance Appraisal: The Problem of Judicial Independence' (1997) 60 *Modern Law Review* 655, 663–6.

[4] The classic text on judicial homogeneity remains J. Griffith, *The Politics of the Judiciary*, 5th edn (London, Fontana, 1997; first published in 1977).

[5] On the courts as 'clubs', see R. Dunn, *Sword and Wig: Memoirs of a Lord Justice* (London: Quiller Press, 1993), p. 231.

to function in a vacuum, with strong informal as well as formal rules ensuring that certain standards of conduct were maintained. It follows that the more formal and regulated systems of internal governance described in this chapter are not a complete break with tradition. And nor was change driven wholly, or perhaps even largely, by the Constitutional Reform Act 2005 (CRA). Although this trend was intensified by developments after 2005, the roots of the transition from a culture of individualism towards a culture of corporatism – with its emphasis on minimum standards of legal knowledge, courtesy and skills of judge-craft – can be traced back over many years.[6]

It was a transition that was driven first and foremost by the growth of the professional judiciary: from 822 in 1950 to 5,570 by 2013. If magistrates are included, the judiciary in England and Wales now comprises approximately 29,000 office-holders.[7] In an expanding and somewhat less homogeneous judiciary, the traditionally informal, and more personalised, system of governance had become less and less sustainable.[8] More recently, moves towards a unified judiciary following the merger of the administration of the tribunal and courts services in 2011 has intensified this process, consigning to the past the relative informality of earlier years. Tribunal judges tend to be much more familiar with, and amenable to, the hands-on management of caseloads and performance appraisal than court judges. As a result, a sizeable proportion of the judiciary now expects more professional management by, and proactive support from, senior colleagues. This move away from a culture of individualism has also been spurred by the development over the last forty years of a judicial career path.

Traditionally, the 'professional' judiciary in England was contrasted with the 'career' judiciaries found in other European countries, with judges drawn from practice rather than specifically educated and trained for a judicial career.[9] The judiciary prided itself on the absence of a career ladder, with no attendant risk that individual judges might be influenced in their decisions by the prospects of promotion; or, as Lord

[6] See generally K. Malleson, *The New Judiciary: The Effects of Expansion and Activism* (Dartmouth: Ashgate, 1999).

[7] See Judicial Office, Overview Data of Judicial Appointments by Type – 2013 (2013); Judicial Office, Magistrates in Post 2013.

[8] On the relative increase in the diversity of judicial backgrounds, see P. Darbyshire, *Sitting in Judgment: The Working Lives of Judges* (Oxford: Hart Publishing, 2011), pp. 44–64.

[9] On the difference between professional and career judiciaries, see C. Guarnieri, P. Pederzoli and C. A. Thomas, *The Power of Judges: A Comparative Study of Courts and Democracy* (Oxford: Oxford University Press, 2002), pp. 66–8.

Denning put it in 1955, 'Once a man becomes a judge, he has nothing to gain from further promotion and does not seek it'.[10] This statement was never wholly true in that there has always been a ladder of promotion from the High Court to the Court of Appeal and from there to the House of Lords. The barrier which existed, though it was never an absolute one, was between the lower ranks (district and circuit bench) and the High Court. Although there is now a policy of actively encouraging promotion up from tribunals, district and circuit bench, in practice this is still relatively rare.[11] Nevertheless, the fact that such promotions are now theoretically possible means that training and appraisal have become more relevant, and the image of individual judges as adjudicative islands has been further eroded.

A system of promotion also presupposes a structural hierarchy of judicial authority. While this has long existed in practice, the CRA accelerated the trend towards more vertical and formal management structures controlled by a more directive leadership from senior judges. Above all, it brought about a change in the way the judges see themselves. From the perspective of one senior civil servant, 'what the Act did ... was to give [the judiciary] a sense – and the very senior judiciary the strong sense – that they were now expected to be the masters of their own fate'. New ways had to be found to garner support for collective positions, to handle internal dissent and to determine what decisions about the organisation and working patterns of the judiciary could be taken, by whom, and at what level in a larger, more complex and increasingly self-governed body. Between 2007 and 2009 the terms of appointment of all judges were changed to make explicit that the Lord Chief Justice (LCJ) ultimately has responsibility for management and could delegate these powers down the judicial hierarchy, so that, for example, resident judges can exercise the delegated powers of the Senior Presiding Judge. This centralisation and formalisation of the management structure has posed a challenge to a traditional culture in which, for many judges, the ideal model of organisation was relatively flat.

The primary goal of this more hierarchical system is to maintain and enhance standards of performance. Among senior judges in particular, there is a heightened willingness to concede that judicial independence has at times served to hide poor performance. As one senior judge put it, 'there is a difference between judicial independence and stopping work at lunchtime'. Another judge commented, 'For far too long the mantra of

[10] Lord Denning, *The Road to Justice* (London: Stevens & Sons, 1955), p. 17.
[11] See Darbyshire, *Sitting in Judgment*, p. 406.

judicial independence has been used as a cloak for judicial incompetence, indolence, inefficiency, insensitivity and ignorance'. The transition described in this chapter has been to a greater sense of collective identity and common working practices in many areas of the judges' work outside their individual decision-making. At the centre of this change is the office of Lord Chief Justice.

## The multiple leadership roles of the Lord Chief Justice

The creation myth of the judiciary as a highly individualistic and non-hierarchical institution has continued in relatively comfortable co-existence with the strengthening leadership role of the Lord Chief Justice. By the end of the twentieth century, the LCJ was already the 'professional head' of the judiciary, even though the Lord Chancellor was its 'constitutional head' until 2006.[12] While the Lord Chancellor had the last word, many issues were decided consensually following consultation with the LCJ. The LCJ was expected to be the outward-looking face of the judiciary, as well as to determine many internal arrangements, including appointing judges to fulfil senior administrative roles, providing guidance and support to individual judges, and maintaining standards of conduct at all levels of the judiciary. Each LCJ had a distinct leadership style, with some leading from the front and others less visibly in control. However, it was widely recognised even before 2005 that all LCJs had real power. As one senior official put it, the pre-2005 LCJs were '*primus inter pares* – but very much *primus*'.

In 2006 the formal leadership of the judiciary passed to the LCJ.[13] While significant in its own right, this change built upon and expanded an already powerful office. Today, the responsibilities attached to the office are so extensive that its 'multi-tasking is exhausting even to contemplate'.[14] Table 6.1 sets out the responsibilities of the LCJ before 2005, and the additional functions conferred since. There are six main responsibilities.

[12] Lord Woolf, 'Judicial Independence Not Judicial Isolation', in *The Pursuit of Justice* (ed. C. Campbell-Holt) (Oxford: Oxford University Press, 2008), p. 167.

[13] Constitutional Reform Act 2005, section 7(1).

[14] N. Andrews, 'Judicial Independence: The British Experience', in S. Shetreet and C. Forsyth (eds.), *The Culture of Judicial Independence: Conceptual Foundations and Practical Challenges* (Leiden: Martinus Nijhoff, 2012), p. 365. Reflecting this multi-tasking, our interviewees described the office of LCJ in various different ways: 'foreman' of the judiciary; 'chief but not master'; '*primus inter pares* – but very much *primus*'; 'commander in chief' and 'first sea lord'.

Table 6.1. *Functions of the Lord Chief Justice in 2003 and 2013*

| Functions of the LCJ in 2003 | Additional functions of the LCJ in 2013 |
|---|---|
| Presiding in Court of Appeal | Head of Judiciary in England and Wales |
| Presiding in Divisional Court | Responsible for welfare, training and guidance |
| Responsible for judicial deployment, through Presiding and other judges | Chairs the Judicial Executive Board |
| Chair of Judges' Council, and Sentencing Guidelines Council | Appoints all Circuit and District Judges |
| Being consulted by Lord Chancellor on judicial appointments | Decides on judicial discipline (jointly with Lord Chancellor) |
| Representing views of judiciary to government | Represents views of judiciary to Parliament, government and public |
| | Responsible for HMCTS (jointly with Lord Chancellor) |

First and foremost – in the eyes of the judiciary at least – the LCJ is a sitting judge entitled to sit in appellate and trial-level courts and in the UK Supreme Court at the invitation of its President. Second, the LCJ must maintain appropriate arrangements for judicial welfare, training and guidance, within the resources made available by the Lord Chancellor.[15] Third, the LCJ is responsible for the deployment of the judiciary and the allocation of work within courts.[16] Fourth, the LCJ is responsible, with the Lord Chancellor, for the exercise of disciplinary powers in relation to judicial conduct.[17] Fifth, following the Crime and Courts Act 2013, the LCJ replaces the Lord Chancellor as the final decision-maker on appointments to all courts below the High Court and is under a statutory duty to take such steps as he or she thinks appropriate 'for the purpose of encouraging judicial diversity'.[18] Sixth, the LCJ represents the views of the judiciary to Parliament, the Lord Chancellor and other ministers.[19] These various tasks coalesce around two leadership roles: managing the judiciary's internal and external relations.

[15] CRA, section 7(2)(b).

[16] CRA, section 7(2)(c).

[17] Crime and Courts Act 2013, Schedule 13, para. 29.

[18] Crime and Courts Act 2013, Schedule 13, para. 11.

[19] CRA, section 7(2)(a).

### *Managing internal relations*

Internally, the LCJ must for the most part exercise power obliquely so as to avoid any suggestion of command and control. Deference towards the LCJ may be normal, but this does not translate into many mechanisms of explicit control. '[T]here is nobody to whom you can give orders … because each judge is not only part of an independent body, but is an independent individual as well' (senior judge). Yet while it is true that LCJs do not command in any crude sense, there are several areas in which they effectively give orders. The most obvious is judicial deployment, with the LCJ under a statutory duty to decide where judges work, both geographically and jurisdictionally. In practice, the LCJ delegates much of the day-to-day decision-making to a senior management team comprising the Senior Presiding Judge, the Senior President of Tribunals and Heads of Division. They, in turn, delegate many detailed decisions to presiding judges, resident judges and the chamber presidents. The LCJ appoints the presiding judges and resident judges (with the concurrence of the Lord Chancellor), and other important leadership posts such as the Senior Presiding Judge. The LCJ retains overall responsibility for deployment and in this must respond to changing caseloads to avoid an under-supply or over-supply of judges with the necessary skills in one area or another. In the past, when this task fell primarily on the Lord Chancellor, the judiciary was often fully stretched and the problem was limited to ensuring that there were enough judges in the right places to cover the work. With workloads dropping in some fields, such as civil justice, but rising in others, such as family proceedings and immigration, the LCJ must now more actively manage the judicial workforce, making potentially unpopular deployment decisions as a result.

The second strand of the LCJ's internal leadership is a diplomatic and consensus-building role. A good example is the response of Lord Judge, when LCJ, to the changes to judicial pensions in 2013, described in Chapter 4. The proposals provoked considerable judicial opposition, including threats of resignation from the bench. Once it became clear that the government would insist on the changes, Lord Judge held seventeen private meetings with judges around the country to explain why he had accepted the proposals. This task could have been delegated to the Senior Presiding Judge, but Lord Judge was concerned about the significant effect that the changes had on morale, particularly among younger judges, and felt that the burden of explaining the outcome of the pension negotiations was one for the LCJ alone. Several judges told us that this sort of personal engagement helps to encourage acceptance of the more structured and hierarchical system of internal management.

### *Managing external relations: Whitehall and Westminster*

The LCJ is responsible for representing the views of the judiciary within Whitehall and Westminster in relation to all judiciary-related policy developments (see Chapters 3 and 4). In recent years this has involved negotiations over court closures, the incorporation of the Tribunals Service into the Courts Service, judicial pensions, funding of the courts and judicial appointments. Each year the LCJ must also agree – or not – the budget for the courts. Punctuating these negotiations are the monthly meetings between the LCJ, the Lord Chancellor and the Permanent Secretary of the Ministry of Justice. Before 2005, the LCJ usually met the Lord Chancellor in the latter's rooms in Parliament. In a small but symbolic change reflective of the post-2005 partnership, the meetings now rotate between the Ministry and the Royal Courts of Justice.

In addition to occasional meetings with the Law Officers and other ministers, there is an emerging practice of the LCJ meeting with the Prime Minister every six months. Previously such meetings were rare, occurring only at moments of heightened tension between the government and the judiciary. One such occasion was in 2001 when a deputation of senior judges met with Tony Blair and dissuaded him from transferring responsibility for the courts from the Lord Chancellor's Department to the Home Office.[20] There were no further meetings with the Prime Minister until around 2012, when (under David Cameron as Prime Minister and Lord Judge as LCJ) this practice of biannual meetings was initiated. Though the LCJ retains the right to request extraordinary meetings, these regular meetings provide an opportunity 'to discuss the strategic interaction of the executive and the judiciary'.[21] They also illustrate the fact that the LCJ has had to step into

[20] Woolf, 'Judicial Independence Not Judicial Isolation', p. 172. In 2006, Lord Falconer said that he was aware of two occasions where the LCJ had requested a meeting with the Prime Minister; 'one was completely unsuccessful and one was successful'. The 2001 meeting was a success insofar as the Prime Minister shelved the proposal. HL Constitution Committee, *Relations between the Executive, the Judiciary and Parliament* (HL 151 2007). See Minutes of Lord Falconer's evidence at Q70 (22 November 2006).

[21] Judicial Office, Lord Chief Justice's Report 2013 (2013) 14.

the vacuum left by the downgraded status of the new-style office of Lord Chancellor. Many judges do not regard the new arrangements as a change for the better, as Lord Judge commented: 'this is a substitution and speaking for myself as the substitute, I can say a pretty poor substitute'.[22] These new arrangements do, however, provide a measure of political accountability in that the Prime Minister is able to ask for explanations of judicial policy from the LCJ as much as the LCJ may seek assurances from the Prime Minister about government policy.

A similar move to more formal and proactive engagement is evident in the way the LCJ manages the judiciary's relations with Parliament (see Chapter 5). The LCJ has the power to lay written representations before Parliament on matters 'of importance relating to the judiciary or otherwise to the administration of justice'.[23] This is now used to lay the LCJ's periodic reviews before Parliament, although the provision is primarily intended to be used to alert Parliament to a threat to the administration of justice, such as a funding crisis.[24] The LCJ also appears before select committees more frequently than do other senior judges.[25] Select committee appearances provide the LCJ with an opportunity to inform parliamentarians of the judicial perspective on policies relating to the administration of justice and to articulate judicial concern about governmental policy; they allow the LCJ to explain and advance the judiciary's views and interests, but they are also important accountability channels through which the LCJ can be asked to explain his or her decisions. The opportunity to appear before select committees is particularly important now that the LCJ is no longer permitted to speak in debates in the House of Lords.[26] Some senior judges feel this loss keenly, and Lord Judge has argued that the LCJ should be given the right to address the Lords in the event that the judiciary does not support a proposed reform to the judicial system.[27]

[22] Lord Judge, 'Constitutional Change: Unfinished Business' (the Constitution Unit, 4 December 2013), para. 21.

[23] Constitutional Reform Act 2005, section 5(1).

[24] As LCJ, Lord Phillips described such a warning as a 'nuclear option': HL Constitution Committee, *Relations between the Executive, the Judiciary and Parliament.* See evidence of Lord Phillips at Qs 48 and 50 (3 May 2006).

[25] Between January 2010 and December 2013 there were six appearances before four committees: the Lords Constitution Committee (three times), the Commons Justice Committee, the Joint Committee on Parliamentary Privilege and the Joint Committee on Human Rights.

[26] CRA, section 137.

[27] Lord Judge, 'Constitutional Change: Unfinished Business', para. 31.

The LCJ can also communicate the judiciary's views to parliamentarians via regular meetings with senior parliamentary officials and, in particular, with the top clerk in the House of Commons, the Clerk of the House. Historically there was very little routine contact between senior judges and parliamentary clerks, with each side largely ignorant of the other's concerns. The appointment in 2011 of a new Clerk of the House, Sir Robert Rogers, led to more regular contact, largely because of his more outward-looking approach. This began with meetings in 2012 between Lord Judge as LCJ, Lord Neuberger as Master of the Rolls, the two Speakers of Parliament and Sir Robert Rogers to discuss judicial concerns about breaches of injunctions in Parliament. The meetings were felt to be very useful and so contact has continued. There are now meetings every four months or so, discussing matters such as the *sub judice* rule and parliamentary privilege.

When the LCJ gives evidence to a committee, it may or may not receive any press coverage. An overarching element of the LCJ's role in managing external relations is to decide when and through which vehicle to make public any concerns. There are set pieces in the legal calendar that typically attract media coverage through which this can be done: the LCJ's annual press conference, the Lord Mayor's Dinner for the Judges where the LCJ makes brief but well-reported comments, and speeches at conferences and universities around the world. Whenever relations with ministers prove problematic, the LCJ must decide whether to raise an issue publicly, and how and where to raise it, always reflecting on whether putting ministers on the spot in public is likely to advance the judicial cause over the long haul.

### *Managing external relations: beyond Whitehall and Westminster*

Relations with a range of bodies fulfilling judiciary-related functions also require the attention of the LCJ, such as the Judicial Conduct Investigations Office, the Judicial Appointments Commission and the Judicial Appointments and Conduct Ombudsman. While much of the day-to-day work is delegated to a senior management team of judges and civil servants, the LCJ has regular personal contact with key officials in these bodies and these contacts are an important part of the routine politics of judicial independence. In 2012, for example, it was proposed that the Crime and Courts Bill include a duty on the LCJ to prepare regulations relating to the power of deployment. Some members of the Judicial Appointments Commission (JAC) considered that such regulations would minimise the likelihood that an LCJ could use the deployment power to place favoured judges in certain posts in a way that circumvents the usual appointment processes. Lord Judge strongly opposed this proposal and, in meetings with the Lord Chancellor and the JAC Chair, he successfully resisted them. Despite some JAC members urging him to challenge the LCJ on this issue, the JAC's Chair refused to do so. Whatever the merits of the arguments for and against the proposal, the fact that Lord Judge blocked it is evidence of the degree of authority that the LCJ exercises when negotiating with judiciary-related bodies.

Perhaps the most important element of these external relations is the LCJ's involvement in judicial appointments. As we explain in Chapter 7, the LCJ's is an influential, and sometimes decisive, voice in appointments at all levels of the judiciary and at various stages of the selection processes. For appointments below the High Court, this now includes the final say whether to accept, reject or request reconsideration of the JAC's recommendations. For the High Court, the LCJ is consulted on every candidate under serious consideration by the JAC, with our interviews suggesting that this can operate as an effective veto for the LCJ. For more senior appointments, the LCJ sits together with another senior judge on the panel that makes the recommendation to the Lord Chancellor. Though there is likely to be (but no guarantee of) a lay majority on these panels, our interviews suggest that the voices of the senior judges are predominant, although the lay members help to ensure that the judicial opinions are evidence-based and well reasoned. In short, the LCJ is a pivotal repeat-player who has many opportunities to ensure that selections at all levels of the judiciary are in line with his or her views.

A different form of authority is evident in the LCJ's dealings with senior judges in the other jurisdictions in the UK, in particular the President of the UK Supreme Court. The formal hierarchy between these two posts is clear: the President is the most senior judge in the UK but has no administrative responsibilities in relation to the three UK jurisdictions. However, the Lord Chief Justice is the leader of by far the largest judiciary in the UK and so arguably wields more power and influence than the President. In practice, the two judges engage as equals. They meet monthly, in addition to regular informal contact. For example, in the wake of comments in 2011 by the Prime Minister and the Home Secretary that were highly critical of a Supreme Court decision, the LCJ and President of the Supreme Court both wrote to the Lord

Chancellor to remind him of the duty on ministers to uphold judicial independence (see Chapter 3). In 2011, the LCJ and President were also in regular contact prior to their joint appearances before the Constitution Committee and the Joint Committee on Human Rights. While they often act in concert, they must each be careful not to stray into the other's territory. The LCJ may express concerns about matters which affect the trial courts, such as the length of Supreme Court judgments, but it would be impolitic for the LCJ to voice such criticisms publicly. In the same way, the President must take care when speaking on issues, such as the televising of trials, which have a bearing on the judiciary as a whole but would not directly affect the Supreme Court itself.

### *Leadership skills of the Lord Chief Justice*

The package of qualities required of the LCJ in carrying out these multiple tasks is a daunting one, encompassing judicial, people and political skills. The LCJ remains, first and foremost, a sitting judge. Given the number and scope of the office's administrative tasks, it is difficult for an outsider to grasp how it is feasible for the LCJ to devote substantial time to sitting in court. Yet for judges, the authority of the office depends on the LCJ remaining regularly engaged with the business of judging at the highest level. Many of our judicial interviewees emphasised that the LCJ must be viewed as the chief judge, not merely as chief administrator, and must set an example to others by taking a lead on the judicial duty to decide cases. For this reason, the LCJ sits not only on high-profile cases, but on more routine appeals as well. This is felt by judges to underscore the LCJ's ability to speak authoritatively on the development of the law as and when necessary. In more practical terms, by sitting on high-profile cases, the LCJ can ensure that such cases are resolved speedily, and with a suitable media strategy in place.

The ability to 'take people along' will be an increasingly important quality as the LCJ needs to nurture the confidence not only of judicial colleagues, but also of the growing number of individuals across many institutions who contribute to the successful running of the judiciary. It is no longer the case that senior judges can expect to have personal knowledge of their colleagues in lower courts, as they did when the judiciary was a fraction of its current size. Nevertheless, there is still a strong cultural imperative for the LCJ to engage, where possible, with individual judges in order to maintain the ideal of the 'judicial family'. One way in which Lord Judge did this (as LCJ) was to travel around the country regularly to meet as many trial judges as possible. He also made a decision to undertake, wherever possible, the task of swearing in all new Circuit and High Court judges. This function passed from the Lord Chancellor in 2005 and could have been delegated to another senior judge. Lord Judge's decision to take on this time-consuming task is an example of how important he considered it to be for the LCJ to remain in touch with judges at a personal level, even if only briefly at the start of a judicial career.

A commitment to continuing as a sitting judge may be a cultural imperative, but its effect is to squeeze the time available to engage in active leadership through planning, organising and making difficult strategic choices.[28] So it is essential that the LCJ delegates administrative functions to a trusted team of senior colleagues. As a senior judge put it, the role of the LCJ now is a 'mega-task'. And the tasks require a wide palate of political skills – political not in the conventional sense, but in the sense of knowing how to operate within the political landscape in its broadest sense, and how to negotiate with the different interest groups.

## The institutional architecture of judicial governance

### *The senior management team*

The Constitutional Reform Act vested all powers in the LCJ, rather than carving out distinct powers for specific Heads of Division.[29] However, it was always intended that many of the powers and duties would be delegated to judicial colleagues and that this would require a more formalised management hierarchy.[30] The development of a more clearly defined internal organisational structure based on line management is difficult to reconcile with the traditional view of the judiciary as a non-hierarchical body. But in reality there has always been a degree of line management of District and Circuit Judges by Presiding Judges, and for Senior Judges by Heads of Division, the Master of the Rolls and the LCJ. The changes necessitated by the CRA built upon and accelerated a process of gradual formalisation which had

[28] See, generally, R. Stupak, 'Court Leadership in Transition: Fast Forward toward the Year 2000' (1991) 15 *Justice System Journal* 617.

[29] Constitutional Reform Act 2005, section 7.

[30] Lord Chief Justice, *Lord Chief Justice's Review of the Administration of Justice in the Courts* (London: HC 448 2008), para. 4.9.

been occurring for many years as the judiciary had grown in size and become more professionalised.[31]

What has changed is that there is now a more general acceptance of the top-down nature of the judicial management structure. The senior judiciary expects to give regular directions to judges in administrative and management roles such as the chief magistrate, resident judges and presiding judges. Though given significant discretion to undertake their administrative responsibilities, they are clear that if the senior judicial leadership felt that they were making mistakes, they would be told. One judge told us that he was in no doubt that, if they disagreed with the way in which he undertook his administrative functions, senior judges would 'steer [him] in a particular direction'. An example of the move towards a more centralised system is the changing role of the Chief Magistrate. Before 2005, the Chief Magistrate exercised considerable discretion when dealing with District Judges in the magistrates' courts, including disciplinary and deployment powers. In 2005, these powers passed to the senior judges, and are now delegated by them back to the Chief Magistrate, and could be taken away if the senior judiciary so chose.

Evidence for the greater formalisation of the management functions is found in the developing roles of the Senior Presiding Judge (SPJ) and the Senior President of Tribunals (SPT). The office of SPJ is held for a three-year, non-renewable term, and with an emerging practice whereby the incoming SPJ is appointed as Deputy SPJ about nine months before the expiry of this term, so as to be able to work into the job with the support of the outgoing SPJ. The SPJ exercises a range of tasks for which the LCJ is responsible. The role is that of 'chief of staff' to the LCJ: 'not only advising him but also exercising many delegated powers in relation to the management and deployment of the judiciary around the country'.[32] Though the SPJ continues to sit in court, finding the time for judicial work is a struggle. The role has both outward- and inward-facing dimensions. In 2006, the SPJ took the lead in developing the judiciary's relationship with the JAC. As a senior judicial member on the Board of HM Courts and Tribunals Service (HMCTS), he or she is closely involved in negotiations with the Lord Chancellor over the budget, while taking on particular responsibility for many aspects of judicial performance. The SPJ brings back from HMCTS board meetings performance data on the

[31] See, generally, Malleson, *The New Judiciary*.

[32] Lord Chief Justice, *Lord Chief Justice's Review of the Administration of Justice in the Courts*, para. 5.3.

different court centres, and then discusses with Presiding Judges and Resident Judges how to improve the speed and efficiency of particular courts. In a recent development, the Crime and Courts Act 2013 transferred the statutory power to appoint magistrates from the Lord Chancellor to the LCJ, who in turn has delegated this power to the SPJ who makes the formal appointments. As before, the recruitment and selection of candidates is carried out by forty-seven local advisory committees composed of existing magistrates and laypeople.

The position of Senior President of Tribunals (SPT) was created under the Tribunals, Courts and Enforcement Act 2007 and is in some ways equivalent to the LCJ and in some ways junior.[33] The SPT leads the tribunals judiciary, with a remit that extends to Scotland and Northern Ireland for tribunals with a UK-wide jurisdiction (e.g. the Asylum and Immigration Tribunal and the Tax Tribunal). Reflecting this, the position is filled from the ranks of existing judges in the Court of Appeal or the equivalent courts in Scotland and Northern Ireland.[34] The SPT has statutory responsibilities for the management and welfare of the tribunal judges similar to those of the LCJ in relation to the courts judiciary. He or she is responsible for representing the views of tribunal judges to the Lord Chancellor, ministers and Parliament, and like the LCJ has the power to make representations to Parliament.[35] Following the Crime and Courts Act 2013, the Lord Chancellor is no longer the final decision-maker for most tribunal appointments, with this power now falling to the SPT. The position of SPT is a burdensome administrative role and also one that demands considerable political skill. It has required the SPT not only to radically transform the internal structures of the tribunal system, but also to maintain good relations with the heads of the judiciaries in England and Wales, Northern Ireland and Scotland, given that the jurisdiction of some tribunals extends across the UK. It is also a critical role for disseminating cultural changes, as the emphasis placed by tribunal judges on user-focus, cost-effectiveness and training percolates through the wider judicial family.

The position of the SPT and its relationship with the LCJ has not yet been fully settled. Initially, in 2005, the intention was that the tribunals would sit within a single judicial system headed by the LCJ. It was envisaged that the judge appointed as SPT would hold a role similar to

[33] Tribunals, Courts and Enforcement Act 2007, section 2(1).

[34] Tribunals, Courts and Enforcement Act 2007, Schedule 1, para. 3.

[35] Tribunals, Courts and Enforcement Act 2007, Schedule 1, paras. 13–14.

the SPJ or a Head of Division under the LCJ.[36] Ultimately, however, this proposal was not carried through, in part because the UK-wide jurisdiction of some tribunals was felt to render it inappropriate for tribunals to be folded into the English and Welsh judiciary. The then Lord Chancellor, Lord Falconer, decided instead that tribunals should remain distinct from the courts, with the 2007 Act creating the SPT as head of the tribunals. Initially, then, the tribunals and tribunal judges were a distinct part of the civil justice system, headed by the SPT and administered not by the Courts Service but separately by the Tribunals Service. This led to the duplication of functions and thus costs. As a result, in 2010, the then Lord Chancellor, Kenneth Clarke, and the LCJ agreed that there should be a single judiciary in England and Wales, with the tribunal judges integrated into a single courts and tribunals service (i.e. HMCTS), and with the LCJ as a single head of both the tribunals and court judiciaries. The statutory underpinning of the SPT's position as head of the tribunal judiciary now means that transfer of the leadership role to the LCJ would require legislation. The UK-wide jurisdiction of some tribunals also makes the prospect that tribunal judges in Scotland and in Northern Ireland might be led from England and Wales, by the LCJ, a politically sensitive one.[37] It was little surprise therefore when, in 2013, the Lord Chancellor announced that the proposal to create a single head of the judiciary had been delayed, with the issue to be kept under review over the next three to four years. For the time being the LCJ and SPT remain heads of court judges and of tribunal judges respectively, with separate but similar statutory responsibilities.

### *The Judicial Executive Board and the Judges' Council*

As the individual management roles performed by particular judges have grown, so has the need for more coherent and effective collective decision-making. This is provided by the Judicial Executive Board (JEB), and the Judges' Council. The former was created in 2005 to act as a form of 'judicial Cabinet'. Prior to 2005, an informal group of senior judges comprising the LCJ and Heads of Division met regularly to discuss and decide issues relating to the judiciary, with their primary function to give advice to the

[36] Lord Justice Thomas, 'The Position of the Judiciaries of the United Kingdom in the Constitutional Changes: Address to the Scottish Sheriffs' Association' (Peebles, 8 March 2008).

[37] The Asylum and Immigration Tribunal, for example, has UK-wide jurisdiction.

Lord Chancellor on judicial appointments.[38] In 2005, this arrangement was formalised and the JEB is now composed of eleven senior judges (listed on the judiciary's website) tasked to play the central role in advising the LCJ on policy decisions affecting the judiciary. While the leadership styles of LCJs vary, and some will be quicker to consult with the JEB than others, its role is increasingly established as a central body in the architecture of the internal governance of the judiciary. It meets regularly; formally once a month for a full day's meeting during the legal term, and once a week more informally.[39] Among its various functions, the JEB approves the annual business plan for the Judicial Office, before it is forwarded to the Ministry. It also considers resources and judicial appointments. Although constitutionally the LCJ has the final say in exercising his statutory powers, a practice is emerging of collective responsibility. The members of the JEB recognise that once a decision has been taken, whether or not they personally supported it, they must take responsibility for its successful implementation. As one JEB member put it to us, 'We advise the LCJ but whatever decision he takes, we're all ultimately responsible with him'.

In contrast to the JEB, the Judges' Council has a long lineage that can be traced back to the creation of the Council of the Judges of the Supreme Court by the Judicature Act 1873. It played a significant role in implementing judicial reform in the nineteenth century, particularly in relation to the circuit system, but its influence had waned in the twentieth century, until it was effectively moribund. The modern Judges' Council dates only from 1988, when the body was re-established to represent the views of the judges in the light of the tensions between the judiciary and the Thatcher government over reforms to the justice system implemented by the then Lord Chancellor, Lord Mackay.[40] Above all, it was intended to be a body that would press for the provision of adequate resources and to this end a resources committee was established in 1990. However, its effectiveness was limited by lack of prior consultation before policy was implemented and the newly revived body worked 'somewhat haphazardly and did not operate consistently or regularly'.[41] In 2001, Lord Woolf proposed reform of the Judges' Council, arguing that it should 'speak

[38] Lord Justice Thomas, 'The Position of the Judiciaries of the United Kingdom in the Constitutional Changes: Address to the Scottish Sheriffs' Association'.

[39] Lord Phillips, 'Constitutional Reform: One Year On' (the Judicial Studies Board Annual Lecture, 22 March 2007).

[40] I. Scott, 'The Council of Judges in the Supreme Court of England and Wales' [1989] *Public Law* 379.

[41] Lord Justice Thomas, 'The Judges' Council' [2005] *Public Law* 608, 623.

for all the judiciary and be a proactive body with terms of reference and identified responsibilities and a driving force in the modernisation of the judiciary'.[42] In 2002, it was reconfigured as a larger representative body chaired by the LCJ. The timing was fortuitous, as it was able to play a useful role in reviewing and commenting on the Constitutional Reform Bill during its parliamentary stages.[43]

Today, the Judges' Council has a membership of around twenty-eight (listed on the judiciary's website), comprising the members of the JEB, representatives from all levels of the judiciary, and a handful of co-opted members.[44] The fact that the members of the JEB are now all *ex officio* members of the Judges' Council represents a tightening of the senior management team's grip on the Council, but it also helped to bridge the gap between senior and junior judiciary that had existed under the prior system. The Judges' Council meets around three times a year, although much of its detailed work is done through its various committees (for example, the Committee on Judicial Support and Welfare, and the Wales Committee).[45] Its role is not to take governance decisions but to be a 'voice' for the wider judiciary and to provide the LCJ with advice. As a senior judge observed, 'in the end it is the JEB and then, ultimately, the Lord Chief Justice who decides'. Yet, 'any LCJ would be mad to ignore the views of the JEB and the Judges' Council'. Successive LCJs have thus understood that the effectiveness of the office is dependent on fruitful relations with judges at different levels across the country. The JEB and the Judges' Council do not challenge the centralisation of power around the LCJ but they do provide forums in which judges can express the views of the judiciary to the LCJ. The LCJ would have to think 'long and hard' (senior judge) before pushing ahead with changes in the face of widespread judicial opposition.

### *The Judicial Office*

The expanded powers of the LCJ and the senior management team can only be exercised if they have a body of administrators to carry out their decisions. The creation of the Judicial Office in 2006 has provided, in

[42] H. Woolf, 'The Needs of a 21st Century Judge: Judicial Studies Board Annual Lecture 2001', in *The Pursuit of Justice*.

[43] See, for example, the Memorandum of the Judges' Council of England and Wales in HL Committee on the Constitutional Reform Bill, *Constitutional Reform Bill [HL]* (HL 125-I 2004).

[44] The current membership of the Judges' Council and the JEB is detailed on the judiciary.gov.uk website.

[45] See, for example, Judges' Council, *Annual Report 2007*, pp. 5–11.

effect, a judicial civil service and represents 'a revolutionary step, but a very quiet revolutionary step', that underlines the more expansive responsibilities assumed by the judiciary for running its own affairs.[46] The Judicial Office's primary role is to provide 'support to the judiciary in discharging its responsibilities under the Constitutional Reform Act',[47] with its strategic goals decided by the JEB.[48] Prior to the Constitutional Reform Act, the LCJ had a private office handling his own immediate affairs, but it consisted of no more than a handful of staff.

The day-to-day work of the Judicial Office includes training, communications, media support, human resources and judicial welfare, and policy advice. In the seven years since its creation, its responsibilities have expanded significantly, notably by incorporating elements of the judicial human resources team that was previously part of the Ministry of Justice. This change was especially important in enabling the development of better support for judges at all ranks of the judiciary with the establishment of much more structured judicial welfare arrangements. Other functions transferred to the Judicial Office include the Civil and Family Justice Councils, the Office for Judicial Complaints, Tribunals training (into the Judicial College), the Tribunals Judicial Office supporting the SPT, the Chief Coroner's Office and the Office of the Judge Advocate General. By 2012, as a result of all these changes, the Judicial Office had grown in size from sixty on its creation to over 200 staff and its organisational structure had transformed into a more formalised hierarchy.[49] This process of transformation is not complete, with the Judicial Office 'growing up as we speak', as a senior judge phrased it.

The impetus for the gradual consolidation of administrative functions within a central Judicial Office was both a push from the Ministry of Justice, which no longer felt it appropriate to be dealing with these judicially related issues, and a pull from the staff supporting the senior judiciary to bring them within its remit. Some in the Ministry of Justice were anxious about losing these functions and questioned whether the Lord Chancellor would get sufficient support for the roles for which the minister retained responsibility. In practice, the process of negotiating the changing remit and staffing of the Judicial Office was relatively

[46] Lord Judge, 'The Judicial Studies Board Lecture 2010' (London, 17 March 2010).

[47] On some processes the Judicial Office support the Lord Chancellor as well as the judiciary, for example, judicial appointments: Judicial Office, *Lord Chief Justice's Report 2013* (2013) 49.

[48] Judicial Office, Business Plan 2011–2012.

[49] Judicial Office, Business Plan 2013–2014, 33.

painless. One reason for this was the underlying drive to reduce spending. Consolidation of the different administrative services in the Judicial Office was one way of making efficiency savings in the Ministry at a time when the Treasury was demanding significant cuts.

The emergence of a civil service to support the judiciary raises issues that may need to be addressed in the future. Although funded by the Ministry of Justice (MoJ) and accountable for financial propriety to Parliament through the Ministry's Permanent Secretary, the civil servants in the Judicial Office are accountable to the LCJ and the SPT. This caused some tensions in the early years. At present, most of the officials in the Judicial Office are seconded from the Ministry, leading to concerns within the MoJ about where their primary loyalties might lie. There was a feeling among some at the MoJ that officials who had been at the Judicial Office might come back, as one interviewee phrased it, 'contaminated'. Some judges felt that the civil servants were the Ministry's 'plants' inside the judiciary and would have divided loyalties. In recent years, suspicions have faded, assisted by the recruitment of staff in the Judicial Office from a wider range of departments (for example, the Crown Prosecution Service and the Government Legal Service). Some have even been recruited from amongst judicial assistants.

### *Judicial Communications Office*

As the judicial leadership has become more active and centralised, the job of managing judicial communications outside the judiciary has become increasingly important. Much of this work is done through the recently developed Judicial Communications Office (JCO).[50] At a policy level, the JCO works with senior judges to develop effective arrangements for managing relations between the media and the judiciary. The growing judicial awareness of the need to engage with the media is illustrated by the occasional meetings that are now held between the LCJ, the SPJ and newspaper editors in order to try to facilitate accurate and balanced media reporting. In addition, there is a 'media panel' consisting of around ten judges who can speak publicly in response to media interest in specific areas. These developments need to be understood as a much larger shift towards a more proactive policy of media engagement.[51]

[50] For an account of its early years, see Lord Phillips, 'Constitutional Reform: One Year On'.
[51] L. Gies, *Law and the Media: The Future of an Uneasy Relationship* (London: Routledge–Cavendish, 2007), pp. 113–16.

On a day-to-day basis, the JCO works with individual judges who are presiding over cases which have attracted media attention or who wish to engage in some form of public communication. Since Lord Mackay abolished the Kilmuir Rules, which imposed restrictions on the extent to which judges could speak in public,[52] it has become much more common for judges to give lectures, interviews and talks. Judges are not required to check with the JCO before making a statement to the press or giving an interview, but it is increasingly common for judges to do so, particularly if the area is sensitive or newsworthy. In such cases they are strongly encouraged to draft what they wish to say in advance and to run it past staff in the JCO for advice before making it publicly available. Resident and Presiding Judges, in particular, will regularly contact the JCO or be alerted by them when an issue has arisen which might need a response, such as media criticism of a sentencing decision. The judges and the JCO will then jointly decide whether and how to respond. In most instances the judges and staff in the JCO work together to protect the reputation of the judiciary. In some cases, however, tensions remain over the extent to which the public statements of individual judges should be checked or monitored.

An example of this arose in 2013 when Mr Justice Coleridge was the subject of a complaint as a result of his public statements about the breakdown of marriage made in the context of his involvement in the Marriage Foundation, a charity he had founded to promote marriage. Following newspaper articles in which he criticised the government's policy on same-sex marriage, the Judicial Conduct and Investigations Office issued a statement announcing that

> having considered all the facts, including the informal advice given to Mr Justice Coleridge last year, the Lord Chancellor and the Lord Chief Justice consider Mr Justice Coleridge's decision to give an interview and to participate in the article to be incompatible with his judicial responsibilities and therefore amounts to judicial misconduct. They have issued Mr Justice Coleridge with a formal warning.[53]

Mr Justice Coleridge subsequently announced he would resign.[54] What was at issue here was tension between the freedom of speech of an

[52] A. Bradley, 'Judges and the Media: The Kilmuir Rules' [1986] *Public Law* 383.

[53] Judicial Conduct and Investigations Office, *Statement from the Judicial Conduct and Investigations Office* (OJC 58/13 2013).

[54] S. Doughty, 'Anger of the Judge Forced to Resign for Championing Marriage: Sir Paul Coleridge Says Only "One or Two" Colleagues Are Opposed to His Views', *Daily Mail*, 19 December 2013.

individual judge, and actions which might call into question his impartiality as a judge of the Family Division. Most judges would now expect to secure advance approval from the JCO or senior judges for the wording of an extra-judicial statement on a controversial issue, just as they are expected to consult the LCJ's Private Office before agreeing to appear before a select committee.[55] Far from being regarded as a threat to judicial independence, many consider that the JCO provides a valuable service that affords judges a measure of protection against unwittingly invoking media hostility or public criticism in their public statements.

## Judicial training

One of the driving rationales for the creation of a more formalised, centralised and top-down management in the judiciary has been to improve efficiency and standards of judicial performance. A key to this process has been the development of judicial training. Most judges would today agree with Lord Judge's view of training as being the judiciary's 'great success story'.[56] Yet when the Judicial Studies Board (JSB) was established in 1979, it generated deep suspicion amongst judges who perceived the very idea of training as a threat to their independence, opening the door to directives about how judges should do their work. These fears were only overcome by establishing the JSB as a body run by judges for judges and by talking opaquely of 'studies' rather than 'training'.[57] In its early years, the training provided by the JSB was relatively informal, amateur and low-key, an example of what one commentator called 'policy-making by stealth'.[58] By the 1990s this had started to change.[59] Whereas training had once been seen as a supplemental and *ad hoc* process, it increasingly came to be regarded as a necessity in order to ensure an appropriately professional judiciary, and particularly when new legislation was introduced. Today it would be difficult to find a judge who views judicial training *per se* as a threat to

55 Judicial Executive Board, Guidance to Judges on Appearances before Select Committees (2012), paras. 20–2.

56 Lord Judge, 'The Judicial Studies Board Lecture 2010'.

57 Speaking in 1996, Lord Bingham remarked that training and education programmes 'no longer need to be disguised as "judicial studies" to make them acceptable': Lord Bingham, *The Business of Judging: Selected Essays and Speeches, 1985–1999* (Oxford: Oxford University Press, 2000), p. 67.

58 M. Partington, 'Training the Judiciary in England and Wales: The Work of the Judicial Studies Board' [1994] *Civil Justice Quarterly* 319, 322.

59 Malleson, *The New Judiciary*, pp. 167–72.

judicial independence, and most regard it as valuable, if not essential.[60] As one judge explained, 'in the late 1980s, there was a view abroad then for judges of a different generation that you really were independent, and that meant that nobody could tell you what to do, they couldn't train you, that training ... breach[ed] judicial independence. That view is long gone'. It is just as likely today for a judge to argue that there is not enough training as to criticise the Judicial College for providing too much.[61] Most judges recognise that judicial training can be related to specific outcomes, such as better-managed and less costly litigation and increased public confidence in the judiciary.[62]

The LCJ and the SPT have a statutory responsibility for training the courts and tribunals judiciaries respectively. In practice, these responsibilities are discharged by the Judicial College, which is the successor to the Judicial Studies Board. In view of the JSB's success in converting the judiciary to the cause of training, the decision to rename it the Judicial College in 2011 was not taken lightly. The change was not, however, simply to the name. With the Judicial College now supported by the Judicial Office, it operates in a more professional manner than the JSB had done. The Judicial College is responsible for training all 29,000 judicial office-holders in England and Wales (including magistrates) and tribunal judges around the UK. Despite significant budget cuts, in a three-month period in 2013, the Judicial College delivered sixty-three courses for tribunal judges, with a total of around 2,130 attendees, and eighteen courses for courts judges, with around 1,250 attendees.[63]

The move to a Judicial College needs to be understood in the context of the merger of the tribunals and courts judiciaries. The introduction of unified training was felt to be a useful way to send the message – especially to tribunal judges – that this change was a merger, not a takeover. The recognition of the equal value of tribunal judges in the judicial training system was particularly important given that tribunal judges generally had more extensive training than the court judiciary. With resources limited at a time of pressure on public spending, the

[60] For a recent empirical review of the changed attitudes to training, see Darbyshire, *Sitting in Judgment*, pp. 103–16.

[61] For example, in 2013, Master Steven Whitaker publicly expressed concern that judges were not being given sufficient training on the implementation of the Jackson reforms to the civil justice process.

[62] See C. Thomas, *Review of Judicial Training and Education in Other Jurisdictions: Report Prepared for the Judicial Studies Board* (2006) 4.

[63] Judicial College, *Performance Report April–June 2013* (2013) 3.

Judicial College is by necessity more flexible and responsive to changing needs than the JSB. In 2011, for example, the JEB agreed that leadership and management training were a priority, and the Judicial College intends to develop this so as to support more effectively the increasing workload of the judicial senior management team. In 2005, the JSB ran a series of compulsory management training courses lasting a day and a half. The courses were cut due to a lack of funding, but, under the leadership of Lady Justice Hallett, the Judicial College decided in 2012 to establish a forum to bring together judges at all levels, from all over the country, to identify the training needs for leadership and management skills. The need for this training has widespread support from the senior judiciary and is seen not as a threat to judicial independence but as a way of preserving it. As a senior judge explained, 'As judges we're not used to managing, we barely can manage ourselves most of us ... we need training in leadership and management skills ... this is not a threat to judicial independence ... it is absolutely essential if we are to preserve our independence.'

## Judicial management and appraisal

While judicial training is now accepted by judges as a necessity in a modern judiciary, the same is not yet true for performance appraisal. The monitoring of judges' work has always been a sensitive issue, and it is in this context that the creation myth of the flat judiciary, in which each judge is envisaged as an adjudicative island, most forcefully confronts the organisational reality of the judiciary today. Although the judiciary still has no formal line-management system of the kind that is found in the civil service or most other professions, there is now, in practice, a much clearer line of responsibility for performance, conduct and welfare. For example, where concerns are raised about the performance or well-being of a Circuit Judge, formal responsibility for responding to the problem falls on the Resident Judge of their court, and from them to the presiding High Court Judges of the circuit and up to the SPJ. This hierarchy has long existed in practice, but what has changed is that the chain of responsibility is now formally established within the job description of each management post. The result is what a Resident Judge described as 'the start of a framework of a managerial structure'. This change is problematic for some longer-serving judges, whereas more recently appointed judges are often relieved that they have some structure and support in their work and that 'they are not just left and told "right, for the next twenty years you do what you want'". The new structure is also less jarring for newly appointed judges who were previously solicitors and were therefore used to working within a formal management structure in marked contrast to the experience of formerly self-employed barristers. As a senior Circuit Judge commented, 'it is very difficult [for a former barrister] to become an employee . . . we've never had an HR department to go to'. The creation of a more structured judicial hierarchy is less of an issue, even for judges at the purist end of the independence spectrum, if its main purpose is for judges to be able to respond more effectively to exceptional cases where the health or conduct of a judge is clearly affecting their judicial performance. More serious tensions can arise when the new management structure is utilised to scrutinise systematically the work of all judges with the aim of improving performance across the board. Performance appraisal was traditionally regarded by judges as a threat to independence. Yet, today, this statement needs qualification, since the degree of opposition depends on what type of appraisal or assessment is proposed: collective or individual.

### *Collective performance*

Most people who have experience of workplace appraisal understand its aim as being to provide a structure of support and supervision, utilising work plans, objectives and monitoring of performance to improve the contribution of an individual employee. Equally important is the deployment of collective assessment mechanisms where the performance of a group within the organisation is monitored and compared to that of an equivalent group or reviewed over time to track improvement or deterioration in its outputs. For the judiciary, collective assessment is increasingly important. Despite the size and cost of the judicial system, the implementation of a coherent system for assessing and comparing the performance of individual courts is a relatively recent development. Some data on issues such as the rate of cracked trials was collected from around the late 1990s onwards, but prior to the year 2000 no systematic data was produced on the work of each Crown Court. It took careful negotiation on the part of the Lord Chancellor's Department and the Courts Service to persuade the judiciary that gathering and reviewing performance data was not a threat to judicial independence.

Today, HMCTS prepares monthly reports covering the performance of each Crown Court, including data such as the number of cases heard and numbers of ineffective trials. These are then scrutinised by the SPJ to determine whether some courts have better performance statistics than others, if so why, and whether changes are needed to improve efficiency. Resident Judges are then asked to analyse this data with their court manager and to discuss it at regular meetings with their trial judges. Thus the system is designed for data on court performance to flow from HMCTS to the senior judiciary for analysis and for a response to flow down to those presiding in court. There remains some resistance from trial judges to more formal and top-down involvement of the senior judiciary. To date, the analysis of court performance has generally been limited to the criminal courts, but the intention is for senior judges to be more closely involved in reviewing court performance across the civil and family courts as well.

The development of this new system of collective appraisal has meant that judges have to engage actively not only with the performance of other judges, but also with the managers and administrators who work in the courts and HMCTS. For the senior judges, this active management has been a steep learning curve. Some took to it with ease, while others had more reservations. Like any management team, judges need 'to be supervised, encouraged, cajoled, and they need constantly to be reminded what their job is' (senior courts service official). Senior judges have not traditionally been trained or expected to take on this role of supervising, cajoling and encouraging those running the courts, and reminding them how to do their job. Nevertheless, most members of the judiciary realise, whether more or less enthusiastically, that if they do not engage actively in this work then it is inevitable that outside officials will sooner or later be given the task of doing so. The days when the judges could resist all collective appraisal on the grounds that it is a threat to independence are long gone. Not only do most judges understand that the review of court performance is required as an element of public accountability, but they also appreciate that the *quid pro quo* of greater powers of self-management is the need to demonstrate that they are responding quickly and effectively to underperformance.

In some instances where monitoring reveals underperformance, this may be directly traced to the work of an individual or a group of individual judges. Given the limited options to remedy the situation through mandatory additional training or directions from the senior judiciary, one possibility is to review the deployment arrangements in the court to consider whether judges should be moved in or out. There is recognition amongst officials at HMCTS that any management problems relating to individual judges fall within the LCJ's responsibility for deployment. Yet the separation of collective from individual performance appraisal is not always clear-cut, and this has the potential to raise serious concerns amongst judges. In April 2013, for example, Sir James Munby, the President of the Family Division, wrote to all the Family Court judges stressing the importance of successful implementation of reforms to the family court system designed to reduce delays. His email stated, 'Failure is not an option.' While his comment was clearly directed at the performance of the Family Courts as a whole, it is difficult to see how this imperative could be upheld without addressing the performance of individual judges dealing with the cases before them. Redeploying judges who are underperforming has led some judges to talk of a breach of Article 6 of the ECHR. But senior judges have generally held firm against any attempt to suggest that performance management against clear and general targets which apply to all judges is a threat to judicial independence.

### *Individual performance*

Interventions by senior judges in cases where problems have arisen do not constitute a system of individual performance appraisal. Aside from some limited pilot schemes in the court judiciary described below, and a more developed system for tribunal judges, there is as yet no formal and systematic use of individual performance appraisal within the judiciary. Traditionally, arguments against individual appraisal centred on the fact that most judges' work is reviewable through the appellate system. It is true that appellate courts have from time to time criticised not just the substantive content, but also the manner, of the judicial work or the style of their judgments.[64] Such comments do not, however, trigger consequences in terms of performance management for individual judges. Thus, although the notion that the judges have been entirely free to conduct their work without any supervision or input is a myth, judges could until recently expect very little formal oversight of their work outside the appellate process, unless there was clear cause for concern about their performance. Even if serious problems were identified, a culture of non-intervention at times meant that the quality of justice was compromised. In a number of controversial instances,

[64] See, for example, the LCJ's criticism of the conduct of Peter Smith J in *Howell & Ors* v. *Lees Millais & Ors* [2007] EWCA Civ 720; and *Jones* v. *Jones* [2011] EWCA (Civ) 41, where the Court of Appeal criticised the judgment of Mr Justice Charles in a divorce case as being 'far too long, too discursive and too unwieldy'.

judges failed to produce judgments for many months, or even years, because of ill-health or incompetence before senior judges intervened.[65] There is now a process whereby the SPJ or relevant Head of Division must be notified by the deciding judge, with reasons, if a decision is or will be outstanding for more than three months (one month for cases involving children). This has helped to reduce the incidence of delayed judgments. Poor performance by judges will normally be addressed through a pastoral response (for example by reducing the workload of a judge in recognition of a health problem). Where there is no obvious reason for poor performance, the judge will be warned that a complaint will be made if his or her performance does not improve. These warnings have generally proved effective, but some judges who have received them have subsequently retired.

For some judges, a hands-off approach is to be welcomed. However, there is increasing acceptance amongst most judges that 'even if [they] start off as the model judge, it is easy to allow our standards to slide' and 'to acquire bad habits'.[66] As one senior District Judge noted, despite several years on the bench, 'No one has ever said "you're slow, you're too fast, you're appealed all the time, you're rude"'. Most recognise, in other words, that all judges can benefit from feedback on their interpersonal skills, listening skills and other skills of judge-craft. There is growing recognition that routine appraisal would not only increase public confidence in the judiciary, but also boost the confidence of individual judges, at least insofar as performance appraisal should emphasise strengths as well as identify weaknesses.[67] The growing acceptance of the need for appraisal is part of the larger shift within the judiciary from a culture of judicial individualism towards a culture of judicial corporatism where stress is placed on consistent standards of judicial professionalism. As one senior judge commented when explaining why appraisal does not endanger judicial independence, 'ensuring the consistency and quality of decision-making is just as much a judicial function as taking the particular decision in the individual case'. As the history of training demonstrates, the way to

[65] Perhaps the best-known example is the resignation of Mr Justice Harman in 1998 following criticism by the Court of Appeal for a twenty-month delay before judgment was given in a personal insolvency case. See *Goose* v. *Wilson Sandford & Co. (No.1)* (1998) 95 LSG. 27.

[66] Woolf, 'The Needs of a 21st Century Judge', p. 187.

[67] HL Constitution Committee, *Judicial Appointments* (HL 272 2012), paras. 181–2. This finding was also reflected in the results of our judicial interviews.

gain acceptance of judicial appraisal across the whole of the judiciary is to ensure that it is carried out by 'judges for judges', even though assessing the work of judges is a labour-intensive process.

Despite the growing acceptance of the potential value of performance appraisal, full-time judges still have no individual feedback on their performance. Deputy District Judges are the only judges within the courts judiciary who are subject to a formal appraisal system. The Deputy District Judge programme involves a full-time District Judge spending a day observing a Deputy in court and then providing feedback. Today, the barrier to the expansion of individual performance appraisal is not the risk that it might impinge on judicial independence, but the more practical problem of limited resources, in terms of both time and money. The judges who conduct the appraisals must themselves be trained and then conduct the appraisal, all of which is time away from their judicial work. A pilot scheme extending appraisal to Recorders on the northern circuit was instigated in 2003–4. It sought to reduce the impact on resources by using judges to read transcripts and listen to tapes of court hearings. But some judges were concerned that audio recordings were a poor substitute for observations of court proceedings and wanted appraising judges to be present in court. Despite these worries, the feedback on the pilot was good and the senior judiciary wanted to roll it out across the whole judiciary. But the cost was deemed by the Ministry of Justice to be prohibitively high and it was shelved. In 2014, a new pilot scheme was instituted, involving fifty Circuit Judges trained as appraisers. It was strongly supported by the Lord Chief Justice, Lord Thomas.

Three factors are driving this push towards individual performance appraisal across the judiciary. The first is the integration of tribunal judges within the larger judicial family. Tribunal judges are more accustomed to management of caseloads and oversight of individual performance than the court judges, and are less likely to see this in terms of a threat to independence.[68] The tribunals judiciary have developed guidance designed to foster consistency of appraisal practice and procedures across chambers and jurisdictions.[69] As one senior judge

[68] In 2001, Sir Andrew Leggatt had recommended that all tribunal chairmen and members should participate in an annual appraisal of their performance while sitting, and that tribunals should strive to recognise a culture of advancement through assessment: *Tribunals for Users – One System, One Series: Report of the Review of Tribunals* (London: TSO, 2001), para. 7.38.

[69] See, for example, Judicial Studies Board, *Appraisal Standards and Appraiser Competences in Tribunals* (2009).

noted, the tribunals judiciary brings with it a far less tolerant perspective on poor performance: 'tribunal users, in a non-deferential age, are not prepared to put up with judicial incompetence, inefficiency, insensitivity and so forth'. A second factor is the use of more specific and formal criteria in judicial appointments. The introduction of standards in appointment cannot be separated from judicial training, appraisal and discipline. As a senior judge commented, 'If you are going to appoint people by reference to competences, and train them by reference to competences, you want to know whether or not it's having any effect, so you need a process of some sort of appraisal'. Finally, it is difficult to see how collective appraisal through the monitoring of court performance data can develop without the creation of an individual appraisal process. Where weaknesses are identified in particular courts that relate to judicial rather than administrative working practices, then these can only be put right by addressing the problems in the performances of the individual judges working in those courts. The traditional response to judges who are underperforming – moving them sideways to a court where they can do less harm – is unlikely to be considered acceptable for much longer.

## Conclusion

The changes in judicial governance outlined in this chapter may not attract the same interest that equivalent root-and-branch reforms of the political branch of government would do, but their long-term impact is no less significant. The reforms set in train by the Constitutional Reform Act 2005, when combined with longer-term changes in the size and composition of the judiciary, have led to more formalised and centralised powers exercised by a more active judicial leadership supported by a new judicial civil service. This effect is to change the 'hidden wiring' of the judiciary in ways which are reshaping its external and internal relationships. This radical development has been achieved with remarkably little internal dissent and the senior judiciary has pulled off a difficult trick in bringing about an institutional shift towards greater corporatism while retaining a culture of individualism. Today the notion of the 'judicial family' remains strong, while in practice the system of internal governance is far more tightly managed and hierarchical.

It has helped that in most cases the changes have not come out of the blue. The origins of the greater emphasis on professionalism and more active management can be traced back to at least the 1980s. The current system is in some ways a hybrid, combining the expectation of individual judicial discretion when things go smoothly with the potential for strong line management if things go wrong. Senior judges understand that the public interest demands that old shibboleths employed to block the management, training and appraisal of judges must be rejected. Yet the creation myth of a flat judiciary in which each judge is an adjudicative island still serves an important function. At all levels judges are acutely alert to the danger of senior judges influencing substantive decision-making, as sometimes occurs in other judicial systems. Our study has shown no evidence of this happening. The line between judicial management, however hands-on, and judicial independence in adjudicative decision-making seems to be as clear as it ever was.

The office of Lord Chief Justice has been pivotal in the process of change, evolving from the head of a relatively small judicial family into the leader of a large corporate entity supported by its own small but expanding civil service. As the formal head of the judiciary, the LCJ has taken over from the Lord Chancellor as the buckle holding together the judiciary and linking it to the political institutions of the state. The new qualities required of the LCJ in order to fulfil these more outward-looking functions are in addition to, not a replacement for, those required for the traditional role since the office now combines both the old and the new aspects of the job. A consequence is that the ever-expanding management role is fast becoming unmanageable, however talented and energetic the individual office-holder. Moreover, the challenge of finding hours in the day and the requisite skills needed to fulfil the current responsibilities of the job of LCJ will seem even more demanding if the judiciary takes over the running of the courts service. If this happens a decision will have to be made as to whether the office of LCJ can continue in its current form or whether it needs to be broken up in some way and divided between two or more people. This will be unavoidable if the holders of the office remain committed to continue to sit in court on more than a token basis.

Either way, more of the burden will need to be shared with the senior management team. Already the members of the Judicial Executive Board and, to a lesser extent, the Judges' Council help to spread the load, and the work could not be done without the support of the Judicial Office. But ultimately the LCJ takes formal responsibility for almost all governance decisions that raise questions about the accountability of the judiciary in relation to its governance. Externally, we have identified both formal and informal lines of accountability from the LCJ and other senior judges to the executive and to Parliament. Appearances before select committees offer an important form of institutional accountability to Parliament, and, through Parliament, to the public. Periodic reports by the LCJ and annual reports on specific jurisdictions by Heads of Division are valuable resources for external scrutiny. The Judicial Office is funded by the Ministry, and is accountable to Parliament through the Ministry's Permanent Secretary. However, gaps remain. It is unclear to what extent the LCJ (and SPT) would have to account for serious maladministration within the Judicial Office – for example, if its staff had the highest rate of absenteeism across Whitehall or if an official lost sensitive information that subsequently appeared in the media. Strictly speaking, it would be for the Chief Executive of the Judicial Office to provide an explanation for such maladministration to the Permanent Secretary. In practice, it is difficult to see how the LCJ could avoid having to account, at some level, to the Lord Chancellor and to the public for serious failures inside the Judicial Office. In addition, judicial reporting is patchy and follows an unpredictable pattern. The LCJ's reviews of the administration of justice are not produced annually; rather, there have been only four since 2005. While the Judicial College produces annual reports and the Judicial Office publishes an annual business plan, the Judges' Council has not published an annual report since 2009. One further area in which there seems to be a considerable accountability gap concerns the new powers of appointment enjoyed by the LCJ for courts below the High Court. It remains to be seen what account will be given of this. At a minimum, the JAC should report exercises by the LCJ of the veto or referral powers, and the LCJ should in his or her annual report make a note of any use of these powers.

However the role of the LCJ and the senior management team develops, and whether or not the courts are run by the judiciary or an independent courts service, the move away from individualism and towards corporatism seems destined to continue. The effects of ongoing cuts in spending will be significant and the pressure to increase efficiency will be greater with increased scrutiny of judges' work. In addition, the inclusion of the tribunal judges within the larger judicial family will further promote a culture of corporatism. While some judges are critical of the moves towards more managerialism, most have been described to us as 'grudgingly accepting', if not positively supportive. Recently appointed judges, in particular, are more likely to value the increased support that they are now offered in doing a difficult and stressful job. Although there is still some nervousness around developments such as performance appraisal, the knee-jerk impulse to view it as an inherent threat to judicial independence now has less of a hold on the judicial mindset. The process of acculturation that judges went through in relation to training is likely to be repeated in the area of performance appraisal. But these cultural shifts take time and the accelerating pace of change can make it difficult for the judiciary to develop a collective long-term view. The reforms to the internal governance are a work in progress, described to us by one senior judge as a process of 'learning as we go on'.

In order to be prepared for further changes ahead, the judiciary will need to ensure that the senior judges who are appointed to positions of management have the skills and expertise to do the job. It is a lot to expect an individual who has excelled as a lawyer in practice and then as a judge in court to have, in addition, a third set of very different high-level management skills which can be produced, fully formed, in late middle age. The selection process for senior judges in leadership positions and the training offered to them once appointed must inevitably take more account of the need for personal skills and qualities. Moreover, where such rare, multi-talented individuals are identified, they are currently asked to fill positions like SPJ for three years, whereas a non-executive director of a large public company would be expected to serve for longer. If the length of time in post increases and the workload continues to grow, it may require a significant change of culture whereby senior judges in management positions acknowledge that this aspect of their role is not just a temporary period out of their day job, but is something closer to a career change.

There are also challenges ahead in relation to the Judicial Office. As it grows in size and expertise, the corresponding judiciary-related staff at the Ministry of Justice shrinks. There are questions about whether the JO should recruit from the MoJ, from the rest of the civil service or from elsewhere. There are also questions about how best to ensure that civil servants in the MoJ retain an appreciation of judicial independence. These questions are all the more important because of the relative retreat of new-style Lord Chancellors from judiciary-related matters. Continuing exchanges of staff between the JO and the MoJ will help to ensure that the MoJ understands the judiciary and judicial independence, and the JO understands the workings of Whitehall.

# 7

# Judicial appointments

Politics, in one sense or another, cannot be removed from judicial appointments. Decisions about whom to select as judges, and how to select them, inevitably have political dimensions, whether in terms of ideological politics, party politics, identity politics, regional politics or institutional politics.[1] The political dimensions will vary from country to country and through time,[2] but there will always be political aspects to the appointment of judges. This chapter charts the evolving politics of appointments in England and Wales (appointments to the UK Supreme Court are discussed in Chapter 8, and appointment processes in Scotland and Northern Ireland in Chapter 9). The old politics were played out on a relatively barren institutional landscape that remained largely untouched for much of the last century, with old-style Lord Chancellors exercising considerable discretion, aided by only a handful of officials and limited chiefly by a requirement to consult senior judges via secret soundings. The new politics unfold on a complex and changing landscape populated by familiar actors performing unfamiliar roles and new bodies tasked with new roles, most obviously the Judicial Appointments Commission (JAC) responsible for selecting candidates for appointment to judicial office.

The essential dynamic of the new politics is the marginalisation of the new-style Lord Chancellors and the high levels of influence by senior judges over judicial appointments. We trace the relative retreat of successive Lord Chancellors, not only from the running of the appointments system as a whole but also from much meaningful involvement in individual appointments. We explain how one consequence of this is that despite

[1] G. Gee, 'The Persistent Politics of Judicial Selection: A Comparative Analysis', in A. Seibert-Fohr (ed.), *Judicial Independence in Transition* (New York and Heidelberg: Springer, 2012), p. 121.

[2] See, for example, G. Gee, 'The Politics of Judicial Appointments in Canada', in *Judicial Appointments: Balancing Independence, Accountability and Legitimacy* (London: Judicial Appointments Commission, 2010).

being created as a recommending body charged merely with identifying suitable candidates for the bench, the JAC now effectively operates as an appointing body, albeit within a detailed statutory scheme that has considerable judicial influence designed into it. Yet, as we explain, the new politics of appointments is not reducible to linear stories of judicial influence rising as political influence wanes, or to straightforward narratives about an increasingly confident JAC evolving into a *de facto* appointing body – it is much more complex than this. Although they have been relatively marginalised, successive Lord Chancellors and officials in the Ministry of Justice have acted in concert with the senior judiciary to minimise the JAC's ability to shape the policy framework on appointments, including the diversity agenda. The Ministry and senior judges have succeeded in emphasising instead the JAC's role as a recruitment agency that must respond to the business needs of the judicial system as determined by the Ministry, HM Courts and Tribunals Service (HMCTS) and the Lord Chief Justice (LCJ).

## Judicial appointments in the twentieth century

Judicial appointments in the twentieth century were characterised by stability, secrecy and informality. At the heart of a system regulated largely by non-legal conventions were the old-style Lord Chancellors, who enjoyed considerable discretion; or what an interviewee called 'a controlling hand'.[3] Strictly speaking, the Lord Chancellor decided all appointments up to the High Court, with more senior appointments made by the Prime Minister, acting on the advice of the Lord Chancellor. In light of their legal backgrounds and role as head of the judiciary, the old Lord Chancellors were said to be uniquely positioned to assess individual candidates, many of whom might be personally known to them. They were assisted by officials in the Lord Chancellor's Department, which had a distinctly legal character (see Chapter 3). By the 1990s, the growing size of the judiciary and an expanding ministerial remit led successive Lord Chancellors to rely heavily on officials to consider the details of individual appointments. The Permanent Secretary canvassed opinions about candidates from judges and barristers and subsequently at monthly meetings the Lord Chancellor consulted senior judges. 'Secret soundings' gave the senior judges

[3] See D. Woodhouse, *The Office of Lord Chancellor* (Oxford: Hart Publishing, 2001), pp. 133–62; R. Stevens, *The Independence of the Judiciary: The View from the Lord Chancellor's Office* (Oxford: Clarendon Press, 1993); G. Drewry, 'Judicial Appointments' [1998] *Public Law* 1.

considerable sway. Only rarely would Lord Chancellors depart from the judicial view.[4] Opinions sometimes differed among senior judges, but most appointments reflected 'the dominant school of thought among the senior judges', as a former official put it.

The result was a ministerial model with a mix of political, legal and judicial influences, in which appointments were formally made by or on the advice of the Lord Chancellor, but with departmental officials and the senior judges exercising considerable influence behind the scenes. By mid-century, most accepted that appointments were made on merit, with no weight attached to partisan considerations. The practice of appointing MPs and even ministers who had maintained close connections between the worlds of law and politics had largely ceased, which helps explain why appointments to even the highest positions attracted little interest outside the legal realm.[5] Cheap and efficient, this process was nevertheless criticised for its informality, secrecy and dependence on old-boy networks. Until the late 1990s, the process had been distinguished by the lack of advertisements, job descriptions, application forms, formal interviews and selection criteria. So secretive and informal was it that even candidates were not always aware that their name was under consideration until receiving a 'tap on the shoulder'.[6] High levels of judicial influence in an informal system translated into judicial self-replication, with those appointed being invariably white, male barristers, who had been privately educated and were from advantaged social backgrounds.

Lack of progress on increasing diversity – and not just in terms of women, minorities and those from less privileged backgrounds, but also in terms of the need to appoint more solicitors and lawyers from non-commercial practices – was one of the main driving forces for change.[7]

[4] One notable exception was in 1996 when the Lord Chancellor appointed Lord Bingham as LCJ against the wishes of senior judges, including the outgoing LCJ. Seventeen judges of the Court of Appeal wrote to the Lord Chancellor, and the LCJ requested a meeting with the Prime Minister. The Lord Chancellor withstood this pressure and Bingham was appointed. See J. Rozenberg, *Trial of Strength: A Battle between Ministers and Judges over Who Makes the Law* (London: Richard Cohen, 1997), pp. 13–17.

[5] R. Stevens, *The English Judges: Their Role in the Changing Constitution* (Oxford: Hart Publishing, 2005), pp. 95–6.

[6] See P. Darbyshire, *Sitting in Judgment: The Working Lives of Judges* (Oxford: Hart Publishing, 2011), pp. 90–5.

[7] See, generally, K. Malleson, 'Prospects for Parity: The Position of Women in the Judiciary in England and Wales', in G. Shaw and U. Schultz (eds.), *Women in the World's Legal Professions* (Oxford: Hart Publishing, 2003), p. 175; K. Malleson, 'Promoting Diversity in the Judiciary: Reforming the Judicial Appointments Process', in P. Thomas (ed.), *Discriminating Lawyers* (London: Cavendish, 2000), p. 221.

Following an independent review, a new scrutinising body known as the Commission for Judicial Appointments (CJA) was established in 2001,[8] with a remit to audit the appointment process, recommend improvements to it and serve as a complaints body. The CJA was not charged with running the appointment process itself, which remained in the hands of the Lord Chancellor. Although the then Lord Chancellor, Lord Irvine, sought to promote promising barristers from non-traditional backgrounds, the CJA in 2002 identified serious and chronic problems, criticising the self-replicating nature of the process and consequent failure to increase diversity, and characterised the use of 'soundings' as a cover for sexism. It therefore recommended creating a new process centred around an independent appointments body.[9] In 2003, the Labour government conceded that tackling diversity required 'fresh approaches' involving a 'major re-engineering of the process for appointment'.[10]

A second driver of change was the Blair government's programme of constitutional reform. Devolution embraced judicial selection processes outside England and Wales: the Justice (Northern Ireland) Act 2002 had outlined a framework for creating an independent appointments commission for Northern Ireland,[11] while a year later the Judicial Appointments Board for Scotland was established.[12] The proposal to replace a ministerial model of judicial appointments in England and Wales with one based on the recommendations of an independent commission thus followed the precedents in Scotland and Northern Ireland. Viewed in this wider context, the 2005 reforms have greater coherence than is generally recognised. The perception that the reforms were drawn up on the back of an envelope arose due to their clumsy introduction and in particular the abrupt dismissal of Lord Irvine and the failure by 10 Downing Street to consult senior judges. Out of sight, the Lord Chancellor's Department had anticipated the pressure for change, preparing contingency plans for a new system involving an independent appointments body many years before this was adopted as government

[8] L. Peach, *Independent Scrutiny of the Appointments Processes of Judges and Queen's Counsel* (London: Lord Chancellor's Department, 1999).

[9] See Q. 1 of HC Constitutional Affairs Committee, *Judicial Appointments and a Supreme Court (Court of Final Appeal): Evidence of Sir Colin Campbell* (HC 1275-i 2003).

[10] Department of Constitutional Affairs, *Constitutional Reform: A New Way of Appointing Judges* (CP 10/03 2003), para. 28.

[11] Justice (Northern Ireland) Act 2002, section 3.

[12] See A. Paterson, 'The Scottish Judicial Appointments Board: New Wine in Old Bottles', in K. Malleson and P. Russell (eds.), *Appointing Judges in an Age of Judicial Power: Critical Perspectives from around the World* (Toronto: University of Toronto Press, 2006), p. 13.

policy. But the lack of consultation by Downing Street led to fears that the reforms were the government's effort to tame a judiciary that had evolved into an important check on governmental power.[13] However, the opposite was nearer the truth. Irvine was dismissed in part because of his reluctance to cede power to an appointments body, while the Concordat negotiations, led on the judicial side by Lord Woolf, helped to ensure that the Constitutional Reform Act achieved a fundamental shift of power away from the government by constructing a wholly new institutional architecture of judicial selection built around the JAC.

## The Judicial Appointments Commission

The JAC is an independent body responsible for identifying candidates for judicial office in courts and tribunals in England and Wales as well as in certain tribunals whose jurisdictions extend to Scotland or Northern Ireland. It manages a long and highly formalised selection process involving advertising, short-listing by tests or paper sifts, interviews and, for some posts, presentations or role-playing. It was created, despite its name, as a recommending body that makes initial selections for judicial office, with the final say whether or not to appoint made by another decision-making authority.[14] However, our findings indicate that the JAC effectively functions more akin to an appointing body. Initially, the JAC only made recommendations to the Lord Chancellor, identifying a single name for each vacancy.[15] The Lord Chancellor could accept or reject this recommendation, or request its reconsideration.[16] In practice, Lord Chancellors almost always accepted the recommendation, with only five occasions from nearly 3,500 recommendations between 2006 and 2013 when this was not so.

Following changes under the Crime and Courts Act 2013, the JAC now makes recommendations to one of three decision-makers who have the ultimate say whether or not to appoint. For most tribunal positions the recommendation is made to the Senior President of Tribunals (SPT).[17]

[13] See, for example, Lord Alexander, 'Is This a Ruthless Grab for Power?' *The Times*, 1 July 2003.

[14] See, generally, K. Malleson, 'Creating a Judicial Appointments Commission: Which Model Works Best?' [2004] *Public Law* 102.

[15] Constitutional Reform Act 2005, section 70(3).

[16] CRA, sections 67–74 and 76–85.

[17] Crime and Courts Act 2013, Schedule 13, para. 30. The only exceptions are appointments outside the first-tier and upper tribunal structure (e.g. Employment Tribunals) where the appointment power remains with the Lord Chancellor.

For courts below the High Court, recommendations are made to the LCJ[18] and for appointments to the High Court recommendations are made to the Lord Chancellor.[19] Separate processes not directly under the JAC's auspices apply for top appointments: the Court of Appeal, Heads of Division and LCJ. The Lord Chancellor has the final say, formally, over these top appointments. We consider the processes in more detail below. The key point is that a highly informal system in which ministerial discretion was lightly regulated by non-legal conventions has been replaced with a formal statutory scheme in which the Lord Chancellor is entirely removed from lower-level appointments and where ministerial discretion for top appointments is, in practice, exceptionally limited.

Making around 600 to 700 recommendations for appointment each year, the JAC has a heavy workload, especially compared to equivalent bodies in Scotland and Northern Ireland.[20] Partly for this reason, it has a relatively large membership by international standards.[21] Commissioners are recruited in an open competition run by the Ministry, except for three senior judicial members who are nominated by the Judges' Council.[22] The commissioners are typically appointed for renewable terms of two or three years, though terms can be for up to five years, subject to a maximum service of ten years.[23] The commissioners shape the JAC's strategy as well as recommend candidates. The JAC's composition is regulated by primary and secondary legislation, with the Lord Chancellor able to alter it with the agreement of the LCJ, provided that there remain more commissioners who do not hold judicial office than those who do.[24]

Striking a suitable balance on an appointments commission between judicial, legal and lay representation is inevitably tricky. As of late 2013, there were fifteen commissioners: seven holding judicial office, six lay members and two legal practitioners.[25] The Chair must be a layperson,

[18] CCA 2013, Schedule 13, para. 29.

[19] CRA, sections 67–74 and 76–85.

[20] The Judicial Appointments Board for Scotland and the Northern Ireland Judicial Appointments Commission make around twenty-seven and forty appointments respectively per year.

[21] K. Malleson, 'The Judicial Appointments Commission in England and Wales: New Wine in New Bottles?' in Malleson and Russell (eds.), *Appointing Judges in an Age of Judicial Power*, p. 48.

[22] The Judicial Appointments Commission Regulations 2013, regs. 9 and 10. The JAC Chair sits on the panels to recruit new Commissioners, and the process is regulated by the Commissioner for Public Appointments.

[23] JAC Regulations 2013, reg. 17.

[24] Schedule 12 to the CRA, Schedule 12, para. 1, as amended by the CCA 2013.

[25] JAC Regulations, reg. 4(1).

which is intended to protect against the risk of excessive judicial influence. Non-judicial members outnumber their judicial counterparts.[26] However, there remains a strong judicial presence, with more judicial than lay commissioners. Commissioners who are judges or practitioners outnumber their lay counterparts and, taken together, form a majority on the JAC. Including lay members was seen as a way of incorporating fresh perspectives on selection processes and as a safeguard against the sort of judicial self-replication that was a feature of the pre-2005 system. Whether they are an effective check in practice against the risk of excessive judicial influence is a matter to which we return below. In comparative terms, the JAC's composition is similar to that of the Northern Ireland Judicial Appointments Commission (NIJAC), where there are six judges, two practitioners and five laypeople. A key difference, however, is that the Lord Chief Justice for Northern Ireland chairs NIJAC. Lay representation on the JAC compares less favourably with the Judicial Appointments Board for Scotland (JABS), where the number of lay members must equal judicial and practitioner members, and the chair must be one of the lay members. With five laypeople, three judges and two practitioners, JABS has the strongest lay representation, and the requirement for an equal number of lay members as judicial and practitioner members is recognition of the likelihood that judges and practitioners will share similar impulses.[27] As we recount in Chapter 9, the high level of lay involvement on JABS was strongly resisted by the Scottish judiciary and has been a running sore ever since.

### *Relations with the Ministry of Justice*

The JAC is an executive non-departmental public body, operating at arm's length from, but within a strategic framework set by, the Ministry of Justice. This relationship is defined formally by legislation and a Framework Document,[28] but also, as with so many of the institutional relationships explored in this book, informally by one-to-one personal relationships. The JAC's lay Chair is accountable to the Lord Chancellor for formulating a strategy to deliver the JAC's main objective of selecting candidates for judicial office. The first Chair was Baroness Usha Prashar, a

[26] In 2013 the two practitioner commissioners were also part-time judges.

[27] See, generally, J. Allan, 'Judicial Appointments in New Zealand: If It Were Done When 'Tis Done, Then 'Twere Well It Were Done Openly and Directly', in Malleson and Russell (eds.), *Appointing Judges in an Age of Judicial Power*, p. 103.

[28] See Ministry of Justice, Framework Document: Ministry of Justice and the Judicial Appointments Commission (2012).

former Civil Service Commissioner, who was succeeded in 2011 by Christopher Stephens, another former Civil Service Commissioner who also had significant experience in human resources in the private sector. The Chair has overall responsibility for ensuring that the JAC's policies support the Lord Chancellor's strategic objectives, but it is the Chief Executive who is responsible for the everyday running of the JAC and managing its staff, which, as of late 2013, numbered around sixty-five.[29] The Chief Executive is appointed by the JAC, but his or her appointment must also be approved by the Lord Chancellor.[30] As accounting officer, the Chief Executive is responsible to Parliament for the efficient use of the JAC's resources.[31]

In its short history, the JAC's relationship with the Ministry has been turbulent, with the years 2006 to 2010 being defined by a series of clashes over both policy and personality. From its very beginning, the JAC had a tense relationship with the Ministry's predecessor, the Department for Constitutional Affairs (DCA). In 2006, when it assumed day-to-day responsibility for appointments, it encountered several challenges: financial, workload and staffing.[32] On top of a 5 per cent budget cut in its first year, the JAC had to manage different types of selection exercise. In its early years, it was responsible not only for selection exercises under the new processes introduced by the Constitutional Reform Act, but also for exercises already under way under the old processes run by the DCA. One practical effect of managing selection exercises under multiple processes without any transition period, at the same time as introducing budget savings, was to remove much opportunity for the JAC to take stock and devise its own procedures. Another effect was delays in actually appointing judges, a problem exacerbated by the lack of reliable forecasting from HMCTS as to the level of vacancies likely to arise in any year. Delays prompted criticism initially from judges and practitioners.[33] Most of the

[29] Judicial Appointments Commission, *Annual Report and Accounts 2011–12* (HC 351 2012) 24.

[30] Constitutional Reform Act 2005, Schedule 12, para. 22(2).

[31] Ministry of Justice, Framework Document: Ministry of Justice and the Judicial Appointments Commission (2012), para. 3.2.

[32] Baroness Prashar, 'Translating Aspirations into Reality: Establishing the Judicial Appointments Commission', in *Judicial Appointments: Balancing Independence, Accountability and Legitimacy* (London: Judicial Appointments Commission, 2010), pp. 46–7.

[33] On the problems experienced by the JAC by lack of proper forecasting from HCMTS, see S. Shetreet and S. Turenne, *Judges on Trial: The Independence and Accountability of the English Judiciary* (Cambridge: Cambridge University Press, 2013), p. 113.

JAC's staff was seconded from the DCA. Secondments were essential given the JAC's inherited responsibility for exercises run under the DCA's processes, but, according to several of our interviewees, were also a source of tension, with some former DCA staff wedded to the traditional system of selecting judges. With criticism from judges, the legal profession and departmental officials, and even from some of its staff, the JAC's first tranche of commissioners felt that they faced 'hostility and suspicion from everyone'.

In the DCA, there was a widely shared feeling that the government had 'responsibility without influence' and that it had 'traded control for nothing terribly visible in return', as two senior officials put it. Formally, the Lord Chancellor was accountable to Parliament for the performance and activities of the JAC; he determined its strategic goals and approved the terms and conditions of its staff, including commissioners, Chair and Chief Executive.[34] In practice, the DCA felt that it had little control over appointments. By the time Jack Straw was appointed Lord Chancellor in 2007, frustration was growing in what was now the Ministry of Justice, especially over the limited ministerial input into the appointment of senior judges, who, as leaders of the justice system, need to engage closely with the government. Although involved at the outset of the process in preparing the vacancy request sent to the JAC which specifies the number and location of posts and the eligibility requirements, there was unease inside the department that at the end of the process the Lord Chancellor was presented with only a single name for each vacancy, with only a very limited right to reject or request reconsideration of that candidate. There was a feeling that the Lord Chancellor no longer had a real choice. Adding to the frustrations was Straw's eagerness to increase diversity on the bench and his belief that the JAC had not made sufficient progress on this, which in turn contributed to a view inside the Ministry that the JAC was inefficient.

### *The JAC's 'near-death experience'*

It is a measure of how quickly unease escalated that the DCA carried out two reviews of the architecture of appointments within the first two years of the JAC's birth, with a total of seven reviews of one type or another

[34] See Department of Constitutional Affairs, *The Judicial Appointments Commission: Framework Document* (2006).

between 2006 and 2012.[35] At least some of the tensions can be explained by competing visions of the JAC's role. By 2007, the Ministry envisaged the JAC as a recruitment agency whose primary responsibility was to respond to the workforce requirements of the judiciary as assessed by the Ministry, HMCTS and the senior judiciary. The JAC's leadership emphasised its role in shaping policy on appointments and driving forward the diversity agenda in particular. These competing visions surfaced in tensions over how the JAC should approach certain critical aspects of the selection processes. Tensions were also born of an increasingly widespread view inside the Ministry that the JAC was too large and expensive and that its processes were too bureaucratic, slow and cumbersome. Within the Ministry, the JAC was widely seen as insufficiently responsive to the concerns and criticisms of the judiciary and the legal professions. Personality clashes inflamed these tensions, with an especially toxic relationship between the JAC's first Chair, Baroness Prashar, and the Ministry of Justice's Permanent Secretary, Sir Suma Chakrabarti. As several interviewees noted, there was a 'very poor relationship' and 'a confrontational attitude on both sides'. Strained personal relationships contributed to criticism heard inside the Ministry that the JAC's leadership was defensive and inflexible, an impression cemented by the Chair and Chief Executive's resistance to a further review in 2010 to examine the JAC's value for money and responsiveness.

Our interviews disclosed that confidence reached such a low point around 2009–10 that the Ministry considered abolishing the JAC outright and bringing appointments back in-house, or alternatively delegating most of the responsibility for appointments to the senior judges. Ultimately, the Ministry concluded that 'the politics of abolishing the JAC were too difficult' and that the best solution was, as an official summed it up, 'to replace the JAC's leadership rather than replace the JAC itself'. Baroness Prashar

[35] These were: (a) the Nooney Review (2007), an internal review of JAC processes with the stated intention of increasing efficiency; (b) the LEAN Review (2008), a further internal review of JAC processes with the stated intention of increasing efficiency; (c) the Constitutional Renewal Bill (2008), later the Constitutional Reform and Governance Bill, where draft clauses that sought to give the Lord Chancellor further controls over the JAC were later removed; (d) the Advisory Panel on Judicial Diversity (2010), established by Jack Straw and led by Baroness Neuberger to examine ways of improving diversity in judicial appointments; (e) End-to-End Review of the Appointment Process (2010), established by the Ministry of Justice; (f) the Constitution Committee's Inquiry into Judicial Appointments (announced in 2011 and reported in 2012); and (g) the Ministry's Consultation Paper on judicial appointments (2011), which culminated in the Crime and Courts Act 2013.

was encouraged to step down as Chair four months before her first term of office expired, around the same time as the JAC's first Chief Executive also left her position. These changes did not immediately secure the JAC's future, however, and in late 2010 the JAC experienced another 'near-death experience', as one official memorably described it. The JAC was included in Schedule 7 of the Public Bodies Bill, which purported to empower, but not require, ministers to restructure or abolish a range of non-departmental bodies. This was a Cabinet Office Bill, with the JAC included in Schedule 7 alongside many other bodies that were subsequently removed from it. The Ministry knew ahead of time that the JAC was to be included in the Bill and warned the Cabinet Office that there would be 'an enormous fuss'. This is what occurred, with senior judges fearing that the JAC's inclusion was evidence of the clear intention at some point in the future to dismantle the new architecture of appointments. The LCJ objected to the Lord Chancellor and representatives from the Law Society and the Bar Council objected publicly. The private intervention by the LCJ, public response by professional associations and the response of prominent peers ensured a rapid reprieve, with the JAC subsequently removed from the Public Bodies Bill.

Relations began to improve in 2011, with Christopher Stephens appointed as the new Chair and Nigel Reeder as a new Chief Executive. Both were more willing to consider how the JAC might become a leaner, cheaper and nimbler operation, working hard to foster more fruitful relationships with the Ministry and judiciary.[36] Occupying what an official characterised as 'a less distressed environment', the ability of the JAC's new leadership to nurture constructive relationships was aided by the resolution of most of the JAC's early teething problems. This coincided with Kenneth Clarke's tenure as Lord Chancellor, during which time much less emphasis was placed by the Ministry on the need for meaningful ministerial involvement in appointments, and more stress on cutting the JAC's size and cost. Clarke described his involvement in appointments to the lower ranks of the judiciary as 'largely ceremonial and ritualistic' – in other words, he went through the motions of reviewing candidates about whom he knew little or nothing.[37] This view informed the policy behind the Crime and

[36] For example, the JAC's budget was reduced by 16 per cent between 2006 and 2013, with its staff reduced from 109 full-time equivalent staff to 79 over the same period: see Judicial Appointments Commission, *Annual Report and Accounts: 2006–7* (HC 632 2007); *Annual Report and Accounts: 2012–13* (HC 495 2013).

[37] See Q. 373 of his evidence to HL Constitution Committee, *Judicial Appointments* (HL 272 2012).

Courts Act 2013 that limited the Lord Chancellor's role to deciding on appointments to the High Court and above, with responsibility for most lower-level tribunal and court appointments passed to the Senior Presiding Judge (SPJ) and LCJ respectively. An illustration of the Ministry's relative retreat was the transfer of its Judicial Appointments Division to the Judicial Office in late 2011. The fifty or so people who had been working on judicial policy in the Ministry in May 2010 had been reduced to around a dozen.

Today, the JAC's relationship with the Ministry is 'as different as night and day', as one interviewee put it. At one level, the struggle between the JAC and the Ministry might appear to have been won by the former. The Ministry's role was, after all, in effect limited to providing support to the Lord Chancellor for whatever residual role he retained in appointments – a role that had been further reduced by the Crime and Courts Act 2013. Day-to-day operations were to be driven by the JAC and the Judicial Office. The Crime and Courts Act has brought more selections within the JAC's remit; for example, deputy High Court judges.[38] It also extended the JAC's involvement in senior appointments. All of this suggests that the JAC occupies a much more stable institutional position. At another level, the JAC might not have been abolished, but it was battle-scarred. Not only was its first leadership effectively forced out early, but most of its first commissioners had been replaced. By extending some commissioners' terms by a single year the Ministry ensured that the majority of the commissioners' terms concluded by early 2012, with a new tranche of commissioners appointed in their place.[39] However, from 2011 the Ministry was in effect dealing with an almost entirely new JAC with new leadership and a new slate of commissioners. This had real consequences insofar as the JAC, in its second phase, seemed less willing to challenge the Ministry, as we explain below.

## JAC selection exercises

So far we have been talking about the new selection processes in general terms, but the devil is in the detail. The sections that follow consider various processes in more depth. We make two main claims. First, there have been important changes in the JAC's approach to key aspects of the selection process during 2006–10 (under its first leadership and first tranche of commissioners) and from 2011 (under its new leadership

[38] Senior Courts Act 1981, section 9 (as amended).
[39] Judicial Appointments Commission, *Annual Report and Accounts 2011–12*, 14.

and new commissioners). The changes suggest that the Ministry's vision of the JAC as a recruitment agency operating on the instructions of the Ministry, HMCTS and the senior judiciary has prevailed over the competing vision favoured by the JAC's first leadership, that stressed the JAC's role in shaping appointments policies in ways that advanced the diversity agenda. In short, the JAC seems less keen to shape the broader policy framework on appointments. Our second claim is that JAC-run processes are characterised by excessively high levels of judicial influence.

### *Pre-selection*

The JAC runs the selection exercises for vacancies up to the High Court. An exercise is triggered when the Lord Chancellor sends a vacancy request to the JAC, which may concern more than one vacancy.[40] Before issuing a request, the Lord Chancellor must consult with the LCJ.[41] This consultation focuses on details of the job description, and in particular whether the Lord Chancellor should specify additional non-statutory eligibility criteria concerning the qualifications, expertise and experience needed for a particular post. Typical is a requirement that candidates applying for a salaried role have fee-paid experience (i.e. experience of sitting in a part-time judicial role while continuing in their day job, for example as a solicitor or barrister).

Between 2006 and 2011, the Lord Chancellor's use of additional selection criteria was the subject of fractious negotiation between the JAC, the Ministry and HMCTS. For the Ministry and HMCTS, there is a 'business need' to ensure that specific posts are filled by those 'best able to do the job'.[42] Requiring those appointed to full-time positions to have prior part-time judicial experience renders it more likely not only that successful applicants will have a good grasp of what judicial office entails, but also that they will require less 'on-the-job' training from the resource-strapped Judicial College. Selecting someone for a salaried judicial office is effectively making an appointment for life, and it is vital that the person appointed is capable of performing the role. The Ministry and HMCTS wanted appointees who could hit the ground running. The senior judges supported the Ministry and HMCTS, arguing that only those responsible

40 Constitutional Reform Act 2005, section 87(3).

41 CRA, section 87(2).

42 Ministry of Justice, *The Governance of Britain: Judicial Appointments* (CP 25/07 2007) 100.

for running the judicial system could determine their business needs, unlike the JAC, which the LCJ likened to a 'recruitment agency' which ought to 'respond to the needs of the clients' business'.[43] The JAC countered that the additional criteria narrowed the pool of eligible candidates and jeopardised its efforts to increase diversity.[44] Candidates from non-traditional backgrounds (solicitors in city firms or high-street practices, for example) might not be able to sit in part-time judicial posts while continuing with their day jobs. So often did the JAC challenge the Ministry over the additional criteria that 'all hell would let loose', resulting in 'trench warfare', as one official put it.

In a sea change from its first few years, since 2011 the JAC has generally accepted the Lord Chancellor's additional selection criteria, only challenging the Ministry over it once or twice a year. As the JAC sees it, there is still flexibility to select a strong exceptional candidate who has gained the relevant skills in some other significant way. This is evidenced by the fact that a small number of candidates without any fee-paid experience have been appointed. However, the JAC no longer challenges the Ministry over the use of additional criteria as frequently or forcefully as it did before. Under its new leadership, the prevailing opinion on the JAC, according to one lay commissioner, is that the criteria 'invariably make good sense', even if they 'might make progress on the diversity agenda more difficult', as a second lay commissioner conceded. There are at least two readings of this. The first is that the JAC's reluctance to confront the Ministry over the criteria is evidence that the earlier clashes tamed the JAC. The JAC's reluctance to persuade the Ministry that it should have a say in deciding whether additional selection criteria are appropriate could be evidence that the Ministry's vision of the JAC as a recruitment agency has prevailed over a view that stressed the JAC's statutory duty to have regard to the need to encourage diversity in the range of persons available for selection.[45] Alternatively, the JAC's new approach could be evidence of its maturing, with the commissioners now more conscious of the resource implications of selecting people who cannot be immediately deployed. The judges on the JAC have succeeded in 'injecting some realism' into their fellow commissioners' views. On this second reading, the commissioners now

[43] See Joint Committee on the Draft Constitutional Renewal Bill, *Draft Constitutional Renewal Bill* (HL 166-I/HC 551-I 2008), para. 174.

[44] Prashar, 'Translating Aspirations into Reality: Establishing the Judicial Appointments Commission', p. 45.

[45] Constitutional Reform Act 2005, section 64(1).

recognise that the Lord Chancellor, in consultation with the LCJ, must have the final say on whether a vacancy requires additional criteria.

### *Short-listing and selection days*

Once the application date has closed, the JAC compiles a short list, through either a qualifying test designed to assess the qualities and abilities required for judicial office or a paper sift.[46] In addition to a reference from someone chosen by the candidate, the JAC requires a reference from a list of specified referees specifically tailored for each exercise, usually judges and leading practitioners in the jurisdiction. Short-listed candidates attend a selection day, which usually comprises an interview, presentation, situational questions replicating challenges of the sort that can arise in judicial work, or role-playing. A three-person panel oversees the selection day: a lay chair, another layperson and a judge from the jurisdiction to which a vacancy relates. The laypeople are selected from a list of lay panellists maintained by the JAC. The panel prepares a report for the commissioners in which each candidate is awarded an overall grade.

The JAC's Chair designates one of the commissioners to oversee the running of each selection exercise and to report the results to the other commissioners. The designated commissioner plans, monitors and moderates the exercise, but usually plays no direct part in either the short-listing or the selection day. An exception is for selections to the High Court, where up to two commissioners are involved in short-listing and interviewing candidates, depending on the number of vacancies to be filled.[47] Unlike in Scotland and Northern Ireland, where all of JABS and NIJAC members are closely involved in every selection, the JAC's workload is so large that most of the commissioners are not involved in short-listing, interviewing or the initial grading of the candidates in the vast majority of selection exercises. One consequence is to confer considerable influence on the selection panels. In the JAC's early years, there were concerns about these panels. Some of the JAC's first commissioners whom we interviewed pointed to the risk of excessive judicial influence on the panels, even though two of three panellists are laypeople. According to two judicial commissioners, it was difficult for

[46] In exceptional circumstances, such as for very small selection exercises, the JAC may not short-list and instead all eligible candidates are invited to the selection day. See Judicial Appointments Commission, *Annual Report and Accounts 2011–12*, 68.

[47] Another exception is for the post of Common Serjeant at the Central Criminal Court.

lay panellists to disagree with 'powerful and robust' judicial panellists. One commissioner commented that 'it was clear that judicial members could, if they chose, influence the outcome'. In 2011, the JAC invested time and money in refreshing and training its cadre of lay panellists.[48] The JAC today observes a large number of panels and speaks to judicial members if they are felt to have dominated a panel's deliberations. Our interviews suggest that there is no longer any concern about the general quality of the selection panels.

### *Statutory consultation*

Before making a recommendation, the JAC must consult with the LCJ for a vacancy in the High Court and, for lower-level appointments, another judge who has relevant experience.[49] Prior to the Crime and Courts Act 2013, the JAC had to consult the LCJ and another judge with relevant experience before making *all* of its recommendations, irrespective of the level of appointment. This has changed, reflecting the fact that the LCJ is now the final decision-maker for lower-level court appointments (and the SPT for tribunal appointments). This process is known as statutory consultation. There is no requirement for the commissioners to follow the views expressed by consultees, but they must give reasons if they do not do so.[50] Our interviews suggest that statutory consultation carries substantial weight. Most commissioners stressed that the quality of the views received in statutory consultation can vary, and that the JAC only relies on 'evidence-based' views; for example, if a consultee reveals that a currently serving judge is unable to manage their lists. For lower-level appointments, senior consultees frequently make no comments. Where comments are made, they are usually positive, and only in a small minority of cases is something negative said. The commissioners we interviewed agreed that the weight ascribed to the views of consultees 'increases exponentially with the seniority of the post'. This means that there is 'real potency' to statutory consultation when opinions are given by senior judges about applicants for the High Court. As discussed in Chapter 6, there is no appraisal process for most judges. The views of senior judges with experience of a candidate's work are thus 'very

[48] Judicial Appointments Commission, *Annual Report and Accounts 2011–12*, 14.

[49] Constitutional Reform Act 2005, section 88. Prior to the Crime and Courts Act 2013, the JAC was required to consult on every recommendation with the LCJ, plus another judge with relevant experience.

[50] CRA, section 89(2).

important' in the absence of appraisal information, as one of the lay commissioners explained.

The Lord Chancellor is unlikely to accept recommendations from the JAC that are at odds with the view expressed by a senior judicial consultee. In 2010, the Ministry told the JAC that the then Lord Chancellor, Kenneth Clarke, would not appoint anyone who had not first been endorsed by the LCJ in statutory consultation. Unsurprisingly, the JAC rarely proceeds with a recommendation that is out of line with the results of statutory consultation. According to one commissioner, there are usually one or two occasions each year when a senior consultee states clearly that a candidate should not be appointed. Interviewees stressed that the JAC may still recommend an exceptional candidate even in the face of the negative opinion of a senior judge, but only after seriously considering that opinion. At the same time, our interviewees struggled to state how often the JAC had done so. One commissioner could not recall any occasion, another said that 'it hardly happens', while a third said that it had only happened once or twice over three years. This implies that statutory consultation very occasionally operates as a *de facto* veto, at least on the small handful of occasions each year when the LCJ or another senior judicial consultee expresses a strongly negative view about a candidate.

Once again, there seem to be different approaches to statutory consultation between the JAC's first and second slate of commissioners. The first tranche were described by an official as being 'more bold' about proceeding with a recommendation that was at odds with statutory consultation, whereas more recently appointed commissioners are said to be more cautious. This can be interpreted as further evidence that the Ministry succeeded in its drive to reshape the JAC into a recruitment agency that responds to the business needs of the justice system as calculated by the Ministry, HMCTS and the senior judiciary. It may also be that the JAC's new leadership team places more emphasis than did their predecessors on the *statutory* nature of the consultation: the fact that statute requires the JAC to consult towards the end of the selection process could be taken to reflect Parliament's intent that substantial weight be attached to the views of the senior judges. Between 2006 and 2010, some commissioners were critical of senior judges using statutory consultation as 'a second bite of the cherry' to influence the JAC's recommendation. Today, there is said to be a shared understanding between the JAC, the senior judges and the Ministry that statutory consultation is an opportunity for a judicial consultee to provide information that is not likely to have been disclosed in the selection process, including information of the 'skeletons-in-the-cupboard variety' that might make individuals unsuitable for judicial office. Where a consultee discloses information of this sort, the JAC will take steps to verify its accuracy.

There seems to be a more widely shared understanding of the purpose of statutory consultation. However, one commissioner, who felt that statutory consultation has 'disproportionate influence', suggested that some (but not all) senior judges who were consultees had grown 'more sophisticated in its use and were able to manipulate the results'. As a consequence, statutory consultation had become 'only a step away from the old tap on the shoulder'. Another interviewee commented on how parts of the senior judiciary could sometimes be 'manipulative', inasmuch as they were very effective in using existing processes to get whatever result they desired. To put it less emotively, judges – senior judicial consultees in particular – who are regular players in JAC-run processes are adept at using their involvement at various stages of a selection exercise to secure their desired outcomes.

### *Recommendations*

The JAC meets around twice monthly to recommend candidates. It is under a statutory duty to select 'solely on merit'[51] and must also ensure that a recommended candidate is 'of good character'.[52] It is also under a statutory duty to 'have regard to the need to encourage diversity in the range of persons available for selection',[53] but this is explicitly stated to be subject to the requirement to select solely on merit.[54] The Crime and Courts Act 2013 clarified that the 'tipping point' provision in the Equality Act 2010 applies to judicial appointments, and that the duty to make selections solely on merit does not prevent the JAC from recommending a candidate on the basis of improving diversity where there are two candidates of equal merit.[55]

In deciding whom to recommend, the commissioners take account of the report of the selection panel, character checks and the statutory

[51] CRA, section 63(2).
[52] CRA, section 63(3).
[53] CRA, section 64(1).
[54] CRA, section 64(2).
[55] Crime and Courts Act 2013, Schedule 13, para. 10, which inserts a new section 63(4) into the Constitutional Reform Act 2005.

consultation. Underlining the extent to which they are rather removed from the detail of the selection process, the commissioners do not routinely review candidates' application forms and references (although these are available if requested). The JAC's workload is generally too large for the commissioners to be closely involved in every recommendation (and, indeed, commissioners are required to attend only half of the meetings where final selections are made, although it is open for them to attend more). At one meeting, for example, the JAC had to make seventy-five recommendations, with the commissioners allocated only fifty minutes to discuss fifty-three recommendations for District Judges and a further fifty minutes to make twenty-two recommendations for Circuit Judges.

Inevitably, therefore, the commissioners accept the evaluation of the selection panels as to who are the strongest candidates, and instead devote most of their discussion to borderline candidates. Interviewees who are involved say that discussion of borderline cases is 'lively' and 'robust', with commissioners casting a 'critical eye' over the panel reports. From time to time, the commissioners will revise the grades awarded by the panels to candidates on the borderline, for example, if the summary of a candidate is not in line with the grade allocated to them, or if new information has come to light through the character checks or statutory consultation. However, we were told that the commissioners only change marks allocated by the selection panels around once or twice a month. This would mean that marks are only changed for a candidate, or a small handful of candidates, for every fifty to a hundred recommendations that the JAC makes. Aside from discussing the borderline applications, much of the commissioners' role involves scrutinising the rigour of the processes and decisions of the selection panels rather than getting involved in the nitty-gritty of the individual applications.

All of the JAC's recommendations are made by consensus, and according to most of those we interviewed there is no discernible difference in views between lay, judicial and legal commissioners. Typical was the following comment that 'outsiders would find it difficult to tell from our contributions who is lay, who is judicial and who is legal'. This might seem puzzling to outsiders, who could reasonably suppose that the lay commissioners defer to their judicial counterparts, particularly on assessments of whether candidates display the particular qualities needed for a post. We found little evidence of this in the JAC-run selection processes up to the High Court. True, one former non-judicial commissioner commented that it was hard not to be influenced by comments from judicial commissioners that particular candidates were 'brilliant' in court. This was an exception, with most saying that all of the commissioners were fully and equally involved in the JAC's selections for lower-level and mid-level judicial appointments.

### *Appointment decisions*

Following changes in 2013, the JAC recommends a single candidate for each vacancy to the SPT, the LCJ or the Lord Chancellor, depending on the level of the judicial vacancy. Until October 2013, all of the JAC's recommendations were made to the Lord Chancellor. The options available to the SPT, the LCJ and the Lord Chancellor are to accept or reject the recommendation, or to request reconsideration of it. The power to reject can only be used if the Lord Chancellor or the SPT or the LCJ (as appropriate) deems the person recommended unsuitable for the office.[56] The power to request reconsideration is only to be used if there is insufficient evidence that the person recommended is suitable for the post or where there is evidence that a person is not the best candidate on merit.[57] In either event, the Lord Chancellor, the SPT or the LCJ must provide the JAC with reasons.[58] In practice, successive Lord Chancellors seldom used either of these powers, rejecting or requesting reconsideration only five times out of around 3,500 recommendations made by the JAC since 2006. With only around 0.15 per cent of their recommendations not accepted, the JAC effectively operates as an appointing body.

By 2012, Kenneth Clarke had concluded that the Lord Chancellor's power to refuse the JAC's recommendations was in effect unusable, which explains why he was relaxed about passing the final say over lower-level appointments to the senior judges.[59] In terms of numbers, the LCJ and the SPT are now the primary decision-makers, making 97 per cent of all judicial appointments between them. It remains to be seen whether the LCJ and the SPT will also regard their powers as effectively unusable. Part of the rationale for this reform was that the LCJ and the SPT would be better able to make an informed evaluation of candidates, and it may follow that these two senior judges will feel more confident in using the powers open to them. In the interests of accountability, it will be important to know if and when they do so – a point we return to at the end.

[56] CRA, section 91(1).
[57] CRA, section 91(2).
[58] CRA, section 91(3).
[59] HL Constitution Committee, *Judicial Appointments*, 423–43.

The dilution of the Lord Chancellor's role represents a fundamental shift from the old ministerial model of appointments. It is also a stark departure from the view that the involvement of the Lord Chancellor injected an important measure of democratic legitimacy into the process of selecting judges. Even if it is argued that democratic legitimacy is less important for appointments to the lower ranks, improving diversity necessitates continued ministerial involvement. Experience in the UK and elsewhere suggests that improving diversity does not happen automatically as the make-up of the legal profession changes.[60] It takes political will to drive change, some of which might not be supported by judges. True, the Crime and Courts Act imposed a statutory duty on the LCJ (and the Lord Chancellor) 'to take such steps as that office-holder consider(s) appropriate for the purpose of encouraging judicial diversity'.[61] However, removing the Lord Chancellor from lower-level appointments removes an opportunity for political will to drive diversity in the judiciary at all levels.

A diluted role in individual appointments does not mean that the Lord Chancellor is without influence. The Lord Chancellor still initiates all appointments and stipulates the number and location of vacancies and any additional criteria (after consulting with the LCJ). The Lord Chancellor also remains responsible for the appointments system, accounting to Parliament for its effectiveness. It must be doubtful, however, whether future Lord Chancellors will exhibit much interest in a system from which they are largely – and increasingly – excluded.

## *Judicial influence on JAC selections*

The relative retreat of the Lord Chancellor from individual appointments decisions, as well as from the day-to-day administration of the system as a whole, contrasts sharply with the increasing influence of the judiciary, and of the senior judges in particular. The senior judges had exerted considerable influence under the old system, with individual appointments rarely made that were out of line with the dominant judicial view. It was unsurprising, then, that when proposals to reform the appointment process were announced, the senior judiciary was fearful that it might lose control, although Lord Woolf secured several

[60] See e.g. J. Resnik, 'Judicial Selection and Democratic Theory: Demand, Supply, and Life Tenure' (2005) 26 no 2 *Cardozo Law Review* 579, 635.

[61] Constitutional Reform Act 2005, section 137A.

victories in the Concordat negotiations that addressed many of their concerns.[62] Initial concerns about the JAC's creation were quickly replaced with criticism of its workings, with judges at all ranks critical that cumbersome processes were leading to delays. The JAC worked with the Ministry and senior judiciary and, over time, delays reduced as the JAC managed its workload more effectively, in part because of better forecasting about judicial vacancies from HMCTS. The JAC's use of qualifying tests was also criticised, with a common complaint from judges that highly qualified applicants who almost certainly would have been appointed under the old system had failed the tests. Given that judges had largely designed and assessed these tests, the JAC had some basis for feeling that the criticisms were unjustified, but this issue too was addressed by the JAC, which worked with judges to adapt the tests so that traditionally qualified candidates at the bar were not disadvantaged.[63] Within a short number of years, most judges had moved from a position of deep suspicion to confidence that the JAC did not jeopardise judicial interests. Emblematic was a senior judge who originally opposed the JAC's creation, but who subsequently self-described 'as a complete and utter convert', and who speaks about the JAC 'with the zealotry of the convert'.

One reason for the widespread change in judicial attitudes is the high level of judicial influence on the JAC. Judges have a legitimate interest and an important role to play in appointments. They are well positioned to evaluate the strengths and potential judge-craft of applicants. However, it is important to highlight how deep judicial influence runs throughout JAC selections. At the very start of the process, the Lord Chancellor must consult the LCJ, who has the chance to press the case for including fee-paid experience as an additional eligibility requirement in vacancy requests sent to the JAC. Judges from jurisdictions to which vacancies relate prepare case studies and qualifying tests that are part of the short-listing process. Judges write references for applicants. On the selection day, a judge sits on the panel that interviews candidates – and,

[62] For example, the judges regarded it as vital that the JAC should select solely on merit, with diversity only a secondary consideration, and sections 63 and 64 of the 2005 Act reflect this. Lord Woolf also insisted that the JAC only recommend a single name rather than presenting the Lord Chancellor with a short list of names from which to pick a preferred candidate. Although he did not secure a judicial majority on the JAC, there is still a strong judicial presence, with legal and judicial members outnumbering their lay counterparts.

[63] See, generally, Shetreet and Turenne, *Judges on Trial: The Independence and Accountability of the English Judiciary*, pp. 111–12.

in practice, these panels have the decisive say over the fate of a candidate's application in all but borderline cases. In statutory consultation, judicial consultees comment on the candidates. On the JAC itself, seven of the fifteen Commissioners are judicial office-holders. Finally, a senior judge – the LCJ or the SPT, depending on the post – has the final say on all lower-level appointments. Even for vacancies in the High Court, where the final decision formally remains with the Lord Chancellor, officials at the Ministry have indicated that the Lord Chancellor expects the JAC's recommendations to be in line with the opinions expressed by the LCJ in statutory consultation.

To be clear, this level of judicial involvement from the very beginning to the very end of the selection process is a statutory requirement, and thus reflects the will of Parliament.[64] It is also true that the type of judicial influence differs at various stages: references written by District Judges are a different, and frankly much less important, type of influence than the LCJ's involvement in shaping additional eligibility criteria and giving opinions on candidates for the High Court via statutory consultation. And views can and do differ between judges, and not just between more senior and more junior judges, or between tribunal and court judges, but also between judges at the same level. It is also important to note the involvement of laypeople at different stages of the process. Laypeople are involved in short-listing and form a majority on the interviewing panel on selection days. Of the fifteen commissioners, six are lay. Involving laypeople introduced fresh perspectives, with their contribution evident in innovations such as insisting on qualifying tests for short-listing in the face of opposition from judges and, as we explain below, insisting on using interviews for appointments to the Court of Appeal.

None of this changes the fact that the JAC-run processes have a very strong judicial flavour to them. Of particular significance is the involvement of senior judges at the very beginning and towards the end of the process. The LCJ exercises real influence on the experience required of candidates by shaping the Lord Chancellor's additional selection criteria at the outset. Towards the end of the process, statutory consultation confers on the LCJ an effective veto over recommendations to the High Court, while for lower-level appointments either the LCJ or the SPT now has the final say over whether to accept JAC recommendations. It remains to be seen how

[64] Although, in reality, the Constitutional Reform Act 2005 reflected the Concordat agreement, with little scope in practice for Parliament to renegotiate the details of the appointments regime envisaged by Lords Falconer and Woolf.

frequently the LCJ or the SPT refuses to accept the JAC's recommendations. But according to our interviews, there have only been a small handful of occasions each year when a senior judge has used statutory consultation to voice serious concerns about a candidate that, in practice, prevented the JAC from making a recommendation. A possible reason is that there has already been such a high level of judicial involvement in the selection process that it is highly unlikely that the JAC will propose a name that will trouble the senior judges. For this reason, there may continue to be only a small number of occasions where JAC recommendations for lower-level appointments are not accepted.

High levels of judicial influence are, then, as much a feature of the new appointments processes as they were under the pre-2005 ministerial model. Of course, high levels of influence do not necessarily equate to excessive levels of influence. However, insofar as judges might tend to favour, whether consciously or otherwise, candidates with conventional backgrounds from the bar and commercial practice, there is a real risk that new appointments will continue to clone the existing judiciary and that progress on diversity will continue to be relatively slow. While senior judges acknowledge the lack of diversity, and appear genuinely keen to see change, they have resisted initiatives that might bring about a much faster transformation; the use of additional selection criteria requiring fee-paid experience is the clearest example. It is true that women constitute around 40 per cent of the nearly 3,500 recommendations made by the JAC, with black and minority ethnic candidates comprising around 10 per cent. It is also true that some recent selection exercises have seen women appointed to senior roles: in 2013, for example, five of fourteen candidates recommended for the High Court were women, while women filled three of ten vacancies on the Court of Appeal. Given the relatively small number of women in the senior judiciary, this might be deemed slow but steady progress. Some judges think so: 'the dam has been broken', as one senior judge put it. However, change in the make-up of the judiciary has been slower than expected and has been largely in the lower ranks, with the upper ranks remaining substantially untouched.[65]

[65] Judicial Appointments Commission, *Annual Report and Accounts: 2006–7*; *Annual Report and Accounts: 2012–13*; K. Malleson and R. Hunter, 'Women Judges: Inconvenient Truth' (letter to the editor) [2014] *Law Society Gazette*; Joint Committee on Human Rights, *Legislative Scrutiny: Crime and Courts Bill* (HL 67/HC 771 2012). JAC statistics from 2013 did, however, suggest some positive movement on diversity. Judicial Appointments Commission, *Judicial Selection and Recommendations for Appointment Statistics, October 2012 to March 2013* (2013).

## Senior appointments

Selecting senior judges – the LCJ, SPT, Heads of Division and judges on the Court of Appeal – falls outside the ordinary JAC-run exercises.[66] The Lord Chancellor triggers the process by sending the JAC a vacancy request,[67] after consulting with the LCJ.[68] The influence of the LCJ at this initial stage should not be underestimated. According to one interviewee, senior judges are 'very good at crafting job descriptions favouring traditional candidates'. This interviewee was 'disgusted and shocked' at how the job description for a Head of Division seemed to have been written in such a way as to disqualify an obvious female candidate, and suggested that senior judges were responsible for it. However, job descriptions are not the sole product of judicial drafting. The Ministry and JAC are involved as well. From time to time, the Lord Chancellor will insist on changes to draft descriptions prepared by judges. According to another interviewee, the job description for the LCJ vacancy in 2013 was 'completely rewritten', with the Lord Chancellor keen for greater emphasis on leadership and management skills.

### *Selection panels*

Upon receipt of the vacancy request, the JAC convenes an *ad hoc* selection panel as required by statute, with its precise composition differing according to the vacancy in question.[69] Until 2013, panels typically comprised four members: the LCJ, another senior judge, the JAC's lay Chair and another JAC lay commissioner. The panels were chaired by the LCJ, who enjoyed the casting vote. In what is regarded within the JAC as an important dilution of judicial control of the process, there must now be an odd number of members on the panels, with the potential – but no guarantee – of a lay majority. Most panels have five members, comprising two senior judges, the JAC's lay Chair, a lay commissioner and a fifth member chosen either by the LCJ (in the case of selections for the Court of Appeal, the SPT and Heads of Division)[70] or by the JAC Chair (in the case of the LCJ).[71] In designating the panel's fifth member, regard must be had to the desirability of having a diverse panel

[66] CRA, sections 67–84, as amended by the 2013 Act.
[67] CRA, sections 69(1) and 78(1).
[68] CRA, sections 59(2) and 78(2).
[69] The Judicial Appointments Regulations 2013, regs. 5, 11, 17 and 23.
[70] Regs. 11(6), 17(6) and 23(6).
[71] Regs. 5, 11, 17 and 23.

with a mix of men and women drawn from a range of racial groups.[72] For this reason it seems likely that in most circumstances the fifth member will be a lay commissioner, and as such there will be a lay majority on most panels.[73]

The panels are free to decide their own processes, subject to requirements to consult the Lord Chancellor, the current office-holder and, in certain cases, some other actors (for example, panels selecting the LCJ must also consult with the First Minister of Wales).[74] In a contrast from the normal selection processes administered by the JAC, these panels initially operated with exceptional levels of informality; for example, interviews were not held for appointments to the Court of Appeal. This led some lay commissioners who sat on these panels to describe the whole process as 'completely futile', with lay involvement 'a token'. Another lay commissioner described a meeting of a selection panel at which the LCJ and the Master of the Rolls effectively told the two lay commissioners who was going to be appointed. Processes have been gradually formalised since 2011, in large part because of efforts by the JAC's second lay Chair, Christopher Stephens, and despite the strong resistance of some senior judges. Today, there are advertisements, application forms, long-listing, short-listing, interviews and feedback for senior posts. There has, in other words, been a distinct move 'from an oblique to a transparent process', as one interviewee put it. This move was 'disruptive' for judges, according to a senior judge. For example, unsuccessful applicants for the Court of Appeal might ask for feedback. This is both tricky and new in a judicial culture where there is no formal appraisal system.

Despite the formalisation of the panels' processes, there remain concerns about the relative influence of the judicial and lay members on it.[75] These concerns are not new; they were anticipated by some of those most closely involved in judicial appointments before the Constitutional Reform Act. For example, writing in 2001, Sir Thomas Legg, the former Permanent Secretary at the Lord Chancellor's Department, suggested that the judicial members

[72] Regs. 5(16), 11(17), 17(18) and 23(14).

[73] The panel that recommended Sir John Thomas to succeed Lord Judge as the Lord Chief Justice in 2013 had a lay majority.

[74] Regs. 6, 12(1)–(2), 18(1)–(2) and 24. For the appointment of Lord Thomas as Lord Chief Justice in 2013, the panel consulted more widely than required by statute; for example; the panel wrote to the Attorney General inviting comments on his views of the applicants.

[75] See, for example, A. Paterson and C. Paterson, *Guarding the Guardians? Towards an Independent, Accountable and Diverse Senior Judiciary* (London: CentreForum, 2012), p. 28.

on an appointments body 'would inevitably have a heavy, and often a predominating, influence'.[76] In its strongest form, the concern is that lay members are expected to defer to the expertise and knowledge of the judicial members as to what is needed in a senior role and who is likely best to fulfil it. In a slightly weaker form, the concern is that lay members view their role as limited primarily to injecting professionalism into the process, ensuring that the candidates are reviewed properly with full and effective discussion, and serving as a check on the final decision reached by the judicial members if they feel that a serious mistake is being made. None of the people with whom we spoke suggested that lay members were expected to defer outright to the judicial members, and some spoke of robust deliberations involving all panel members. However, several of our interviews suggested that the lay members perform this limited, secondary role of corroborating the senior judges' assessment of the candidates. If acting in this way, lay members can still play an important role in helping the senior judges understand the importance of leadership skills and people management. What it means, however, is that changes in the composition of selection panels and the formalisation of the selection processes are likely to result in limited changes to the appointments made, and that senior judges will continue to have a strong influence, with traditional appreciation of merit continuing to prevail.[77] It is, of course, impossible to know with certainty how the private panel deliberations are conducted, and even then the dynamics between lay and judicial members will always be open to rival and opposing interpretations.

There remain serious gaps in the formalisation of the most senior appointments. Strictly speaking, anyone in the Supreme Court, Court of Appeal or High Court – or for that matter anyone who satisfies the basic eligibility requirement for judicial office of seven years' standing in the legal profession – could be appointed LCJ.[78] In reality, the cohort of potential candidates is small. The emergence of key management roles means that there now exists a more formal career path for those aspiring to the office of LCJ. At the point at which an LCJ retires, there are unlikely to be more than three or four candidates with sufficient leadership and management experience. Though this has the advantage of providing for more structured succession planning, it might also have the effect of

[76] T. Legg, 'Judges for the New Century' [2001] *Public Law* 62, 73.

[77] Note, however, the promotion of three women High Court judges to the Court of Appeal in early 2013. J. Rozenberg, 'Three Women and Seven Men Promoted to Court of Appeal', *Guardian*, 28 March 2013.

[78] Senior Courts Act 1981, section 10(3).

reducing the appointments process to a choice between a mere handful of candidates at best, and a rubber stamp at worst. Of particular note is that the two most recent LCJs had both served as Senior Presiding Judge. The SPJ, as discussed in Chapters 4 and 6, is an important management role. Despite its importance, the SPJ is not selected by a formal, externally regulated process, but is chosen by the LCJ with the concurrence of the Lord Chancellor.

### *The Lord Chancellor's powers*

The selection panels make recommendations to the Lord Chancellor, who, as in the normal JAC-run exercises, can accept or reject, or request that the panel reconsider. In practice, the Lord Chancellor has accepted all of the recommendations for senior posts, except one. In 2010, Jack Straw requested reconsideration of the selection of Sir Nicholas Wall to be the President of the Family Division. Having initiated the Norgrove Review of the family justice system, Straw doubted Wall's capacity to lead the family judges through a major reform process. The story leaked in the press, with speculation that Straw sought to block the appointment because of earlier criticisms that Wall had made about the funding of the family courts and the general approach of the government to family justice.[79] Straw and his officials felt that 'the politics' of rejecting Wall were 'too difficult' with a general election imminent in May 2010, and that it would be unwise to leave the Family Division without a President for too long. The recommendation was subsequently confirmed after reconsideration. In his Hamlyn Lectures in 2012, and without naming any names, Straw indicated that he had only sought to block the appointment because he felt that there were 'grounds within the [Constitutional Reform Act] for doing so'. Straw went on to imply that there were in fact 'good grounds' for doing so, 'as many can now see'.[80] As we read it, this episode confirms how marginalised Lord Chancellors have become in individual decisions for even the most senior appointments.

[79] Lord Justice Wall, 'Justice for Children: Welfare or Farewell?' (Annual Conference of the Association of Lawyers for Children, Manchester, 19 November 2009).

[80] J. Straw, *Aspects of Law Reform: An Insider's Perspective (The Hamlyn Lectures)* (Cambridge: Cambridge University Press, 2013), pp. 58–9. Sir Nicholas Wall subsequently resigned on grounds of ill health. Straw had reportedly wanted to appointed Lady Justice Heather Hallett: see J. Rozenberg, 'Jack Straw on Judicial Appointments: "Labour Went Too Far"', *Guardian*, 4 December 2012.

In 2012, Kenneth Clarke sought more 'meaningful input' for the Lord Chancellor in the selection of the LCJ.[81] He proposed that the Lord Chancellor sit on the panel that selects the person to be recommended, but opposition from the senior judiciary, the JAC and the House of Lords persuaded Clarke's successor as Lord Chancellor, Chris Grayling, to drop the proposal. Instead, a requirement was introduced for the panel to consult with the Lord Chancellor at the outset of the selection process (and not only for the appointment of the LCJ, but for all of the senior posts). This provides the Lord Chancellor with an opportunity to explain to the panel the qualities the Ministry seeks in the candidate for the judicial leadership. For the selection of the new LCJ in 2013, Grayling addressed the selection panel in its planning stage, when he emphasised the need for leadership and management skills. The panel found Grayling's comments 'instructive and helpful' and produced a report recommending Lord Thomas, which Grayling accepted.

While this consultation requirement is welcome, it does little to reverse the retreat of Lord Chancellors from individual appointment decisions. The Constitutional Reform Act 2005 resulted in much greater administrative responsibilities for judicial leaders, such as the LCJ and Heads of Division, and it is unsurprising that ministers and officials feel that the government should have a meaningful role in their selection. Yet although the Ministry has at times been frustrated that its views on the sort of people who are suitable for senior posts have not been given sufficient weight, there is little prospect of Lord Chancellors becoming more forceful in using their powers to reject or request reconsideration of panel recommendations. As a result, the judicial influence on the selection of the senior judiciary – in shaping the job descriptions and on the selection panels – is likely to remain very high. This is problematic since '[n]o branch of government should be effectively self-perpetuating'.[82]

## Accountability

Several mechanisms are designed to secure the accountability of the JAC, including a statutory duty to publish an annual report,[83] publication of the minutes of meetings of the JAC's board, and the responsibility of the

81 Ministry of Justice, *Appointments and Diversity: A Judiciary for the 21st Century: Response to Public Consultation* (CP19/2011 2012), para. 58.

82 Legg, 'Judges for the New Century', 73.

83 CRA 2005, Schedule 12, para. 32(4).

Chief Executive as accounting officer for the efficient use of resources.[84] The Chair, commissioners and Chief Executive have also given evidence several times to select committees.[85] That said, there are real concerns about a developing democratic deficit. Formally, the Lord Chancellor is responsible for the overall appointments process. The Lord Chancellor is accountable to Parliament for the activities and performance of the JAC,[86] and Lord Chancellors have appeared before the Justice Committee and the Constitution Committee to discuss aspects of the appointments system.[87] However, as we have seen, successive Lord Chancellors have transferred most of their day-to-day functions to the JAC, which runs the vast majority of selection exercises, with the final say over most appointments now exercised by the LCJ and the SPT. Since the judiciary are now the most prominent players in the system, they need to be called to account for the workings of the appointment process just as much and as routinely as the Lord Chancellor and the JAC. The Lord Chief Justice, in particular, is under a statutory duty to take such steps as he or she deems appropriate for the purpose of encouraging diversity.[88] In a 2012 report on appointments, many of the Constitution Committee's recommendations on diversity were directed specifically at the judiciary, although the broad thrust of the report implicitly endorsed high levels of judicial involvement in JAC-run processes.[89] Select committees are not always good at following up, and it remains to be seen whether the committee will pursue these matters in its annual sessions with the LCJ.

Parliament has shown sporadic interest in shaping the overall system, but no desire to influence individual appointments. It created the system's statutory framework, and the inquiries of Select Committees have from time to time encompassed the workings of the system.[90] But it has shown no interest in scrutinising individual appointments, even

[84] Ministry of Justice, *Framework Document: Ministry of Justice and the Judicial Appointments Commission*, 3.2.

[85] To the Commons Justice Committee on 7 September 2010 and to its predecessor, the Constitutional Affairs Committee, on 20 March and 20 June 2007.

[86] Ministry of Justice, *Framework Document: Ministry of Justice and the Judicial Appointments Commission*, 3.3.

[87] HL Constitution Committee, QQ. 373–401; HC Justice Committee, *The Budget and Structure of the Ministry of Justice* (HC 97-II 2012), QQ. 443–4.

[88] Constitutional Reform Act 2005, section 137A.

[89] HL Constitution Committee.

[90] A notable example was in 2008 when a Joint Committee helped the JAC to resist reforms proposed by the Lord Chancellor during the period of rocky relations between the JAC and the Ministry: Joint Committee on the Draft Constitutional Renewal Bill, *Draft Constitutional Renewal Bill*, paras. 134–201.

though it developed systems for scrutinising other senior public appointments. Interest might resurface as the use of such hearings develops in Parliament for other senior public appointments, and as other common law countries experiment with pre-appointment hearings for senior judges.[91] One channel through which Parliament exercises its scrutiny of the appointments process is parliamentary questions. Between 2008 and 2011, fifty-nine questions were asked by MPs about the appointments process, almost all of which were on judicial diversity or detailed queries about spending by the commission. These links with Parliament provide a two-way communication that not only ensures public accountability, but also provides a means through which the JAC can voice concerns about resources or relations with the executive. In 2011, the Justice Committee held a pre-appointment hearing for Christopher Stephens, who at that point was the candidate to replace Baroness Prashar as JAC Chair.[92] This hearing was seen as a useful way for the JAC to develop its relationship with Parliament, and the inquiry in 2011 by the Lords Constitution Committee was welcomed by the JAC for similar reasons. However, the risk is that Parliament's interest may decline. In the JAC's early years, the Justice Committee paid considerable attention to judicial appointments, but they are a small part of its overall work. As one interviewee put it, the worry is that the JAC may become 'lost in the noise' of Parliament.

There are accountability mechanisms for individuals who feel JAC-run processes have not worked fairly. The Constitutional Reform Act created the Judicial Appointments and Conduct Ombudsman (JACO) to investigate complaints about the appointment process and judicial conduct and make recommendations to the Lord Chancellor.[93] JACO's staff of ten performs a second-tier investigatory function.[94] Over 90 per cent of complaints to JACO are about conduct, with less than 10 per cent about judicial appointments. Nevertheless there is a steady stream of complaints, with on average some forty complaints received each year by

[91] For pre-appointment scrutiny hearings in the House of Commons, see HC Liaison Committee, *Select Committees and Public Appointments* (HC 830 2011); and P. Waller and M. Chalmers, *Evaluation of Pre-appointment Scrutiny Hearings* (London: The Constitution Unit, 2010). Recent years have seen experiments with pre-appointment hearings for appointments to the Supreme Court of Canada: see Gee, 'The Politics of Judicial Appointments in Canada', 108–13.

[92] HC Justice Committee, Appointment of the Chair of the Judicial Appointments Commission (HC 770 2011).

[93] See section 62 and Schedule 13 of CRA 2005.

[94] Judicial Appointments and Conduct Ombudsman, *Business Plan 2011–2012*, pp. 1–3.

the JAC, and a dozen referred on to JACO. Of the sixty complaints referred to JACO between 2007 and 2012, only four were partially upheld, suggesting that the JAC's first-tier investigation is generally effective. An example of a partially upheld complaint was where JACO found that the JAC's written response had not addressed every issue raised by the complainant. The Lord Chancellor and the JAC have always accepted JACO's recommendations.[95] Overall, then, JACO provides a useful, albeit limited, check that picks up process errors in a small number of cases.

## Conclusion

Politics has not been removed from judicial appointments, nor could it be. It has merely changed its form. Under the old system, power was formally concentrated in the hands of the old-style Lord Chancellor, who took soundings from the senior judges and placed great weight on their views. It was a closed, narrow but stable system in which the judges, the Lord Chancellor and his senior officials all came from similar legal and judicial cultures. The Lord Chancellor almost never went against the wishes of the senior judges. The changes in the Constitutional Reform Act 2005 threatened to derail this system by replacing it with a detailed statutory scheme involving a wide array of actors from different backgrounds. The new processes are much more transparent, with open competition for most posts from the bottom to the top of the hierarchy, although there are anomalies such as the selection of the Senior Presiding Judge, which remains largely untouched by the more formal approach to appointments. The new processes are also extraordinarily complex. From the ways in which the JAC's Commissioners are chosen to the differing make-up of selection panels and selection criteria, the new processes are difficult to grasp, even for insiders. This has knock-on effects on the accountability of the system as a whole. Despite Parliament's early interest in appointments, these complexities make it very hard for select committees to hold those who operate the system to account, and almost impossible for the public to understand or engage with it.

The involvement of more actors in the appointments processes also creates greater scope for confusion and contestation. In practice, while there have been numerous clashes over the procedures, conflicts about individual appointments have been rare. The initial years after 2006 were

[95] CRA, section 103(3).

marked by serious tensions between the JAC, the Ministry of Justice and the judiciary over policy, aggravated by personality clashes; but the fraught relations between the Ministry and the JAC did not spill over into individual appointments. Tensions eased after the JAC's first tranche of leadership was replaced in 2010, which coincided with an acceleration of the Ministry's retreat during Kenneth Clarke's and then Chris Grayling's tenures as Lord Chancellor. The legacy of the early problems presents a curious contrast. On the one hand, the JAC now functions as a *de facto* appointing body, with almost all of its recommendations accepted by successive Lord Chancellors, who have withdrawn in effect from decisions about individual appointments. On the other hand, the JAC is today less willing to challenge the use of additional selection criteria, and less willing to make recommendations at odds with statutory consultation. This suggests that the Ministry's vision of the JAC as a recruitment agency has prevailed over the competing vision that emphasised the JAC's duty to drive forward the diversity agenda. Across all of the various actors, there is now a more pragmatic, businesslike approach, with less fussing about the constitutional boundaries now that the transition from the old ministerial model has been completed. In this sense, conceiving of the JAC as akin to a recruiting agency with a *de facto* power to appoint and not merely select judges is a very functional response to the need to ensure that judges can be immediately deployed on appointment, but it may mean that progress on increasing diversity continues to be slower than had been hoped. There are also dangers if, over time, officials inside the Ministry underestimate the importance of the JAC's constitutional role.

Reflecting the victories that Lord Woolf secured during the Concordat negotiations, judicial influence is built into the new processes at almost every stage, especially over the most senior appointments. Our interviews suggest that senior judges have grown adept at using statutory processes to secure maximum – and, as we see it, disproportionate – influence. Senior judges are pivotal repeat players, especially by contrast with the shorter tenure of new-style Lord Chancellors, the rapid turnover of staff within the Ministry and the relatively short terms of the commissioners.[96] The ability of the senior judges to exert considerable

[96] Commissioners can be appointed for up to five years, with the possibility of reappointment for a maximum of ten years. The JAC's first leadership and Commissioners were replaced in 2011, after five years. New appointments have typically been for periods of two or three years, but this may be to ensure that the commissioners do not all finish their terms at the same time.

influence helps to account for a shift in judicial attitudes towards the JAC, from suspicion, and even outright hostility, when it was first established to a determination to fight for its survival in 2009–10. This is not the only reason for the evolution of judicial attitudes: the JAC had done important work to streamline its processes, reshaping them to address judicial concerns. But the ability of senior judges to exert considerable influence over appointments was, perhaps, the most important factor.

Pointing to the high levels of judicial influence is not to deny that laypeople perform key roles, not only in individual appointments but also in shaping the JAC's broader strategy. Rather, it is merely to note that judges play important parts in shaping the job descriptions, designing qualifying tests and role-play activities, writing references and sitting on selection panels, and in statutory consultation. This is in addition to the fact that seven of the fifteen commissioners are judges. That the level of judicial influence is high is undeniable. Significant influence from beginning to end was designed into the selection processes by the Constitutional Reform Act, which reflected the result of the Concordat negotiations between Lords Falconer and Woolf. We believe that it is too high, not least because there is no effective check on this influence. It is unrealistic to expect laypeople to check against the risk of 'judges appointing judges', especially in the very top appointments. Laypeople make a valuable contribution to the new processes, but they cannot compensate for lack of meaningful involvement by politicians.

Senior judges exercised considerable judicial influence under the pre-2005 selection process, but subject to the controlling influence of the Lord Chancellor. With the final say over lower-level appointments now lying with either the Senior Presiding Judge or the Lord Chief Justice, the vast majority of all appointments are now made the ultimate responsibility of senior judges with no direct democratic accountability. For the highest appointments, it is also difficult to avoid the conclusion that judges are appointing judges, albeit via more formal processes. This places the senior judiciary in a bind. The tighter they hold onto the reins, the longer progress on diversity is likely to be stalled, and pressure to reform the system will mount. On the other hand, it is understandable that the senior judges might feel unwilling to cede control given future uncertainties, especially if future Lord Chancellors bring a different view to judicial appointments, and feel little responsibility for a system in which they have very limited involvement.

There are two main risks associated with the dynamic discussed in this chapter of the retreat of the Lord Chancellor coinciding with increasing judicial influence. The first is a growing accountability gap. Judicial influence is increasing, especially over the most senior posts, but there is little appetite at Westminster for holding them to account effectively and, given the complexity of the new processes, little capacity to hold them to meaningful account. The second risk is that Lord Chancellors will retreat more and more from the appointments system. With the JAC now functioning as a *de facto* appointing body in a densely regulated statutory scheme that has extensive judicial influence engineered into it, the judiciary may feel initially even better protected, but ultimately they may be left exposed to future political attacks. A recurring theme in this book is that judicial independence depends on political machinery that understands and respects the role of the judiciary and the courts. Over the long term, the retreat of politicians from the appointments process may pose more of a threat to judicial independence than a system in which engaged and well-informed politicians play a more equal part.

8

# The UK Supreme Court

This book opened by claiming that judicial independence is a political achievement. In many ways, the creation of the UK Supreme Court can be similarly characterised, for the government's proposal in 2003 to create a new top court was not the result of a long-standing campaign by senior judges, few of whom had called for the removal of the Law Lords from the Westminster Parliament.[1] Rather, it was, for better or worse, a political project. It was conceived in private, and without consulting a single judge, by the then Prime Minister, Tony Blair. The proposal was closely scrutinised in Parliament, particularly by a special select committee of the House of Lords that took detailed evidence from a range of judges, politicians, practitioners and academics from across the UK, with the first new-style Lord Chancellor, Lord Falconer, accepting several amendments that strengthened the proposal. Subsequently, government officials worked closely with the Law Lords to identify Middlesex Guildhall on Parliament Square as a suitably dignified, spacious and accessible building to house the Court, all the while conscious of the political imperative to keep costs down.[2] Despite the Prime Minister's cavalier attitude towards the reform of the very apex of the judicial system, the creation of the Supreme Court – in terms of its origins, parliamentary passage and realisation – was a distinctively political achievement. The detailed story of the Court's creation has been well documented elsewhere.[3] Our purpose is instead to

1 Notable exceptions include Lord Steyn, 'The Case for a Supreme Court' (2002) 118 *Law Quarterly Review* 382; Lord Bingham, 'The Evolving Constitution' [2002] *European Human Rights Law Review* 1. Elements of the legal elite had called for a new court: see, for example, the submission by JUSTICE to the Royal Commission on the Reform of the House of Lords, *A House for the Future* (Cm 4534 2000).

2 See, generally, Lord Hope, 'A Phoenix from the Ashes? Accommodating a New Supreme Court' (2005) 121 *Law Quarterly Review* 253.

3 See A. Le Sueur, 'From Appellate Committee to Supreme Court: A Narrative', in Blom-Cooper, Dickson and Drewry, *The Judicial House of Lords, 1876–2009*; Lord Windlesham, 'The Constitutional Reform Act: The Politics of Constitutional Reform – Part 2' [2006] *Public Law* 35.

discuss how politicians, judges and officials have built on this to negotiate the parameters of the Court's independence.

During the passage of the Constitutional Reform Act 2005, Lord Falconer said that 'special arrangements' would apply to reflect the Court's 'unique status'.[4] In practice, the Court's early years have been marked by a behind-the-scenes struggle to translate this status into the everyday requirements of independence and accountability, leading to tensions between the Court and the Ministry of Justice. When located inside Parliament, the top court was insulated from governmental interference, with the arcane workings of the House of Lords serving as a buffer that bolstered the administrative and financial independence of the Law Lords. Following its relocation to Middlesex Guildhall, relations with the Ministry on a number of financial and administrative issues in the Court's early years were characterised by 'strains and stresses', as one Justice put it. In this chapter we consider some of the reasons for and consequences of these strains and stresses. In particular, we explain how the politics of independence of the top court have changed since 2009, shifting from a limited and insular politics defined by the arcane practices of the House of Lords to a more expansive, multi-faceted politics moulded primarily by the priorities, routines and rigours of Whitehall, though it also has important and at times turbulent devolutionary dimensions.

## Organisation, management and leadership

At first blush, it might be thought that the Court is essentially the same institution as its predecessor. The Court's composition is little different in terms of the number and backgrounds of the Justices, although by late 2013 only four of the twelve had previously sat as Law Lords, so that the institutional memory of the Court's previous incarnation is fast disappearing. It enjoys broadly the same powers, combining the jurisdiction of the Appellate Committee with the responsibility for devolution cases that previously lay with the Judicial Committee of the Privy Council.[5] It also handles a similar caseload.[6] It is true that some commentators suggested that the Court's creation might transform the

[4] *Hansard*, HL, vol. 417, col. 926, 9 February 2004.

[5] Constitutional Reform Act 2005, section 40(4)(a)–(b) and Schedule 9.

[6] The Court receives between 230 and 280 applications for permission to appeal each year, granting an average of seventy or so, or around 66–75 per cent, broadly consistent with the refusal rate of the Appellate Committee. See, generally, A. Paterson, *Final Judgment* (Oxford: Hart Publishing, 2013).

role of the UK's top judges, with speculation that this might even culminate in the Justices assuming a general power to enforce legal limits on the UK Parliament's ability to legislate.[7] But the Court's decisions since it began its work in October 2009 suggest that this speculation has been 'wide of the mark',[8] at least in the short term, with any change to the role of the Justices likely to be evolutionary.[9] On closer inspection, however, the assessment that the Court is essentially the same as the Appellate Committee holds true only if it is narrowly defined in judicial terms.[10] It is less accurate if the Court is more broadly defined to include its administrative as well as judicial activities. In administrative terms, the Court is a larger, more active and businesslike institution with a much higher public profile. Removed from Parliament, there is both more scope and more need for the Court to manage its own activities. As one Justice observed, 'We are very much more running our own affairs. There are things that were done completely unseen in the House of Lords, which we now have to organise ourselves.'

Assisting the Justices in the Supreme Court is a larger staff. Although still a small institution with around forty permanent staff, all of whom are civil servants, plus a further eight temporary staff, the Court's administrative operation is twice the size of the Appellate Committee's, where the staff were parliamentary officials and thus not part of the civil service. The Court's larger administrative operation also has a different character, one shaped by mission statements, business plans and annual reports; it is more reflective, in other words, of the culture of Whitehall than that of Westminster. The Court is very much 'a twenty-first century institution steeped in the businesslike culture of new public management'.[11] It is also more visible, incorporating a communications office that, among other things, issues press releases summarising

[7] See, generally, R. Masterman and J. Murkens, 'Skirting Supremacy and Subordination: The Constitutional Authority of the UK Supreme Court' [2013] *Public Law* 800; A. Kavanagh, 'From Appellate Committee to Supreme Court: Independence, Activism and Transparency', in J. Lee (ed.), *From House of Lords to Supreme Court: Judges, Jurists and the Process of Judging* (Oxford: Hart Publishing, 2011), p. 35.

[8] B. Dickson, *Human Rights and the UK Supreme Court* (Oxford: Oxford University Press, 2013), p. 3. See also the detailed discussion of the government's success rate in various different types of case in Paterson, *Final Judgment*, pp. 288–90.

[9] K. Malleson, 'The Evolving Role of the UK Supreme Court' [2011] *Public Law* 754.

[10] As of early 2014, only four of the sitting Justices had previously sat in the Appellate Committee: Lord Neuberger, Lady Hale, Lord Mance and Lord Kerr (who was appointed in June 2009, only four months before the Court began its work).

[11] G. Drewry, 'The UK Supreme Court: A Fine New Vintage or Just a Smart New Label on a Dusty Old Bottle?' (2011) 3 *International Journal for Court Administration* 20, 31.

judgments and oversees the live streaming of hearings online. The Law Lords, by contrast, had no communications team, merely releasing their judgments in line with the Standing Orders of the House of Lords.[12] Underscoring its commitment to be a more visible and accessible institution, the Court encourages the public to visit: 250,000 did so between 2009 and 2013.[13] Central to running the Court in a professional, businesslike and accessible manner is its 'leadership trinity'[14] consisting of the President, the Deputy President and the Chief Executive.

## *Judicial leadership: the President and Deputy President*

The Constitutional Reform Act 2005 established two new offices of President and Deputy President to head the Court. The first occupants were the Senior Law Lord and the Second Senior Law Lord, Lords Phillips and Hope respectively.[15] That the occupants of the two senior roles in the Appellate Committee were transferred to the twin leadership roles in the Supreme Court might be taken to suggest that the offices were not intended to be different. In practice, the new posts are quite distinct. For much of the twentieth century, Senior Law Lords exercised relatively limited leadership.[16] The position was traditionally occupied on the basis of seniority. It was only in 1984 that the seniority rule was changed to enable Lord Diplock, who was in poor health, to step down as Senior Law Lord while continuing to serve in the Appellate Committee.[17] It was not until Lord Bingham's appointment in the year 2000 that the role took on greater significance. This was the product in part of the gradual

[12] R. Cornes, 'A Constitutional Disaster in the Making? The Communications Challenge Facing the United Kingdom's Supreme Court' [2013] *Public Law* 266, 268.

[13] UK Supreme Court, *Annual Report and Accounts 2012–13* (London: HC 3 2013), p. 37.

[14] R. Cornes, 'Gains (and Dangers of Losses) in Translation: The Leadership Function in the United Kingdom's Supreme Court, Parameters and Prospects' [2011] *Public Law* 509, 517.

[15] Constitutional Reform Act 2005, section 24(b) and (c).

[16] J. Vallance White, 'The Judicial Office', in Blom-Cooper, Dickson and Drewry, *The Judicial House of Lords, 1876–2009*, pp. 35–6. This bold statement is of course subject to exceptions: see, for example, Paterson's accounts of the influence of Lord Reid and Lord Diplock as Senior Law Lord in A. Paterson, *The Law Lords* (London: Macmillan, 1982), pp. 154–89; and A. Paterson, *Lawyers and the Public Good: Democracy in Action?* (Cambridge: Cambridge University Press, 2012), pp. 176–84.

[17] For an account of the episode that led to the departure from the seniority rule, see A. Paterson, 'Scottish Lords of Appeal 1876–1988' [1988] *Juridical Review* 235, 251–2 (n. 59).

realisation that the workings of the top court required careful management in much the same way as any other court. It was also the result of Lord Bingham's awareness of the potential for a judicial leader to make his or her mark.[18] No previous judge had been appointed Senior Law Lord with as much leadership experience as Lord Bingham, who had previously served for a total of eight years first as the Master of the Rolls and then as Lord Chief Justice. Even then, Lord Bingham's influence was perhaps more jurisprudential than administrative, deriving more from his intellectual gifts than from a defined leadership role.[19]

The roles of President and Deputy are more clearly defined. The Constitutional Reform Act confers several responsibilities on the offices. A number are conferred directly on the President alone, reflecting the fact that this office has a heavier mix of outward-facing and inward-facing functions. In practice, the President and Deputy work closely on issues relating to the Court's judicial role, with both working with the Chief Executive on non-judicial matters. There are five key responsibilities for the President and/or the Deputy President relating to judicial business over and above sitting in and presiding over hearings. First, the President and Deputy President determine the composition of the panels that hear applications for permission to appeal and full hearings. Second, the President may request senior appellate judges from England and Wales, Scotland and Northern Ireland to serve as an 'acting judge' in the Court on a temporary basis.[20] The President may also ask members of a supplementary panel of retired appellate judges to sit.[21] Third, the President is responsible for making the Court's Rules. In practice, the Court's first President delegated much of this task to the Deputy President.[22] Fourth, the President has an important role relating to complaints and discipline.[23] Fifth, the President sits – and, until 2013, the Deputy President also sat – on the Commission that recommends to the Lord Chancellor candidates for appointment as Justices whenever

[18] B. Dickson, 'A Hard Act to Follow: The Bingham Court, 2000–2008', in Blom-Cooper, Dickson and Drewry, *The Judicial House of Lords, 1876–2009*, p. 257.

[19] See, generally, Baroness Hale, 'A Supreme Judicial Leader', in M. Andenas and D. Fairgrieve (eds.), *Tom Bingham and the Transformation of the Law: A Liber Amicorum* (Oxford: Oxford University Press, 2009) 209; Paterson, *Lawyers and the Public Good: Democracy in Action?*, pp. 176–90.

[20] CRA, section 38(1).

[21] CRA, section 39(1)–(4).

[22] CRA, section 45(1).

[23] UK Supreme Court, *Judicial Complaints Procedure*.

vacancies arise.[24] These roles do not exhaust the ways that the President and Deputy can shape the running of the Court, but they point to the formalisation of the leadership of the top court.[25]

It is not just the more formal definition of their responsibilities that distinguishes the offices of President and Deputy President. The Court's judicial leadership operates in a more inclusive and transparent way, with more extensive obligations to consult, report and account. Take, for example, their responsibility for determining the composition of the Court's panels. The Registrar prepares draft panels taking account of, among other things, the need for expertise and an even workload across the Justices. The Registrar submits these for approval by the President and Deputy President. The Court's first two Presidents – Lords Phillips and Neuberger – usually accepted the Registrar's suggestions, although Lord Hope made changes from time to time.[26] All of this is broadly similar to the latter years of the Law Lords, where the Principal Clerk of the Judicial Office in the House of Lords presented draft lists to the Senior Law Lord and Second Senior Law Lord. Like the Court's first two Presidents, Lord Bingham typically accepted the lists.[27] No other Law Lords were involved, with no mechanism for outsiders to comment on the Court's broad approach to the size of panels. Today, there is a more inclusive and accountable approach. Internally, the Court's policy on panel size has been discussed at meetings of the Justices.

A significant departure is the more frequent use of panels of seven or nine for full hearings. This reflects, among other things, that the Court's more spacious accommodation affords them the flexibility to sit in larger panels, the assumption being that in especially controversial cases added legitimacy attaches to the decision of a larger panel; and the concern to minimise the potential criticism that a differently composed panel might have reached a different decision. Between the year 2000 and 2009, the Law Lords sat in panels of more than five only thirteen times.[28] In contrast, between 2010 and 2013, the Court sat in panels of more than

[24] CRA, sections 25–31 and Schedule 8, as amended by the Crime and Courts Act 2013.

[25] For example, one consequence of the fact that the President and the Deputy generally preside is that they also decide who writes the lead judgment. This is especially significant given that the Court now issues more single judgments than the Appellate Committee: Paterson, *Final Judgment*, pp. 91–7.

[26] Paterson, *Final Judgment*, p. 72.

[27] See B. Dickson, 'The Processing of Appeals in the House of Lords' (2007) 123 *Law Quarterly Review* 571, 589.

[28] Paterson, *Final Judgment*, p. 72 (n 35).

five on fifty-seven occasions, sixteen involving panels of nine.[29] In a further departure, the Justices have published the criteria for the circumstances in which more than five should sit.[30] Greater use of larger panels and the publication of these criteria are best viewed as collective decisions of the Court as a whole. Externally, the Court's User Group (a consultative body that comprises solicitors, barristers and representatives from the Law Society, the Bar Council and similar bodies) has discussed the more frequent use of larger panels, including the difficulties that can arise as a result of such panels sometimes taking longer to reach a decision.[31] The suggestion, then, is that although the mechanics of determining the make-up of individual panels exhibit an underlying continuity with the Appellate Committee, the Court's judicial leaders now engage more actively with other Justices, practitioners and professional bodies to shape the policy on the size of panels.

Something similar can be seen in the President's responsibility for making the Court's Rules. The Rules take the form of a statutory instrument, and any changes involve a laborious process of laying a statutory instrument before Parliament, with the President required to consult with the Lord Chancellor and professional associations throughout the UK. The Court has therefore created Practice Directions to supplement the Rules, which are revisable at the Court's discretion. Revisions have been made to the Practice Directions, but most are 'unremarkable' and of 'interest only to the poor souls who must ensure that they file the correct number of copies produced in the approved manner'.[32] While the procedures are broadly similar,[33] the Court's approach to making changes is more inclusive than that of the Appellate Committee, where the Senior Law Lord discussed changes to

[29] For criticism of this, see A. Burrows, 'Numbers Sitting in the Supreme Court' (2013) 129 *Law Quarterly Review* 305. See also R. Buxton, 'Sitting En Banc in the New Supreme Court' (2009) 125 *Law Quarterly Review* 288. The use of larger panels seems to have lessened under the leadership of Lord Neuberger: A. Paterson, 'The Supreme Court Today' [2012] *Counsel* 34, 36.

[30] These are: (a) if the Court is being asked to depart or may decide to depart from a previous decision; (b) a case of high constitutional importance; (c) a case of great public importance; (d) a case where a conflict between decisions in the House of Lords, Privy Council and/or the Supreme Court has to be reconciled; and (e) a case raising an important point in relation to the European Convention on Human Rights. Though vague, these criteria provide at least some sense of the factors that influence the size of panels.

[31] UK Supreme Court, Note of the UKSC/JCPC User Group Meeting (UKSC, 2013) 4.

[32] C. Knight, 'The Supreme Court Gives Its Reasons' (2012) 128 *Law Quarterly Review* 477, 477.

[33] UK Supreme Court, *Annual Report and Accounts 2012–13*, p. 19.

the Standing Orders and Practice Directions that governed the judicial business of the House of Lords with colleagues and outsiders only as he saw fit, and in practice perhaps not at all. Today, the User Group has a central role, providing valuable feedback on the Practice Directions and reviewing proposed changes to them. Equally significant is the Court's more flexible application of its Rules and Practice Directions. By the 2000s, there was a 'gradual but perceptible increase in the belligerence displayed' by practitioners to the detailed and rigidly applied rules of the Appellate Committee.[34] The Court's approach is different and more businesslike; as an official put it, 'the whole ethos of the Court is to assist practitioners ... and to operate a much more flexible and friendly approach'. This is enshrined in the Rules themselves, which require the Court to apply them with a view to ensuring that 'the Court is accessible, fair and efficient and that unnecessary disputes over procedural matters are discouraged'.[35]

One final example of how stronger judicial leadership is professionalising the running of the UK's top court is the introduction of a complaints process where the Appellate Committee had none. In matters of discipline, the Court is largely self-regulating. The Constitutional Reform Act provides that the Justices hold office during good behaviour, but may be removed from it on the address of both Houses of Parliament.[36] Given that no judge has been removed by Parliament since 1830, this is a measure of last resort that is unlikely to be used. Although not required by statute to do so, the Court's first leadership team introduced a complaints procedure. Complaints relating to the effects of the Court's judicial decisions are inadmissible, but any disclosing grounds for further consideration are referred to the President, who can decide to take no action or to resolve the complaint informally.[37] If formal disciplinary action is considered, the President

[34] Vallance White, 'The Judicial Office', in Blom-Cooper, Dickson and G. Drewry, *The Judicial House of Lords, 1876–2009*, p. 44.

[35] The Supreme Court Rules, SI 2009/1603.

[36] CRA, section 33.

[37] UK Supreme Court, *Judicial Complaints Procedure*, paras. 1–3. If the complaint relates to the President, then it is passed to the Deputy, and where it relates to both, it is passed to the next most senior Justice. This occurred when a complaint was made that involved both the President's former role as Master of the Rolls and the Deputy's involvement as chair of a panel which refused permission to appeal. This complaint was also entwined in an application to set aside the decision of a panel deciding permissions to appeal, which usefully illustrates how the line between complaints about judicial decisions and judicial conduct is not always clear.

must consult with the Lord Chancellor. Formal action involves a tribunal consisting of the Lord Chief Justice, the Lord Chief Justice of Northern Ireland and the Lord President (head of the Scottish judiciary), plus two independent members nominated by the Lord Chancellor. After the tribunal delivers its report, the Lord Chancellor must decide whether to remove the Justice by laying the necessary resolution before both Houses of Parliament.[38] To date, most complaints have related to the effects of the Court's decisions and therefore no action has been taken. What is noteworthy, however, is that introducing a procedure where the Law Lords had none is recognition by the Court's judicial leadership that any professional and well-run organisation requires a formal complaints procedure. That the procedure envisages substantial external input where serious misconduct is alleged is a small but significant symbol of the Court's greater external accountability.

### *Administrative leadership: the Chief Executive*

At the heart of the top court's transformation into a more professional and businesslike institution is the Court's Chief Executive. The President appoints the Chief Executive,[39] to whom responsibility is delegated for the management of the Court's administrative operation.[40] The Constitutional Reform Act 2005 had provided for the Lord Chancellor to appoint the Chief Executive, after consulting with the President. Following changes in the Crime and Courts Act 2013 and for reasons that will become apparent below, the Lord Chancellor has now been removed from the appointment process.[41] The Court's first Chief Executive was Jenny Rowe, a civil servant with considerable experience in the Lord Chancellor's Department and the Attorney General's Office. Operating at the direction of and answerable to the President,[42] the Chief Executive performs three main functions.

First, and above all, the Chief Executive is responsible for the financial running of the Court. This includes preparing the Court's bid for funds from the UK government, negotiating with officials from the Ministry and, in austere times, advising the President on the reductions to

[38] UK Supreme Court, *Judicial Complaints Procedure*, paras. 5–7.

[39] CRA, section 48(2), as amended by the Crime and Courts Act 2013.

[40] CRA, section 48(3). See G. Gee, 'Guarding the Guardians: The Chief Executive of the UK Supreme Court' [2013] *Public Law* 538.

[41] CCA, section 29(1).

[42] CRA, sections 48(4) and 49(2).

expenditure that can be achieved without jeopardising the Court's activities. In doing so, the Chief Executive must comply with a statutory duty to ensure that resources are employed 'to provide an efficient and effective system to support the Court in carrying out its business'.[43] To assist with this, the Chief Executive established an internal governance structure headed by a Management Board, the Remuneration Committee and an Audit Committee, all of which include non-executive directors. The Chief Executive chairs the Management Board's monthly meetings, at which discussions include the Court's financial performance, with its minutes published on the Court's website. The Remuneration Committee is responsible for considering the pay of the Court's staff. The primary responsibility of the Audit Committee is to assist the Chief Executive as the Court's Accounting Officer. Designation as Accounting Officer means that the Chief Executive is accountable directly to Parliament for stewardship of public monies, rather than indirectly via the Ministry's Permanent Secretary. Thus the Chief Executive is the key office-holder for ensuring that the funds allocated to the Court are employed 'efficiently, economically and effectively, avoiding waste and extravagance'.[44] With the accounts for which she is responsible audited by the National Audit Office, and as the Accounting Officer who can be called before the House of Commons' Public Accounts Committee, the Chief Executive personifies the increased accountability for the Court's financial and administrative running.

Second, the Chief Executive appoints and manages the Court's non-judicial staff.[45] The Constitutional Reform Act initially required the Lord Chancellor to agree the numbers of staff at the Court and their terms of appointment. This assumed that the Lord Chancellor and the officials at the Ministry of Justice would have a detailed understanding of the Court's staffing needs. In practice, however, there is a relatively detached relationship between the Court and the Ministry, with only twice-yearly formal meetings between the President and the Lord Chancellor in the Court's early years and monthly meetings between the Chief Executive and counterparts at the Ministry.[46] The Crime and Courts Act 2013 therefore removed the Lord Chancellor's role, with the Chief Executive becoming responsible for all staffing decisions instead.

[43] CRA, section 51(1).

[44] HM Treasury, *Managing Public Money* (2013), para. 3.3.

[45] These powers the President delegates to the Chief Executive.

[46] The practice in the Court's early years has been for the Deputy President to attend these meetings as well.

Even without any involvement of the Lord Chancellor, the power to appoint staff is constrained by the Court's budget, which, as described below, is subject to approval by the Treasury. The power to appoint must also be exercised in line with the Chief Executive's statutory duty to ensure the efficient use of public monies. As Accounting Officer, the Chief Executive is also liable to be called before the Public Accounts Committee in the House of Commons to justify her staffing decisions. There is therefore a triple lock that disciplines the Chief Executive's decisions.

Third, the Chief Executive performs an important diplomatic function, internally and externally. As one interviewee put it, this diplomatic role is 'upward-facing' and addresses issues of concern to the Justices, for example in 2010 when the Chief Executive prepared a paper on the possible impact on the Court of the coalition government's constitutional reform agenda. It is also 'outward-facing' in that it covers responsibility for the Court's education and outreach activities. But its most important aspect is maintaining positive relations with judges, politicians and officials across the UK, and especially in the devolved jurisdictions. There is a formal aspect to this: reflecting the fact that the politics of the Court's independence and accountability are today more clearly multi-dimensional, the Chief Executive has a statutory duty to submit an annual report to the Lord Chancellor and the First Ministers in Scotland, Wales and Northern Ireland.[47] There is an informal aspect as well. The first Chief Executive was aware of the need 'to build relationships with all parts of the UK', conscious that 'politics do not start and stop at Westminster'.[48] Through frequent trips to Edinburgh, Belfast and Cardiff, the Chief Executive seeks to acquire a better sense of the political contexts in which the Court operates, speaking privately with politicians whom the Justices might be reluctant to meet. As we will see below, there is, however, potential for the administrative politics of the Court's running to get swept up in the larger devolutionary politics of the UK as a whole.

## Financial independence

Given that the Court is a larger, more active and more visible institution than the Appellate Committee of the House of Lords, it is little surprise

[47] CRA, sections 54(1) and (2).

[48] J. Rowe, 'Speech to Government Legal Service Scotland' (26 March 2010).

that the Court's operating costs are also significantly higher, amounting to just under £13m each year. At approximately £1.1m per year, the operating costs of the Appellate Committee were astonishingly small.[49] Sharing overheads with the rest of the House of Lords and a modest staff kept costs low. In another respect, keeping these costs low was also the Law Lords' choice, since there were effectively no budgetary constraints. So long as the senior clerk in the Lords was satisfied that a request was reasonable, the Law Lords received whatever funds they had requested.[50] There was no governmental involvement in the funding of the Appellate Committee, and therefore no scope for the Treasury to impose limits or in-year changes to the budget. The Law Lords enjoyed 'the complete detachment and benevolent protection of the legislature'.[51]

By contrast, the funding arrangements for the Court have proved, in the words of one interviewee, a source of 'constant tension' between the Court, the Treasury and the Ministry of Justice. At one level, this is scarcely surprising given that the Court was 'unlucky to have been born into a harsh world of economic crisis'.[52] However, the tensions have concerned not only the level of funding, but also the structure of the funding arrangements themselves. There are three sources of funding for the Court. First, there are the sums agreed with the UK government as part of the annual bid process in Whitehall (£6.8m in 2012–13). Second, there are fees from the Court's users (£0.9m in 2012–13), plus contributions received from HMCTS (£5.7m), the Northern Ireland Courts Service (£0.2m) and the Scottish government (£0.5m). Third, there is a small income from market initiatives, such as income from

[49] This estimate combines the costs of the Judicial Office's salaries and office costs with its apportioned share of costs such as utilities, telephones and accommodation and for the use of staff employed by the wider House of Lords, such as library staff. Salaries of the Law Lords were paid directly from the Consolidated Fund. This estimate does not include any contribution towards the upkeep of the Palace of Westminster. Discussions of the differing costs of the Appellate Committee and the Court must take into account that the latter's budget includes sums allocated for renting and maintaining Middlesex Guildhall, a Grade II star listed building. Additionally, though the salaries for the Justices come directly from the Consolidated Fund, they are now included in the Court's budget. See, generally, HL Committee on the Constitutional Reform Bill, *Constitutional Reform Bill [HL]* (HL 125-I 2004), para. 109.

[50] Vallance White, 'The Judicial Office', in Blom-Cooper, Dickson and Drewry, *The Judicial House of Lords, 1876–2009*, pp. 42–3.

[51] See Q. 62 of Lord Howe's evidence to HL Committee on the Constitutional Reform Bill, *Constitutional Reform Bill [HL]* (HL 125-I 2004), para. 109.

[52] Drewry, 'The UK Supreme Court: A Fine New Vintage or Just a Smart New Label on a Dusty Old Bottle?', 31.

the Court's gift shop and the hiring out of its premises (£0.1m). The first and second sources have proved problematic in the Court's short history, with problems stemming as much from the arrangements themselves as from cuts to public spending.

### *Central funding*

The Court's funding arrangements were the subject of debate during the passage of the Constitutional Reform Act 2005. The former Chancellor of the Exchequer (and QC) Lord Howe argued for a system in which funds would be allocated directly from Parliament to safeguard the Court's financial independence.[53] Lord Falconer, then Lord Chancellor, resisted this, arguing that democratic accountability required ministerial responsibility for funding.[54] Nevertheless, the final arrangements sought to provide protection for the Court within the confines of Whitehall's budget process. Lord Falconer had outlined a process to 'ring-fence' the Court's bid for funding to ensure that it 'cannot be touched by Ministers'.[55] The Chief Executive and President now determine the funds required by the Court, before submitting their bid to the Lord Chancellor, who includes it without alteration within the Ministry's bid to the Treasury. The Lord Chancellor is to be a mere conduit for the Court's bid, but if necessary deals directly with the Treasury to secure the funds that the Court has sought. Once it has approved the Ministry's bid, the Treasury passes it to the House of Commons as part of the government's overall estimates, with the Court assigned its own estimate. Since it is allocated its own estimate, the Court's resources are transferred directly from the Consolidated Fund, not indirectly via the Ministry.

Lord Falconer had concluded that, under the new system, 'It is hard to imagine more financial independence'. The process that Falconer outlined was not reflected on the face of the Constitutional Reform Act, although it was summarised in the Explanatory Notes.[56] Rather, section 50(1)(b) merely states that the Lord Chancellor must ensure that the Court is provided with the funds that the Lord Chancellor 'thinks are

[53] See evidence Q. 62 of HL Committee on the Constitutional Reform Bill, *Constitutional Reform Bill [HL]* (HL 125-I 2004), para. 109.

[54] Q. 65 of report, HL Committee on the Constitutional Reform Bill, *Constitutional Reform Bill [HL]* (HL 125-I 2004), para. 109.

[55] *Hansard*, HL, vol. 667, col. 1235, 14 December 2004.

[56] The process is set out in the Explanatory Notes.

appropriate for the Court to carry on its business'.[57] As the Court's first President, Lord Phillips, has observed, 'it is difficult to recognise in section 50(1)(b) the scheme that Lord Falconer . . . described'.[58] More particularly, it is difficult to square this section with the suggestion that the Lord Chancellor is supposed to be little more than the conduit for the Court's bid. Even putting section 50(1)(b) aside, the mere fact that the Court's bid is enveloped within the Ministry's bid inevitably interposes the Lord Chancellor between the Court and the Treasury, which risks precluding the Chief Executive from dealing directly with officials at the Treasury. This in turn creates scope for interference by the Lord Chancellor in the Court's determination as to the resources required. Alternatively, the Lord Chancellor might engage in only perfunctory advocacy on the Court's behalf once its bid is passed to the Treasury. In 2013, the Court and Ministry agreed that while the Lord Chancellor must submit the Court's bid to the Treasury without alteration, he can 'add any accompanying comment he wishes regarding the merits of the bid, having first discussed his comments with the President'. It was further agreed that though the Lord Chancellor deals directly with the Treasury to secure the Court's resources, the Court also retains the right 'to discuss matters at official level with Treasury officials'.[59]

Even if future Lord Chancellors forswear from interfering with the Court's bid, the Treasury retains a powerful role and can impose reductions on the Court. When the risk of Treasury cuts was raised in 2004, Lord Falconer had suggested that while the Treasury would review the Court's bid, the reality was that the resources requested by the Court would not create 'significant issues' since its bid would form such a small proportion of overall public expenditure.[60] As it turned out, Lord Falconer was overly optimistic. The Court negotiated 'a satisfactory budget'[61] for its first year in 2009–10, but in 2010 the Ministry notified the Court that it would receive only £12.8m for 2010–2011, a reduction of

[57] CRA, section 50(1)(b).

[58] Lord Phillips, 'Judicial Independence and Accountability: A View from the Supreme Court' (the Constitution Unit, 8 February 2011).

[59] This was reflected in the agreement reached in October 2013 which sought to formalise, in very broad terms, relations between the Court and the Ministry: *Concordat between: The Ministry of Justice (MOJ) and the Supreme Court of the United Kingdom (The Court)* (DEP2014–0133 2013) 5–6.

[60] *Hansard*, HL, vol. 667, col. 1245, 14 December 2004.

[61] Lord Phillips, 'Judicial Independence and Accountability: A View from the Supreme Court'.

£1m against the Court's initial bid.[62] Recognising that the Court could not be insulated against Whitehall's wider imperative to reduce costs, the Chief Executive sought to identify cuts in expenditure, while at the same time negotiating with the Ministry about the levels of savings required. Agreement was eventually reached after fraught negotiations, but only once the Chief Executive confirmed to the President that the cuts would not adversely affect the Court's judicial functions.[63]

We return to other aspects of these fraught negotiations below. For now, it is important to note the very real scope under the current arrangements for the Treasury to impose cuts unilaterally on the Court, which in turn injects uncertainty into the Court's financial planning. This is not a problem unique to the Court: it is common for public bodies to complain that the Whitehall budget process creates uncertainty in financial planning. However, it is new for the top court: no longer sheltered inside Westminster, the Supreme Court is now exposed to the harsh realities and unavoidable uncertainties of Whitehall funding. At the same time, the funding arrangements inject a measure of accountability for the financial running of the Court that was largely absent from the Appellate Committee, though it was arguably not much needed given the small levels of expenditure incurred by the Law Lords. Today, the Court must justify its budget to the Ministry and the Treasury.

### *Fees and territorial contributions*

It is not only the process of bidding for central funds that has created uncertainty in the Court's financial arrangements. The same is true of the system for recovering the costs of the Court's civil business. In line with the UK government's policy for other parts of the judicial system, the Court is required to recover all of the costs of its civil business. These costs are borne in part by the Court's users but in order to meet the full costs of running the Court's civil business, contributions are also received from HMCTS, the Northern Ireland Courts and Tribunals Service and the Scottish government. This reflects the fact that the Court not only is the final court of appeal for individual civil cases, but also has a responsibility for developing the civil law, so that the benefits of its decisions accrue to all civil litigants, irrespective of whether their case reaches the Court.

[62] UK Supreme Court, Management Board: Minutes of the Meeting Held on 23 March 2010, para. 8.1.

[63] Lord Phillips, 'Judicial Independence and Accountability: A View from the Supreme Court'.

To date, there have been two principal problems with this contribution system. First, it has proven 'difficult to operate in practice', as one senior official put it, and this has led to uncertainty. In the years 2009–10 and 2010–11, sizeable contributions were due from HMCS, as the courts service for England and Wales and predecessor to HMCTS was then known. In both years, HMCS was unable to meet its contributions, with the Ministry of Justice initially refusing to make up the shortfall. At one point, this led to such a serious shortfall that the Court was a matter of days away from being unable to pay its staff. Only after the Chief Executive wrote to the Ministry's Permanent Secretary to convey the seriousness of the Court's financial position did the Lord Chancellor agree to make up the shortfall. There was, in other words, considerable uncertainty in the Court's first few years about whether those required to contribute would do so in full and on time and what would happen if one or more failed to do so. Admittedly, the Lord Chancellor always made up the deficits (although it may be that by continuing to underwrite missing contributions, this actually encouraged HMCS to default again). But for the first few years of the Court's life, there was no guarantee that the Lord Chancellor would in fact step in. In January 2011, however, the Court and the Ministry reached an agreement whereby the Lord Chancellor would guarantee to cover HMCTS's contribution. This avoids what one of the Justices called 'the continuous distraction' of worrying whether the contribution due from HMCTS would be forthcoming.

Second, the contribution system is open to manipulation by politicians. That this is so was illustrated by the response of Scottish National Party (SNP) politicians to the Court's decisions in *Cadder*[64] and *Fraser*.[65] The relevant background is that the Court has no general jurisdiction over Scottish criminal appeals.[66] The High Court of Justiciary in Edinburgh, prior to 1998, was the final appellate court in Scottish criminal matters. However, one unintended consequence of the Scotland Act 1998 was to create a *de facto* appeal route to the Privy Council (and, since 2009, the Supreme Court) in Scottish criminal cases. Section 57(2) of the Scotland Act provides that Scottish ministers must not act incompatibly with the European Convention on Human Rights. Because prosecutions in Scotland are taken in the name of the Lord Advocate – who is a minister in the Scottish government – a right of

[64] *Cadder* v. *H.M. Advocate* [2010] UKSC 43.

[65] *Fraser* v. *H.M. Advocate* [2011] UKSC 24.

[66] CRA, section 40(3). See generally Paterson, *Final Judgment*, pp. 233–46.

appeal was effectively created in criminal cases. Defendants could seek judicial review of the Lord Advocate's decision to prosecute if there was an arguable breach of the right to a fair trial in Article 6 of the ECHR. The number of appeals reaching either the Privy Council or the Court via this route has been comparatively small, with only twenty-nine full appeals between 1999 and 2011.[67] However, the appeals have provoked fierce criticism within the Scottish political and legal spheres, including among the Scottish judiciary, reflecting the importance traditionally placed on the independence of the Scottish legal system.[68]

This criticism became particularly toxic in 2010 following *Cadder*, when a seven-judge panel of the Supreme Court unanimously agreed to overturn the decision of the High Court of Justiciary by holding that interviewing suspects in the absence of a solicitor in the six hours while being detained was incompatible with Article 6.[69] In 2011, *Fraser* provoked an even stronger reaction amongst SNP politicians after the Court quashed a conviction following non-disclosure of evidence that raised an issue of whether there had been a fair trial within the meaning of Article 6. Within a week of the decision in *Fraser*, Kenny MacAskill, the Scottish government's Justice Secretary, threatened to withhold the contribution for the Court's funding from the Scottish government on the grounds that Scottish ministers viewed the Supreme Court's exercise of its jurisdiction under section 57(2) as an illegitimate interference in Scotland's criminal justice system, saying, 'He who pays the piper . . . calls the tune'.[70] As it happens, the Scottish government have always been fastidious in paying the Court the sums owed by them, both before and after MacAskill's comments. Yet regardless of whether MacAskill sought to pressurise the Court into revising its approach to accepting Scottish criminal appeals or merely intended to inflame separatist sentiment ahead of the independence referendum in 2014, his comments illustrate how the contribution system can be used as a political weapon.[71]

[67] UK Supreme Court, *Scottish Criminal Cases and the UK Supreme Court* (2012).

[68] Submission by the Judiciary in the Court of Session to the Commission on Scottish Devolution (10 October 2008), para. 13.

[69] See generally Lord Hope, 'Scots Law Seen from South of the Border' (2012) 16 *Edinburgh Law Review* 58, 72–5.

[70] 'MacAskill Threat to End Supreme Court Funding', *Herald*, 31 May 2011.

[71] In response to concerns about the Court's devolution jurisdiction in Scottish criminal appeals, the Scotland Act 2012 introduced a new 'compatibility' procedure for raising ECHR or EU law issues that arise in criminal cases (which is somewhat similar to the Preliminary Reference procedure whereby national courts can refer questions of EU law to the European Court of Justice). The Supreme Court may determine a compatibility

## Administrative independence

### *A proposed merger with HMCTS*

We have already noted that, though twice the size of the Judicial Office of the House of Lords, the Court's administrative operation remains relatively small.[72] If this simplifies the internal management roles of the President, Deputy President and Chief Executive, it complicates relations with the UK government, insofar as the Court's comparatively small size has at times led officials at the Ministry and Treasury to attach insufficient weight to arrangements designed to secure the Court's independence. We noted earlier that the Court's officials are not part of HMCTS, the Scottish Court Service or the Northern Ireland Courts and Tribunals Service. Rather, the Court's administrative operation was effectively created as a small and independent courts service in its own right. During budget negotiations in 2010, the Ministry proposed amalgamating the Court's administration with HMCTS.

For the government, a merger with the much larger operation at HMCTS would reduce costs and also be more convenient insofar as the Ministry would only have to negotiate funding with HMCTS, and not with the Court as well. From the Court's vantage point, the proposal inappropriately prioritised administrative convenience over the constitutional status of the Court. As Lord Phillips noted in a subsequent public lecture, a merger was 'totally unacceptable' to the Justices,[73] who viewed the independence of its administration limb as underscoring their own independence. The Court was established, in the lexicon of Whitehall, as a non-ministerial government department (NMGD); that is, as a separate department in its own right, with its own budget. The nature of the relationship between an NMGD and ministers varies according to context, but it signals an absence of direct ministerial control and oversight. Ministers are not responsible for an NMGD's performance. NMGDs are typically responsible for their own accounts and deployment of funds. Other examples include the Crown

issue only and must then remit proceedings to the High Court of Justiciary for the case to be concluded. Prior to the 2012 Act, it had been for the Supreme Court to decide whether to make such order and to decide the content of that order.

[72] The Court's administration also incorporates that of the Judicial Committee of the Privy Council.

[73] Lord Phillips, 'Judicial Independence and Accountability: A View from the Supreme Court'.

Prosecution Service, the Charity Commission and the UK Statistics Authority. For the Justices, this status as an NMGD was an expression of the Court's independence from the Lord Chancellor and the Ministry of Justice. HMCTS, by contrast, is an executive agency of, and therefore has a much closer relationship with, the Ministry. So, whereas the Court's Chief Executive is directly accountable to Parliament for use of public monies, the HMCTS's chief executive is accountable to the Ministry's Permanent Secretary, with HMCTS subject to the possibility of audit by the Ministry's Internal Audit Division.[74] The proposal to merge the Court's administrative limb with HMCTS was therefore viewed by the Justices as threatening an unacceptable diminution in the Court's independence from the Ministry.

Above all, the opposition of the Justices to a proposed merger rested on the Court's status as a UK institution with a UK-wide jurisdiction, including over the politically contentious category of devolution cases such as *Cadder* and *Fraser* that had provoked such fury among SNP politicians in particular. The primary responsibility of HMCTS, on the other hand, is to provide resources, support and infrastructure for courts in England and Wales.[75] Because the administration of the UK's top court would have become subsumed within an executive agency responsible for and identified with the courts in England and Wales, the Justices viewed the merger as politically ill-advised as well as constitutionally inappropriate.[76] Their concern was to avoid administrative arrangements that could lead critics to caricature the Court as an 'English' institution.

The proposed merger with HMCTS was only one part of the fraught negotiations in 2010 between the Court, the Ministry and the Treasury discussed above. Although ultimately successful in persuading the Ministry to abandon the proposal after intense behind-the-scenes negotiations, the Court had to accept the budget cuts. For these purposes, what is noteworthy is that in the face of the propensity of the Ministry to favour administrative convenience over constitutional principle, the Court had to work hard to insist on its proper place in

[74] Ministry of Justice, *HM Courts and Tribunals Service Framework Document* (Cm 8043 2011), paras. 3.4 and 8.2.

[75] HMCTS also provides resources to non-devolved tribunals throughout the UK for which the Lord Chancellor is responsible, but it is still primarily identified with courts in England and Wales.

[76] Similar concerns were raised during the passage of the Constitutional Reform Bill: see e.g. HC Constitutional Affairs Committee, *Judicial Appointments and a Supreme Court (Court of Final Appeal)* (HC 48-I 2004), paras. 96 and 99.

the new institutional landscape and to manage consequent relationships with government officials. Not only did this entail opposing the merger with HMCTS, it also involved more mundane matters as well. The Chief Executive, for example, had to remind government officials that the Court, as an NMGD, albeit a small one, is entitled to respond directly to the Cabinet Office on issues such as the security of data stored at the Court and not indirectly via the Ministry. Thus the Court has not only sought to resist large structural reforms, it has also made use of the minutiae of more mundane institutional interactions to underline the Court's distinct status in Whitehall.[77] In doing so, the Court's officials have sought to encourage their counterparts throughout Whitehall to attach due weight in their everyday work to arrangements that safeguard the appearance as well as the reality of the Court's independence. This insistence on constitutional principle over administrative convenience on issues large and small has led some at the Ministry to complain privately that the Court has 'sharp elbows'. Or, in the words of one official, the early relations between officials from the Court and the Ministry proved 'very, very scratchy'.

### *The accountability of the Chief Executive*

Relations between officials at the Court and the Ministry reached their lowest ebb in 2010–11 following a fracas involving the Chief Executive and the Ministry's Permanent Secretary. During the passage of the Constitutional Reform Act 2005, the Lord Chancellor, Lord Falconer, had explained that the Chief Executive would be 'answerable to the President, in accordance with whose directions [she] will be required to act in carrying out [her] functions'.[78] In 2011, in a public lecture outlining his concerns about the fine details of the Court's financial and administrative independence, Lord Phillips quoted Falconer's statement, arguing that it was essential to the independence of the Justices that the Chief Executive owed her primary loyalty to the President, and not to the Lord Chancellor.[79] As Lord Phillips saw it, 'there are those within the Ministry who do not appreciate this' and

[77] On how ritualised institutional interactions manage relations in Whitehall, see R. Rhodes, *Everyday Life in British Government* (Oxford: Oxford University Press, 2011).

[78] *Hansard*, HL, vol. 667, col. 1239, 14 December 2004.

[79] Lord Phillips, 'Judicial Independence and Accountability: A View from the Supreme Court'.

instead 'treat it as axiomatic that civil servants' duties are inevitably owed to Ministers'.[80] Within a matter of hours of Phillips's lecture, the current Lord Chancellor, Kenneth Clarke, was on the radio stressing that the Chief Executive is a civil servant who, though accountable to the President, 'is also part of the government' and by implication owes a duty to the UK government akin to that of a departmental civil servant.[81]

To grasp the significance of this exchange, it is necessary to consider events that occurred one year earlier in the shadow of the Constitutional Reform and Governance Act 2010. This Act put the Civil Service Code on a statutory footing. Paragraph 14 of the Code provides that civil servants must 'serve the Government, whatever its political persuasion', and must do so 'in a way which deserves and retains the confidence of Ministers'. In early 2010, and while the Constitutional Reform and Governance Bill was before Parliament, the President sought confirmation from the then Lord Chancellor, Jack Straw, that the Court's permanent staff would not owe a duty of loyalty to ministers. Echoing Lord Falconer's earlier statement, Straw confirmed in an exchange of letters that the Court's staff reported to the Chief Executive, who in turn worked at the direction of the President and did not report to the government of the day.[82] The Chief Executive sought to have the Bill amended to reflect this, but was told by officials in the Ministry that there was insufficient time to do so in view of the impending General Election. The Court secured instead a ministerial statement in the Lords clarifying that the general duty of loyalty owed by civil servants to ministers did 'not affect civil servants who are on loan to or directly employed by bodies such as the Supreme Court . . . whose duty is to serve the organisation they are seconded to or employed by'.[83]

A few months later, at a press conference in July 2010, the Chief Executive was asked about proposed cuts of 40 per cent to the Court's budget. Noting that 62 per cent of the Court's expenditure was fixed, the Chief Executive suggested that the Court 'couldn't actually deal with any casework . . . with a 40 per cent cut'. Although emphasising that she 'didn't want to negotiate in public', the Chief Executive said that

80 Lord Phillips, 'Judicial Independence and Accountability: A View from the Supreme Court'.

81 H. Mulholland, 'Kenneth Clarke Rejects Claim of Threat to Supreme Court Independence', *Guardian*, 9 February 2011.

82 UK Supreme Court, Management Board: Minutes of the Meeting Held on 23 March 2010, para. 3.2.

83 *Hansard*, HL, vol. 718, col. 960 (Lord Bach), 24 March 2010. This is reflected in the version of the Code laid before Parliament in 2010, which acknowledges that some civil servants are answerable to the office-holder of their organisation.

preserving monies to support casework would be the priority but that the Court's public engagement work would be 'more vulnerable'.[84] Not long after the press conference, the Permanent Secretary at the Ministry complained to the President that the Chief Executive had breached the Civil Service Code by criticising the government in public and informed him that the Ministry was considering whether to take disciplinary action against her. As an official at the Ministry commented, there was 'enormous pushback' from the President at the suggestion that the Chief Executive had breached the Code. The President told the Ministry that the Chief Executive had spoken at the press conference at his direction, stressing that the Chief Executive served the Court, not the government. In the face of the President's defence of the Chief Executive, the Ministry chose not to pursue the matter further. This low point in relations with the Ministry created an environment that was, as an official put it, 'very, very corrosive'. While relations later improved, in part as abrasive personalities moved on to other roles outside the Ministry, this confrontation reinforced the sense in the Court that its leadership must be vigilant against any threats to their administrative independence.

At one level, this dispute over the accountability lines of the Chief Executive was a consequence of the fact that the Ministry's assumptions about the role did not reflect the reality of the office's functions.[85] On a day-to-day basis, it was clear that the Chief Executive works under and reports to the President, and not the Lord Chancellor. As one Justice told us, there is no doubt that the Chief Executive 'bats for the judges'. The Chief Executive in practice decides how the budget is allocated and is accountable for this to the Public Accounts Committee, and thus arguably it was entirely appropriate for her to spell out in public the implications of any budget cuts. At the same time, it could be argued that it was imprudent for the Chief Executive to appear to be publicly criticising the Ministry, even if invited to do so by the President. Comments on such sensitive matters are perhaps best left to the President, and even then only once it has become clear that negotiations in private with the Ministry have failed. Alternatively, it might be suggested that the Chief Executive, as the Court's accountable officer, bears ultimate responsibility for the Court's financial health and should use all available tools to press the Court's case for more resources.

[84] N. Hanman, 'Cuts "Would Close Supreme Court"', *Guardian*, 29 July 2010.

[85] For the argument that the dispute was also a reflection of the mixed 'constitutional' and 'bureaucratic' visions of the office of Chief Executive in the Constitutional Reform Act 2005, see Gee, 'Guarding the Guardians: The Chief Executive of the UK Supreme Court'.

In doing so, the Chief Executive can serve as a buffer between the Justices and the Ministry, though it is preferable that any backlash from the Ministry should be focused on her public comments rather than on those of the President.

At another level, the dispute demonstrates that it is now more difficult to establish and maintain shared understandings between the top judges, politicians and officials in a more formally separated institutional landscape. While the Lord Chief Justice and staff in the Judicial Office interact frequently with the Lord Chancellor and Ministry officials on a very wide range of issues (including funding, deployment, discipline and appointments), the Court only interacts with the Ministry on a narrow range of issues, principally funding. The level of contacts between officials from the Court and the Ministry is accordingly much less extensive than between the Judicial Office and the Ministry. There is much less contact between principals as well: the Lord Chief Justice and Lord Chancellor meet monthly, but the President and the Lord Chancellor have tended to meet formally only twice yearly. The challenge of nurturing constructive relationships with the government has been compounded by the relatively rapid turnover of staff within the Ministry (although, then again, this rapid turnover can be useful, if it means that tensions over the loyalty of the Chief Executive ease after certain officials move on). Most of the tension between the Court and the Ministry has occurred at an official level and appears to be a by-product of officials treating the Court as if it were a run-of-the-mill executive agency subject to close oversight by the Ministry. Tensions have tended to be more bureaucratic than political. For the most part, they have not been caused directly by the decisions or actions of any of the new-style Lord Chancellors.

The political tensions which arose over the question of the Chief Executive's loyalty and accountability also illustrate how the leadership team must be creative when defending the Court's interests. For example, there was private pushback in 2010 by the President when the Ministry complained about the Chief Executive's public criticism of cuts to the Court's funding. Several months later the President used a public speech to articulate, albeit in rather oblique terms, his concerns about the incident. Two years later, the Court's new President, Lord Neuberger, encouraged his predecessor, Lord Phillips, to propose amendments in the House of Lords to the Crime and Courts Bill that would remove the Lord Chancellor from the process of selecting the Chief Executive and also any role in the Court's staffing decisions. The government eventually accepted these amendments. The Court's creative approach to defending its interests requires political skill and an ability to play the long game. This is the more important given that the Court's President lacks some of the formal protections available to the heads of the other judiciaries in the UK; for example, the President does not have a power to lay representations before Parliament on matters of concern to the Court equivalent to that enjoyed by the Lord Chief Justice.[86]

## Appointments

One further area where there have been tensions and a significant degree of change is the process of selecting the Court's Justices. The central feature of the new system is the creation of an *ad hoc* Supreme Court appointments commission to be convened if a vacancy arises on the Court.[87] The new body was intended to be independent of the executive, with the Lord Chancellor's role reduced to accepting, rejecting or requesting reconsideration of the recommendation made by the selection commission. In practice, this *de facto* veto is exercisable in limited circumstances which mirror the Lord Chancellor's powers to reject the selections of the JAC.[88] Initially, the five-member commission comprised the President, the Deputy President and three members of the territorial appointments bodies (i.e. the JAC in England and Wales, JABS in Scotland and NIJAC in Northern Ireland), with one of these three required to be a layperson. Participation by members of the various appointments commissions was intended to reflect that the Court is a UK-wide institution, ensuring that all three jurisdictions were involved in the selection of the Justices. Although the Constitutional Reform Act did not establish in statute that there must be at least two Scottish judges and one from Northern Ireland,[89] this now seems firmly embedded as a convention (and it is one that might be expanded to require the appointment of a Welsh judge if and when Wales develops into a more formally separate jurisdiction).[90]

86 CRA, section 5. As of the start of 2014, the possibility of giving the President a similar power was being considered.

87 See Schedule 8 to the 2005 Act.

88 CRA, sections 29–31 and 73–5.

89 In making its recommendation, the commission must ensure that 'between them [the Court's Justices] will have knowledge of, and experience of practice in, the law of each part of the [UK]': 2005 Act, section 27(8).

90 See, for example, Welsh Government, *Evidence Submitted by the Welsh Government to the Commission on Devolution in Wales* (2003) 25; Lord Neuberger, 'Judges and Policy: A Delicate Balance' (Institute for Government, 18 June 2013), para. 20.

During the passage of the Constitutional Reform Act 2005, the judges fought hard to retain a central role in the new system. The involvement of the President and the Deputy President as members of the selection commission, combined with the fact that only one of the remaining three members needed to be a lay member, meant that the body had a high level of judicial influence. The views of the two top members of the Court would and – according to our interviews – did, inevitably, carry great weight. Over and above this, each of the serving Justices is individually consulted as part of the appointments process.[91] An example of the influence of serving Justices was evident in the opposition of some of their number to Jonathan Sumption QC – his appointment was derailed in 2008, although he was later appointed in 2011.[92] The selection commission must also consult with the Lord Chancellor, the First Ministers in Scotland and Wales and the Chairman of NIJAC.[93] At the same time, the limited decision-making role retained by the Lord Chancellor seems, in practice, to be little more than a rubber stamp. The result was that the Constitutional Reform Act transferred considerable influence over top appointments from the Lord Chancellor to the Court's leadership. In the light of the seemingly token involvement of the Lord Chancellor, the Court's leadership was relaxed about continued ministerial involvement, recognising that conferring the final say, formally at least, on the Lord Chancellor performed an important accountability function.[94] It seems less likely that senior judges would have been as sanguine about a continuing ministerial role had one of the Lord Chancellors rejected a recommendation of the selection commissions. As the Court's first President, Lord Phillips, acknowledged, the system allows for only limited political involvement, which (as he saw it) played a 'significant part in guaranteeing [the Court's] institutional independence'.[95] In light of this view, it was perhaps surprising that Lord Phillips was amenable to the proposal made by Kenneth Clarke that the Lord Chancellor should be a member of the commission that considers candidates for appointment to the

[91] CRA, sections 27(2)(a) and 60(1).

[92] Paterson and Paterson, *Guarding the Guardians?*, p. 31; F. Gibb, 'Judges Oppose Appointment of Sumption, QC, to the Supreme Court', *The Times*, 15 October 2009.

[93] CRA, section 27(2).

[94] Lord Phillips, 'Judicial Independence and Accountability: A View from the Supreme Court'.

[95] Lord Phillips, 'Judicial Independence and Accountability: A View from the Supreme Court'.

position of President.[96] This proposal was, however, strongly resisted during debates on the floor of the Lords.[97]

This balance between judicial influence on the one hand and political and lay influence on the other might have been applauded by the Justices as protecting the independence of the Court, but some commentators have criticised the accountability gap, pointing to the danger of self-replication in the participation of both the President and the Deputy in the *ad hoc* commissions.[98] This danger is intensified, in turn, by the requirement that the commission consult all of the current Justices, eleven of whom were white men in early 2014, and statutory consultees in leading judicial and political offices, most of whom are also typically white men. By 2012, Phillips himself had acknowledged that the participation of the President and the Deputy President in the selection of their respective successors was problematic, and he supported the provision in the Crime and Courts Act 2013 that removed the role of the two top judges in this aspect of the process. Under the Act, the commission is now made up of an odd number of members (no less than five), including at least one serving Supreme Court justice, at least one lay member and at least one member each from the JAC, JABS and NIJAC. In effect, the Deputy has been removed from the commission, with neither the President nor the Deputy entitled to sit on a commission selecting their respective successors. Given the appointment in 2013 of Lady Hale as Deputy, removing the Deputy from the commissions might seem, as one Justice put it, 'an own goal'.

While the influence of the Court's leadership has been reduced, it seems unlikely that these changes will make a significant difference to the relative influence of the judges and lay members. As we explained in Chapter 7, our interviews suggest that the lay members on senior appointments panels have an understandable tendency to defer to the expertise of the judicial members on the most senior appointments. They do not see it as their function to lead from the front and frame the basis on which the candidates should be considered. As one interviewee explained, the approach of the lay members is in effect to ask the President 'what do you need?', reflecting the 'overwhelming view of the

96 See Q. 170 of his evidence to HL Constitution Committee, *Judicial Appointments* (HL 272 2012).

97 See HL Constitution Committee, *Crime and Courts Bill [HL]* (HL 17 2012), para. 16.

98 See, for example, Paterson and Paterson, *Guarding the Guardians?*, p. 28; *The Report of the Advisory Panel on Judicial Diversity 2010*; HL Constitution Committee, *Judicial Appointments*, paras. 144–7.

judiciary . . . that judges know best'.[99] Nor is it clear that removing the President and Deputy from participating in the selection of their respective successors will have much effect. In appointing a new Deputy, the President might be expected to consult closely with and attach considerable weight to the view of the outgoing Deputy. It seems likely that appointment commissions will continue to be considerably influenced by senior judges, with only a supporting role played by the lay members, while the Lord Chancellor can be expected to continue to rubber-stamp its decisions. The refusal of a Lord Chancellor to accept a person recommended by an appointment commission would indicate a serious rift. It would suggest, in Lord Phillips's words, that the commission was putting forward for appointment 'a judge in whom the government had no confidence'. It is difficult to imagine the basis on which the Lord Chancellor might make such a claim of someone who would, in all likelihood, already be a very senior serving judge. What this means, then, is that the stakes have been raised so high that the Lord Chancellor's right to reject or request reconsideration of a recommendation may have become unusable other than in wholly exceptional circumstances. Nor is there any prospect in the near future of enhancing accountability through the involvement of Parliament in the appointments process of the Justices. As we explained in Chapter 7, the arguments for any form of scrutiny hearing, though supported by some academics, are resisted by almost all senior judges and have been rejected by Parliament. This is so even though the Court's selection commission could be characterised as a closed shop, with only eleven different people sitting on the four commissions that identified eight candidates for appointment to the Court.

## Conclusion

The impact of relocating the UK's top court from the Westminster Parliament was difficult to predict in 2005. The Blair government had suggested that the change would enhance the judges' independence. Critics countered that there would be greater scope for political interference in the everyday running of the top court once it was no longer 'cocooned in the comfortable archaism of parliamentary procedure'.[100] The evidence to date suggests that both supporters and

[99] See also the evidence of Lord Justice Etherton at Q. 53 of the HL Constitution Committee, *Judicial Appointments*.

[100] Drewry, 'The UK Supreme Court: A Fine New Vintage or Just a Smart New Label on a Dusty Old Bottle?', 31.

critics can claim to have been right, at least to some degree. The new building, with enhanced and more spacious facilities, and the development of leadership roles, in the form of the President, Deputy President and Chief Executive, that are exercised in a more inclusive and transparent fashion, alongside a more outward-looking profile, have created conditions likely to secure the independence of the Supreme Court over the long term. But these advantages have been hard won and have come at a cost. The removal of the buffer of the House of Lords has, as was feared, forced the Court into a much closer and at times strained relationship with the UK government, and the Ministry of Justice and the Treasury in particular. This has coincided with larger political developments that have catapulted the Court into difficult political waters, most obviously in the context of its devolution jurisdiction and political debates about the Strasbourg Court and the status of the European Convention on Human Rights.[101] Yet, despite sporadic bursts of tension when ministers from the Scottish government and the UK government have criticised this or that decision, the first phase of the Court's life has witnessed more politics off the bench than on it.

This is not to say that the Court's decisions have been wholly immune from political controversy. Criticism by SNP politicians of the decisions in *Fraser* and *Cadder* and by the Prime Minister and Home Secretary of the Court's decision in *R(F)*[102] on the sex offenders' register are obvious examples. But on both occasions there was also a political response to the criticisms. In the former example, political opponents of the SNP rallied to the Court's defence and criticised the comments of the Scottish Ministers, while in the second example the Lord Chancellor wrote to the Prime Minister and the Home Secretary to remind them of their duty to uphold the independence of the Court. Similar flare-ups would almost certainly have occurred had the Appellate Committee been retained or if the Privy Council had retained its devolution jurisdiction. The expansion of the role of the courts in determining human rights issues and the increasing scope and intensity of judicial review have put senior judges on a collision course with politicians for some years – but there is no evidence that the creation of the Supreme Court has by itself accelerated this. In contrast, the politics of judicial independence played out behind the scenes have become more intense and the stakes for the Court have

[101] On the Court's relationship with the Strasbourg Court see Paterson, *Final Judgment*, pp. 222–3.

[102] *R(F)* v. *Secretary of State for the Home Department* [2010] UKSC 17.

been high. The increased number of potential rubbing points between the judges and politicians is an inevitable by-product of the fact that the Court must now interact with the government on a range of financial and administrative matters. Equally important is the fact that much of these politics now occurs on the Whitehall stage. The workings of the top court are no longer shaped by the parliamentary culture at Westminster, where the arcane procedures of the Lords precluded ministerial involvement in the daily running of the Appellate Committee. Rather, the politics of the Court's independence are today shaped in large measure by the culture, pressures and priorities of Whitehall.

The more intense politics played out off the bench are a direct result of removing the top court from Parliament. In the Court's early years, this posed a challenge inasmuch as officials at the Ministry sometimes downplayed the Court's unique constitutional status, envisaging it as akin to an executive agency responsible for the delivery of services under the control of central government. While this was less a nefarious ploy by government officials, and more a reflection of the propensity of officials to employ familiar practices when liaising with new institutional actors, the upshot was that the Supreme Court's leadership team had to work hard when negotiating the finer details of the Court's independence. The leadership has succeeded in furthering the Court's interests on structural matters, such as fending off the proposed merger with HMCTS and successfully arguing for the removal of any role for the Lord Chancellor in the Court's staffing decisions. At the same time, the Court has had to accept a series of budget cuts. Lacking some of the formal protections available to the LCJ, the leadership team has had to be creative when furthering the Court's interests, using not only behind-the-scenes negotiations, but also more public tools such as lectures and media interviews. Knowing how best to advance the Court's interests inside Whitehall and which tools to deploy requires political judgement and diplomacy. It is probably no accident that both of the Court's first two Presidents – Lords Phillips and Neuberger – had considerable prior leadership experience.

Leadership – both judicial and administrative – has moulded the top court into a more responsive, transparent, inclusive and accountable body than the Appellate Committee. Internal management of issues such as the making of Rules and Practice Directions, the size of panels and the creation of the User Group reveal a judicial leadership concerned not only to engage the legal community in shaping the workings of the Court, but also to offer a narrative to the public at large. From public tours of the Court's building to an annual report with detailed accounts, this sort of accountability also defines the Court's administration, in matters large and small. The Court's budgetary process is more transparent. The Court's leadership may lament the passing of the funding system in the House of Lords under which the Law Lords received all the sums they requested, but the new arrangements help to instil financial discipline. The arrangements also carry greater accountability for the financial management of the Court, which must now justify its budget to the Ministry and Treasury. Rather out of line with this greater emphasis on accountability are appointments to the Court. True, the selection process is now more formal and in some respects both more transparent (for example, clear selection criteria and formal processes that replace the old 'tap on the shoulder') and inclusive (for example, the inclusion of laypeople), but the Lord Chancellor's role has become vestigial. No use has been made of the Lord Chancellor's power to reject or request reconsideration of the recommendations made by the *ad hoc* selection commissions on which, according to our interviews, senior judges hold sway. If remaining unused, these powers may in effect become unusable. These commissions will become *de facto* appointing bodies, with the Lord Chancellor offering a veneer of accountability, but little in reality.

We opened this chapter by noting that in terms of its origins, parliamentary passage and implementation, the Court's creation was primarily a political achievement. The same can be said of the negotiation of its working arrangements. The Constitutional Reform Act 2005 outlined the basic statutory framework within which the Court operates, but how this actually works in practice has depended on sometimes very tense negotiations between civil servants from the Court and the Ministry of Justice. In common with other issues examined in this book, personalities were significant in shaping these negotiations. Although not always straightforward, the negotiations succeeded for the most part in furnishing the Court with a stable foundation for discharging its judicial role. While commentators had pointed to the paradox that a more formally separate top court might start becoming more enmeshed in politics via its substantive decision-making,[103] the theme of our chapter is that even in terms of its administrative role, the

[103] See, for example, D. Woodhouse, 'Judicial Independence and Accountability within the United Kingdom's New Constitutional Settlement', in G. Canivet, M. Andenas and D. Fairgrieve (eds.), *Independence, Accountability and the Judiciary* (London: BIICL, 2006), p. 128; R. Masterman, *The Separation of Powers in the Contemporary Constitution* (Cambridge: Cambridge University Press, 2011), p. 246.

Court is more obviously part of Whitehall politics, where close negotiation and engagement with officials from the Ministry and Treasury are required to define and then maintain a formal separation. The negotiation of the Court's formal separation is not a one-off event. It is an ongoing activity requiring active political engagement on both sides. This is true not only in the very concrete sense of the Court and the Ministry engaging year-in and year-out over the former's budget. It is also true inasmuch as the Court's leadership must nurture among the political elites – not only in Whitehall and Westminster but in the devolved jurisdictions as well – a continued appreciation of the importance of the Court's independence.

# 9

# Scotland and Northern Ireland

As the largest jurisdiction in the UK, England and Wales has tended to dominate debates about the relationship between judges and politicians. But the politics of judicial independence have been played out just as intensely in Scotland and Northern Ireland in recent years, although responses to similar issues have sometimes been quite different. This is particularly evident in three key areas that form the focus of this chapter: the running of the courts, judicial complaints and discipline, and judicial appointments. This chapter builds on the discussion of these areas in England and Wales to illustrate the spectrum of arrangements that now exists within the UK and the process of political negotiation that led to them. In relation to these three areas it asks: where does control lie between the executive and judiciary? Who are the main guardians of judicial independence and accountability in each system? How much accountability is there and who is accountable to whom and for what?

To anticipate our conclusions, the Scottish and Northern Irish judiciaries are more firmly in control of judicial appointments and discipline than in England and Wales. In Scotland the judiciary has also taken the lead in managing the Court Service, unlike the partnership model in England and Wales; while in Northern Ireland the Courts Service is still managed by the executive, but may in time follow the Scottish model. So in Scotland and in Northern Ireland the judiciary has greater institutional independence than in England and Wales, and more limited accountability. Despite this lack of accountability, Scottish and Northern Irish politicians have shown little interest in the judicial system, and, so far, no desire to hold the judiciary more robustly to account.

## Judges in devolved politics

While Lord Judge could quite legitimately describe the Constitutional Reform Act 2005 (CRA) as a 'constitutional revolution' in relation to

England and Wales,[1] the Act had much less significance in Scotland and Northern Ireland, where the Lord Chancellor's power and influence were more limited. In both jurisdictions, the real constitutional revolutions took place with the devolution settlements of 1998. Each devolution settlement produced different answers to the questions the CRA had to resolve for England and Wales. The differences are partly a product of the different scales and sizes of the jurisdictions. Whereas England and Wales has 1,984 judges, the judiciaries in Scotland and Northern Ireland comprise 185 and 122 judges respectively.[2] These differences in scale have practical and cultural effects. In Scotland and Northern Ireland, unlike in England and Wales, those who apply for office (particularly at the higher levels) are likely to be familiar to most of those in political and legal leadership roles. A recurring theme in our interviews in Edinburgh and Belfast was that the small political and legal communities there mean that all those involved in running the courts and the judiciary belong to the same interconnected professional and social groups. The legal worlds of both Scotland and Northern Ireland are 'villages'; though that in Scotland was described by an interviewee as a village 'where nobody talks'. Individual personalities of those in leadership roles play an even more influential part in the politics of judicial independence in Scotland and Northern Ireland: 'because it's a small country . . . big personalities can absolutely dominate and can set a particular course', as one Scottish advocate put it.

Size is not the only significant variable setting Scotland and Northern Ireland apart. The political and constitutional contexts, in both the short term and the longer term, are quite different. The long period of political conflict and violence in Northern Ireland has inevitably been a defining feature of the institutional and cultural shape of the judiciary. From the introduction of direct rule in 1972 there has been a consensus that there should be minimal political interference in judicial affairs provided that justice was delivered fairly to both sides of the community. This has persisted under the power-sharing arrangements established by the 1998 Belfast Agreement.

[1] In his Introduction to 'Lord Chief Justice's Report 2013', 5.

[2] These figures are for the number of paid court-based members of the judiciary and exclude tribunal judges and lay magistrates. Figures for England and Wales and Scotland are taken from 'Evaluation Report on European Judicial Systems' (European Commission for the Efficiency of Justice 2012), 144. The figure for Northern Ireland was taken from 'A Guide to Judicial Careers in Northern Ireland' (Northern Ireland Judicial Appointments Commission 2013), 58–60.

In Scotland, by contrast, the distinctiveness and independence of the legal system survived political union with England and was guaranteed under the Act of Union 1707. 'Legal nationalism' – the commitment to the independence and standing of the Scottish legal system – runs deep and transcends the political spectrum. One effect of this was an unlikely shared understanding between the normally unionist legal establishment and the Scottish National Party administration that came to power in 2007. There is a belief that, as an advocate put it to us, 'Scots law is the crucible of the nation . . . and the judges regard themselves as custodians of Scottishness'. This was especially true prior to devolution: while politics was primarily transacted in London, Scottish legal institutions remained north of the border. Scottish judges were geographically and socially distant from Scottish politicians. One consequence of devolution has been that post-devolution local politicians may not always fully grasp what judicial independence entails. As one judge we interviewed put it, the local political class is 'new and there is perhaps very little understanding of what judicial independence is really all about. It's easy to subscribe to in abstract; it is very often that the problem is what its consequences are in practice'.[3]

Conversely, however, the esteem in which the Scottish legal system is held across the political spectrum has enhanced its status and the quality (and independence) of the Scottish judiciary. Judicial review is also less prevalent in Scotland than it is in England and Wales and as a result the executive finds itself in conflict with the judiciary less frequently.[4] The politics of judicial independence have not, therefore, been tested to the same degree that they have been in England and Wales. There is concern that if they are, politicians in Scotland may be more committed to the idea of judicial independence in theory than in practice: '[the SNP] don't have within their DNA as yet the idea that there are limits on what they should be doing', as an advocate we interviewed put it. The threats to the budget of the Supreme Court made by the Scottish government in connection with the *Cadder* and *Fraser* cases may support this reading of Scottish politics (see Chapter 8).[5] The Scottish judiciary offered little

[3] Interviewees in Northern Ireland made similar observations about their own politics (discussed below).

[4] Per capita, the rate of judicial review in Scotland is about one-third that of England and Wales, with 342 applications in Scotland in the 2010–11 legal year as against 11,200 in England and Wales in the 2011 calendar year: A. McHarg, 'Access to Judicial Review in Scotland', at ukconstitutionallaw.org, accessed 30 July 2013.

[5] *Cadder* v. *H.M. Advocate* [2010] UKSC 43; *Fraser* v. *H.M. Advocate* [2011] UKSC 24. See also A. Paterson, *Final Judgment* (Oxford: Hart Publishing, 2013), Chapter 6.

public defence of the Supreme Court because judges largely shared the Scottish government's discontent with the substance of the decisions. If similar threats were made against a Scottish court, it is likely that the judges would take a very different view.

In Northern Ireland there is a similar detachment between judges and politicians, compounded by the history of inter-community conflict. Under direct rule, the judiciary became much more representative of both communities than they had been under the old unionist-dominated Stormont system. Judges were perceived to be legitimate and impartial long before the Belfast Agreement of 1998, despite the pressure they came under for applying anti-terrorist laws in non-jury Diplock courts.[6] Their legitimacy was gained, however, at the cost of being almost completely detached from local politics and politicians. This culture of detachment persists even after the devolution of justice powers to Northern Ireland in 2010. Officials feel that judges are not fully engaged in essential conversations about the efficient running of the courts while, as in Scotland, judges complain that politicians have not fully grasped the concept of judicial independence.

Politicians finally agreed on the devolution of policing and justice powers to Northern Ireland in 2010, more than a decade after other powers had been transferred. Debate had concentrated on policing arrangements and paramilitary disarmament. No one asked 'what is our new relationship with the judges going to be?' as an Assembly official framed the question. One judge noted that in advance of devolution, 'some politicians believed that it would be possible, for instance, to give directions to the judiciary in relation to sentencing and so on'. This confusion is acknowledged by some politicians. As one put it, 'I'm not that much clear what judicial independence is . . . At times it could be a duty to criticise a judge'. A senior politician noted that criticism of judges by politicians sometimes goes too far because 'the personalisation of politics carries over into personalisation in comments on judicial issues'. To attempt to address this, the Lord Chief Justice of

[6] Livingstone argues that the Northern Irish Court of Appeal performed better from a human rights standpoint than did the Appellate Committee of the House of Lords during the conflict in Northern Ireland, and Dickson says that 'the judges in Northern Ireland actually preserved human rights in the face of quite severe executive and Parliamentary pressure'. S. Livingstone, 'The House of Lords and the Northern Ireland Conflict' (1994) 57 *Modern Law Review* 333, 334; B. Dickson, 'The Protection of Human Rights: Lessons from Northern Ireland' (Paul Sieghart Memorial Lecture, British Institute of Human Rights, 6 April 2000), 8.

Northern Ireland, Sir Declan Morgan, sought to educate politicians about the proper boundaries between politics and the judiciary through engagement with the Stormont Assembly and public speeches. In interview, he stressed the need to develop a partnership between judges and politicians: 'judicial independence doesn't mean judicial isolation. We have a role to play in working in partnership with many other groups and with both the executive and, to some extent, the legislature.'

The chair of the Committee for Justice, Paul Givan, interpreted his interventions as 'a marker being put down: "Don't come near us, we're independent"'. Similarly, in advance of the Chief Justice's appearance before the Assembly's Committee for Justice, the Department of Justice circulated a warning that committee members should not encroach upon judicial independence and this was construed by the committee 'as a signal to get their tanks off the judges' lawn', as a senior civil servant put it. The basis of any judicial partnership with the legislature is affected by the more limited privilege rules operating in the Assembly, with more limited protection from contempt of court than at Westminster.[7] Moreover, there is relatively little interest in judicial matters among members of the Assembly, only a handful of whom are lawyers by training. In 2011, the Attorney organised a seminar on judicial independence, inviting the Assembly members. Not a single member turned up.

If understandings differ in Scotland and in Northern Ireland, so also do the substantive politics of judicial independence. One example of this is in the Scottish attitude to the Supreme Court, which is bound up with nationalist politics. Criticism of the Supreme Court is a win–win proposition for Scottish nationalists. Even if they lose the argument, they can present the continuing jurisdiction of the Court as an unwanted imposition. There was also a clear divergence in attitudes between Westminster and Belfast in connection with the prosecution in 2012 of former Northern Ireland Secretary Peter Hain for criticising a judge. In his memoir, *Outside In*, Hain described Lord Justice Girvan as 'off his rocker' and as 'going out of his way legally to damage me' in relation to the granting of a specific application for judicial review against Hain's department.[8] In response, the Northern Ireland Attorney General, who is independent of Northern Ireland politics,

[7] The Northern Ireland Act 1998 provides absolute privilege against defamation and a limited form of protection from contempt of court. Protection from the strict liability rule for contempt of court applies only during the passage of legislation (section 50).

[8] P. Hain, *Outside In* (London: Biteback Publishing, 2012), pp. 332–3.

began a prosecution for scandalising the court (a form of contempt) against Hain and his publisher. The use of this moribund common law crime was extremely controversial in Westminster. It prompted an early day motion in support of Hain and, subsequently, led to the abolition of the crime in England and Wales in the Crime and Courts Act 2013. In Northern Ireland, however, the Attorney General had more support. One member of the Assembly's Justice Committee noted that '[i]t shows [the Attorney General] in the role he was mandated to do', while another commented, '[t]he more I look at what Hain said, the more serious it is'. The prosecution was ultimately dropped and the crime of scandalising the court was abolished in Northern Ireland.[9] Nonetheless, the incident indicates a degree of sensitivity that is not present in Scotland or at Westminster. This may have something to do with the deep fault lines that still run through Northern Irish society. In 2013, following unionist criticisms that judges were applying different standards to loyalists and republicans in granting bail, the Lord Chief Justice for Northern Ireland responded with an unprecedented and carefully nuanced television interview that sought to defuse tensions.[10]

To sum up, the judicial systems in Scotland and Northern Ireland are much smaller than that of England and Wales. Measured by the number of paid court-based judges, they are roughly 10 per cent and 6 per cent, respectively, of the size of that of England and Wales. Judges in Scotland and Northern Ireland are more detached from the political world, with very little political interference, and there are fewer tensions as a result. Judicial independence has not come under strain, and politicians and judges are still testing where the boundaries lie. Despite these differences, there is an important commonality between all three jurisdictions. In all three, the judiciary dealt with constitutional change by mustering a very effective response that protected and in some areas strengthened judicial interests. This was done to greatest effect in Scotland. The Scottish judiciary did not seek greater institutional independence, but fought hard and successfully for greater control when greater responsibility was thrust upon them. This was particularly the case with the Court Service, which has become the most judge-led in the UK.

[9] Criminal Justice (Northern Ireland) Act 2013, section 12.

[10] V. Kearney, 'Sir Declan Morgan Responds to Bail Decision Criticisms' *BBC News*, 11 March 2013.

## The Court Service in Scotland

Since 2010 the Scottish Court Service (SCS) has operated as a fully independent judge-led service without any power of ministerial direction.[11] The SCS's board has a judicial majority. It is made up of thirteen members: seven judicial members, two lawyers, three laypeople and the Chief Executive. The Lord President, who is the head of the Scottish judiciary, chairs the board and is responsible for making all the remaining appointments, other than that of the Lord Justice Clerk (the second most senior Scottish judge), who is a member *ex officio*. Before 2010, SCS was an executive-run body and broadly similar in structure to the courts service in England and Wales.[12] The appointment of Eleanor Emberson as Chief Executive in 2004 triggered a re-evaluation of the system. Her view was that the system was fundamentally flawed because the judiciary was semi-detached. The relationship between the judges and SCS was 'tetchy': judges stood back from strategic decision-making, SCS management did not always understand their views, and both sides would complain when things went wrong. Emberson was strongly attracted to a judge-led model along the lines of that in the Republic of Ireland. She initiated a review of the Court Service which produced a cautious report recommending that judges should have some involvement in running the courts but that change should be introduced gradually.[13] The judiciary had mixed feelings about moving to greater judicial control. Some judges had visited the Republic of Ireland and were impressed by the system there. Others were more sceptical about whether they had the skills and resources to run a court service.

In 2005, therefore, it seemed that change would be incremental, with judges slowly becoming more involved. This plan was 'blown out of the water' (according to an official) in February 2006 when the Scottish government published a consultation paper, influenced by changes in England and Wales, which proposed unifying the courts system in Scotland under the Lord President. The proposal was driven by the desire of the Scottish government to improve the efficiency of the

[11] The Scottish Government originally sought a power of direction, but was ultimately convinced that lines of responsibility were better protected by the absence of such a power.

[12] Established in 1995 and administered as an agency of the UK Government until devolution and thereafter by the new Scottish Executive.

[13] D. Osler, *Agency Review of the Scottish Court Service* (Scottish Executive, 2006).

courts and justice system. Previously, the Scottish justice system had been fragmented. The Lord President had responsibility for the Court of Session, but not for the lower courts (Sheriff Courts and Justices of the Peace), for which responsibility rested ultimately with the government. The government wanted to make the Lord President head of the whole judiciary and transfer to him responsibility for training, welfare and discipline across the system. The judiciary was alarmed by this, fearing that under the proposal the role of Lord President would come with huge responsibilities but without the power necessary to meet them.[14] The judges realised that they would need to have a strong voice in the Court Service to counter this danger. Having initially been sceptical about a court service on the judge-led model, the then Lord President, Lord Hamilton, became a strong supporter of the proposal and joined forces with Eleanor Emberson to push for the change. The judge-led SCS model therefore emerged as the *quid pro quo* for the structural changes to the courts sought by the Scottish government. Although the Scottish government was concerned that it was 'selling the family silver', as one official put it, it came to accept that this was an arrangement that could work. This belief was facilitated by a meeting in February 2010, three months before the changes were due to be implemented, between the judiciary, the Court Service and the Scottish government. All the parties at the meeting 'had exactly the same sort of nervousness that the others were suddenly going to become rabid'. The Court Service feared that the judges 'would be demanding all sorts of unreasonable things . . . wanting their offices completely refurbished'. The judges were worried that they would be absorbed into the civil service, while the Scottish government, as a senior Court Service official put it, 'were just worried that the other two were going to gallop off into the sunset and leave them far behind.' These fears were allayed by establishing good channels of communication between the three parties which continued after 2010.

One effect of the reform of the new SCS was to improve the scope for strategic thinking about the courts and to allow the judiciary to take ownership of decision-making in areas such as judicial deployment; as another senior court official put it, 'to ask hard questions about where we're going and what we should be doing'. The board of the SCS meets every two months and relations between the lay and judicial members work

[14] One judicial response to the Consultation paper came from the Judicial Council of Court of Session, another from a minority of judges who felt that the latter did not deal with their concerns. A third was produced by the Lord President.

well, largely because there is an acceptance on both sides of their relative areas of expertise. Lay members bring with them knowledge and experience of issues such as corporate plans, budgets and performance review. When these areas are being discussed, the judicial members 'mostly shut up and listen', but 'will weigh in and correct if there's a misunderstanding about how the justice system works or what the needs of the courts are', according to a senior court official. The Chief Executive is a key figure in the new arrangements and is a full member of the board. The other members of the board do not interfere in the day-to-day running of the courts, leaving this for the Chief Executive to manage. As Eleanor Emberson explained, the Chief Executive's job had previously been 'to make sure it all ran smoothly so the minister didn't have to think about it', but now it 'is to make it all run smoothly so the board doesn't have to think about it'.

The effect of the creation of the new SCS on the relationship between the judiciary and the executive can be seen in negotiations around court closures. In September 2012, SCS issued a consultation paper on future court structures, exploring what Scotland needed in terms of court provision. A considerable amount of informal negotiation had been undertaken between the SCS and the judiciary in advance so that there was a degree of consensus around the proposals. This contrasts with the position in England and Wales, where in 2010 the programme of court closures incurred public criticism by the then LCJ, Lord Judge, and the then SPJ, Lord Goldring (see Chapter 4). Judicial fears that the new system would weaken the financial bargaining power of the courts have not been realised, however. The SCS budget is negotiated with government as a separate budget item and ring-fenced once Parliament has voted on it. The evidence seems to be that the Scottish judiciary has negotiated its budget successfully. Although, as in England and Wales and Northern Ireland, there have been cuts in recent years, these compare favourably with those imposed on other similar organisations. (As we note in Chapter 4, the same may be said of the courts in England and Wales.) Overall, the evidence suggests that the new arrangements have improved the way the judges, the government and officials work together to manage the courts.

The downside of the new arrangement is that these benefits have been achieved at some cost to accountability. The Judiciary and Courts (Scotland) Act 2008 provides for a fail-safe mechanism whereby ministers can take over SCS in the event of a serious failure by the service to perform its functions.[15] Short of this scenario, 'there is

[15] Judiciary and Courts (Scotland) Act 2008, section 70.

probably no other public agency that has a freer hand', according to a senior official. The Chief Executive is the accountable officer[16] and so must lay the SCS's accounts before Parliament. She or he will also appear before the Public Audit Committee from time to time and, more regularly, before the Justice Committee when called to explain the work of the SCS. Board members, both judicial and lay, are also eligible to give evidence, but have not to date been called. The Scotland Act 1998 specifically precludes the Scottish Parliament from summoning judges before it. During the passage of the Judiciary and Courts (Scotland) Bill, there was, however, considerable debate about whether there should be a convention that judicial members of the SCS board could be summoned to appear. In the end, the Parliament accepted that it could only invite, rather than summon, the judges. The consensus seems to be that the Lord President will, as a senior court official put it, 'think very, very hard before refusing' and will do so only if he or she feels that the invitation was a pretext to raise questions about a judgment in a particular case.[17] In practice, it seems unlikely that this dilemma will arise, given the generally low level of interest amongst Scottish parliamentarians in the day-to-day work of the courts and judiciary.

## The Courts Service in Northern Ireland

If the Scottish model is the most independent and judge-led in the UK, the Courts Service in Northern Ireland is subject to the most direct form of executive control (with the partnership model in England and Wales falling somewhere between the two). The Northern Ireland judiciary is in a bind. The judges feel strongly that they do not have enough influence over their courts service, yet they consider that they are too few in number to manage the service alone. Nor is there internal agreement about what is required. Some judges are in favour of having a much greater role in running the courts service, others think that that is 'a dangerous route', as a senior judge put it. Prior to the Constitutional Reform Act 2005, the Northern Ireland Courts Service effectively operated as a local branch of the old Lord Chancellor's Department.

[16] The equivalent of the Accounting Officer in England and Wales.

[17] Note, however, that in 2013 the Lord President refused to appear before the Public Petitions Committee to discuss a register of judicial interests (see Chapter 5). He subsequently agreed to meet two members of the Committee in private. R. Findlay, 'Scotland's Most Senior Judge Finally Agrees to Meet MSPs after Snubbing Parliament', *Daily Record*, 2 February 2014.

The Lord Chancellor was formally the head of the Northern Irish judiciary until the CRA, and was responsible for running the courts, but a concordat negotiated in 1979 gave the Lord Chief Justice of Northern Ireland (LCJ-NI) and his colleagues day-to-day control over court staff. Given their distance from London and the distinct jurisdictional framework, the senior judiciary in Northern Ireland operated with a significant degree of independence, with the Lord Chief Justice's office being akin, as a senior civil servant put it, to 'the Vatican City . . . a state within a state'. The passage of the CRA made the LCJ-NI head of the judiciary, and the devolution of justice in 2010 led to the creation of the Northern Ireland Courts and Tribunals Service (NICTS), which was established as an agency of the new Department of Justice of the Northern Ireland Executive. As in Scotland, the judiciary was involved in early negotiations about the shape of a new courts service but the outcome was quite different. Some judges supported a move to a judge-led system. Sir Brian Kerr, as the LCJ-NI, was strongly in favour of running the courts service as a non-ministerial department. In evidence to the Assembly and Executive Review Committee in 2007, he argued that 'that model provides the maximum safeguard for judicial independence, and it will also provide administrative efficiency'.[18] He felt that the judiciary was best placed to devise realistic targets and goals for the courts service. However, Kerr's successor was initially lukewarm about the idea. Sir Declan Morgan and other judges worried that the Northern Irish judiciary was simply too small to run a courts service, given that the senior judiciary in Northern Ireland (High Court and Court of Appeal) comprised only fourteen judges in total. Many of the arguments that pointed Scotland towards the judge-led model seem to have pointed Northern Irish judges and officials away from it. Judges felt that under such a system they would end up with responsibilities that went beyond their remit. Officials worried that an independent court service would be a 'nobody's child', as one put it, without a champion in the Executive. With cuts in public spending, the judges could be left exposed: 'who bats for them; who is their voice at the Cabinet table when resourcing decisions are being made?' (senior civil servant). As a result of these different opinions, judicial involvement with the new NICTS was fudged. Day-to-day governance is the responsibility of the NICTS board, chaired by the Chief Executive of the organisation. While four judges sit

[18] Assembly and Executive Review Committee, *Inquiry into the Devolution of Policing and Justice Matters: Evidence of Sir Brian Kerr* (22/07/08R (Session 2007–08) 2007).

on its board, they are there as observers only and do not participate in decision-making. Their primary role is to liaise between the board and the Chief Justice.

These management arrangements for NICTS are a relatively minor alteration of the arrangements that existed prior to 2010 and today NICTS remains an executive agency. But although the judges are not in control, this arrangement allows them to exercise considerable influence over areas such as court provision and resources and allows them to be consulted on key decisions such as court closures.[19] It seems likely that the judiciary could have had a judge-led model had they – like the Scottish judges – pushed for it. In evidence before the Stormont Assembly and Executive Review Committee in 2007, David Lavery, then director of the Courts Service and later director of NICTS, was confident that this model was possible in Northern Ireland.[20] Instead, the judiciary has, to date, worked to achieve a gradual increase in its involvement with administration. The LCJ-NI argued in 2011 that he did not 'have the oversight which is needed in matters of strategic importance such as the budget and priorities for the courts'.[21] In 2013, the Framework Document was revised to give the LCJ-NI a significant role as a consultee in relation to the budget and the power to make representations to the Minister if the LCJ-NI felt that the budgetary allocation to NICTS was inadequate. The LCJ-NI was also given a consultative role in relation to issues such as courts policy, budget and staffing. The aim, as a senior politician put it, was 'to enhance the input, the influence of the judges, while not handing off to an entirely separate department which would have no friends in terms of how it's managed'. Sir Declan explained that under the new arrangements the Chief Justice has three options when responding to the proposed budget: 'The first letter is, "The budget is fine". The second one is, "I'm not too sure", and the third one is constitutional crisis.'

This change will not necessarily guarantee that the NICTS budget is wholly protected, any more than it has been in Scotland or in England and Wales, but it could be a small step towards greater formal judicial involvement, but with an awareness on all sides that 'there is actually a

[19] A judge with experience of the NICTS board described being consulted on court closures and concluded that the proposal was improved by judicial input.

[20] Assembly and Executive Review Committee, *Inquiry into the Devolution of Policing and Justice Matters: Evidence of David Lavery* (22/07/08R (Session 2007–08) 2007).

[21] Sir Declan Morgan, 'Judicial Independence in the Twenty-First Century', Attorney General's Conference on Judicial Independence, Belfast, 24 June 2011.

benefit for the Courts and Tribunals Service to be part of the [Department of Justice] budgeting process and to have a minister to defend it', according to a senior politician. Nonetheless there are some indications of support building amongst both judges and officials for a judge-led system along Scottish lines.[22] Interviewees suggested that the Assembly election in 2016 might provide the opportunity for such a system to be implemented in Northern Ireland.

## Judicial complaints and discipline

Judges in Scotland and Northern Ireland enjoy much greater autonomy over judicial complaints and discipline than do their counterparts in England and Wales. In each jurisdiction, the investigation of complaints against judges is run for the most part by the judiciary. However, a key difference is that in England and Wales the Lord Chancellor still plays a central role: the Lord Chief Justice and the Lord Chancellor have to co-operate both in the making of rules and in reaching disciplinary decisions. The judiciary in Scotland and Northern Ireland have no equivalent oversight. They set the rules and exercise greater control over the process. As in the case of England and Wales, reforms in the last decade were intended to put judicial discipline in Scotland and Northern Ireland on a formal footing. In Scotland, it had an additional purpose. The fragmented Scottish justice system made a disciplinary system difficult – the Lord President was responsible only for discipline in the Court of Session. At the lower levels, each Sheriff Principal was responsible for the conduct of sheriffs within his or her jurisdiction. The 2008 reforms unified the judiciary and formalised disciplinary procedures under a single head: the Lord President.

The processes in Scotland and Northern Ireland are similar. Officials (overseen in Scotland by a designated judge of the Court of Session) determine whether there is a valid complaint. Where a complaint is substantiated, there is a range of possible responses from 'no action taken' to formal warnings and restrictions on judicial work. In Scotland, the Lord President also retains the discretion to deal with a complaint informally. For allegations of serious misbehaviour, inability or neglect of duty, a tribunal will be convened. In Scotland, this process has significant political involvement: the tribunal is convened by and

[22] For example, NI Assembly Justice Committee, *Briefing from the Lord Chief Justice* (2013).

reports to the First Minister.[23] Judges of the Court of Session and the Chairman of the Scottish Land Court may only be removed by the Queen, following a vote by the Scottish Parliament on a motion made by the First Minister.[24] Sheriffs and temporary judges may be removed by the First Minister directly if the report of the removal tribunal concludes that the person is unfit to hold office. No vote of the Scottish Parliament is required, although the First Minister must lay the report of the removal tribunal before the Parliament.[25]

In Northern Ireland, the judiciary retains significant influence at all stages of the process.[26] Judges below High Court level may be suspended or removed only with the agreement of the LCJ-NI. If the tribunal recommends suspension or dismissal of a High Court or Court of Appeal judge, the advice of the LCJ-NI must be taken and the matter then goes to the Prime Minister and Lord Chancellor. Judges at this level may be dismissed only by the UK Parliament, using the address procedure that applies to judges in England and Wales. Northern Ireland possesses a special process for complaints against the LCJ-NI. Serious complaints will be referred to a senior UK judge for investigation (the Lord President, the LCJ of England and Wales, or a Justice of the Supreme Court).

By contrast, although there is a statutory procedure for dismissing the Lord President in Scotland, there is no procedure for investigating complaints against him or her. The Scottish judiciary appears to have had particularly deep concerns about the prospect of a new formalised disciplinary process.[27] The judges ultimately agreed to the new approach on condition that the Lord President would have complete control over the system. The result has been that the Lord President has what amounts to absolute authority to issue rules and manage the complaints and disciplinary system. The Lord President is not obliged to publish the results of an investigation or the decision made. The 2008 Act also leaves the Lord President with discretion to deal with disciplinary cases

[23] Judiciary and Courts (Scotland) Act 2008, section 28; and the Complaints against the Judiciary (Scotland) Rules 2013. The judge is dismissed by the monarch on the recommendation of the First Minister: see Scotland Act 1998, section 95.

[24] Scotland Act 1998, section 95.

[25] Judiciary and Courts (Scotland) Act 2008, section 39; and the Sheriff Courts (Scotland) Act 1971, section 12E.

[26] See 'Complaints about the Conduct of Judicial Office Holders' (Lord Chief Justice's Office, 2013).

[27] J. Harrison, 'Judging the Judges: The New Scheme of Judicial Conduct and Discipline in Scotland' [2009] *Edinburgh Law Review* 427, 433.

informally if he or she sees fit. There is limited oversight by a Judicial Complaints Reviewer. Individuals who feel that their judicial complaint has not been dealt with properly can complain to the Reviewer, who can examine whether the investigation was conducted fairly.[28] The Reviewer may also make written representations to the Lord President about disciplinary procedures and (if requested by the Scottish government) may make a report. The judiciary was very hostile to the proposal for a Complaints Reviewer, arguing that 'it is a sorry day if one cannot trust the Lord President to operate complaints procedures effectively' and that it would give people 'opportunities to mock the judicial system'.[29] The powers of the Reviewer are significantly weaker than those of the Judicial Appointments and Conduct Ombudsman (JACO) in England and Wales and rely on the willingness of the Lord President to follow her recommendations. The Reviewer's budget of £2,000 per year compared very unfavourably with the JACO's budget of £500,000. The first Reviewer, Moi Ali, declined to seek a second term of office, complaining that the position was 'tokenistic' and lacked sufficient power to implement change.[30]

## Judicial appointments

Judicial power in all three jurisdictions has increased most markedly in relation to judicial appointments. Politicians have been marginalised and, in Northern Ireland, removed altogether. All three jurisdictions have undergone root-and-branch reform of their judicial appointments process within the last decade. Beginning with Scotland in 2002, they have moved from systems of executive control with strong input from judges through the consultations process, to systems in which an independent appointing body has primary responsibility for appointments. These bodies differ in their composition, powers and procedures, but in one crucial respect they are similar. In all three, judges have continued to play a leading role. The new systems were intended to replace the old 'tap on the shoulder' appointment model with something more structured, transparent and formal. In terms of procedural rigour and the inclusion of external involvement through lay participation, the appointing bodies have achieved their goal, being more open and having adopted more

[28] Harrison, 'Judging the Judges' 436–41.
[29] Harrison, 'Judging the Judges' 437.
[30] P. Hutcheon, 'Judicial Watchdog Quits from "Straightjacket" Role', *Sunday Herald*, 26 January 2014.

professional recruitment processes. But in all three jurisdictions the judges pushed very strongly when the new systems were set up for minimal government involvement and strong judicial input, arguing that political involvement in appointments was inimical to judicial independence and that assessment of judicial skill is a matter for judges alone. In this effort, they were largely successful. Politicians have more or less withdrawn themselves from judicial appointments.

### *Northern Ireland*

The Northern Ireland Judicial Appointments Commission (NIJAC) was set up in 2005 under the Justice (Northern Ireland) Acts 2002 and 2004.[31] Of the three appointment bodies, NIJAC has the strongest judicial representation; it is chaired by the LCJ-NI and six out of the thirteen commissioners are judges. Of the seven non-judicial members, two are drawn from the legal professions and five are lay members. NIJAC has responsibility for judicial appointments up to High Court level. For the appointment of the Lord Chief Justice and Court of Appeal, appointments are made by the Prime Minister after consultation with the LCJ-NI and NIJAC.[32] The process is not set out in the statute, and so a non-statutory process must be agreed between the Prime Minister, LCJ-NI and NIJAC.[33]

The numerical dominance of the judiciary on NIJAC is in large part due to the divided communities of Northern Ireland and the importance of demonstrating publicly that there is no political bias in judicial appointments. The 2000 Criminal Justice Review proposed that political responsibility and accountability for judicial appointments should lie with the Office of the First Minister and Deputy First Minister (OFMDFM), but this was dropped because unionist politicians, and the DUP in particular, were unwilling to trust Sinn Féin with judicial appointments. They

[31] The statutory provisions implemented the recommendations of the 2000 Northern Ireland Criminal Justice Review, which in turn flowed from the 1998 Belfast Agreement.

[32] There have been no appointments under this system, which was created by the Northern Ireland Act 2009, at the time of writing. The previous process generally appointed judges to the Court of Appeal on the basis of seniority, but the post-2009 processes seem likely to do so on the basis of merit. See NI Assembly Justice Committee, *Review of Judicial Appointments: Evidence of Sir Declan Morgan* (NIA 38/11–15 (Session 2011–15) 2012).

[33] The appointment exercise agreed for the appointment of the last LCJ-NI prior to the 2009 Act involved a committee made up of two senior Northern Irish judges, together with a lay member of NIJAC and the Chair of the JAC (of England and Wales). This committee produced a recommendation for the Prime Minister. The non-statutory process for appointments under the 2009 Act is likely to be similar.

particularly abhorred the prospect of Deputy First Minister and former IRA commander Martin McGuinness having any role in judicial appointments. One politician interviewed commented that 'in a normal democracy where you didn't have that factor I suspect we wouldn't have gone as far as we have in removing politicians from the role of selecting the judiciary'. The judiciary was therefore pushing at an open door when it sought to remove political influences from the new process. From the beginning, the central role played by the LCJ-NI's new role as head of the judiciary was evident: 'Sir Brian Kerr ruled [NIJAC] and the legal system utterly. It wouldn't have worked without him', as one former NIJAC member commented.

Until the devolution of justice in 2010, the Lord Chancellor had the power to refuse or request reconsideration of a NIJAC recommendation. The power of refusal was exercised only once, in respect of Mark Orr QC. Coincidentally, this occurred in 2010 in connection with the last appointment for which the Lord Chancellor held this power, which made it all the more controversial. The decision generated considerable publicity and annoyance in legal circles. Under the Northern Ireland Act 2009, this power was removed and the Lord Chancellor has effectively become a postbox to the Queen for NIJAC recommendations. NIJAC is therefore now essentially a judicial appointing body led by the Chief Justice and run by the judiciary with limited external oversight. As a remnant of the original proposal to involve the First Minister and Deputy First Minister, NIJAC's sponsoring department is not the Justice department but OFMDFM, whose role is one of oversight and ensuring accountability for its governance and finance arrangements. In addition, it produces an annual report and its decisions and procedures can be reviewed by the Northern Ireland Judicial Appointments Ombudsman, but there are few other checks and with the removal of the Lord Chancellor from the process little external accountability remains in the judicial appointments system. One episode of accountability, however, stands out. Rather surprisingly, in November 2013, the Stormont Justice Committee took evidence from a disappointed candidate in the same 2010 selection exercise that had recommended Mark Orr QC, and later heard from the Northern Ireland Judicial Appointments Ombudsman in response.[34] For politicians to take evidence from a disappointed individual sets a dangerous precedent, even if

[34] D. Marrinan, 'Judicial Appointments and Competition for a High Court Judge', Justice Committee of the Northern Ireland Assembly, 7 November 2013; K. Singh, 'Judicial Appointments and Competition for a High Court Judge: Northern Ireland Judicial Appointments Ombudsman', Justice Committee of the Northern Ireland Assembly, 16 January 2014.

the Ombudsman's view was also heard in response. In a letter to the Committee, the LCJ-NI refused to give evidence on the matter and characterised the Committee's approach to the investigation as 'unconstitutional conduct'.[35]

Apart from this incident, politicians appear to have withdrawn from the process. This has attracted criticism. In 2012, the Northern Ireland Attorney General, John Larkin, argued for the reintroduction of a degree of direct political accountability and an end to the perception of 'judges appointing judges'. In evidence to the Justice Committee in its 2012 review of the appointments process, Larkin argued that 'NIJAC is a hermetically sealed body as presently constituted and should be reformed over time to allow political input'. Some members of the Committee clearly had sympathy for this view. One argued for full-throated political involvement, with the replacement of the lay members of NIJAC with five politicians, on the grounds that it is not good for an 'important constitutional body like the judiciary [to] be completely detached from the political process'. The judges, while acknowledging that the system has an unusual degree of insulation from the political process, argued that this was both a necessary and an effective arrangement given the political context of Northern Ireland. In his evidence to the Justice Committee, Sir Declan Morgan stated, 'On one view, [the system] might be regarded as unusual as such appointments are more routinely a matter for Ministers. That said, the arrangement appears to have worked perfectly well in practice.' The Committee's report broadly agreed with this conclusion and recommended that the status quo be retained. It did, however, question NIJAC's role in determining the number of judges and asked if the Department of Justice should not have some scrutiny role in NIJAC's operations. But beyond posing such questions, the Assembly decided to go no further in injecting greater democratic accountability into the system and there is little sign that any significant political input will come about in the foreseeable future. A dominant sentiment in the judicial appointments process is the 'fear of the other' – a fear that a political or sectarian opponent will gain responsibility for selecting judges. There is also concern amongst judges and lawyers that political input would introduce political controversy. This has led to a consensus that the judicial appointments process should remain firmly in judicial hands and that the politicians should observe a self-denying ordinance and refrain from commenting on appointments.

[35] 'MLAs Criticise NI Lord Chief Justice Sir Declan Morgan', *BBC News*, 20 February 2014.

John Larkin's concern in 2012 about the lack of democratic accountability in the judicial appointments process was not limited to the relative input of judges and politicians, but also queried the role of the lay members: 'The present lay members should ask: what am I doing here?' He adverted to the 'danger of the creation of a self-perpetuating mandarin class of judges appointing themselves'.[36] Others have expressed similar concerns that the lay members would have limited influence in a body so dominated by judicial and legal interests. A lawyer warned one lay member when she joined NIJAC that she would be 'involved in a cover-up and providing a face'. The fact that the LCJ-NI chairs NIJAC has also led to claims that this gives the judiciary a much stronger position compared to that of England and Wales and Scotland where they have lay Chairs. Sir Declan Morgan strongly rejected this claim in 2012 in evidence to the Justice Committee:

> I am aware that there is a perception that NIJAC is dominated by the judiciary. That impression does a serious disservice to the very real contribution that the lay members make to the selection process. A lay member sits on all our schemes and makes as weighty a contribution as anyone else. All members of the commission have an equal status and contribute equally to the selection process.

He also argued that his own role was not a dominant one:

> Anyone who attends a NIJAC meeting is bound to come away understanding that what I, as chairman, seek to do is to bring all the skills forward with a view to ensuring that we achieve better outcomes in everything we do.[37]

Lay members made clear to us that they did not feel excluded from the decision-making and believed that their views had been taken into account. Conversely, one judge commented that judges who do not have direct involvement with NIJAC feel that *their* views are ignored. One possible reform which has been mooted is for the Chair of NIJAC to become a layperson. Our research suggests that the judiciary is unlikely to resist this proposal if it is taken forward.

[36] NI Assembly Justice Committee, *Review of Judicial Appointments in Northern Ireland: Evidence of the Attorney General for Northern Ireland* (NIA 38/11–15 (Session 2011–15) 2012).

[37] See NI Assembly Justice Committee, *Review of Judicial Appointments: Evidence of Sir Declan Morgan* (NIA 38/11–15 (Session 2011–15) 2012).

## *Scotland*

Before 2002, when the Judicial Appointments Board for Scotland (JABS) was created, the Lord Advocate had been responsible for appointments in Scotland: 'He appointed all the judges and usually then appointed himself to the highest office when he felt like it', as an advocate put it. The creation of JABS was therefore a radical reform. The impetus for the change was less about greater separation of powers and more about the perceived need to create a fairer and more transparent appointment process and in so doing to protect against allegations of cronyism. The decision to push ahead with a new system was driven by a few individuals, in particular the then Lord Advocate, Andrew Hardie; the Justice Secretary, Jim Wallace; and the civil servant in charge of the reform, David Stewart.

JABS is a small body compared to the JAC, and as a result its board members are directly involved in decision-making: 'Ten people who cut the wood and carry the water themselves', as a former board member put it. The board considers all full-time appointments other than the Lord President and Lord Justice Clerk. For these two top appointments, an *ad hoc* board is convened comprising two lay members of JABS and two judges nominated by the First Minister.[38] Like the JAC, JABS is formally a recommending rather than appointing body and it makes recommendations for appointment to a minister of the Scottish government (the First Minister) who may accept or reject them. Once accepted, the recommendation is formally made to the Queen. If the recommendation of JABS is rejected by the First Minister, the Board must reconsider it and make a further recommendation (which may be of the same individual).[39] Of the hundreds of recommendations made to date, the government has sought reconsideration only once and this was on a procedural rather than substantive issue.[40]

Relations between the Scottish government and JABS are generally good, although in the early days of its existence there were tensions around delays and leaks. The judicial members were also concerned about interactions with the government and, according to one

[38] Judiciary and Courts (Scotland) Act 2008, section 19(2) and Schedule 2. The JABS does not appoint temporary High Court judges and does not have a role in the promotion of judges from the Outer House to the Inner House of the Court of Session (the equivalent of appointment from High Court to Court of Appeal).

[39] Judiciary and Courts (Scotland) Act 2008, section 11.

[40] The candidate concerned was subsequently appointed to a judicial post.

interviewee, were prone to misinterpret ordinary institutional interactions as government interference. JABS was initially vulnerable in that it was not set up through primary legislation and could therefore have been dismantled relatively easily. In 2009, it was given statutory basis as a non-departmental public body and the danger of any threat to its continued existence passed.[41] Criticism subsided with the passage of time and changes in personnel, although administrative members of JABS still sometimes feel the need to 'translate' contact with the Scottish government for the judiciary. The budget for JABS is negotiated directly with the Scottish government but, at less than £0.5m, is small enough to be uncontroversial. In common with NIJAC, there is little contact between JABS and the devolved legislature, although JABS is obliged to provide an annual report to the Scottish Parliament. Similarly, there is little interest in judicial appointments amongst Scottish parliamentarians. The general view is that as long as the judicial appointments process is 'a dog that's not barking', the Parliament is content to leave it alone.

In common with the JAC and NIJAC, the relative influence of judicial and lay members on JABS remains a live issue. Of the three bodies, JABS is the only one with an equal number of lay members and judicial and legal members.[42] Of its ten members three are judicial, two are legal and five (including the chair) are lay. This composition was achieved in the teeth of judicial opposition. Most judges and lawyers felt that if the government was going to create a partial vacuum by stepping back and giving appointments to an independent commission, then the judiciary was 'the obvious choice to fill that vacuum' (former board member). The judges saw dangers in letting laypeople, as another former member put it, 'get their hands on the process' and they sought a judicial majority when the board was originally created and did so again in the debates over the 2008 Act. The government resisted this demand on both occasions. A senior judge put the judicial argument to us as follows:

> There ought to be a coherent judicial view as to the type of person who is best suited to judicial appointments at each level, and what the characteristics are that are being looked for. I don't know if those would be the characteristics that the lay members of the board would look for. In all probability they wouldn't.

[41] Judiciary and Courts (Scotland) Act 2008, section 9.
[42] Judiciary and Courts (Scotland) Act 2008, Schedule 1 and paras. 4 and 9.

The failure of the judges to persuade the executive to increase the judicial representation on the board meant that they decided that 'if they couldn't change Jim Wallace [the Justice Minister], they would try and change the board from within', according to a former Board member. As a *quid pro quo* for accepting the composition, the judges lobbied successfully for the inclusion in the 2008 legislation of a provision[43] making assessment of the legal skills of candidates a matter for the legal members of the Board. This formalised an existing practice and was intended to ensure, a board member told us, that 'senior and experienced lawyers make the judgement of whether somebody is a sufficiently senior, experienced and competent lawyer'. The practice had previously been used not as a legal veto but as a backstop for rare cases when a majority of the judicial members felt that 'X simply hasn't got it; this is too big a risk'. Once this practice was given statutory authority, some members of the board sought to give it a much wider interpretation by creating a two-stage process with an effective veto for judicial and legal members: an initial 'sift' of candidates in which lay members would not participate. Lay members resisted this, and a new practice has instead developed of the legal and judicial members conducting this sift in the presence of the lay members (who do not participate in the discussion). The scrutiny of the legal skills by the judicial and legal members is just one stage at which the judicial view on the competence of the candidates is put forward. It has influence but is not determinative. Much will depend on other assessments, including the references. However, these too will often have a strong judicial input and are taken seriously. In relation to the appointment of Senators, the board also seeks references from the Lord President and from a Sheriff Principal under whom the applicant has served. These references are usually written by the judges personally and so, inevitably, carry considerable weight.

### *The politics of judicial diversity*

The most politically sensitive issue in relation to judicial appointments, and the only issue to attract any significant attention outside the legal establishments of all three jurisdictions, has been the need to increase diversity in the composition of the judiciary. The lack of judicial diversity was a factor in the decisions to establish NIJAC and JABS as much as the JAC. In Northern Ireland, the main focus of the diversity issue in the past

[43] Judiciary and Courts (Scotland) Act 2008, section 13.

had been on the underrepresentation of judges from Catholic backgrounds. Before the 1970s almost all senior judges came from Protestant backgrounds. However, under direct rule (which began in 1972), the Lord Chancellor and the Westminster government made a conscious effort to engage in positive discrimination and sectarian discrimination was eliminated long before NIJAC's creation. Sir Declan Morgan is the second Catholic Lord Chief Justice in succession. In 2013, 52 per cent of judges were from a Protestant community background, 42 per cent from a Catholic background and 6 per cent from neither.[44] This roughly mirrors the make-up of the population and is also reflected in the statistical breakdown of those appointed by NIJAC.[45] However, there is a serious gender disparity. Men comprised 83 per cent of appointees in 2012–13 and Northern Ireland has never had a female judge at High Court level or above (women are somewhat better represented at lower levels of the judiciary). In Scotland, the focus has similarly been on the lack of women in the judiciary, particularly in the upper ranks, with a secondary concern over the absence of black and minority ethnic judges.

The starting point in all three jurisdictions has been the same: to require that appointments be made 'solely on merit'.[46] Many of the explanations for the continuing lack of diversity in Scotland and Northern Ireland are the same as those heard in England and Wales – that the judicial appointments process applies a narrow conception of merit and that women are underrepresented at the top of the legal profession from which the judiciary is appointed.[47] Despite policies in all three bodies designed to attract a wider range of candidates, across the UK there is growing concern that the removal of politicians from the appointments processes and the reinforcement of the role of the judiciary, while strengthening judicial independence, may have come at the cost of reducing the prospects for improving judicial diversity. Although senior judges in all three jurisdictions express a wish for greater diversity in relation to the gender, ethnic and social backgrounds of the judges, none has to date been willing to undertake positive action actively to seek out

[44] 'A Guide to Judicial Careers in Northern Ireland', 49.

[45] 'NIJAC Annual Report and Accounts 2012–2013' (Northern Ireland Judicial Appointments Commission, 2013) 23. Of those appointed by the NIJAC in 2012–13, 52 per cent identified themselves as having a Protestant community background, 35 per cent as Catholic and 13 per cent as neither.

[46] Section 12 of the 2008 Act in Scotland and section 5(8) of the Justice (Northern Ireland) Act 2002 in Northern Ireland.

[47] P. Leith and J. Morison, 'Rewarding Merit in Judicial Appointments?' (Belfast, QUB/ Northern Ireland Judicial Appointments Commission, 2013).

and argue for the appointment of non-traditional candidates, of the kind which was implemented in Northern Ireland to ensure balanced community representation on the bench. As an advocate noted in relation to Scotland, 'by giving the [legal and] judicial members a veto, what you get is judicial cloning. So the paradox is you get less diversity because it's now judges re-creating themselves rather than the Lord Advocate before saying, "Try this one, try that one"'. For this reason, one Northern Irish politician favoured some political role short of direct involvement in appointment, noting that without this 'the choice of women will never happen'. The appointment of three women, including the Chief Justice, to the Irish Supreme Court in recent years under a far more politicised appointments process lends weight to this claim.

In response to criticisms that they have been resistant to moves to ensure that more women are appointed to the bench, the judges argue that the removal of the 'tap on the shoulder' has stripped them of the ability to 'tap on the underrepresented shoulder'. As Lord President, Lord Hamilton publicly regretted the ending of the 'tap on the shoulder' system in connection with some temporary judge appointments, in part because it had enabled him to identify people who had real potential.[48] Today, the judges can only encourage non-traditional candidates to apply but they cannot guarantee that they will be appointed. This argument would be more powerful if the evidence suggested that senior judges had gone to any great effort to encourage such applications in the past. In this area, as in so many others, much depends on the commitments and views of individuals in leadership positions. We saw that in England and Wales Lord Irvine and Jack Straw both had a strong commitment to appointing a more diverse judiciary, whereas Kenneth Clarke was less interested. Similarly amongst the judges, some are known for taking the problem seriously, while others do little more than pay lip-service to the need for change. JABS limited the use of 'judicial soundings' in its work because these were felt to encourage judicial self-replication. However, the impetus for this came from the lay members and ultimately this procedural change has not been enough in itself to make a significant difference. As one former board member put it,

> The only way you can do more, this is what I would say in England and Wales too, is that you have to have the government having the political will to say, as they did in Canada, 'Well, you are going to do something about this, you are going to take gender into account.'

[48] Scottish Parliament Justice Committee, *Stage 1 Report on the Judiciary and Courts (Scotland) Bill: Evidence of Lord Hamilton* (SP Paper 91 (Session 3) 2008).

In the light of the effective removal of politicians from the process in all three jurisdictions, a change of personnel amongst the lay members of the appointment bodies and the senior ranks of the judiciary who are willing to 'do something about this' is therefore likely to have a more significant impact than many of the procedural changes which have been introduced over the years in the hope of bringing about greater diversity. Once again, personalities play a far more significant role in the politics of judicial appointments than is often acknowledged.

## Conclusion

The politics of judicial independence in Scotland and Northern Ireland are played out against the backdrop of their very particular legal and political traditions within small, tight-knit legal and political worlds. Individual personalities – whether judges, politicians, officials or laypeople – have an even greater influence than in England and Wales. We have noted the contributions in Scotland of officials like Eleanor Emberson and David Stewart, and in Northern Ireland of judges like Sir Brian Kerr and Sir Declan Morgan. The smaller scale also allows for more informal and personal engagement to smooth potential tensions. The suspicion generated within the judiciary in England and Wales by the way in which the Constitutional Reform Act 2005 was introduced was not replicated with the introduction of reforms in the rest of the UK. Relations between judges and politicians in Scotland and in Northern Ireland have generally been easier than they have been in England and Wales.

The politics of judicial independence are no less dynamic in Scotland and Northern Ireland. The mutually respectful relationship between Scottish judges and politicians has yet to be as seriously tested as it has been in England and Wales. If judicial review of government decisions becomes a bigger feature of the Scottish institutional landscape, the Scottish judiciary might find itself more exposed. So far the Supreme Court has served as a lightning rod deflecting political criticism away from the local judiciary. If Scotland withdraws from the jurisdiction of that court, its judges will find themselves in the media and political firing line more often. Their failure to defend Lord Hope more forcefully and publicly against the criticisms he faced after the *Cadder* and *Fraser* cases may come back to haunt them.

In Northern Ireland, judges have been insulated from politics because politicians on all sides of the political divide have observed a self-denying ordinance in respect of the judicial system. This has largely protected the judiciary from the bitter hostility that is still a feature of partisan politics. Politicians regard judicial control of the appointments process as the least objectionable option: better for judges to recruit judges than for a perceived political enemy to do so. This political retreat has, however, meant that politicians are sometimes poorly informed about the requirements of judicial independence and judges are semi-detached from the administrative politics of running the courts. The removal of the Lord Chancellor from the system has also come at a cost. He served a number of useful functions: a 'moderating influence and a protective role', a conduit for messages to flow to the Cabinet at Westminster and back again, and a 'decompression chamber' for reducing tensions between judges and politicians, according to a senior civil servant. He was also someone who could get judges onside for necessary reforms, if need be saying to the Lord Chief Justice, 'Look, get over it, suck it up. That's the way it is', as a judicial official put it.

The trend towards disengagement by politicians from the running of the courts and the appointment of judges has also come at the cost of a lack of political and democratic accountability for these activities in both jurisdictions. This accountability gap is problematic in its own right. But it also has longer-term implications for judicial independence. As we have emphasised throughout this work, the willingness of politicians to retreat from the justice system may do longterm damage. It means that the main guardians of judicial independence are the judges themselves. In Scotland, the role of the Lord Advocate has changed from that of a political figure who 'knew how to negotiate with the political class' to something closer to that of a career civil servant. This has left a vacuum which has not been filled by Parliament and 'because of a habit of neglect' (advocate) judges have got used to this. In Northern Ireland, judicial accountability is 'a work in progress . . . and neither side's played it particularly well so far, neither the judges nor the assembly' (senior civil servant).

All three jurisdictions have struggled with the question of how best to ensure that court budgets are protected. Judges are sensitive to the danger of being swamped by more politically pressing concerns (such as the far larger prison budget), and to the importance of having a voice at the Cabinet table when resources are tight. The partnership model in England and Wales sometimes gives rise to tensions but it has the benefit of requiring politicians to work closely with senior judges and of ensuring that they are familiar with judicial concerns. If the systems in

Northern Ireland and in England and Wales move to a judge-led Scottish model, the process of political retreat from the judicial system will increase in pace. The implications of this trend are potentially serious. Politicians appear relatively unconcerned about pushing for greater judicial accountability. If, however, judges assume greater control over the administration of the courts, over judicial appointments and over judicial conduct, 'responsibility without control' may be replaced by 'control without responsibility'. So long as everything runs smoothly in all areas this accountability gap is likely to remain under the public radar. But in the event of a crisis, such as the exposure of financial mismanagement in the courts service, or growing impatience at the failure to increase judicial diversity, judges risk finding themselves seriously exposed, with no one else to take the blame.

# 10

# Conclusion

The central argument of this book is that judicial independence is necessarily a political achievement. Because the principle of judicial independence is contextual and contested, we can only understand its place in the constitutional arrangements of the UK today by examining the ways in which politicians, judges and officials negotiate and renegotiate its precise meaning and its limits. In the early years of the twenty-first century, the context in which these politics were played out involved radical reforms to the institutional and constitutional landscape. Some change had started to happen; but those reforms brought about a big shift in the politics of judicial independence, in all three jurisdictions of the UK. This final chapter focuses mainly on England and Wales, with comparisons with Scotland and Northern Ireland where appropriate. It begins by summarising the main characteristics of the new politics of judicial independence, before considering the challenges ahead for the judiciary and the politicians responsible for the justice system.

The old politics were largely informal, closed and consensual. The relationship between judges and politicians was built on very similar understandings of what judicial independence required in practice and relations were highly collaborative, with neither side keen to change the system. They were also stable, until the removal of Lord Irvine in 2003 abruptly ended the old system, and ended it forever. Some of these features are still evident. The new politics still depend on informal contacts between judges and politicians to cement good relations. Like the old, the new politics rely on personalities to help smooth over tensions; while the particular approach of individual office-holders is still instrumental in shaping the relationships and developing the reform agenda itself. But there are important differences. Today, the new politics of judicial independence are more formalised, and fragmented. There has also been a retreat by politicians from running the judicial system, paralleled by greater involvement by judges and a consequent increase in judicial self-governance.

## The new politics: formalised and fragmented

A defining feature of the old politics of judicial independence was that the judicial and political worlds were interconnected and governed substantially by tradition and convention. Today, the two operate in increasingly distinct spheres. The greater separation of powers introduced by the Constitutional Reform Act 2005 required more formal structures and processes to handle the relationships between more separate branches of government, most notably in the area of judicial appointments and conduct, the management of the courts and the judicial governance structure. Some of these processes were created by the Constitutional Reform Act itself, while others have emerged subsequently. More formal processes are also evident in the detailed procedures laid down in the 2004 Concordat between the Lord Chief Justice and the Lord Chancellor, and in the later Framework Documents 2008 and 2011 which covered the management of the Courts Service. Although the smaller size of the jurisdictions of Northern Ireland and Scotland have allowed informal arrangements to continue in both systems to a greater degree than in England and Wales, there too new bodies and new rules have been created in relation to the judicial appointments process, judicial discipline and the courts services.

The system of communications between the judiciary in England and Wales and the outside world has also been formalised with the creation of the Judicial Communications Office and the willingness of judges to be guided and supported in managing their communications in a faster and less deferential world. Similarly, while many of the informal meetings and communications through which the politics of judicial independence were traditionally conducted still take place, the judiciary's channels of communications with politicians have become more formalised with meetings at regular and fixed intervals between the senior judges and politicians. Parliament has also been a focus for the development of more formal relations through the regular appearances by senior judges before Parliamentary Select Committees and *ad hoc* inquiries by committees into particular aspects of the justice system.

This more formalised politics of judicial independence has also become more fragmented. Because there is less reliance on the Lord

Chancellor alone as the buckle between the judiciary and the government, a wider range of actors are involved in negotiations and interactions which shape the politics of judicial independence. Some have long played important roles, albeit out of sight, hidden behind the Whitehall and Westminster curtains. These have been joined by new actors, in particular lay members appointed to bodies such as HMCTS and the Judicial Appointments Commission. Involving laypeople in decisions previously taken by civil servants and politicians is not unique to the judicial sphere, but it has further dispersed responsibility for safeguarding judicial independence and for negotiating its meaning and boundaries.

The internal governance of the judiciary has undergone a similar process of formalisation, again most notably in England and Wales, where the expansion of the judiciary and the courts service to embrace the whole of the tribunals system has been a radical, if relatively neglected, change. The stronger leadership role of the Lord Chief Justice as the new head of the judiciary has been accompanied by the formal delegation of important administrative and managerial tasks to dozens of other judges. This senior management team now operates through the Judicial Executive Board as a form of judicial Cabinet, supported by the revitalised Judges' Council, which provides a stronger 'voice' for the whole judiciary.

## Political retreat and judicial advance

The main consequence of the formalisation and fragmentation of the politics of judicial independence has been the increasing disengagement of ministers from judiciary-related matters and the growing importance of the judicial leadership in filling this vacuum. The very purpose of the Constitutional Reform Act 2005 (CRA) was to increase the formal separation of powers between the political and judicial branches of government and to reduce the role of the executive in judicial matters. The flip side of political retreat has been judicial advance. In response to the changing role of the Lord Chancellor, the first three Lord Chief Justices to be head of the judiciary in England and Wales – Lord Woolf, Lord Phillips and Lord Judge – worked hard to strengthen the institutional autonomy of the judiciary and heightened their influence in the running of the judicial system. Political retreat and judicial advance have taken different forms. In some areas, such as judicial discipline, which used to be a matter exclusively for the Lord Chancellor, responsibility is now formally shared between the Lord Chancellor and the LCJ. Likewise, the Courts Service was reconfigured as a partnership to be run jointly between the executive and the judiciary. The transformation of the Judicial Office into a *de facto* judicial civil service was an important factor in allowing the judiciary to share much of the day-to-day management of the judiciary with the Ministry of Justice.

The marginalisation of the executive has also shaped judicial appointments, where a highly informal system built around largely unfettered ministerial discretion has been replaced by a closely regulated statutory system managed by an independent body, in which the Lord Chancellor plays only a limited role. The transfer of the final say over lower-level appointments from the Lord Chancellor to the Lord Chief Justice and the Senior President of Tribunals is symbolic of the shift in power from ministers to senior judges in respect of individual appointment decisions. The Lord Chancellor is now formally responsible for making just 3 per cent of judicial appointments. Though still having a veto power over appointments to the High Court and above, Lord Chancellors in practice almost always accept the recommendations made to them, and instead input earlier in the selection processes. Over and above this, judges are involved at all stages of the selection processes. In the JAC-run processes, judicial influence is present through all aspects of a complex process. This is not to deny that lay members play an important role, especially in injecting fresh insights from their different backgrounds in the public sector, private sector, human resources and so on. It is simply to recognise that the CRA has engineered considerable judicial influence throughout the selection processes. As repeat players in the process, senior judges are adept at using additional selection criteria and statutory consultation to ensure that weight is attached to their viewpoints. The Crime and Courts Act 2013 increased lay involvement in the most senior appointments in England and Wales, but judicial influence remains particularly high at the top levels.

This broad pattern can be seen in all three jurisdictions: highly formal processes are run by arm's-length bodies, with limited ministerial involvement. The Northern Ireland Judicial Appointments Commission (NIJAC) is the most strongly judge-led, being chaired by the Chief Justice, with only five lay members out of thirteen commissioners. Because of the reluctance in Northern Ireland to allow politicians near judicial appointments, NIJAC is *de facto* the appointing body – a system depicted by the Northern Ireland Attorney General as 'judges appointing judges'. In Scotland, the Judicial Appointments Board (JABS) has equal numbers of lay and legal/judicial members; but with only one recommendation ever queried, it too is *de facto* an appointing body.

The transfer of appointments from the Lord Chancellor to judges and laypeople was explicit and has been the subject of considerable debate, including in Parliament. In contrast, the decision to merge the courts and tribunals judiciaries has attracted almost no attention outside the legal world, although it may prove to be the most important driver in this process of political retreat. Tribunals are a large and increasingly important part of the judicial system. They used to be wholly dependent on their sponsoring government departments for their funding and for the appointment of Tribunal members. Now the appointments are all made by the JAC and the Senior President of Tribunals, independently of government, and the funding of Tribunals comes from HMCTS.

At the other end of the court hierarchy, a related but different shift in power has taken place. The creation of the new Supreme Court detached the highest-profile element of the court system from the legislature. Having been constitutionally, financially and administratively embedded in the House of Lords, its successor has its own building, its own budget and its own staff, with extensive institutional freedom to run its own affairs headed by the President, Deputy President and Chief Executive. Yet, paradoxically, a consequence of this detachment from Parliament has been to require the Supreme Court Justices to engage more closely with the executive on issues such as budgets and administration. Separation from Westminster has led to closer connections to Whitehall than was ever the case for the Law Lords.

In Scotland and Northern Ireland there has been a similar political retreat and judicial advance. We have already noted how in both countries judicial appointments have been transferred to an independent appointing body, with politicians effectively being removed from the process. Scotland has seen a similar shift in the running of the Court Service. The Scottish Court Service (SCS) was an executive-run body, but since 2010 has been judge-led, with the Lord President chairing the board and appointing the other board members, including six other judges. This judge-led model has given the judges much greater ownership of planning and running the courts. The Northern Ireland judiciary seems likely to go down the same road after 2016. As for complaints and discipline, here too there has been political retreat and judicial advance, which has gone even further in Scotland and

Northern Ireland. With no equivalent to the involvement of the Lord Chancellor, the judiciary in Scotland and Northern Ireland sets the disciplinary rules and exercises greater control over the process.

## The challenges ahead

In this more formalised and fragmented politics of judicial independence, in which power has shifted from politicians to judges, new boundaries and ground rules are being constructed. The following issues are likely to be particularly important in the years ahead.

### *Accountability*

Throughout the book we have traced the changes in accountability in tandem with independence, arguing that an independent judiciary presupposes a degree of democratic accountability. The changes summarised above have as much significance for the day-to-day politics of judicial accountability as they do for judicial independence. Our findings show that judicial accountability has increased in many areas, sometimes quite dramatically. The senior judiciary has shown itself to be far less conservative than might be expected in its willingness to embrace greater transparency. A wide array of information on the functioning of the courts is now published by the judiciary through websites and reports. Much judicial business which was previously conducted behind closed doors in the old Lord Chancellor's Department is now out in the open; annual reports and statistics are produced by the Ministry of Justice and the judiciary-related bodies. This is not just a consequence of the constitutional changes, but results from wider initiatives in Whitehall and Westminster to make government more open and accountable.

The increasing trend for the senior judiciary to give evidence to select committees has also been facilitated by the creation of two new specialist select committees: the Lords Constitution Committee and the Commons Justice Committee, both of which have produced several reports on judicial matters. The administrative and operational side of the justice system is also accountable through investigations by the National Audit Office (NAO) and the Ombudsman. These are some of the formal channels through which accountability has been developed. Equally important are the 'soft' accountability processes by which the courts and judiciary engage more generally with the media and the public.

Here, very significant changes are also evident, most strikingly in the Supreme Court, which has pursued an outward-facing and user-friendly approach unprecedented in the UK courts, with a new building, website, television coverage and public outreach work.

These examples are all evidence of narrative or explanatory accountability, whereby those responsible for the judicial system offer an account of its different parts and explain how they function. On a day-to-day basis it is this explanatory accountability that forms the bedrock of accountability in a democratic system. The counterpart is accountability in the classic 'sacrificial' sense of a decision-maker taking ultimate responsibility for their decisions or conduct. Individual judges are now more accountable for their behaviour beyond their judicial decision-making. The complaints and disciplinary system has become more visible and is much more frequently used. Judges are more often reprimanded for poor conduct, not because standards have fallen, but because there is now a more effective and responsive system for identifying conduct which falls short.

But our findings also reveal some potential problems as clear lines of responsibility have become more blurred as a result of greater fragmentation. For example, it would no longer be possible to argue that a Lord Chancellor should resign if it was discovered that a judge was appointed as a result of a serious mistake in the judicial appointments process, given how little responsibility the Lord Chancellor now has for that process. Similarly, since judicial independence has traditionally and rightly required a high threshold before judges can be removed from office, it is equally hard to imagine that Parliament would call for the resignation or dismissal of the LCJ as head of the judiciary should serious mismanagement be discovered in the Judicial Office, or a serious error of judgement made in the appointment of a Circuit Judge. In short, it is hard to determine where, in relation to decision-making in areas such as judicial appointments and the management of the judiciary and of the Courts Service, the accountability buck now stops. The greater fragmentation described above may have the advantage that judicial independence is safeguarded by more individuals in more places, and it may also increase the scope for effective mechanisms of explanatory accountability when things run smoothly, but it runs the risk that no one individual office-holder is ultimately responsible when things go wrong.

There are also weaknesses in the degree and quality of accountability provided by Parliament. Select committees can be fickle and patchy in their coverage: they have shown much initial interest in judicial appointments, but ignored the running of the Courts Service. They do, at times, criticise the courts, and judges in turn have sought to address these concerns. But the boundaries of this process of accountability are not yet clear and to date there have been no examples of serious or sustained pressure on a senior judge in relation to management decisions. This may be because no senior judge has ever made any serious management mistakes, or, more likely, because they are dealt with internally and out of sight.

An example of the potential dangers of this accountability gap is in the area of judicial diversity. Many senior judges explicitly and genuinely wish to see greater diversity in the composition of the judiciary, not just in relation to gender and ethnicity but also in terms of the balance between former barristers and solicitors and the range of legal expertise which appointees bring to the bench. But they have found it hard to recognise the implicit self-replication that can inform assessments of what constitutes merit in the appointments process, and, in turn, the role that this plays in inhibiting significant change. In the absence of a politician who is responsible to the electorate to take forward the diversity agenda, the expectation has been that the lay members of the appointments bodies will fulfil this role. Our evidence suggests that even when individual lay members are committed to the need for change, they do not have the authority that comes with elected office which they would need to push back hard enough against judicial preferences. Laypeople lack that electoral mandate, but are expected to substitute for politicians in being a check on 'judges appointing judges'. The inclusion of laypeople further reduces accountability: they bring different expertise, but cannot begin to provide the accountability which only politicians can supply.

### *Finding a new equilibrium*

Lawyers tend to conceive of judicial independence as a fixed principle. But as we demonstrated in Chapter 2, attitudes to and definitions of judicial independence have changed down the ages – and they are still changing. The expansion of training and the introduction of performance appraisal for judges, both once viewed by the judiciary as a fundamental breach of judicial independence, are now enthusiastically supported by many in the senior judiciary. It is through debate, discussion, negotiation and renegotiation between judges, politicians, officials, laypeople and the public (via the media) that new understandings of how the principle of judicial independence should play out in practice are forged.

New understandings of judicial independence traditionally emerged slowly, in the evolutionary manner which characterises change to the UK's constitutional arrangements. In contrast, the research which underpins this book was carried out at an unusually dynamic and unstable moment in the politics of judicial independence. Some of our findings are inevitably specific to that time. It is still too early to say whether we are now entering a new period of stability in which institutional changes will be allowed to bed down. In the short term, the stability of the old arrangements has been lost. But in the longer term, several institutions now exist on a surer and more independent footing, the most obvious being the Supreme Court. After initial tensions with the Ministry of Justice over its funding and administration, and despite occasional criticism from ministers north and south of the border, the Supreme Court has established itself as a confident and well-respected body. Similarly, after a bumpy first few years marked by fraught tensions with the Ministry of Justice, culminating in its 'near-death experience', the Judicial Appointments Commission's position in the institutional landscape now seems settled.

Another positive indicator of the emergence of a new equilibrium and a more stable foundation underpinning the new politics of judicial independence is the effect of the painful funding cuts to the justice system in the wake of the 2007 economic crisis. Despite severe reductions in court funding, a freeze on judicial salaries and adverse changes to judicial pensions, senior judges and the executive managed to negotiate a budget which each side could live with. This is not to suggest that negotiating these issues was easy. But it does perhaps indicate that the working relationship has been stress-tested and found to be strong enough to survive.

It also indicates that, at least amongst the senior judiciary, there is a growing acceptance that judicial independence does not protect the judiciary from its share of public spending cuts and that there is a distinction between the public interest and judicial self-interest. The cuts have been hard for the judiciary to bear, but no senior judge has yet come out and said that they threaten the independence of the courts. It is unlikely that if Lord Mackay was Lord Chancellor today, and sought to end lawyers' restrictive practices, he would be attacked by the judges, as he was in the 1990s, as posing a fundamental threat to judicial independence and the rule of law.

But while stability might be emerging in some areas, in at least one respect the signs are that further major change may lie ahead. In England

and Wales, the judiciary and the government spent most of 2013 negotiating the possibility of a much more autonomous court system. If this is implemented, the knock-on effects of this change for the politics of judicial independence will be significant. For one thing the accountability deficit will become more glaring and less acceptable. If the judiciary comes to assume the lead in running the new courts service, Parliament will need to eschew its deferential approach and scrutinise the senior judiciary as keenly as it would the leaders of any other major public service. The judiciary, for its part, would have to supply a full account of its stewardship of public resources and be willing to be held to account for any failings. At the same time, the proportion of the work of the Ministry of Justice which relates to the courts would shrink further and the Lord Chancellor would have even less reason to prioritise the needs of the judiciary. This raises the question of what role the office of Lord Chancellor will play in safeguarding judicial independence in the years ahead.

### *Filling the vacuum of the Lord Chancellor*

The judges have sometimes been guilty of having selective memories in cherishing the unqualified vigilance of the old Lord Chancellors as guardians of judicial independence. Nevertheless, they are right to worry about the potential implications of the reform of that office. New Lord Chancellors are no longer expected to be senior lawyers and politicians towards the end of their careers, but are ministers of justice, no different in status from any other politician in Cabinet, and with one eye on the next job. At the same time, the Ministry of Justice has grown into a large department where the judiciary and courts account for less than a fifth of its budget. The faster turnover of staff also means that officials have less opportunity to develop a sophisticated appreciation of the culture of judicial independence and judicial accountability.

The judges view all these changes as for the worse. They fear that under the new system they do not have such a strong voice at the Cabinet table. Our findings do not reveal any evidence to show that the changes to the office of Lord Chancellor have – as yet – weakened support for judicial independence. Assessing whether or not this is likely to happen in the future requires a distinction to be drawn between judicial interests and judicial independence. Future Lord Chancellors may fail to defend the interests of the judges over issues like judicial salaries and pensions, while at the same time being effective guardians of judicial independence. Only when an issue arises which has clear implications for judicial independence will we know whether the new Lord Chancellors will step up to the plate. As ever, much is likely to depend on the individual personality of the person in post at the time.

Although the judiciary may have overstated the threat to judicial independence from the reform of the office of Lord Chancellor, any further disconnection between the Lord Chancellor and the judges risks further reducing the personal responsibility of Lord Chancellors for the administration of justice. Given the uncertainties, judges are right to continue to assume that they, and the LCJ in particular, will be required to take a more central role in the politics of judicial independence. However, as Lord Judge noted, the LCJ is a 'poor substitute' for the Lord Chancellor and cannot carry that role alone. The fragmentation described above means that a wider range of politicians and officials must be ready to engage. In the short term, the retreat of the politicians and the reduced role of the Lord Chancellor could appear to work to the advantage of the judges, since they will become the 'repeat players' who remain in post while Lord Chancellors come and go. This will allow them to cement their influence and interests over the running of the courts as they have done for judicial appointments and discipline. In the longer term, however, if Lord Chancellors and their officials retreat from judiciary-related matters, and if more limited contact between judges and politicians makes it more difficult to nurture positive personal relationships, the political understanding of why judicial independence matters might atrophy. Over time, Lord Chancellors might not take seriously their personal responsibility for the efficient and effective working of the judicial system and might take less care when exercising their residual discretion over judiciary-related issues. Without good examples set by the Lord Chancellor, there is a danger that other politicians will in turn become less mindful of constitutional proprieties. Arguably, the primary challenge of the future is, paradoxically, to strengthen the ministerial side of the judicial–political partnership, to find ways of reminding politicians of the stake that they share in a system of independent courts.

### *Separation, not divorce*

A key finding of this work is that, counterintuitively, the greater constitutional separation between judges and politicians since 2005 requires more day-to-day contact between them in order to negotiate and maintain the terms of that separation. A healthy politics of judicial independence requires that politicians do not regard judicial independence simply as an inconvenience, or seek to hive off responsibility for those parts of the justice system which have little political purchase. At the same time, judges must continue to develop their political acumen, showing the same skill with which they have navigated the constitutional changes of recent years. A series of successful rearguard actions has seen them retain, and indeed enhance, their role in crucial decision-making in areas such as judicial appointments, complaints and discipline, court management and budgetary negotiations. In deciding when to tackle the government in the future, the judges need to be astute about which issues to fight and which to drop. They must choose battles which they are likely to win, on issues which are likely to command parliamentary and public support. This may not be easy for judges whose only professional experience is the world of the law and life on the bench. The worlds of politics and the law have become much more separate than they used to be, with the result that there is a risk of a growing gulf in understanding. As the judiciary becomes a more separate branch of government, the judges must be careful not to isolate themselves, but must rather redouble their efforts to engage with the political branches. The danger is not that they have been marginalised, as they first feared, but instead that they may get all they wished for. If they find that the executive has retreated from the running of the courts and the judicial appointments process, leaving the field to them, the partnership will exist in name alone. The Constitutional Reform Act was designed to produce greater separation, but not divorce. It sought to create a new form of partnership, very different from the traditional relationship, but one which had the potential to form the basis of a new culture in which judicial independence is valued as a political achievement.

The rules, structures and processes must help politicians to grasp that an independent judiciary is an indispensable part of a democratic system, even if from time to time courts render politically unpopular decisions. Those same arrangements must also help judges to see that an effective partnership between the political and judicial branches requires that ministers are interested in and concerned about the financial and administrative health of the judicial system. Judges should never forget that judicial independence is not shorthand for saying that politicians must defer to the judges on questions relating to the running of the judicial system, and they cannot expect to exercise a veto on issues such as the budgets of the courts. Related to this, judges must recognise the need for heightened judicial accountability at the same time as they exercise increased power over the management and funding of the judicial system. The reason why all of this matters is because, no matter how formalised the politics of judicial independence become, the boundaries between the political and judicial branches are not and never can be fixed. They will always be contested. Politicians and judges can and do legitimately hold different opinions about where the boundaries ought to lie. What matters is not that politicians or judges know the right answer, or that the former always defer to the views of the latter, but that both negotiate in good faith as informed and respectful participants in the politics of judicial independence.

# BIBLIOGRAPHY

## Official documents and reports

Assembly and Executive Review Committee, *Inquiry into the Devolution of Policing and Justice Matters: Evidence of David Lavery* (22/07/08R (Session 2007–08) 2007)

Assembly and Executive Review Committee, *Inquiry into the Devolution of Policing and Justice Matters: Evidence of Sir Brian Kerr* (22/07/08R (Session 2007–08) 2007)

Cabinet Office, *Executive Agencies: A Guide for Departments* (2006)

Canadian Judicial Council, *Alternative Models of Court Administration* (Ottawa, ON, 2006)

Chen, A., *The Determination and Revision of Judicial Remuneration* (Hong Kong, Report for the Hong Kong Standing Committee on Judicial Salaries and Conditions of Service, 2008)

Church, T. W. and Sallmann, P., *Governing Australia's Courts* (Carlton South, Vic., Australia, Australian Institute of Judicial Administration, 1991)

Committee on Super-Injunctions, *Super-Injunctions, Anonymised Injunctions and Open Justice* (2011)

*Commonwealth (Latimer House) Principles on the Three Branches of Government* (2003)

Commonwealth Secretariat, *Commonwealth Principles on the Accountability of and the Relationship between the Three Branches of Government* ([S.1], Commonwealth Secretariat, 2003)

*Concordat between: The Ministry of Justice (MOJ) and the Supreme Court of the United Kingdom (The Court)* (DEP2014-0133 2013)

Council of HM Circuit Judges, *Convicting Rapists and Protecting Victims: A Consultation* (2006)

Court Service Agency, *Framework Document* (1995)

Cribb, J. and others, *Living Standards, Poverty and Inequality in the UK: 2013* (Institute for Fiscal Studies, 2013)

Department of Constitutional Affairs, *Constitutional Reform: A New Way of Appointing Judges* (CP 10/03 2003)

Department of Constitutional Affairs, *Constitutional Reform: A Supreme Court for the United Kingdom* (CP 11/03 2003)

Department of Constitutional Affairs, *Constitutional Reform: The Lord Chancellor's Judiciary Related Functions: Proposals ('the Concordat')* (2004)

Department of Constitutional Affairs, *The Judicial Appointments Commission: Framework Document* (2006)

European Commission for the Efficiency of Justice, *Evaluation Report on European Judicial Systems* (2012)

Gay, O. /House of Commons Parliament and Constitution Centre, *Role of the Lord Chancellor* (SN/PC/2105 2003)

Genn, H., *The Attractiveness of Senior Judicial Appointment to Highly Qualified Practitioners: A Report to the Judicial Executive Board* (2008)

HC Constitutional Affairs Committee, *Asylum and Immigration Tribunal: The Appeals Process* (HC 1006-I 2006)

HC Constitutional Affairs Committee, *The Creation of the Ministry of Justice* (HC 466 2007)

HC Constitutional Affairs Committee, *Judicial Appointments and a Supreme Court (Court of Final Appeal)* (HC 48-I 2004)

HC Constitutional Affairs Committee, *Judicial Appointments and a Supreme Court (Court of Final Appeal): Evidence of Sir Colin Campbell* (HC 1275-i 2003)

HC Constitutional Affairs Committee, *Judicial Appointments and a Supreme Court (Court of Final Appeal) – Minutes of Evidence* (HC 48-II 2004)

HC Constitutional Affairs Committee, *Judicial Appointments Commission – Minutes of Evidence* (HC 416-I 2007)

HC Constitutional Affairs Committee, *Judicial Appointments Commission – Minutes of Evidence* (HC 416-II 2007)

HC Culture, Media and Sport Committee, *Press Standards, Privacy and Libel* (HC 362-I 2010)

HC Home Affairs Committee, *The US–UK Extradition Treaty* (HC 644 2012)

HC Justice Committee, *Appointment of the Chair of the Judicial Appointments Commission* (HC 770 2011)

HC Justice Committee, *The Budget and Structure of the Ministry of Justice* (HC 97-II 2012)

HC Justice Committee, *Operation of the Family Courts* (HC 518-I 2011)

HC Justice Committee, *Operation of the Family Courts – Oral and Written Evidence* (HC 518-II 2011)

HC Justice Committee, *Towards Effective Sentencing* (HC 184-I 2008)

HC Justice Committee, *Towards Effective Sentencing: Oral and Written Evidence* (HC 184-II 2008)

HC Justice Committee, *The Work of the Judicial Appointments Commission – Oral Evidence Taken on 7 September 2010* (HC 449-I 2010)

HC Justice Committee, *The Work of the Legal Services Commission – Uncorrected Evidence – 30 November 2010* (HC 649-I 2012)

HC Justice Committee, *The Work of the Lord Chief Justice – Oral Evidence – 26 October 2010* (HC 521-I 2012)

HC Liaison Committee, *Select Committees and Public Appointments* (HC 830 2012)

HC Procedure Committee, *The Sub Judice Rule of the House of Commons* (HC 125 2005)

HC Public Administration Committee, *Government by Inquiry – Minutes of Evidence* (HC 51-II 2005)

HL Committee on the Constitutional Reform Bill, *Constitutional Reform Bill [HL]* (HL 125-I 2004)

HL Committee on the Constitutional Reform Bill, *Constitutional Reform Bill [HL] – Volume II: Evidence* (HL 125-II 2004)

HL Constitution Committee, *Coroners and Justice Bill* (HL 96 2009)

HL Constitution Committee, *Counter-terrorism Bill: The Role of Ministers, Parliament and the Judiciary* (HL 167 2008)

HL Constitution Committee, *Crime and Courts Bill [HL]* (HL 17 2012)

HL Constitution Committee, *Judicial Appointments* (HL 272 2012)

HL Constitution Committee, *Justice (Northern Ireland) Bill* (HL 40 2004)

HL Constitution Committee, *Justice and Security (Northern Ireland) Bill* (HL 54 2007)

HL Constitution Committee, *Meetings with the Lord Chief Justice and the Lord Chancellor* (HL 89 2011)

HL Constitution Committee, 'Memorandum by Lord Irvine of Lairg', *The Cabinet Office and the Centre of Government* (HL 30 2009)

HL Constitution Committee, *Northern Ireland Bill* (HL 50 2009)

HL Constitution Committee, *Parliamentary Standards Bill: Implications for Parliament and the Courts* (HL 134 2009)

HL Constitution Committee, *Relations between the Executive, the Judiciary and Parliament* (HL 151 2007)

HL Constitution Committee, *Relations between the Executive, the Judiciary and Parliament: Follow-up Report* (HL 177 2008)

HL Constitution Committee, *Welfare Reform Bill* (HL 79 2009)

HM Courts and Tribunals Service, *Annual Report and Accounts 2011–12* (HC 323 2012)

HM Courts and Tribunals Service, *Annual Report and Accounts 2012–13* (HC 239 2013)

HM Treasury, *Spending Review 2010* (London: TSO, 2010)

HM Treasury, *Spending Round 2013* (London: TSO, 2013)

HM Treasury, *Managing Public Money* (2013)

House of Commons, *Matters Sub Judice: Resolution of 15 November 2001*

House of Lords, *The Grey Book: Who Does What in the House of Lords* (2014)

International Bar Association, *Minimum Standards of Judicial Independence* (1982)

Joint Colloquium on Parliamentary Supremacy and Judicial Independence – towards a Commonwealth Model, *Parliamentary Supremacy, Judicial Independence: Latimer House Guidelines for the Commonwealth* (Oxford: Latimer House, 1998)

Joint Committee on Human Rights, *Enhancing Parliament's Role in Relation to Human Rights Judgments* (HL 85/HC 455 2010)

Joint Committee on Human Rights, *Human Rights Judgments: Minutes of Evidence (Uncorrected Transcript of Oral Evidence)* (HC 873-II 2011)

Joint Committee on Human Rights, *Legislative Scrutiny: Crime and Courts Bill* (HL 67/HC 771 2012)

Joint Committee on Parliamentary Privilege, *Parliamentary Privilege* (HL 30/HC 100 2013)

Joint Committee on Privacy and Injunctions, *Privacy and Injunctions* (HL 273/HC 1443 2012)

Joint Committee on the Draft Constitutional Renewal Bill, *Draft Constitutional Renewal Bill* (HL 166-I/HC 551-I 2008)

Judges' Council, *Annual Report 2007*

Judges' Council, *First Progress Report of the Standing Committee of the Judges' Council – Judicial Support and Welfare* (2007)

Judges' Council, *Guide to Judicial Conduct* (2008)

Judicial Appointments and Conduct Ombudsman, *Business Plan 2011–2012*

Judicial Appointments Commission, *Annual Report and Accounts: 2006–7* (HC 632 2007)

Judicial Appointments Commission, *Annual Report and Accounts 2009–10* (HC 219 2010)

Judicial Appointments Commission, *Annual Report and Accounts 2011–12* (HC 351 2012)

Judicial Appointments Commission, *Annual Report and Accounts: 2012–13* (HC 495 2013)

Judicial Appointments Commission, *Judicial Selection and Recommendations for Appointment Statistics, England and Wales, April 2010 to September 2010: Judicial Appointments Commission: Statistics Bulletin* (2010)

Judicial Appointments Commission, *Judicial Selection and Recommendations for Appointment Statistics, April to September 2011: Judicial Appointments Commission Statistics Bulletin* (2011)

Judicial Appointments Commission, *Judicial Selection and Recommendations for Appointment Statistics, October 2011 to March 2012: Judicial Appointments Commission Statistics Bulletin* (2012)

Judicial Appointments Commission, *Judicial Selection and Recommendations for Appointment Statistics, October 2012 to March 2013* (2013)

Judicial College, *Performance Report April–June 2013* (2013)

Judicial Conduct and Investigations Office, *Statement from the Judicial Conduct and Investigations Office* (OJC 58/13 2013)

Judicial Executive Board, *Guidance for Judges Appearing before or Providing Written Evidence to Parliamentary Committees* (2008)

Judicial Executive Board, *Guidance to Judges on Appearances before Select Committees* (2012)

Judicial Independence Project, 'The Abolition of the Office of Lord Chancellor: 10 Years On: Note of Seminar Held at Queen Mary, University of London' (12 June 2013)

Judicial Independence Project, 'Judicial Independence in Northern Ireland: Note of Seminar Held in Belfast' (6 November 2012)

Judicial Office, *Business Plan 2011–2012*

Judicial Office, *Business Plan 2013–2014*

Judicial Office, *Lord Chief Justice's Report 2013* (2013)

Judicial Office, *Magistrates in Post 2013*

Judicial Office, *Overview Data of Judicial Appointments by Type – 2013* (2013)

Judicial Studies Board, *Appraisal Standards and Appraiser Competences in Tribunals* (2009)

Judiciary of England and Wales, 'The Accountability of the Judiciary' (2007)

Leggatt, S. A., *Tribunals for Users – One System, One Series: Report of the Review of Tribunals* (London: TSO, 2001)

Leith, P. and Morison, J., *Rewarding Merit in Judicial Appointments?* (Belfast: QUB/Northern Ireland Judicial Appointments Commission, 2013)

Letter from Lord Gill to the Convenor of the Public Petitions Committee (28 May 2013)

Letter from Lord Judge to Keith Vaz MP (6 July 2013)

Lord Chief Justice, *Lord Chief Justice's Review of the Administration of Justice in the Courts* (HC 448 2008)

Lord Chief Justice, *The Lord Chief Justice's Review of the Administration of Justice in the Courts* (London: TSO, 2010)

Lord Chief Justice's Office, *Complaints about the Conduct of Judicial Office Holders* (2013)

Lord President of the Court of Session, *Complaints about the Judiciary (Scotland) Rules 2013* (2013)

Ministry of Justice, *Appointments and Diversity: A Judiciary for the 21st Century: Response to Public Consultation* (CP19/2011 2012)

Ministry of Justice, *Fee Increases in the United Kingdom Supreme Court* (CP4/2011 2011)

Ministry of Justice, *Framework Document: Ministry of Justice and the Judicial Appointments Commission* (2012)

Ministry of Justice, *The Governance of Britain: Judicial Appointments* (CP 25/07 2007)

Ministry of Justice, *HM Courts and Tribunals Service Framework Document* (Cm 8043 2011)

Ministry of Justice, *HM Courts Service Framework Document* (Cm 7350 2008)

Ministry of Justice, *Judicial Pension Scheme Memorandum on Single Supplementary Estimate 2012–13* (2013)

Ministry of Justice, *Judicial Salaries 2013–14* (2013)

Ministry of Justice, *A Judiciary for the 21st Century* (2011)

National Audit Office, *The Performance of the Ministry of Justice 2012–13* (2013)

NI Assembly Justice Committee, *Briefing from the Lord Chief Justice* (2013)

NI Assembly Justice Committee, *Judicial Appointments and Competition for a High Court Judge: Evidence of HH Judge Desmond Marrinan* (2013)

NI Assembly Justice Committee, *Judicial Appointments and Competition for a High Court Judge: Evidence of Karamjit Singh* (2014)

NI Assembly Justice Committee, *Review of Judicial Appointments: Evidence of Sir Declan Morgan* (NIA 38/11–15 (Session 2011–15) 2012)

NI Assembly Justice Committee, *Review of Judicial Appointments in Northern Ireland: Evidence of the Attorney General for Northern Ireland* (NIA 38/11–15 (Session 2011–15) 2012)

Northern Ireland Judicial Appointments Commission, *Annual Report and Accounts 2012–2013* (2013)

Northern Ireland Judicial Appointments Commission, *A Guide to Judicial Careers in Northern Ireland* (2013)

Office for Budget Responsibility, *Fiscal Sustainability Report – July 2013* (2013)

Osler, D., *Agency Review of the Scottish Court Service* (Scottish Executive, 2006)

Paterson, A. and Paterson, C., *Guarding the Guardians? Towards an Independent, Accountable and Diverse Senior Judiciary* (London: CentreForum, 2012)

Peach, L., *Independent Scrutiny of the Appointments Processes of Judges and Queen's Counsel* (1999)

Pensions Policy Institute, *The Implications of the Coalition Government's Reforms for Members of the Public Service Pension Schemes* (2012)

Potter, M., *Do the Media Influence the Judiciary?* (Oxford: Foundation for Law, Justice and Society, 2011)

*The Report of the Advisory Panel on Judicial Diversity 2010*

Review Body on Senior Salaries, *25th Report on Senior Salaries: Report No. 54* (Cm 5718 2003)

Review Body on Senior Salaries, *33rd Annual Report on Senior Salaries: Report No. 77* (Cm 8026 2011)

Review Body on Senior Salaries, *35th Annual Report on Senior Salaries: Report No. 81* (Cm 8569 2013)

Royal Commission on the Reform of the House of Lords, *A House for the Future* (Cm 4534 2000)

Russell, M. and Benton, M., *Analysis of Existing Data on the Breadth of Expertise and Experience in the House of Lords* (London: The Constitution Unit, 2010)

Scottish Government, *Civil Judicial Statistics 2009–10* (2010)

Scottish Government, *Civil Judicial Statistics 2010–11* (2011)

Scottish Parliament Justice Committee, *Stage 1 Report on the Judiciary and Courts (Scotland) Bill: Evidence of Lord Hamilton* (SP Paper 91 (Session 3) 2008)

Senior Presiding Judge, *HMCTS Reform: Judicial Overview* (2013)

Senior Presiding Judge, *Response: Proposals on the Provision of Court Services in England and Wales* (2010)

Simson-Caird, J., Hazell, R. and Oliver, D., *The Constitutional Standards of the House of Lords Select Committee on the Constitution* (London: The Constitution Unit, 2014)

Submission by the Judiciary in the Court of Session to the Commission on Scottish Devolution (10 October 2008)

Thomas, C., *Review of Judicial Training and Education in Other Jurisdictions: Report Prepared for the Judicial Studies Board* (2006)

*Tokyo Principles on the Independence of the Judiciary in the LAWASIA Region* (1982)

UK Supreme Court, *Annual Report and Accounts 2012–13* (London, HC 3 2013)

UK Supreme Court, *Judicial Complaints Procedure*

UK Supreme Court, Minutes of the Management Board: April 2010 (2010)

UK Supreme Court, Minutes of the Management Board: May 2010 (2010)

UK Supreme Court, Note of the UKSC/JCPC User Group Meeting (UKSC, 2013)

UK Supreme Court, *Scottish Criminal Cases and the UK Supreme Court* (2012)

UK Supreme Court, Management Board: Minutes of the Meeting Held on 23 March 2010

UN Congress on the Prevention of Crime and the Treatment of Offenders, *Basic Principles on the Independence of the Judiciary* (UN Doc A/CONF.121/22/Rev.1 1985)

UN General Assembly, *UN Basic Principles on the Independence of the Judiciary* (1985)

UN Office on Drugs and Crime: Judicial Integrity Group, *Bangalore Principles of Judicial Independence* (The Hague, 2002)

Waller, P. and Chalmers, M., *Evaluation of Pre-appointment Scrutiny Hearings* (London: The Constitution Unit, 2010)

Welsh Government, *Evidence Submitted by the Welsh Government to the Commission on Devolution in Wales* (2003)

## Books and journal articles

Allan, J., 'Judicial Appointments in New Zealand: If It Were Done When 'Tis Done, Then 'Twere Well It Were Done Openly and Directly', in K. Malleson and

P. Russell (eds.), *Appointing Judges in an Age of Judicial Power: Critical Perspectives from around the World* (Toronto: University of Toronto Press, 2006)

Andrews, N., 'Judicial Independence: The British Experience', in S. Shetreet and C. Forsyth (eds.), *The Culture of Judicial Independence: Conceptual Foundations and Practical Challenges* (Leiden: Martinus Nijhoff, 2012)

Baker, R., 'The New Courts Administration: A Case for a Systems Theory Approach' (1974) 52 *Public Administration* 285

Bell, J., 'Judicial Cultures and Judicial Independence' (2001) 4 *Cambridge Yearbook of European Legal Studies* 47

Bell, J., *Judiciaries within Europe: A Comparative Review* (Cambridge: Cambridge University Press, 2006)

Bellamy, R., *Political Constitutionalism* (Cambridge: Cambridge University Press, 2007)

Beloff, M. J., 'Paying Judges: Why, Who, Whom, How Much? Neill Lecture 2006' [2006] *Denning Law Journal* 1

Berlinksi, S., Dewan, T. and Dowding, K., *Accounting for Ministers: Scandal and Survival in British Government 1945–2007* (Cambridge: Cambridge University Press, 2012)

Bevir, M., 'The Westminster Model, Governance and Judicial Reform' (2008) 61 *Parliamentary Affairs* 559

Bingham, T., *The Business of Judging: Selected Essays and Speeches, 1985–1999* (Oxford: Oxford University Press, 2000)

Bingham, T., 'The Evolving Constitution' [2002] *European Human Rights Law Review* 1

Bingham, T., *Lives of the Law: Selected Essays and Speeches: 2000–2010* (Oxford: Oxford University Press, 2011)

Blair, T., *The Journey* (London: Hutchinson, 2010)

Blom-Cooper, L., 'Who Is the Most Senior Judge?' [2008] *Public Law* 413

Blom-Cooper, L., Dickson, B. and Drewry, G. (eds.), *The Judicial House of Lords, 1876–2009* (Oxford: Oxford University Press, 2009)

Blom-Cooper, L. and Drewry, G., *Final Appeal* (Oxford: Oxford University Press, 1972)

Bonneau, C. and Gann Hall, M., *In Defense of Judicial Elections* (Abingdon: Routledge, 2009)

Bovens, M., 'Analysing and Assessing Accountability: A Conceptual Framework' (2007) 13 *European Law Journal* 447

Bovens, M., 'Two Concepts of Accountability: Accountability as a Virtue and as a Mechanism' (2010) 33 *West European Politics* 946

Bradley, A., 'Judges and the Media: The Kilmuir Rules' [1986] *Public Law* 383

Brazier, R., *Ministers of the Crown* (Oxford: Clarendon Press, 1997)

Brody, D., 'The Use of Judicial Performance Evaluation to Enhance Judicial Accountability, Judicial Independence, and Public Trust' (2008) 86 *Denver University Law Review* 115

Browne-Wilkinson, N., 'The Independence of the Judiciary in the 1980s' [1988] *Public Law* 44

Burbank, S., 'The Architecture of Judicial Independence' (1999) 72 *Southern California Law Review* 315

Burbank, S., 'What Do We Mean by "Judicial Independence"?' 64 *Ohio State Law Journal* 323

Burbank, S. and Friedman, B. (eds.), *Judicial Independence at the Crossroads: An Interdisciplinary Approach* (Thousand Oaks: Sage, 2002)

Burbank, S. and Friedman, B. 'Reconsidering Judicial Independence', in S. Burbank and B. Friedman (eds.), *Judicial Independence at the Crossroads: An Interdisciplinary Approach* (Thousand Oaks: Sage, 2002)

Burrows, A., 'Numbers Sitting in the Supreme Court' (2013) 129 *Law Quarterly Review* 305

Buxton, R., 'Sitting En Banc in the New Supreme Court' (2009) 125 *Law Quarterly Review* 288

Cameron, C., 'Judicial Independence: How Can You Tell It When You See It? And Who Cares?', in S. Burbank and B. Friedman (eds.), *Judicial Independence at the Crossroads: An Interdisciplinary Approach* (Thousand Oaks: Sage, 2002)

Cooke, R., 'The Law Lords: An Endangered Heritage' (2003) 119 *Law Quarterly Review* 49

Cornes, R., 'A Constitutional Disaster in the Making? The Communications Challenge Facing the United Kingdom's Supreme Court' [2013] *Public Law* 266

Cornes, R., 'Gains (and Dangers of Losses) in Translation: The Leadership Function in the United Kingdom's Supreme Court, Parameters and Prospects' [2011] *Public Law* 509

Cranston, R., 'Lawyers, MPs and Judges', in D. Feldman (ed.), *Law in Politics, Politics in Law* (Oxford: Hart Publishing, 2013)

Dalton, R., *Democratic Challenges, Democratic Choices* (Oxford: Oxford University Press, 2004)

Darbyshire, P., *Sitting in Judgment: The Working Lives of Judges* (Oxford: Hart Publishing, 2011)

Darbyshire, P., 'Where Do English and Welsh Judges Come from?' (2007) 66 *Cambridge Law Journal* 365

Denning, Lord, *The Road to Justice* (London: Stevens & Sons, 1955)

Dickson, B., 'A Hard Act to Follow: The Bingham Court, 2000–2008', in L. Blom-Cooper, B. Dickson and G. Drewry (eds.), *The Judicial House of Lords, 1876–2009* (Oxford: Oxford University Press, 2009)

Dickson, B., *Human Rights and the UK Supreme Court* (Oxford: Oxford University Press, 2013)

Dickson, B., 'The Processing of Appeals in the House of Lords' (2007) 123 *Law Quarterly Review* 571

Dodek, A. and Sossin, L., 'Introduction', in A. Dodek and L. Sossin (eds.), *Judicial Independence in Context* (Toronto: Irwin Law, 2010)

Dodek, A. and Sossin, L. (eds.), *Judicial Independence in Context* (Toronto: Irwin Law, 2010)

Donaldson, J. and Scott, I., 'Court Administration in England and Wales', in G. Moloney (ed.), *Seminar on Constitutional and Administrative Responsibilities for the Administration of Justice: The Partnership of Judiciary and Executive* (Canberra: Australian Institute of Judicial Administration, 1985)

Drewry, G., 'The Executive: Towards Accountable Government and Effective Governance?', in J. Jowell and D. Oliver (eds.), *The Changing Constitution*, 6th edn (Oxford: Oxford University Press, 2007)

Drewry, G., 'Judicial Appointments' [1998] *Public Law* 1

Drewry, G., 'Ministers, Parliament and the Courts' (1992) 142 *New Law Journal* 50

Drewry, G., 'Parliamentary Accountability for the Administration of Justice', in A. Horne, G. Drewry and D. Oliver (eds.), *Parliament and the Law* (Oxford: Hart Publishing, 2013)

Drewry, G., 'The UK Supreme Court: A Fine New Vintage or Just a Smart New Label on a Dusty Old Bottle?' (2011) 3 *International Journal for Court Administration* 20

Drewry, G. and Oliver, D., 'Parliamentary Accountability for the Administration of Justice', in D. Oliver and G. Drewry (eds.), *The Law and Parliament* (London: Butterworths, 1998)

Dunn, R., *Sword and Wig: Memoirs of a Lord Justice* (London: Quiller Press, 1993)

Elliot, M., 'Ombudsmen, Tribunals, Inquiries: Re-fashioning Accountability beyond the Courts', in N. Bamforth and P. Leyland (eds.), *Accountability in the Contemporary Constitution* (Oxford: Oxford University Press, 2013)

Feldman, D., '"Which in Your Case You Have Not Got": Constitutionalism, at Home and Abroad' (2011) 64 *Current Legal Problems* 117

Ferejohn, J. and Kramer, L., 'Independent Judges, Dependent Judiciary: Institutionalising Judicial Restraint' (2002) 77 *NYU Law Review* 962

Finn, J., 'The Rule of Law and Judicial Independence in Newly Democratic Regimes' (2004) 13 *The Good Society* 12

Garapon, A., 'A New Approach for Promoting Judicial Independence', in R. Peerenboom (ed.), *Judicial Independence in China: Lessons for Global Rule of Law Promotion* (Cambridge: Cambridge University Press, 2010)

Gardbaum, S., 'Reassessing the New Commonwealth Model of Constitutionalism' (2010) 8 *International Journal of Constitutional Law* 167

Gardner, J., 'The Mark of Responsibility', in M. Dowdle (ed.), *Public Accountability: Designs, Dilemmas and Experiences* (Cambridge: Cambridge University Press, 2006)

Gee, G., 'Defending Judicial Independence in the British Constitution', in A. Dodek and L. Sossin (eds.), *Judicial Independence in Context* (Toronto: Irwin Law, 2010)

Gee, G., 'Guarding the Guardians: The Chief Executive of the UK Supreme Court' [2013] *Public Law* 538

Gee, G., 'The Persistent Politics of Judicial Selection: A Comparative Analysis', in A. Seibert-Fohr (ed.), *Judicial Independence in Transition* (New York and Heidelberg: Springer, 2012)

Gee, G., 'The Politics of Judicial Appointments in Canada', in *Judicial Appointments: Balancing Independence, Accountability and Legitimacy* (London: Judicial Appointments Commission, 2010)

Geyh, C., 'Rescuing Judicial Accountability from the Realm of Political Rhetoric' (2006) 56 *Case Western Law Review* 911

Gies, L., *Law and the Media: The Future of an Uneasy Relationship* (London: Routledge-Cavendish, 2007)

Green, G., 'The Rationale and Some Aspects of Judicial Independence' (1985) 59 *Australian Law Journal* 135

Griffith, J., 'Here Come the Judges' [2000] *Times Literary Supplement* 14

Griffith, J., *The Politics of the Judiciary*, 5th edn (London: Fontana, 1997)

Guarnieri, C., Pederzoli, P. and Thomas, C. A., *The Power of Judges: A Comparative Study of Courts and Democracy* (Oxford: Oxford University Press, 2002)

Hailsham, Lord, 'The Office of Lord Chancellor and the Separation of Powers' [1989] *Civil Justice Quarterly* 308

Hain, P., *Outside In* (London: Biteback Publishing, 2012)

Hale, B., 'A Supreme Judicial Leader', in M. Andenas and D. Fairgrieve (eds.), *Tom Bingham and the Transformation of the Law: A Liber Amicorum* (Oxford: Oxford University Press, 2009)

Hall, J. and Martin, D., *Yes, Lord Chancellor: A Biography of Lord Schuster* (Chichester: Barry Rose Law, 2003)

Harlow, C. (ed.), *Public Law and Politics* (London: Sweet and Maxwell, 1986)

Harlow, C. 'Refurbishing the Judicial Service', in C. Harlow (ed.), *Public Law and Politics* (London: Sweet and Maxwell, 1986)

Harlow, C. and Rawlings, R., 'Promoting Accountability in Multi-level Governance: A Network Approach' (2007) 13 *European Law Journal* 542

Harrison, J., 'Judging the Judges: The New Scheme of Judicial Conduct and Discipline in Scotland' [2009] *Edinburgh Law Review* 427

Hayo, B. and Voigt, S., 'Explaining De Facto Judicial Independence' (2007) 28 *International Review of Law and Economics* 269

Hazell, R., 'Who Is the Guardian of Legal Values in the Legislative Process: Parliament or the Executive?' [2004] *Public Law* 495

Helmke, G. and Rosenbluth, F., 'Regimes and the Rule of Law: Judicial Independence in Comparative Perspective' (2009) 12 *Annual Review of Political Science* 345

Heuston, R., *Lives of the Lord Chancellors: 1940–1970* (Oxford: Clarendon Press, 1997)

Hogg, P., 'The Bad Idea of Unwritten Constitutional Principles: Protecting Judicial Salaries', in A. Dodek and L. Sossin (eds.), *Judicial Independence in Context* (Toronto: Irwin Law, 2010)

Holdsworth, W., 'The Constitutional Position of the Judges' (1932) 48 *Law Quarterly Review* 29

Holmes, S., 'Judicial Independence as Ambiguous Reality and Insidious Illusion', in R. Dworkin (ed.), *From Liberal Values to Democratic Transition: Essays in Honor of Janos Kis* (Budapest and New York: Central European University Press, 2004)

Hope, Lord, 'A Phoenix from the Ashes? Accommodating a New Supreme Court' (2005) 121 *Law Quarterly Review* 253

Hope, Lord, 'Scots Law Seen from South of the Border' (2012) 16 *Edinburgh Law Review* 58

Hope, Lord, 'Voices from the Past: The Law Lords' Contribution to the Legislative Process' (2007) 123 *Law Quarterly Review* 547

Howarth, D., 'Lawyers in the House of Commons', in D. Feldman (ed.), *Law in Politics, Politics in Law* (Oxford: Hart Publishing, 2013)

Hunt, M., 'The Joint Committee on Human Rights', in A. Horne, G. Drewry and D. Oliver (eds.), *Parliament and the Law* (Oxford: Hart Publishing, 2013)

Hutchinson, A., 'Judges and Politics: An Essay from Canada' (2004) 24 *Legal Studies* 275

Jack, M. and others (eds.), *Erskine May: Parliamentary Practice*, 24th edn (London: LexisNexis Butterworths, 2011)

Jackson, V., 'Judicial Independence: Structure, Context, Attitude', in A. Seibert-Fohr (ed.), *Judicial Independence in Transition* (New York and Heidelberg: Springer, 2012)

Jennings Peretti, T., 'Does Judicial Independence Exist? The Lessons of Social Science Research', in S. Burbank and B. Friedman (eds.), *Judicial Independence at the Crossroads: An Interdisciplinary Approach* (Charlottesville: University Press of Virginia, 2002)

Kavanagh, A., 'From Appellate Committee to Supreme Court: Independence, Activism and Transparency', in J. Lee (ed.), *From House of Lords to Supreme Court: Judges, Jurists and the Process of Judging* (Oxford: Hart Publishing, 2011)

Kavanagh, A., 'A New Supreme Court for the United Kingdom: Some Reflections on Judicial Independence, Activism and Transparency', Paper No. 58/2010, University of Oxford Legal Research Series

Kelly, R., 'Select Committees: Powers and Functions', in A. Horne, G. Drewry and D. Oliver (eds.), *Parliament and the Law* (Oxford: Hart Publishing, 2013)

Knight, C., 'The Supreme Court Gives Its Reasons' (2012) 128 *Law Quarterly Review* 477

Knight, J. and Epstein, L., 'The Norm of *Stare Decisis*' (1996) 40 *American Journal of Political Science* 1018

Kosar, D., 'The Least Accountable Branch' (2013) 11 *International Journal of Constitutional Law* 234

Kotzian, P., 'Public Support for Liberal Democracy' (2011) 32 *International Political Science Review* 23

Kwak, J., 'Cultural Capture and the Financial Crisis', in D. Carpenter and D. Moss (eds.), *Preventing Regulatory Capture: Special Interest Influence and How to Limit it* (Cambridge: Cambridge University Press, 2014)

Larkins, C., 'Judicial Independence and Democratization: A Theoretical and Conceptual Analysis' (1996) 44 *American Journal of Comparative Law* 605

Lee, S., *Judging Judges* (London: Faber, 1988)

Legg, T., 'Judges for the New Century' [2001] *Public Law* 62

Le Sueur, A., 'Developing Mechanisms for Judicial Accountability in the UK' (2004) 24 *Legal Studies* 73

Le Sueur, A., 'Parliamentary Accountability and the Judicial System', in N. Bamforth and P. Leyland (eds.), *Accountability in the Contemporary Constitution* (Oxford: Oxford University Press, 2013)

Livingstone, S., 'The House of Lords and the Northern Ireland Conflict' (1994) 57 *Modern Law Review* 333

Lukes, S., *Power: A Radical View* (London: Macmillan, 1974)

Mackay, Lord, 'The Lord Chancellor's Role within Government' (1995) 145 *New Law Journal* 1650

Malleson, K., 'Creating a Judicial Appointments Commission: Which Model Works Best?' [2004] *Public Law* 102

Malleson, K., 'The Evolving Role of the UK Supreme Court' [2011] *Public Law* 754

Malleson, K., 'The Judicial Appointments Commission in England and Wales: New Wine in New Bottles?', in K. Malleson and P. Russell (eds.), *Appointing Judges in an Age of Judicial Power: Critical Perspectives from around the World* (Toronto: University of Toronto Press, 2006)

Malleson, K., 'Judicial Training and Performance Appraisal: The Problem of Judicial Independence' (1997) 60 *Modern Law Review* 655

Malleson, K., 'The New Judicial Appointments Commission in England and Wales', in K. Malleson and P. Russell (eds.), *Appointing Judges in an Age of Judicial Power: Critical Perspectives from around the World* (Toronto: University of Toronto Press, 2006)

Malleson, K., *The New Judiciary: The Effects of Expansion and Activism* (London: Ashgate, 1999)

Malleson, K., 'Promoting Diversity in the Judiciary: Reforming the Judicial Appointments Process' in P. Thomas (ed.), *Discriminating Lawyers* (London: Cavendish, 2000)

Malleson, K., 'Prospects for Parity: The Position of Women in the Judiciary in England and Wales', in U. Shultz and G. Shaw (eds.), *Women in the World's Legal Professions* (Oxford: Hart Publishing, 2003)

Malleson, K. and Russell, P. (eds.), *Appointing Judges in an Age of Judicial Power: Critical Perspectives from around the World* (Toronto: University of Toronto Press, 2006)

Marsh, D., 'Towards a Framework for Establishing Policy Success' (2010) 88 *Public Administration* 564

Mashaw, J., 'Accountability and Institutional Design: Some Thoughts on the Grammar of Governance', in M. Dowdle (ed.), *Public Accountability: Designs, Dilemmas and Experiences* (Cambridge: Cambridge University Press, 2006)

Masterman, R., 'Labour's "Juridification of the Constitution"' (2009) 62 *Parliamentary Affairs* 476

Masterman, R., *The Separation of Powers in the Contemporary Constitution* (Cambridge: Cambridge University Press, 2011)

Masterman, R. and Murkens, J., 'Skirting Supremacy and Subordination: The Constitutional Authority of the UK Supreme Court' [2013] *Public Law* 800

Millar, P. S. and Baar, C., *Judicial Administration in Canada* (Montreal: McGill-Queen's University Press, 1981)

Moran, L., 'Mass-Mediated "Open Justice": Court and Judicial Reports in the Press in England and Wales' (2014) 34 *Legal Studies* 143

Muller, L., 'Judicial Administration in Transitional Eastern Countries', in A. Seibert-Fohr (ed.), *Judicial Independence in Transition* (New York and Heidelberg: Springer, 2012)

Nergelius, J., *Constitutional Law in Sweden* (Alphen aan den Rijn: Kluwer Law International, 2011)

Normanton, E., *The Accountability and Audit of Governments: A Comparative Study* (Manchester: University of Manchester Press, 1966)

O'Brien, P., 'Change to Judicial Appointments in the Crime and Courts Act 2013' [2014] *Public Law* 179

Oliver, D., *Constitutional Reform in the United Kingdom* (Oxford: Oxford University Press, 2003)

Oliver, D., 'Constitutionalism and the Abolition of the Office of Lord Chancellor' (2004) 57 *Parliamentary Affairs* 754

Oliver, D., 'The Lord Chancellor's Department and the Judges' [1994] *Public Law* 157

Olowofoyeku, A., *Suing Judges: A Study of Judicial Immunity* (Oxford: Clarendon Press, 1993)

Partington, M., 'Training the Judiciary in England and Wales: The Work of the Judicial Studies Board' [1994] *Civil Justice Quarterly* 319

Paterson, A., *Final Judgment* (Oxford: Hart Publishing, 2013)

Paterson, A., *The Law Lords* (London: Macmillan, 1982)

Paterson, A., *Lawyers and the Public Good: Democracy in Action?* (Cambridge: Cambridge University Press, 2012)

Paterson, A., 'The Scottish Judicial Appointments Board: New Wine in Old Bottles', in K. Malleson and P. Russell (eds.), *Appointing Judges in an Age of Judicial Power: Critical Perspectives from around the World* (Toronto: University of Toronto Press, 2006)

Paterson, A., 'Scottish Lords of Appeal 1876–1988' [1988] *Juridical Review* 235

Paterson, A., 'The Supreme Court Today' [2012] *Counsel* 34

Peerenboom, R. (ed.), *Judicial Independence in China: Lessons for Global Rule of Law Promotion* (Cambridge: Cambridge University Press, 2010)

Polden, P., *Guide to the Records of the Lord Chancellor's Department* (London: HMSO, 1988)

Powell, J., *The New Machiavelli: How to Wield Power in the Modern World* (London: Vintage, 2010)

Prashar, Baroness, 'Translating Aspirations into Reality: Establishing the Judicial Appointments Commission', in *Judicial Appointments: Balancing Independence, Accountability and Legitimacy* (London: Judicial Appointments Commission, 2010)

Prince, S., 'Law and Politics: Rumours of the Demise of the Lord Chancellor Have Been Exaggerated . . .' (2005) 58 *Parliamentary Affairs* 248

Prince, S., 'The Law and Politics: Upsetting the Judicial Apple-Cart' (2004) 57 *Parliamentary Affairs* 228

Purchas, F., 'The Constitution in the Market Place' (1993) 143 *New Law Journal* 1604

Purchas, F., 'Lord Mackay and the Judiciary' (1994) 144 *New Law Journal* 527

Purchas, F., 'What Is Happening to Judicial Independence?' (1994) 144 *New Law Journal* 1306

Resnik, J., 'Judicial Selection and Democratic Theory: Demand, Supply, and Life Tenure' (2005) 26 no. 2 *Cardozo Law Review* 579

Rhodes, R., *Control and Power in Central–Local Government Relations* (Aldershot: Gower, 1981)

Rhodes, R., *Everyday Life in British Government* (Oxford: Oxford University Press, 2011)

Robertson, D., *Judicial Discretion in the House of Lords* (Oxford: Clarendon Press, 1998)

Rozenberg, J., *Trial of Strength* (London: Richard Cohen, 1997)

Rush, M. and Baldwin, N., 'Lawyers in Parliament', in D. Oliver and G. Drewry (eds.), *The Law and Parliament* (London: Butterworths, 1998)

Russell, P., 'Judicial Independence in the Age of Democracy', in P. Russell and D. O'Brien (eds.), *Judicial Independence in the Age of Democracy* (Charlottesville: University Press of Virginia, 2001)

Russell, P., 'Towards a General Theory of Judicial Independence', in P. Russell and D. O'Brien (eds.), *Judicial Independence in the Age of Democracy* (Charlottesville: University Press of Virginia, 2001)

Russell, P. and O'Brien, D. (eds.), *Judicial Independence in the Age of Democracy* (Charlottesville: University Press of Virginia, 2001)

Sackville, R., 'The Judicial Appointments Process in Australia: Towards Independence and Accountability' (2007) 16 *Journal of Judicial Administration* 125

Sallmann, P., 'Courts Governance: A Thorn in the Crown of Judicial Independence?' (2007) 16 *Journal of Judicial Administration* 139

Sallmann, P. and Smith, T., 'Constitutionalism and Managerial Effectiveness: Revisiting Australian Courts' Governance', in Australasian Institute of Judicial Administration (ed.), *Australian Courts: Serving Democracy and Its Publics* (Melbourne, 2013)

Schuster, Lord, 'The Office of the Lord Chancellor' (1948) 10 *Cambridge Law Journal* 175

Scott, C., 'Accountability in the Regulatory State' (2000) 27 *Journal of Law and Society* 38

Scott, I., 'Judicial Involvement in Court Administration' [1988] *Civil Justice Quarterly* 153

Scott, I., 'The Council of Judges in the Supreme Court of England and Wales' [1989] *Public Law* 379

Sedley, S., 'Beware Kite-Flyers' (2013) 35 *London Review of Books* 13

Segal, J. and Spaeth, H., *The Supreme Court and the Attitudinal Model* (Cambridge: Cambridge University Press, 1993)

Segal, J. and Spaeth, H., *The Supreme Court and the Attitudinal Model Revisited* (Cambridge: Cambridge University Press, 2002)

Shapiro, M., *Courts: A Comparative and Political Analysis* (Chicago: The University of Chicago Press, 1981)

Shapiro, M., 'Political Jurisprudence' (1963) 52 *Kentucky Law Journal* 294

Shetreet, S., 'Judicial Independence: New Conceptual Dimensions and Contemporary Challenges', in S. Shetreet and J. Deschênes (eds.), *Judicial Independence: The Contemporary Debate* (Dordrecht: Martinus Nijhoff, 1985)

Shetreet, S., 'The Normative Cycle of Shaping Judicial Independence in Domestic and International Law' (2009) 10 *Chicago Journal of International Law* 275

Shetreet, S. and Deschênes, J. (eds.), *Judicial Independence: The Contemporary Debate* (Dordrecht: Martinus Nijhoff, 1985)

Shetreet, S. and Forsyth, C. (eds.), *The Culture of Judicial Independence: Conceptual Foundations and Practical Challenges* (Leiden: Martinus Nijhoff, 2012)

Shetreet, S. and Turenne, S., *Judges on Trial: The Independence and Accountability of the English Judiciary* (Cambridge: Cambridge University Press, 2013)

Simson-Caird, J., 'Parliamentary Constitutional Review: Ten Years of the House of Lords Select Committee on the Constitution' [2012] *Public Law* 4

Simson-Caird, J., Hazell, R. and Oliver, D., *The Constitutional Standards of the House of Lords Select Committee on the Constitution* (London: The Constitution Unit, 2014)

Spiller, P. and Tomasi, M., 'Judicial Decision-Making in Unstable Environments: Argentina 1935–1998' (2002) 46 *American Journal of Political Science* 699

Steele, D., 'The Judicial House of Lords: Abolition and Restoration 1873–6', in L. Blom-Cooper, B. Dickson and G. Drewry (eds.), *The Judicial House of Lords, 1876–2009* (Oxford: Oxford University Press, 2009)

Stevens, R., *The English Judges: Their Role in the Changing Constitution* (Oxford: Hart Publishing, 2005)

Stevens, R., *The Independence of the Judiciary: The View from the Lord Chancellor's Office* (Oxford: Clarendon Press, 1993)

Stevens, R., 'Judicial Independence in England: A Loss of Innocence', in P. Russell and D. O'Brien (eds.), *Judicial Independence in the Age of Democracy: Critical Perspectives from around the World* (Charlottesville: University Press of Virginia, 2001)

Stevens, R., 'Judicial Salaries: Financial Independence in the Age of Equality' (1992) 13 *Legal History* 155

Stevens, R., 'A Loss of Innocence and the Separation of Powers' (1999) 19 *Oxford Journal of Legal Studies* 365

Steyn, Lord, 'The Case for a Supreme Court' (2002) 118 *Law Quarterly Review* 382

Straw, J., *Aspects of Law Reform: An Insider's Perspective (The Hamlyn Lectures)* (Cambridge: Cambridge University Press, 2013)

Straw, J., *Last Man Standing: Memoirs of a Political Survivor* (London: Macmillan, 2012)

Stupak, R., 'Court Leadership in Transition: Fast Forward toward the Year 2000' (1991) 15 *Justice System Journal* 617

Sunkin, M., 'Judicialization of Politics in the United Kingdom' (1994) 15 *International Political Science Review* 125

Thomas, Lord Justice, 'The Judges' Council' [2005] *Public Law* 608

Tushnet, M., 'Judicial Accountability in Comparative Perspective', in N. Bamforth and P. Leyland (eds.), *Accountability in the Contemporary Constitution* (Oxford: Oxford University Press, 2013)

Underhill, N., *The Lord Chancellor* (Lavenham: Terence Dalton, 1978)

Vallance White, J., 'The Judicial Office', in L. Blom-Cooper, B. Dickson and G. Drewry (eds.), *The Judicial House of Lords, 1876–2009* (Oxford: Oxford University Press, 2009)

Vyas, Y., 'The Independence of the Judiciary: A Third World Perspective' (1992) 11 *Third World Legal Studies* 127

Watson, R. and Wolfe, M., 'Comparing Judicial Compensation: Apples, Oranges and Cherry Picking' [2008] SSRN Duke Law Working Paper Series

Widner, J., *Building the Rule of Law: Francis Nyalali and the Road to Judicial Independence in Africa* (London: W. W. Norton, 2001)

Windlesham, Lord, 'The Constitutional Reform Act: The Politics of Constitutional Reform – Part 2' [2006] *Public Law* 35

Woodhouse, D., 'The Constitutional Reform Act 2005: Defending Judicial Independence the English Way' (2007) 5 *International Journal of Constitutional Law* 153

Woodhouse, D., 'Judicial Independence and Accountability within the United Kingdom's New Constitutional Settlement', in G. Canivet, M. Andenas and D. Fairgrieve (eds.), *Independence, Accountability and the Judiciary* (London: BIICL, 2006)

Woodhouse, D., *The Office of Lord Chancellor* (Oxford: Hart Publishing, 2001)

Woodhouse, D., 'The Office of Lord Chancellor: Time to Abandon the Judicial Role – the Rest Will Follow' (2002) 22 *Legal Studies* 128

Woodhouse, D., 'The Reconstruction of Constitutional Accountability' [2002] *Public Law* 73

Woolf, Lord, 'The Needs of a 21st Century Judge: Judicial Studies Board Annual Lecture 2001', in *The Pursuit of Justice* (Oxford: Oxford University Press, 2008)

Woolf, Lord, 'Judicial Independence Not Judicial Isolation', in *The Pursuit of Justice* (Oxford: Oxford University Press, 2008)

Woolf, Lord, *The Pursuit of Justice* (ed. C. Campbell-Holt) (Oxford: Oxford University Press 2008)

Zuckerman, A., 'Civil Litigation: A Public Service for the Enforcement of Civil Rights' (2007) 26 *Civil Justice Quarterly* 1

# INDEX

Lightning Source UK Ltd.
Milton Keynes UK
UKOW05n0024040315

247231UK00003B/42/P